United States. Office of the Comptroller of the Currency

Annual Report of the Comptroller of the Currency

Third Session of the Fortififth Congress

United States. Office of the Comptroller of the Currency

Annual Report of the Comptroller of the Currency
Third Session of the Fortififth Congress

ISBN/EAN: 9783741182426

Manufactured in Europe, USA, Canada, Australia, Japa

Cover: Foto ©Andreas Hilbeck / pixelio.de

Manufactured and distributed by brebook publishing software
(www.brebook.com)

United States. Office of the Comptroller of the Currency

Annual Report of the Comptroller of the Currency

With the Compliments of

Comptroller.

OF THE

COMPTROLLER OF THE CURRENCY

TO THE

THIRD SESSION OF THE FORTY-FIFTH CONGRESS

OF THE

UNITED STATES.

DECEMBER 2, 1878.

WASHINGTON:
GOVERNMENT PRINTING OFFICE.
1878.

REPORT

OF

THE COMPTROLLER OF THE CURRENCY.

TREASURY DEPARTMENT,
OFFICE OF COMPTROLLER OF THE CURRENCY,
Washington, November 25, 1878.

I have the honor to submit for the consideration of Congress the sixteenth annual report of the Comptroller of the Currency, in compliance with section three hundred and thirty-three of the Revised Statutes of the United States. This section provides that the Comptroller shall make annually a report to Congress at the commencement of its session exhibiting—

1st. A summary of the state and condition of every association from which reports have been received during the preceding year, at the several dates to which such reports refer, with an abstract of the whole amount of banking capital returned by them, of the whole amount of their debts and liabilities, the amount of circulating notes outstanding, and the total amount of means and resources, specifying the amount of lawful money held by them at the times of their several returns, and such other information in relation to such associations as, in his judgment, may be useful.

2d. A statement of the associations whose business has been closed during the year, with the amount of their circulation redeemed and the amount outstanding.

3d. Any amendment to the laws relative to banking by which the system may be improved and the security of the holders of its notes and other creditors may be increased.

This section further provides that a statement shall be prepared by the Comptroller, exhibiting, under appropriate heads, the resources and liabilities and condition of the banks, banking companies, and savings-banks organized under the laws of the several States and Territories; such information to be obtained by the Comptroller from the reports made by such banks, banking-companies, and savings-banks to the legislatures or officers of the different States and Territories, and where such reports cannot be obtained, the deficiency to be supplied from such other authentic sources as may be available.

This last provision became a law by act of February 19, 1873, but owing to the defective legislation of the several States it has thus far been found impracticable to procure reliable statistics showing the condition of all the banks organized under State laws. All private bankers and banking associations, however, of whatever nature other than national, are required by law, for purposes of taxation, to make semi-annual returns to the Commissioner of Internal Revenue of the average amount of their capital and deposits. From these returns the following table has been compiled in this Office, exhibiting in a concise form, by geographical divisions, the total average capital and deposits of all State and savings-banks and private bankers in the country, for the six months ending May 31, 1878:

Geographical divisions.	State banks and trust companies.		Private bankers.		Savings-banks with capital.		Savings-banks without capital.	
	No.	Capital.	Deposits.	No.	Capital.	Deposits.	No.	Capital.	Deposits.	No.	Deposits.
		Millions.	*Millions.*		*Millions.*	*Millions.*		*Millions.*	*Millions.*		*Millions.*
New England States.	42	8.19	15.06	71	2.86	3.23	1	0.07	1.14	441	403.43
Middle States.......	217	42.45	122.10	916	34.48	61.92	3	0.16	1.37	190	358.68
Southern States.....	233	27.38	30.67	280	7.30	13.68	4	0.88	1.28	3	2.14
Western States and Territories........	361	46.33	61.65	1,589	33.16	105.00	15	2.13	22.39	34	39.05
United States...	853	124.35	229.48	2,856	77.80	183.83	23	3.24	26.18	668	803.30

The capital of the 2,056 national banks in operation on June 29, 1878, as will be seen by a subsequent table, was $470,393,366, not including surplus, which latter fund amounted at that date to more than 118 millions; while the average capital of all the State banks, private banks, and savings-banks having capital stock, for the six months ending May 31 previously, was, as seen below, but $205,382,832; which amount is considerably less than one-half that of the national banks. The net deposits of the national banks were $677,159,298, while the average deposits of all other banks and bankers, including savings-banks, were $1,242,794,903. The average deposits for the same period of 668 savings-banks having no capital stock were $803,299,345.

The table below exhibits the aggregate average capital and deposits for the period named of all banks other than national, together with the capital and deposits of the national banks on June 29 following:

Geographical divisions.	State banks, savings-banks, private bankers, &c.			National banks.			Total.		
	No.	Capital.	Deposits.	No.	Capital.	Deposits.	No.	Capital.	Deposits.
		Millions.	*Millions.*		*Millions.*	*Millions.*		*Millions.*	*Millions.*
New England States.	555	11.12	422.86	542	166.52	128.83	1,097	177.64	551.69
Middle States........	1,326	77.09	544.07	634	177.18	374.89	1,960	254.27	918.96
Southern States......	520	35.55	47.77	176	31.49	35.94	696	67.04	83.71
Western States and Territories.........	1,999	81.62	228.09	704	95.20	137.50	2,703	176.82	365.59
United States......	4,400	205.38	1,242.79	2,056	470.39	677.16	6,456	675.77	1,919.95

From this table it will be seen that the total number of banks and bankers in the country at the dates named was 6,456, with a total banking capital of $675,776,198, and total deposits of $1,919,954,201.

Tables similar to the foregoing for previous periods, together with other tables giving the assets and liabilities of State institutions during the past year, so far as they could be obtained from the official reports of the several States, will be found in the appendix.

A table arranged by States and principal cities, giving the number, capital and deposits, and the tax on capital and deposits, of all banking institutions other than national, for the six months ending May 31, 1878, will be found on page 54 of this report. Similar tables for previous years are printed in the appendix.

The total number of national banks organized, from the establishment of the national banking system on February 25, 1863, to November 1 of the present year, is 2,400. Of these, 273 have gone into voluntary liquidation by vote of shareholders owning two-thirds of their respective capitals, and 74 have been placed in the hands of receivers for the purpose of closing up their affairs, leaving 2,053 in existence on November 1 of this year. Included in the number organized are nine national gold banks, in the State of California, with an aggregate capital of $4,300,000, and circulation of $1,468,920, which redeem their circulating-notes in gold coin at their places of issue and in the city of San Francisco.

During the past year twenty-eight banks have been organized, with an authorized capital of $2,775,000, to which $1,598,800 in circulating-notes has been issued. Fifteen banks have failed within this period, having an aggregate capital of $2,712,500, and forty-one banks, with a total capital of $5,200,000, have voluntarily discontinued business.

The following table exhibits the resources and liabilities of the banks on the 1st day of October, 1878, the returns from New York, from Boston, Philadelphia, and Baltimore, from the other reserve cities, and from the remaining banks of the country, being tabulated separately:

	New York City.	Boston, Philadelphia, and Baltimore.	*Other reserve cities.	Country banks.	Aggregate.
	47 banks.	99 banks.	85 banks.	1,822 banks.	2,053 banks.
RESOURCES.					
Loans and discounts				$430,184,396	$830,521,542
On U. S. bonds on demand	$7,003,085	$1,140,581	$735,243		
On other stocks, bonds, &c., on demand	57,904,202	19,766,710	7,874,762		
Payable in gold	6,752,181	3,053	1,247,996		
On single-name paper without other security	17,297,474	10,583,112	6,699,583		
All other loans	80,625,038	120,030,184	62,669,942		
Overdrafts	130,973	81,090	347,495	2,907,350	3,466,908
Bonds for circulation	24,195,500	50,113,200	23,076,800	250,171,150	347,556,650
Bonds for deposits	26,715,550	6,402,300	3,990,900	10,829,000	47,936,850
U. S. bonds on hand	11,463,900	7,903,450	6,005,850	21,412,400	46,785,600
Other stocks and bonds	9,193,664	3,726,212	2,552,158	21,387,501	36,859,535
Due from reserve agents		16,375,643	12,684,211	56,023,565	85,083,419
Due from other national banks	11,366,000	8,636,970	4,466,954	17,022,995	41,492,919
Due from other banks and bankers	2,981,297	894,272	2,470,311	5,968,818	12,314,698
Real estate, furniture and fixtures	9,465,820	7,082,539	4,825,685	25,328,432	46,702,476
Current expenses	995,333	780,220	731,401	3,765,613	6,272,567
Premiums	1,767,167	1,021,048	608,474	3,738,047	7,134,736
Checks and other cash items	1,765,188	874,554	857,598	7,485,093	10,982,433
Exchanges for clearing-house	62,454,792	15,148,067	4,769,079		82,372,538
Bills of other national banks	1,560,623	2,523,054	2,195,325	10,650,719	16,929,721
Fractional currency	67,703	36,187	55,171	356,600	515,661
Specie	13,294,602	5,987,189	3,417,524	7,988,991	30,686,866
Legal-tender notes	14,893,468	8,300,930	11,154,895	30,079,307	64,428,600
U. S. certificates of deposit	21,660,000	7,370,000	2,665,000	995,000	32,690,000
Five per cent. redemption fund	1,073,505	2,178,355	980,741	10,972,940	15,205,541
Due from U. S. Treasury	147,702	265,393	108,187	816,941	1,338,133
Totals	384,778,767	297,224,523	167,190,985	918,084,858	1,767,279,133
LIABILITIES.					
Capital stock	53,800,000	78,526,310	40,725,500	293,095,626	466,147,436
Surplus fund	15,920,230	19,968,943	10,892,787	70,445,820	116,897,780
Undivided profits	8,659,800	3,899,846	3,323,613	25,052,984	40,936,213
National-bank notes outstanding	20,025,864	42,986,571	19,658,749	219,216,911	301,888,092
State bank notes outstanding	73,339	80,757	4,245	255,582	413,913
Dividends unpaid	190,705	1,037,172	188,612	1,701,216	3,118,390
Individual deposits	172,411,669	108,863,331	62,156,122	276,775,055	629,236,177
U. S. deposits	26,090,297	6,255,785	2,465,341	6,843,389	41,654,812
Deposits of U. S. disbursing officers	131,225	20,271	1,631,935	2,159,364	3,342,795
Due to national banks	68,125,944	27,787,067	15,226,442	11,357,064	122,496,544
Due to other banks and bankers	19,314,700	6,591,905	10,347,506	6,385,592	42,636,703
Notes and bills rediscounted		37,537	183,808	2,785,980	3,007,325
Bills payable	8,000	1,168,758	1,015,950	2,310,275	4,502,983
Totals	384,778,767	297,224,523	167,190,985	918,084,858	1,767,279,133

The reserve cities, in addition to New York, Boston, Philadelphia, and Baltimore, are Albany, Pittsburgh, Washington, New Orleans, Louisville, Cincinnati, Cleveland, Chicago, Detroit, Milwaukee, Saint Louis, and San Francisco.

The following table exhibits the resources and liabilities of the national banks in operation at nearly similar dates for the last nine years:

	Oct. 8, 1870.	Oct. 2, 1871.	Oct. 3, 1872.	Sept. 12, 1873.	Oct. 2, 1874.	Oct. 1, 1875.	Oct. 2, 1876.	Oct. 1, 1877.	Oct. 1, 1878.
	1,615 banks.	1,767 banks.	1,919 banks.	1,976 banks.	2,004 banks.	2,087 banks.	2,089 banks.	2,080 banks.	2,053 banks.
RESOURCES.	*Millions.*	*Millions.*	*Millions.*	*Millions.*	*Millions.*	*Millions.*	*Millions.*	*Millions.*	*Millions.*
Loans	716.0	831.0	877.2	944.2	954.4	984.7	931.3	891.9	834.0
Bonds for circulation	340.6	364.5	382.0	388.3	383.3	370.3	337.2	336.8	347.6
Other U. S. bonds	37.7	45.8	27.6	23.6	28.0	28.1	47.8	45.0	94.7
Other stocks, bonds, &c	23.6	24.5	23.5	23.7	27.8	33.5	34.4	34.5	36.9
Due from other banks	109.5	143.2	128.2	149.5	134.8	144.7	146.9	129.9	138.9
Real estate	27.5	30.1	32.3	34.7	38.1	42.4	43.1	45.2	46.7
Specie	18.5	13.2	10.2	19.9	21.2	8.1	21.4	22.7	30.7
Legal-tender notes	77.2	107.0	102.1	92.4	80.0	76.5	84.2	66.9	64.4
National-bank notes	12.6	14.3	15.8	16.1	18.5	18.5	15.9	15.6	16.9
Clearing-house exchanges	91.6	115.2	125.0	100.3	109.7	87.9	100.0	74.5	82.4
U. S. certificates of deposit			6.7	20.6	42.8	48.8	29.2	33.4	32.7
Due from U. S. Treasurer					20.3	19.6	16.7	16.0	16.5
Other resources	55.9	41.2	25.2	17.3	18.3	19.1	19.1	28.7	24.9
Totals	1,510.7	1,730.6	1,755.8	1,830.6	1,877.2	1,882.2	1,827.2	1,741.1	1,767.3
LIABILITIES.									
Capital stock	430.4	458.3	479.6	491.0	493.8	504.8	499.8	479.5	466.2
Surplus fund	94.1	101.1	110.3	120.3	129.0	134.4	132.2	122.8	116.9
Undivided profits	38.6	42.0	46.6	54.5	51.5	53.0	46.4	44.5	40.9
Circulation	293.9	317.4	335.1	340.3	334.2	319.1	292.2	291.9	301.0
Due to depositors	515.3	631.4	628.9	640.0	683.8	679.4	666.2	630.4	608.4
Due to other banks	130.0	171.9	143.8	173.0	175.8	179.7	179.8	161.6	165.1
Other liabilities	8.4	8.5	11.5	11.5	9.1	11.8	10.6	10.4	7.9
Totals	1,510.7	1,730.6	1,755.8	1,830.6	1,877.2	1,882.2	1,827.2	1,741.1	1,767.3

THE NATIONAL BANKING SYSTEM.

The Comptroller, in his report for 1876, in addition to the usual national-bank statistics, gave an historical sketch of the two Banks of the United States, and also of the several State systems of banking, with tables showing, by geographical divisions and by States, so far as they could be obtained from official sources, the resources and liabilities of the State banks from the earliest dates to that of the organization of the national system, together with a comparative view of the State and national systems of banking.

In his report to Congress for the year 1875 he sketched the origin and growth of the national-banking system, and answered the principal arguments advanced against its continuance. The establishment of the system was not advocated in the interest of any political party, and it has been free from the control of partisan or sectional influence, its benefits being now open to all who desire to engage in the business of banking. The opportunity occasioned by a great war was seized upon, in the interest of the government, to get rid of a circulation issued by authority of many different States, which had been, almost from the beginning of the government, a grievous tax upon the business and the commerce of this country. It was shown, from the discussions in Congress at the time of the passage of the legal-tender act, from the reports of this department, and from the uniform legislation since that time, that the national-banking system was intended to be permanent, the institutions organized under it being, by the express terms of the law, authorized to continue for a term of twenty years; while it was equally evident that the Treasury notes issued and still in circulation were intended to be funded, to constitute a temporary currency, issued from necessity, and to furnish the government with the means to save itself from destruction; that the amount was not to be increased, but to be withdrawn from circulation as rapidly as possible.

It was further shown that the system was not a monopoly, its privileges being free to all, but that it uprooted many real banking monopolies authorized by the several States, and which had been in existence almost from the foundation of the government; that the profits upon circulation were small, and that the earnings of the banks were not too great a compensation for the risks incident to the business of banking, to which capital loaned directly on mortgage security is not subject; that the taxation imposed upon the banks is unequaled in the history of monetary institutions; that the losses by failures had been insignificant in proportion to the liabilities; and that the losses on circulation had not been one dollar; that the restrictions of the act are such as experience has shown to be necessary for the success of great banking systems; that publicity is one of the principal features of the national system; that a surplus of more than one hundred millions of dollars—equal to one-fourth of the capital, and derived largely from profits accruing from transactions during the war—had accumulated and remained as a security to stockholders and depositors during times of revulsion and panic.

This report, which, since its publication, has been constantly in demand, is out of print. The proposition for the substitution of Treasury notes in place of national-bank notes having been again revived and discussed, it is thought advisable again to answer the principal objections urged against the national banking-system, even at the risk of repeating to some extent, although with more recent data, what has already appeared in previous reports.

The chief reasons urged in favor of the substitution of Treasury notes for national-bank notes are, that the banks in the national system are a favored class, enjoying special privileges at the cost of the people; that they derive a large profit from the issue of circulating-notes; and that a large amount of money may be saved to the government by authorizing it to issue all the paper currency of the country.

Before the passage of the act of June 20, 1874, no national bank could reduce its circulation and take up its bonds except by returning a proportionate amount of its own circulating-notes, and these were usually difficult to obtain; and prior to the act of January 14, 1875, the total amount of circulation authorized to be issued was limited to 354 millions. But these acts provided both for a reduction of circulation and withdrawal of bonds at the pleasure of the banks, upon a deposit by them of lawful money in sums of not less than $9,000, and for an issue of bank-notes to any association organized in conformity with law. Under the law, then, as it now stands, any number of persons not less than five, in any part of the country, who together may have $50,000 of capital at command, may organize a national bank and receive circulating-notes equal in amount to 90 per cent. of such capital—the law discriminating in the latter respect only against the large instititutions, as no bank organized since the passage of the act of July 12, 1870, is entitled to circulation in excess of $500,000. A bank organized prior to that time, and having a capital of between $500,000 and $1,000,000, can receive in circulating-notes but 80 per cent. thereon; if between $1,000,000 and $3,000,000, it can receive but 75 per cent.; and if over $3,000,000, but 60 per cent.

Since the passage of the act of June 20, 1874, the national banks, so far from considering the privilege of issuing circulation a profitable monopoly, have voluntarily surrendered $66,237,323 of their notes, which is $29,463,467 more than has been issued to all of the banks organized since that date, while 144 banks, with capital stock amounting to $15,517,000, and a circulation of $9,190,718, have gone into voluntary liquidation.

The capital stock of the national banks is not largely in the hands of capitalists. Among their shareholders may be found persons in every station of life, and great numbers of women and children rely for their support upon the successful management of these institutions. The elaborate tables which appeared in the Comptroller's Report for 1876 showed that there were then only 767 persons anywhere who held as much as $50,000 each of national-bank stock; that more than one-half of the whole number of shareholders in these associations held, each, but $1,000, or less, of such stock; and that, taking the whole number of shareholders together, the average amount held by each one was but $3,100. Of shareholders owning not more than $1,000 each, there were 32,235 in Massachusetts alone, 12,784 in New York, 14,621 in Pennsylvania, 1,441 in Kentucky, 2,388 in Ohio, 1,608 in Illinois, 832 in Georgia, and 617 in Virginia. Of those holding the stock in amounts ranging between $2,000 and $3,000 there were 17,743 in the New England States, 15,614 in the Middle States, 2,305 in the Southern States, and 3,422 in the Western States. Moreover, citizens of the Western States held 26,455 shares, and citizens of the Southern States 13,319 shares, of the stock of banks located in the Eastern and Middle States. It is not probable that the stock of any other class of corporations in the country is more widely distributed among people of moderate means than is that of the national banks. It is also largely distributed among members of all political parties, and, as a rule, is free from the control of partisan influence.

The national banks have not at any time monopolized the business of banking, nor do they at the present time. On May 31 of this year there were in existence more than 3,700 State banks and private banking-houses, having an aggregate capital of 202 millions of dollars, and deposits of 413 millions. These banking establishments are located in all of the principal cities and villages of the country, and it is to be presumed that if the privilege of issuing circulating-notes were so great as it is persistently claimed to be, these associations and individuals, who are already engaged in the business of banking, and who are free to enter the national system, would hasten to organize under that system.

The amount of interest accruing annually upon the bonds held by the national banks on November 1—less the tax paid by them upon their circulation—is $14,544,692 only, while the annual profit upon the entire circulation of the national banks, as will be shown in another place in this report, is but $8,961,519, or less than two and one-half per centum upon their capital. As the 3,700 banks and bankers mentioned still continue to transact their business as State banks or private associations, it seems very clear that this annual profit of $2,500 only, upon a capital of $100,000, does not present to them, or any of them, a sufficient inducement to transfer their business to the national system. The reason is obvious. The laws governing the national banks contain numerous and burdensome restrictions, and impose many and severe penalties for their violation. On the one hand they authorize the issue of circulating notes, but on the other they require that the business of banking shall be conducted under a uniform system, which insures the greatest possible degree of safety to the depositor and bill-holder and prompt and certain convertibility to the circulating note. If, on the one hand, the right to issue circulating notes is given, on the other, wholesome restraints are insisted upon as a condition of that privilege. These legal prohibitions and restrictions, which are the compensations that the public receive from these corporations in return for their right to issue circulating notes, are too numerous to be given here in detail. But it is proposed now to notice specially some of the more important of the restrictions, and to give a general summary of the whole of them, for the information of the public, in a subsequent portion of this report.

CAPITAL STOCK.

One of the most important requirements of the national-bank act is that the capital stock of all institutions organized thereunder shall be fully paid in. The organization of banks without capital was one of the great abuses of previous banking systems. The history of banking in this country is full of instances of institutions of this character, which were not only permitted to receive deposits and transact a general banking business, but were authorized to issue circulating notes; and to the frequent failures of these associations may be attributed, in a great degree, the prejudice still existing in this country against all banking corporations.

When the national system was established especial care was exercised in the framing of the banking act, not alone to insure the safety and convertibility of the circulating notes, but also to guard against the organization of banks without *bona fide* capital. At least fifty per cent. of the capital stock of a national bank must be paid in before it can be authorized to commence business, and the remainder must be thereafter paid in installments of not less than one-fifth monthly, the payment of each installment being certified to this office, under oath, by the president or cashier of the association.

It is frequently stated, and it seems to be believed by many, that banks of circulation, only, may be organized under the act—that is, that a bank may use its circulating notes either to increase its existing capital or to assist in organizing other banks without real capital. The law carefully guards against such an abuse. In the first place, as has been already stated, the officers and directors are required at the outset to certify under oath to the Comptroller the amount of stock which has been paid into the bank as permanent capital, while subsequent install-ments must be similarly certified. In addition to this, section 5203 of the Revised Statutes provides that "no association shall, either directly or indirectly, pledge or hypothecate any of its notes of circulation for the purpose of procuring money to be paid in on its capital stock, or to be used in its banking operations or otherwise ; nor shall any association use its circulating notes, or any part thereof, in any manner or form to create or increase its capital stock." The Comptroller is also author-ized to examine every banking association before granting it authority to commence business, in order to ascertain whether or not its capital has been actually paid in. It is impossible, therefore, for a bank of circulation only, without capital, to be organized under the national sys-tem, if proper precaution be exercised and the examiner is competent and faithful in the performance of his duty.

Neither can an association increase its circulation at pleasure, for the circulation can never exceed a certain proportion of the paid up cap-ital. There never has been an instance of the organization of one na-tional bank by the use of the circulation issued to another. Such an illegitimate transaction could scarcely fail to be at once detected and the facts reported to the United States district attorney for his action thereon.

If any association fails to pay up its capital stock, as required by law, or if its capital shall become impaired, an assessment must be made upon the shareholders, *pro rata*, for the amount of the deficiency or impairment, the interest upon the bonds held as security for its circulation being in the mean time withheld by the Treasurer, while a receiver may be appointed by the Comptroller if the capital be not restored after three months' notice by him to the association.

The proportion of capital, and of capital and surplus, to liabilities, is much greater in this country than elsewhere, which is undoubtedly owing to the fact that our law requires that the full amount of authorized capital shall be actually paid in. In England, as a rule, only a portion of the capital is paid in, but the stockholders are individually liable for the full amount of their subscriptions. This restricted liability is true of the limited banks only, the stockholders of other corporations not limited being each liable for all of the debts of the corporation.

The following table, compiled from statements in the London Economist of October 19, 1878, exhibits the amount of capital, reserve and liabilities, and the ratio of capital, and of capital and reserve, to liabilities, of 3,417 banks (141 banks and 3,276 branches) of the United Kingdom:

Banks.	Number of—			Capital.	Reserve fund and undivided profits.	Total.	Liabilities.	Ratio to liabilities of—	
	Bks	Br'chs.	Total.					Capital.	Capital and profits.
								Pr. ct.	*Pr. ct.*
England and Wales	72	1,144	1,216	£26,046,420	£13,761,814	£39,808,234	£223,679,548	11.64	17.80
Bank of England	1	10	11	14,553,000	3,768,531	18,321,531	51,611,899	28.20	35.50
Isle of Man	2	7	9	60,904	29,895	90,799	539,268	11.29	16.82
Scotland	10	809	819	9,045,780	4,857,882	13,903,662	82,093,497	11.02	16.94
Ireland	9	270	279	2,950,000	1,374,141	4,324,141	20,800,649	14.18	20.79
Colonial with London offices	27	969	996	20,430,136	7,336,415	27,766,551	121,905,216	16.76	22.78
Foreign with London offices	20	67	87	17,563,130	2,840,444	20,403,574	39,623,424	44.33	51.49
Totals	141	3,276	3,417	90,649,370	33,969,122	124,618,492	540,253,501	16.78	23.07

National banks.

October 1, 1878			2,053	$466,147,436	$157,833,993	$623,981,429	$1,140,179,314	40.88	54.73

A comparison of this table with a similar statement regarding the national banks, which is also given above, shows the ratio of capital to liabilities of the 3,417 banks in the United Kingdom to be 16.78 per cent., and the ratio of their capital and reserve to liabilities to be 23.07 per cent.; while the corresponding ratios of the national-banks are 40.88, and 54.73; the ratios of the national banks being in each instance more than double those of the United Kingdom. In the national banking system the existing ratio of capital to liabilities is nearly four times greater than is that of the 1,216 banks in England and Wales; while the ratio of the combined capital and reserve of the former banks to their liabilities is more than three times greater than that of the latter.

CONVERTIBILITY OF THE NOTE.

Previous to the passage of the national bank act, the circulating notes of banks located elsewhere than in New York or New England were not redeemable except at the counters of the issuing banks. As only about one-third of the circulation of the country consisted of New York and New England notes, it may be said that the remaining two-thirds had practically no general system of redemption. The legislation of the New England States provided only for redemption at the counter, although what was known as the Suffolk system compelled redemption in the city of Boston also. The New York law required redemption at the counter at par, and also in New York, Albany or Troy at one-fourth of 1 per cent. discount. The New England currency, therefore, consisted of unsecured notes redeemable at par at the place of issue and in the city of Boston, while the New York currency was a secured note redeemable at par at its counter, and at a discount at its agency. The notes of the national banks constitute the only secured circulation* ever required by law to be redeemed at par at a central agency, as well as at their place of issue.

If the New York system of redemption were to be applied to the national-bank circulation, in place of the existing method, it would probably at once raise the price of exchange to the rate current under that system, which was generally one-half of one per cent. The Suffolk system was excellent, as a voluntary arrangement entered into by 500 banks, having an aggregate circulation of fifty millions only, and all located within the comparatively moderate area of the six New England States; but it would not be a practicable one if extended to more than 2,000 banks, distributed, as are the national banks, throughout all the States of the Union, and having a circulation more than six times as great as that of the New England banks. So large a volume of circulating notes, issued at points so remote from each other, could not be made uniformly convertible by the legislative action of separate States, nor by the agency of individual corporations. Congressional action alone is adequate to accomplish this; and accordingly full provision was made by Congress for the convertibility of the national-bank circulation, by providing for its redemption at par, both at its place of issue and at the Treasury of the United States. For the latter purpose the banks are, by a late act, required to keep on deposit with the Treasurer an amount of lawful money equal to five per cent. of their circulation.

At the time of the passage of the last-named act a very large propor.

* The following extract from the London Economist of October 26, 1878, clearly illustrates the superiority of the national banking system of this country, so far as the safety of circulating notes is concerned, over the systems of Great Britain. The closing sentence, contrasting the superior system of the Isle of Man with those of the United Kingdom, is significant :

"A curious detail in the business of the City of Glasgow Bank has been brought to light. The Bank of Mona, an institution in the Isle of Man, was incorporated with it, and a large circulation of notes existed in that island. The House of Keys, which regulates these matters with more foresight than the House of Commons, in 1845 required adequate security on real estate to be held, not only against every note which was issued, but against every note signed by the authorities of the bank, whether held by them or by the public. The manager of the Bank of Mona, faithful to his trust while his superiors at Glasgow were so unmindful of theirs, has published a statement that the security is intact and immediately available. The gold which the City of Glasgow Bank should but does not hold would have been no security to the note-holder more than to any other creditor of the bank. The annual migrations of sovereigns to the north, in accordance with the act of 1845, is a continual inconvenience to the Bank of England, and but little benefit to any one. One is tempted to ask whether something like the precedent set by the House of Keys might not be followed with advantage in Great Britain."

The London Bankers' Magazine for November of the present year, in referring to this bank failure, says :

"At all events, a strong argument in favor of the deposit of government securities, instead of the dispatch of gold to meet the periodical expansion of the Scotch circulation, is desirable from what has happened."

tion of the notes of the national banks was in a worn and mutilated condition, but within eighteen months thereafter more than $248,000,000 in such notes were received at the Treasury for redemption. For this amount about $177,000,000 of new currency was issued by the Comptroller to replace the mutilated portion, the remainder, which was fit for circulation, being returned to the banks.

In transmitting national-bank notes to the Treasury for redemption, they may be sent unassorted, that is, without reference to denominations or banks of issue, the only restriction being that they shall be presented in sums of $1,000 or a multiple thereof, while the only expense to the sender is the cost of transportation to the place of redemption. Under this system the notes of the national banks, wherever located, have possessed a uniform value, and the prices of exchange have ruled at the lowest rate. The rates of exchange between Saint Louis, Cincinnati, Chicago, and New York have been frequently at par and under, not exceeding, say, 80 cents for $1,000, instead of from ten to fifteen dollars per thousand, as was common under previous systems. Redemptions have not been so frequent under this as under the previous systems of New York and New England, for the reason that the notes are more fully secured, and also because the demand for Treasury notes has not been so great as was formerly the demand for gold under similar circumstances. The machinery of the law is, however, in operation, and the frequency of redemptions will, to a great extent, depend upon the demand for gold after specie payment shall have been resumed. But the notes of the banks being secure beyond peradventure, this demand will, in all probability, be much less than under former systems of unsecured currency.

PROFITS AND LOSSES.

The law provides that no association shall, during the time it continues its banking operations, withdraw or permit to be withdrawn, in dividends or otherwise, any portion of its capital, and that no dividend shall ever be made to an amount greater than the net profits then on hand, deducting therefrom losses and bad debts. With these restrictions, the banks are permitted to declare dividends semi-annually from their net profits, but are also required, before making any such dividend, to carry to surplus fund one-tenth part of their net profits of the preceding half year, until this fund shall equal twenty per cent. of their capital stock. The law thus designates three uses for the profits of the national banks: First, for building up a surplus fund; secondly, to protect the capital stock from impairment by losses in business, by the use of such fund when the other profits are insufficient; and, thirdly, for the declaration of dividends out of any remaining profits. As a rule, the banks in the national system have not made excessive dividends. In determining the true ratio of their profits, their accumulated surplus, as well as what is technically known as capital, must be considered, as it is from the use of both capital and surplus that their profits are derived. Even during the most prosperous years of the system, the ratio of annual earnings to the combined capital and surplus of the banks was not greatly in excess of the usual legal rates of interest in the States where they were located, while during the last two years this ratio has been less than six per cent. on the combined capital and surplus.

The surplus of the national banks amounted on October 1 to nearly $117,000,000. A part of this sum represents the profits earned by former State banks previous to their conversion into national organizations, and brought by them into the system. The greater portion was, however, accumulated by the banks during the years of business prosperity immediately succeeding the close of the war. The following table exhibits the amount of surplus held by the banks on or near the 1st day of January and July in each year since 1863, as shown by their reports for the dates nearest thereto, together with the semi-annual increase or decrease therein:

Dates.	Surplus.		Dates.	Surplus.	
	Amount.	Semi-annual increase or decrease.		Amount.	Semi-annual increase or decrease.
		Increase.			Increase.
July 4, 1864	$1,129,910		December 16, 1871 ..	$101,573,154	$3,250,950
January 2, 1865	8,663,311	$7,533,401	June 10, 1872	105,181,943	3,608,789
July 3, 1865	31,303,566	22,640,255	December 27, 1872 ...	111,410,249	6,228,306
January 1, 1866	43,000,371	11,696,805	June 13, 1873	116,847,455	5,437,206
July 2, 1866	50,151,992	7,151,621	December 26, 1873 ...	120,961,268	4,113,813
January 7, 1867	59,992,875	9,840,883	June 26, 1874	126,239,308	5,278,040
July 1, 1867	63,232,811	3,239,936	December 31, 1874 ...	130,485,641	4,246,333
January 6, 1868	70,586,126	7,253,315	June 30, 1875	133,169,095	2,683,454
July 6, 1868	75,840,119	5,253,993			Decrease.
January 4, 1869	81,169,937	5,329,818	December 17, 1875 ...	133,085,422	$83,673
June 12, 1869	82,218,576	1,048,639	June 30, 1876	131,897,107	1,188,225
January 22, 1870	90,174,281	7,955,705	December 22, 1876 ...	131,390,605	506,532
June 9, 1870	91,689,834	1,515,553	June 22, 1877	124,714,073	6,676,592
December 28, 1870	94,705,740	3,015,906	December 28, 1877 ...	121,568,455	3,145,618
June 10, 1871	98,322,204	3,616,464	June 29, 1878	118,178,531	3,389,924

It will be seen that the maximum surplus was reached in June, 1875, and that there has since then been a gradual diminution of this fund. The diminution has been caused by charging thereto, from time to time, portions of the losses sustained by the national banks, such losses aggregating, during the last three years, the large sum of $64,119,415, as shown in the following table:

Six months ending—	New England States.		Middle States.		Southern States.		Western States and Territories.		United States.	
	No.	Amount.	No.	Amount.	No.	Amount.	No.	Amount.	No.	Amount.
March 1, 1876	201	$1,485,532	268	$3,553,129	67	$308,861	270	$1,153,648	806	$6,501,170
September 1, 1876	282	3,074,128	344	7,156,349	90	896,891	318	2,090,489	1,034	13,217,857
Total, 1876		4,559,660		10,709,478		1,205,752		3,244,137		19,719,027
March 1, 1877	289	2,465,328	314	3,462,684	80	478,252	297	1,769,697	980	8,175,961
September 1, 1877	312	4,825,040	353	3,945,806	86	511,841	357	2,474,940	1,108	11,757,627
Total, 1877		7,290,368		7,408,490		990,093		4,244,637		19,933,588
March 1, 1878	327	3,344,012	417	4,506,813	124	672,032	436	2,380,288		10,903,145
September 1, 1878	399	4,016,814	449	5,502,770	140	1,225,602	442	2,818,409	1,430	13,563,655
Total, 1878		7,360,826		10,009,583		1,897,634		5,198,757		24,466,800
Total for 3 years		19,210,854		28,127,551		4,093,479		12,687,531		64,119,415

Of the $36,224,427 of loans charged off within the last eighteen months, as shown above, $5,326,072 was on account of depreciation in the premium on the United States bonds held by the banks.

The total losses thus charged off equal nearly fourteen per cent. of the entire capital of the banks. Although the charging up of losses has very considerably reduced the surplus of the banks, yet if the total losses incurred had been wholly charged to this fund it would have been still more largely diminished. The greater portion of the losses mentioned has been canceled by charging it to the account of current profits, in consequence of which 357 banks, with an aggregate capital of $58,736,950, have, in the last six months, paid no dividends at all; while during the last three years the average number of banks semi-annually passing dividends on account of losses has been 288. This number is equal to about one-seventh of the whole number now in operation. The average amount of capital upon which no dividends have been paid during that time is $44,583,515; from which it follows that for a continuous period of three years more than one-tenth of the total capital of the national banks has been without profit to its owners. This is exhibited in the following table:

Geographical divisions.	Six months ending—				Average for the year.	
	March 1, 1878.		September 1, 1878.			
	No. of banks.	Capital.	No. of banks.	Capital.	No. of banks.	Capital.
New England States...............	37	$9,389,500	51	$14,870,000	44	$12,129,750
Middle States	95	17,244,400	114	22,454,850	105	19,849,625
Southern States..................	36	5,266,000	44	6,867,000	40	6,066,500
Western States and Territories....	160	16,898,000	148	14,545,100	154	15,721,550
Totals for 1878	328	48,797,900	357	58,736,950	343	53,767,425
Totals for 1877	245	40,452,000	288	41,166,200	266	40,809,100
Totals for 1876	235	34,290,320	273	44,057,725	254	39,174,022
Average for three years	269	41,180,073	306	47,986,958	288	44,583,515

Many of the banks, also, which have declared dividends within the last three years have done so wholly or in part out of profits other than surplus previously accumulated by them, and not out of their current earnings.

The following table shows by geographical divisions the ratio to capital and surplus of the dividends declared by all the national banks during the last nine years:

Geographical divisions.	Ratio of dividends to capital and surplus.									
	1870.	1871.	1872.	1873.	1874.	1875.	1876.	1877.	1878.	Average.
	Per ct.	Per ct.	Per ct.	Per ct.	Per ct.	Per ct.	Per ct.	Per ct.	Per ct.	Per ct.
New England States	8.4	8.3	8.1	8.2	7.7	7.6	6.7	6.0	5.5	7.4
Middle States....................	8.1	7.9	7.9	7.9	7.6	7.6	7.7	6.6	6.1	7.5
Southern States..................	10.7	10.1	9.5	8.8	8.2	7.7	7.6	7.1	6.2	8.4
Western States	8.5	8.9	9.3	9.0	8.6	8.6	8.1	9.6	7.7	8.7
United States	8.4	8.3	8.3	8.3	7.9	7.8	7.5	7.1	6.2	7.7

The ratio to capital and surplus of the total net earnings of all the national banks was, in 1876, 6.9 per cent., in 1877, 5.6 per cent., and in 1878, 5.1 per cent.

The average ratio of dividends to capital in the New England and Middle States, where the greater portion of the capital of the national banks is held, was during the last three years 8.2 per cent. In the same States the ratio of dividends to the combined capital and surplus was 6.5 per cent., and the ratio of the net earnings to capital and surplus was 5.1 per cent.

The belief, so widely entertained, that the profits made by the national banks are excessive, is in great part due to the exceptionally large dividends paid by a few banks which are favorably located and have a large surplus, and which make large returns to their shareholders on the amount of their nominal capital. The profits of these banks are not to any considerable extent derived from their circulation, but from surplus and deposits. Many of the banks making these exceptional dividends have a much less amount of circulation than those making moderate dividends only, while a few of them have no circulation whatever.

If the bank act gives to the national banks the privilege of circulation, it also provides for a United States tax upon circulation, deposits and capital, and for a State tax upon the shares of each bank, to be determined by the legislature of each State, at a rate estimated to be not greater than is assessed upon other money capital in the hands of individual citizens of each State. The total amount of United States taxes collected from the commencement of the system to the present time is as follows:

On circulation.	On deposits.	On capital.	Total.
$39,775,817 35	$40,328,256 32	$5,929,480 73	$86,033,554 40

The annual amount of taxation, national and State, has for the last four years been as follows:

Years.	National.	State.	Total.
1874	$7,256,083	$9,620,326	$16,876,409
1875	7,317,531	10,058,122	17,375,653
1876	7,076,087	9,701,732	16,777,819
1877	6,902,573	8,829,304	15,731,877
Totals	28,552,274	38,209,484	66,761,758

More complete tables, showing the amount of taxes collected from the banks of each State and principal city of the Union, will be found upon subsequent pages of this report. The rate of taxation upon the banks in the city of New York and in other cities has averaged more than five per cent. annually during the past four years, and there is no doubt that the annual taxes collected from these institutions has been greatly in excess of the rate collected upon the capital of other corporations, private firms, and individuals, which cannot be as accurately determined as is that of the national banks from their published statements.

NATIONAL BANK FAILURES.

The failures in this country of State banks and private bankers are known to have been numerous and frequent; but information as to their numbers, or to the consequent losses to their stockholders or creditors, has not been attainable by the Comptroller. The bank departments of the different States give no information on this subject except as to the losses upon bank currency, and even that information has been of a scanty character. As a rule, under the different State laws, the affairs of insolvent institutions have been liquidated by a receiver appointed by the court, and the receiver has not reported to any State officer, but to the court which appointed him. Full information with reference to these insolvent institutions is therefore in most cases unattainable. The losses upon currency are estimated to have been five per cent. annually upon the amount issued, but no estimate has ever been made of the losses to creditors and shareholders. Under the national-bank system, however, the losses as well as profits of each bank are reported to this Office. If a bank becomes insolvent, the Comptroller, by law, appoints the receiver, and exercises full supervision over the closing up of its affairs. The files of this Office, therefore, contain a complete record of everything pertaining to the settlement of the business of such associations. The following table exhibits the number of failures of national banks in each State, together with their capital, amount of claims proved, the amount of dividends paid, and the estimated losses to creditors, from the organization of the system to July 1 of the present year:

State.	No. of banks.	Capital.	Claims proved.	Dividends paid.	Estimated losses.	Percentage of dividends paid.
Connecticut	1	$60,000	$97,541	$82,910	$10,000	85.
New York	16	4,076,100	5,722,248	5,060,536	320,498	88,43
Pennsylvania	8	1,312,000	1,558,564	898,103	416,850	57.62
District of Columbia	2	700,000	2,288,828	1,785,173	503,655	78.
Virginia	4	800,000	1,679,045	646,818	931,789	38.52
Alabama	1	100,000	289,407	121,551	167,856	42.
Mississippi	1	50,000	33,562	11,746	20,900	35.
Louisiana	3	1,600,000	2,981,554	1,805,060	922,900	61.02
Texas	1	50,000	60,330		60,000	
Arkansas	1	50,000	15,142	15,142		100.
Tennessee	1	100,000	376,932	65,335	311,597	17.33
Missouri	3	3,100,000	2,683,083	951,918	740,000	35.48
Ohio	3	250,000	422,891	190,557	189,800	45.06
Indiana	4	282,000	505,531	239,893	178,800	47.45
Illinois	8	2,250,000	3,366,767	1,414,368	1,096,198	42.01
Wisconsin	1	50,000	134,445	47,055	70,000	35.00
Iowa	3	200,000	290,477	181,128	90,998	62.35
Minnesota	2	200,000	313,429	210,016	61,000	67.
Kansas	2	160,000	141,576	84,195	57,381	59.47
Nevada	1	250,000	170,012	153,011	17,001	90.
Colorado	2	225,000	178,135	32,418	177,000	18.19
Utah	1	150,000	89,200	13,380	71,200	15.
Totals	69	16,015,100	23,398,709	14,010,313	6,415,423	59.88

From the above table it will be seen that the total amount of capital of all the insolvent national banks is $16,015,100; amount of claims proved, $23,398,709; of dividends paid, $14,010,313; while the estimated losses are but $6,415,423. The average number of failures during each of the past fifteen years has been less than five, and the average annual loss less than $430,000.

The City of Glasgow Bank, which recently failed in Scotland, had a capital and surplus of less than $8,000,000, and liabilities of more than $50,000,000. It loaned to four debtors of the bank more than $28,000,000, upon which there is a loss of more than $21,000,000. The deficiency in the assets is nearly $26,000,000, which is four times as great as the losses to all the creditors of national banks which have failed since the organization of the system. The bank superintendent of the State of New York reports the liabilities of twenty-two savings banks which have failed in that State during the last six and one-half years at $12,188,777, and estimates the losses to their creditors at $4,303,616, which is more than one-third of their entire indebtedness. He estimates the losses during the last three years at $3,400,000, which is more than one-half of the estimated losses to the creditors of all the national banks in the United States from the beginning of the system until now. The losses from five State banks in the city of Chicago during the last two years, which banks were organized under special charters, under which neither State supervision nor reports were required, is estimated to be $3,819,500, on liabilities of $5,785,572. The losses from the State and savings banks of the country during the last two years only are known to have been greater than the total loss resulting from all the failures which have occurred of national banking associations. The government has had large amounts on deposit continually with a great number of national banks throughout the country, for its convenience in making disbursements, but has suffered no loss during the past twelve years. Upon the circulating notes of the national banks there has been no loss whatever.

PUBLIC STATEMENTS AND EXAMINATIONS.

One of the most important provisions of law relating to the national banks is that requiring statements of their resources and liabilities to be made at such times and in such manner as the Comptroller may direct, and the publication of these statements in the daily newspapers of the country. The banks are also required to make returns to the Comptroller, semi-annually, of their earnings, losses and dividends; and all of these returns are compiled by him and annually transmitted to Congress. The Comptroller has authority to call upon the banks for any and all information concerning their affairs which may be thought of value; and it is his endeavor to communicate annually to Congress and the people the fullest possible knowledge attainable upon every question of interest connected with the business of banking. Letters, also, from whatever source, asking for proper information on these subjects, are always fully answered. The annual reports which have been issued from this Office are themselves evidence of the great amount and value of the information to be derived from the returns made by the national banks.

The law also provides for a thorough examination of the banks by competent persons as frequently as the Comptroller may think desirable. This feature of the law was at first exceedingly unpopular, but it is now generally approved by the banks themselves, and has been attended with the best results. Irregularities are not so likely to be allowed when it is known that they may be exposed by a competent examiner. In numerous instances unlawful dividends have been prevented, impaired capital discovered and its restoration compelled, and large losses to both shareholders and creditors avoided, by the prompt action of this office, based upon the report of an examiner. The excellent system now in operation is in strong contrast with the generally lax systems of bank reports and supervision which prevailed previous to the passage of the national-bank act.

The Comptroller, in his report for 1876, made an effort to collect from official sources the general bank statistics of the country. Only two balanced statements of the first Bank of the United States could be found, and previous to 1832 the published bank statistics consisted mainly of estimates made, or statements unofficially compiled, by individuals. Subsequently statements were obtained by this department from the several State officials, and were compiled annually for the use of Congress. But the State laws differed widely in their requirements, both as to the nature of the returns to be made by the banks and the dates which they should bear. Instead of a uniform time and similarity in form being required by all the States, as is now required under the national system, there was great diversity in both date and form, so that when the compilation of the reports was completed by this department the work was very unsatisfactory, and it was found impracticable to give anything like a just or true presentment of the condition of the banks of the country on or near any given day.

For the last five years the Comptroller, in obedience to an act of Congress, has endeavored to compile annually the returns made by the State banks to the different State officials; but the same difficulties in this regard exist now that existed before the establishment of the national-banking system. The constitution of the State of Illinois provides "that every banking association now and which may hereafter be organized under the laws of the State, shall make and publish a full and accurate quarterly statement of its affairs, which shall be certified to under oath by one or more of its officers"; but although bills designed to carry out this provision of the constitution have been often introduced into the legislature, they have thus far failed to be enacted in the form of law. Many other States have no laws whatever upon the subject, and complete returns can be obtained from not more than one-half of the States in the Union.

For many years past there has been a growing desire to obtain the fullest data possible concerning the condition of all public corporations, and especially of all financial institutions; but if the present homogeneous system, which has accomplished so much in this direction, be now abolished, all further hope of obtaining full and reliable banking statistics may be at once abandoned.

The London Economist of October 26, 1878, in commenting upon the report of the directors of the City of Glasgow Bank, says:

A more complete publication of banking accounts, as well as a more rigid audit, will probably be insisted on for the future. A real audit of such accounts is most difficult to make, but some authentication by qualified persons outside the business is obviously required. Though publication of accounts is not by any means a complete safeguard, yet a more thorough statement of the position of the business would have prevented much of the mischief.

In contrast with the beneficial workings of the national system in this respect, the Comptroller presents below an extract from the London Bankers' Magazine for May, 1877, commenting upon the statement contained in a previous annual report to Congress. The editor says:

Our last number contained a statement as to the position of banking in the United States of America. It is not possible, as our readers know, to publish any similar statement as to banking in England. No private bank in England has, we believe, ever put forward any authorized statement as to the position of its accounts, and it is barely possible to imagine a time in which such an innovation on the established practice could occur. Most of the joint-stock banks in England now publish their accounts; even among them, however, the custom is far from universal, though the number of those who prefer to keep the state of their affairs in privacy is steadily on the decrease; and it is very desirable that this should be the case. It cannot be doubted that a statement of the position of the main facts of banking would be often of service. In times of pressure a reliable official statement would tend to allay anxiety among many, and the careful banker would obtain from it information ready to his hand which might assist him in shaping his course at such periods. No such statement, however, is possible in England at the present time. The nearest approach to any such return was made in 1875, when a great many English banks, both private and joint-stock, sent returns to Sir Stafford Northcote, in connection with the proceedings before the select committee of the House of Commons on banks of issue in that year. But the manner in which this return was made, and the fact that many banks abstained from making it, and that it was impossible to supply the names either of those banks which complied with the request, or of those who did not, render the return of no value as a basis for estimating the deposits held by English banks at the present time.

FUNDING THE NATIONAL DEBT.

One of the chief objects in view in the organization of the national system was, not only to furnish bank-notes which were safe and convertible, but to supply a steady market for and facilitate the negotiation of United States bonds; and there is no doubt that the credit of the government and its ability to borrow money at low rates of interest have been greatly increased by making its bonds a basis for the issue of national-bank notes.

Of the United States bonds held by the national banks on November 1, 1868, and deposited with the Treasurer as security for their circulating notes, nearly three-fourths bore interest at the rate of six per cent. The amount of this class of bonds has since been gradually reduced, until it is now less than one-fourth of all the bonds held, while nearly one-fourth of the whole amount bears interest at the rate of four and one-half and four per cent. only. About one-fifth of the entire issues of the latter classes of bonds is now held by the national banks. This will be seen from the following table, which exhibits the amount and classes of bonds held as security for circulation on the 1st day of November, for each year since 1865, and the rate of interest which they respectively bear:

Date.	6 per cent. bonds.	5 per cent. bonds.	4½ per cent. bonds.	4 per cent. bonds.	Total.
November 1, 1865	$202,523,350	$78,619,950			$281,143,300
November 1, 1866	244,993,200	90,076,450			335,069,650
November 1, 1867	251,274,800	91,376,450			342,651,250
November 1, 1868	252,623,750	88,888,750			341,512,500
November 1, 1869	249,724,650	92,731,300			342,455,950
November 1, 1870	247,460,950	97,284,600			344,745,550
November 1, 1871	181,158,600	185,955,850			367,114,450
November 1, 1872	173,303,100	211,665,800			384,968,900
November 1, 1873	157,834,950	235,017,150			392,852,100
November 1, 1874	145,981,650	239,440,100			385,421,750
November 1, 1875	128,503,212	239,046,200			367,549,412
November 1, 1876	103,819,300	223,602,700	$10,305,800		337,727,800
November 1, 1877	81,984,550	200,090,500	45,089,700	$15,884,150	343,048,900
November 1, 1878	72,829,750	196,615,600	49,397,250	30,566,300	349,408,900

The government has still outstanding more than 693 millions of six per cent. and more than 703 millions of five per cent. bonds. The reduction of the interest on this amount to four per cent. would s ve to the government nearly 21 millions of interest annually. The funding of the six per cent. bonds into four per cents. has made rapid progress during the last year, and the banks have been of great service to the government in this process of refunding, by negotiating and absorbing a very considerable part of the new issues. Should the national system continue there is no doubt that the present rapid reduction in the burden of interest will continue also. If the national-bank system is to be abolished, and an additional amount of United States notes is to be issued, all hope of reducing the rate of interest on the public debt must be abandoned.

The larger portion of the five and six per cent. gold-bearing bonds of the United States is payable at the option of the government, and the remainder will be payable in 1881—two years hence. As already stated, 21 millions yearly may be saved to the government by funding these bonds into four per cents., while the amount which it is claimed may be annually saved by the repeal of the national-bank act and the issue of 320 millions of unconvertible Treasury notes, is 13 millions only.*

With the issue of this large amount of government notes the funding of the public debt will be rendered impossible; for the pledges of the government will then be violated and its credit permanently injured.

---

* The currency value of the interest upon the bonds deposited as security for circulation is $17,689,372, as is shown in a table on the next page. If from this amount be deducted ten per cent., $1,768,937, which is the interest upon that portion of the bonds on which the banks receive no circulation, and the tax upon the circulation issued, $3,144,680, there will remain $12,775,755, which is the net amount of currency interest received by the banks upon ninety per cent. of the bonds deposited as security for their circulating notes.

Which is the wiser course—to continue the work of funding the debt, which has so successfully progressed during the present year, thus saving the greater amount of interest named, while adding to the credit of the country, or to attempt, by the repeal of the national-bank act, to save the less amount, and at the loss, as well, of reputation and credit? Is there not danger that attempts to remove an imaginary evil may be followed by the introduction of a real and much greater evil? Success in funding the national debt through the co-operation of two thousand of the principal monetary institutions of the country may be assured, but the effects of the issue of a large amount of irredeemable government currency cannot be foretold.

VALUE OF CIRCULATION TO THE NATIONAL BANKS.

The profit to the national banks derived from the issue of circulating notes is not great, as is frequently asserted, being but about $2\frac{1}{2}$ per cent. more per annum on the capital invested in the bonds pledged to secure the circulation than could be obtained by lending directly the same amount of capital. The table below shows the amount of bonds deposited in the Treasury on November 1, 1878, to secure national bank circulation, their various classes, their currency value, the circulation issuable thereon, and the annual interest upon them:

Class of bonds.	Par value.	Currency value.	Circulation issuable.	Annual gold interest.	Currency value of interest.
Sixes of 1881	$56,483,450	$61,072,730	$50,835,105	$3,380,007	$3,397,480
Five-twenties of 1865, 2d series	825,700	851,503	743,130	49,542	49,666
Five-twenties of 1865, 3d series, 1867s	8,172,100	8,672,641	7,354,890	490,326	491,552
Five-twenties of 1865, 4th series, 1868s	1,764,500	1,905,660	1,588,050	105,870	106,135
Ten-forties of 1864	70,688,850	75,195,264	63,619,965	3,534,443	3,543,279
Fives of 1881, funded 1881s	125,926,750	132,223,088	113,334,075	6,296,337	6,312,078
Four-and-one-halfs of 1891, funded 1891s	49,397,250	51,311,393	44,457,525	2,222,876	2,228,433
Fours of 1907, consols of 1907	30,566,300	30,506,300	27,509,670	1,222,652	1,225,709
Pacific Railroad bonds	5,584,000	6,735,700	5,025,600		335,040
Total	349,408,900	368,534,279	314,468,010	17,311,053	17,689,372

It will be seen that the currency value of the bonds, which represents the amount of capital invested in their purchase, is $368,534,279. If this amount of capital were placed at interest at eight per cent. per annum, estimated as the average rate of interest obtainable throughout the country, it would produce $29,482,742. The annual interest on the bonds of the banks amounts, as shown by the table, to $17,311,053 in gold and $335,040 in currency, the total currency value of the interest on November 1, 1878 (gold being quoted at the New York stock exchange on that date at one-quarter of one per cent. premium), being $17,689,372, which is the whole amount received annually by the banks; but as they are required to pay into the Treasury of the United States a tax of one per cent. per annum upon their circulation, which, upon the amount issuable, is $3,144,680, the net amount of interest received by them is thereby reduced to $14,544,692. This amount, together with the interest which the banks receive on the amount of their circulation available for use, gives the whole income derived by them from their circulation and the bonds deposited to secure it.

The amount available for use is that issuable (being 90 per cent. of the par value of the bonds pledged), less an amount equal to five per cent. thereof, which the banks are required, by the act of June 20, 1874, to place with the Treasurer of the United States, as a redemption fund. Therefore, even if the banks could keep loaned out all the time the whole of their circulation available for use, which is in practice an impossibility, they could have free for loaning but $298,744,610 of the $314,468,010 issuable upon their bonds; and that amount loaned at the rate named, eight per cent. per annum, would produce $23,899,569, which, together with the net interest received on the bonds, makes $38,444,261 as the income derived by the banks from their bonds and circulation, as against $29,482,742 that would be produced by lending the capital invested in the bonds directly at the same rate of interest. The difference between the two sums, which is $8,961,519, or 2.43 per cent. on the capital invested, represents the true amount of profit that the banks can, under the most favorable circumstances, receive from their circulation.

To recapitulate:

The interest at 8 per cent. per annum on the loanable amount of circulation, which, as shown above, is $298,744.610, is	$23, 899, 569
The currency value of the interest on the bonds deposited to secure the circulation is	17, 689, 372
Gross amount received by the banks from bonds and loanable circulation..	41, 588, 941
From which deduct one per cent. of the issuable amount of circulation as the tax thereon	3, 144, 680
Net income upon the capital employed	38, 444, 261
The capital necessary to purchase the bonds pledged by the banks, which, as shown above, is $368.534.279, loaned at 8 per cent. per annum would produce	29, 482, 742
Difference, representing the profit on circulation if the whole amount available for use be loaned continually throughout the year.	8, 961, 519

Two and forty-three hundredths per cent. on the capital employed ($368,534,279) is $8,955,383, which, as shown above, is about the value of circulation to the national banks if they could keep the whole amount of their issues loaned out all the time.

In the above calculation no deduction is made for the costs of the redemption of the bank circulation, which lessens by so much the profits on circulation. The cost of redemption for the fiscal year ending June 30, 1878, was $317,942.48; for the year ending June 30, 1877, it was $357,066.10; for the year ending June 30, 1876, $365,193.31; and for the year ending June 30, 1875, $290,965.37.

In localities where the annual rate of interest is seven per cent., the value of circulation is about two and sixty-two hundredths per cent. per annum, and where the rate is ten per cent., its value is about two and five-hundredths per cent.

The large margin ($54,066,269) between the value of the bonds owned by the banks and the circulation issuable thereon, would, in case of disaster, be available as a reserve for the payment of the depositors or other creditors; and this is an additional argument in favor of issuing circulation under the restrictions of the law as now provided.

Another thing that should be considered in estimating the value of circulation is, that the banks held their bonds at a premium, which, though it has been greatly reduced in the past, still appears among their assets for a large amount, and which will disappear when the bonds shall mature and be paid by the United States. The amount of premium appearing as an asset of the banks on October 1, 1878, the date of the last report of their condition, is $7,134,736.

If all of the bonds of the banks necessary to secure their circulation were converted into four per cent. bonds, the value of circulation, taking the same amounts of bonds and circulation as are used above, would be shown as follows:

Interest on $298,744,610 of circulation, loaned at 8 per cent. per annum .. $23, 899, 569
Currency value of interest on bonds 14, 011, 297
                                                                           _____
    Total 37, 910, 866
Less tax on circulation 3, 144, 680
                                                                           _____
    Total profit on capital employed 34, 766, 186
The same capital loaned directly at 8 per cent. per annum would earn... 29, 482, 742
                                                                           _____
Difference, representing profit on circulation when the whole issue is kept
    loaned out 5, 283, 444
which is 1 43/100 per cent. on the capital employed.

The average rate of State taxation upon the capital of the national banks is about two per cent. per annum; and if they should go into liquidation, and the owners of the bonds should continue to hold them, the amount of State taxation saved to them would nearly or quite equal the benefit they now derive from circulation.

NO SAVING TO THE GOVERNMENT BY THE SUBSTITUTION OF TREASURY FOR NATIONAL-BANK NOTES.

The amount of legal-tender notes outstanding is 346 millions; of national bank notes, 322 millions; making a total of 668 millions. It is not probable that additional legal-tender notes can be constitutionally issued. If, therefore, Treasury notes shall be substituted for the present national-bank notes, it is doubtful if they can be made a legal tender in the payment of all debts. Two kinds of Treasury notes will then be in circulation, one of which will be a full legal tender and the other not, even between national banks, as is now the case with their own notes. The full legal-tender notes will be of greater value than the other class, unless both are alike redeemable in gold at the commercial centers.

The banks hold among their resources 830 millions in bills receivable, and an equally large amount of other assets, a large proportion of which is readily convertible into money. Their deposits and bank balances amount to more than 600 millions, and their circulating notes are promptly redeemed, with but little expense to the holders, through the use of their assets, which represent their capital, surplus, and deposits. If more notes are issued to the banks than are necessary for the requirements of business, they can be easily retired. If a larger amount is desired, they can be readily obtained upon application in the manner provided by law. On the other hand, if the entire circulation of the country is to be issued by the government, its amount must be fixed by Congress, and can be neither increased nor diminished except by its action. The Treasury note represents no business capital, and the volume of the currency will be controlled, not by the demands of business and the wants of the country, but by the views and action of political parties and of Congress.

The government, unlike the banks, does not receive deposits nor loan money, and it must therefore provide for the redemption of its notes from its own resources. If it issues a small amount of currency, the amount of reserve required and the expense of redemption will be small; but if it issues the whole paper currency of the country, it must, when specie payments are reached, maintain a ratio of reserve equal to that of the Bank of England or the Bank of France, which is not less in either case than one-third of the amount of its issues. If the amount of government issues should reach 668 millions, which is the present volume of the currency, a reserve of 223 millions in coin must be kept on hand. The interest upon this amount of reserve, at the lowest government rate (4 per cent.), would be $8,920,000. The expense of issuing the notes and the cost of redemption would also be large, and the total cost to the government, including the hazards attending the issue of so large an amount of money, would not probably be less than 10 millions of dollars annually. This amount is but three millions less than that of the net annual interest received by the national banks upon their bonds, and is much greater than the profits derived by them from their entire circulation.

If the amount of Treasury notes should be largely increased, and be subject, as they will, to additional increase by each successive Congress, the ability of the government to redeem them will in time be questioned, and the amount and proportion of reserve required will need to be increased, thus adding materially to the expense attending the issue. If United States Treasury notes are substituted for the national-bank notes and specie payments are resumed, it is evident that the government will save but little, if anything, by the transaction. If not convertible, two kinds of Treasury notes, as before stated, will then be in circulation. The old legal-tender note will be preferred, separate accounts of each kind of notes will be kept, and the difference of exchange, which has practically disappeared under the present system, will again appear in every business transaction.

Nearly all of the United States bonds held by the national banks are, by the explicit terms of the acts under which they were issued, payable, both principal and interest, in coin. These coin-bearing bonds will bear a high premium in the market, in comparison with the new issues of inconvertible Treasury notes. Only three years ago, in 1875, the five and six per cent. bonds of the United States were at a premium of from 15 to 20 per cent. in Treasury notes, which were a full legal tender, and which were limited in the amount of issue. The issue of the new Treasury notes in place of national-bank notes will therefore be attended with an advance in premium upon the bonds of the government held by the banks, in amount not less than from fifty to sixty millions of dollars, and probably exceeding that sum; and if the bonds held by the banks are purchased with the proposed new issue of Treasury notes, this loss of premium must at the outset be borne by the government.

It is believed by the Comptroller that this proposed substitution is impracticable, and that the repeal of the national-bank act will result, not in an additional issue of Treasury notes, but in the restoration of State systems similar to those which were previously in operation. Secretary Chase, in his report for 1861, said that the establishment of the national-bank system would "avoid the evils of a great and sudden change in the currency, by offering inducements to solvent existing institutions to withdraw the circulation issued under State authority, and substitute that provided by the authority of the Union"; and that "through the voluntary action of the existing institutions, ordered by wise legislation, the great transition from a currency heterogeneous, unequal, and unsafe, to one uniform, equal, and safe, may be speedily and almost imperceptibly accomplished."

The national-bank act became a law on February 25, 1863, but the inducements offered by the Secretary were not sufficient to bring about, to any great extent, the conversion of existing State into national associations. Subsequently, on March 3, 1865, an act was passed, which provided "that every national banking association, State bank, or State banking association, shall pay a tax of ten per centum on the amount of notes of any State bank or State banking association paid out by them after the first day of July, 1866." As soon as it became apparent that this bill, in effect taxing out of existence the State bank notes, would become a law, the State banks of New York, New England, and of other States, surrendered their old charters and entered into the national system; not as a matter of choice, but either because they foresaw that the banks in the national system would, in the future, possess a higher character than that of other similar institutions, or because, having always had the privilege of issuing circulating notes, they desired to retain that privilege.

According to the Comptroller's report for December, 1865, 731 State banks became national associations during the year preceding the report, and of the 1,601 national banks in operation at the close of the year named, 922 were conversions. These banks, however, almost without exception, came into the system reluctantly, but with the expectation of a continuance of their charters for twenty years, as provided in the act. They had conducted a successful business as State associations for many years previous to and during the war. They had loaned gold dollars to the people and received in return the greenback, which purchased the bonds now held as security for their circulating notes; and, therefore, contrary to the existing general belief, they did not realize large profits upon the purchase of these bonds. The restrictions of the act were burdensome and unpopular with the banks. Experience has shown them to be good, and the banks have become habituated to those prohibitions which at first were so objectionable. The strong banks, with their large surplus and deposits and loans, do not ask for a change; but others, comprising a large class, not so favorably located nor so prosperous, would welcome again the condition they once enjoyed of freedom from legal restrictions and official supervision.

The national banks, as a class, are by no means enthusiastic advocates of the national system, as is implied in the assertions of those who proclaim that these banks will form a combination or union for its defense at any hazard. No formidable combination can be organized among them to save the system from repeal. On the contrary, it will be found that large numbers of the banks will quietly acquiesce in such repeal, provided they shall be satisfied that the old State systems are certain to be revived. Bills for the repeal of the act of March 3, 1865, which taxed the State bank circulation out of existence, have been already introduced in Congress, speeches favoring this measure have, during the late canvas, been made by representatives of many States, and resolutions of chambers of commerce in many of the principal Southern cities ask for the repeal of the 10 per cent. prohibition. The national-banking system, with its restrictions and wise provisions, may, under the excitement of an unfounded prejudice, be destroyed, but its destruction will soon be followed by a revival of the old objectionable State systems, with all the evils which formerly accompanied them, and from which they are inseparable.

In New York and Massachusetts, Wisconsin, Minnesota, Iowa, and other States, provisions either of law or of the constitution now exist, which prohibit the issue of circulating notes, unless secured in a manner similar to those issued under the provisions of the national banking system. As a consequence of these laws and constitutional provisions, the bonds now held in the Treasury at Washington will be largely transferred to the capitals of many of the States, the result being that while, contrary to the expectation of many, no great saving of interest to the government will ensue, the circulating notes of State associations, secured and unsecured, will soon fill the places now occupied by the uniform circulation of the national banks. But even if this circulation shall all be well secured, it will be impossible, under the varying legislation of different States, to secure the issue of a homogeneous currency of equal value throughout the country. Many useful restrictions may be adopted, but it would be hopeless to expect all the States to agree upon a central point of redemption outside of their own respective boundaries, or upon a uniform system of cash reserve, or upon similarity in form of public statements. State lines, as formerly, will bound the field of circulation of many of the Southern and Western issues, while the notes of New York and New England will not only monopolize the field within their own boundaries, but will successfully contest the privilege of circulation in those States remote from the commercial centers, which have no Eastern agency for the redemption of their notes. Eastern communities will suffer comparatively little from the unsound issues of other States, but those which are less favored with capital will, as of old, be the chosen field for the establishment of illegitimate corporations. The cost of exchange, which under the present system has, during the last fifteen years, nearly disappeared, will be again revived. The rate will not, perhaps, be so large as in former times, but yet large enough to be a grievous burden upon the business of the country.

Few persons have a just conception of the many advantages possessed by a homogeneous currency, fully secured, the issue of a single system, redeemable at a common point, and exempt from the discount occasioned by an irregularity of value in different localities. Great pains have been taken to obtain an estimate of the amount of exchange issued annually upon New York by the Western and Southern States. The amount drawn upon New York alone is estimated at nearly three thousand millions of dollars annually; and it will not probably be an exaggeration to say that not less than four thousand millions of dollars are annually drawn in exchange by the West and South upon the East. The amounts drawn upon each other by the banks in the commercial cities and States of the East is also great. In 1859 the average cost of Southern and Western exchange upon New York, was not less than from 1 to 1¼ per cent. If this latter rate should be restored, the cost of exchange alone would be sixty millions annually; while if the rate were but one-half of one per cent., which was the current rate in the State of New York in the year 1860, a loss in exchange of twenty millions annually would ensue, to say nothing of the loss upon the issues of banks not properly organized.

The overthrow of the present well-established system, with its abundant capital and reserve, its large surplus, and its wise provisions, will be succeeded, either by two kinds of government notes, one or both at a discount for gold and of unequal current value, or by circulating notes issued under State authority. Either system will be bad. The one will be subject to the changing opinion of each successive Congress, and the other to the independent caprice of the legislatures of forty States.

The proposition is, to save money to the government by placing the principal existing monetary institutions of the country in liquidation at a time when specie payment is assured. There will be no saving to the government, but a loss of millions of dollars annually to the people, which loss will increase yearly with the growth of business and commerce between the different States.

Since 1863 the measure of value has been subject to such frequent changes that business men, no matter how careful their calculations or prudent their arrangements, have been continually deceived by the false regulator which measures every transaction. If any single day is selected, for the purpose of comparison, from the business days of each of the last sixteen years, the measure of value will be found to have been as variable as the thermometer. This will be clearly seen in the following table, which gives the value, in standard gold coin, of the legal-tender paper dollar on July 1 of each year from 1864 to 1878, and also its value on November 18 of the present year:

1864.	1865.	1866.	1867.	1868.	1869.	1870.	1871.	1872.	1873.	1874.	1875.	1876.	1877.	1878.	1878.
Cts.	Cts.	Cts.	Cts.	Cts.	Cts.	Cts.	Cts.	Cts.	Cts.	Cts.	Cts.	Cts.	Cts.	Cts.	Cts.
38. 7	70. 4	66. 0	71. 7	70. 1	73. 5	85. 6	89. 0	87. 5	86. 4	91. 0	87. 2	89. 2	94. 5	99. 4	99. 8

In 1864 the value both of the Treasury note and the national-bank note was less than thirty-nine cents to the dollar. They are now alike worth ninety-nine and eighty-seven hundredths cents. It is within the province of the present Congress to discountenance henceforth in this country the use of a false and fluctuating measure of value, and to insure in its stead the use of a measure which is everywhere recognized as honest and true. The business interests of this country demand a permanent system of finance, free from the influence of political parties and from the ever-varying opinions of legislative bodies.

President Lincoln, in his annual message to Congress of December 1, 1862, said :

The condition of the finances will claim your most diligent consideration. The vast expenditures incident to the military and naval operations required for the suppression of the rebellion, have hitherto been met with promptitude, and certainty, unusual in similar circumstances; and the public credit has been fully maintained. The continuance of the war, however, and the increased disbursements made necessary by the augmented forces now in the field, demand your best reflections as to the best modes of providing the necessary revenue, without injury to business, and with the least possible burdens upon labor.

The suspension of specie payments by the banks, soon after the commencement of your last session, made large issues of United States notes unavoidable. In no other way could the payment of the troops, and the satisfaction of other just demands, be so economically, or so well provided for. The judicious legislation of Congress, securing the receivability of these notes for loans and internal duties, and making them a legal tender for other debts, has made them an universal currency; and has satisfied, partially, at least and for the time, the long-felt want of an uniform circulating medium, saving thereby to the people, immense sums in discounts and exchanges.

A return to specie payments, however, at the earliest period compatible with due regard to all interests concerned, should ever be kept in view. Fluctuations in the value of currency are always injurious, and to reduce these fluctuations to the lowest possible point will always be a leading purpose in wise legislation. Convertibility, prompt and certain convertibility into coin, is generally acknowledged to be the best and surest safeguard against them; and it is extremely doubtful whether a circulation of United States notes, payable in coin, and sufficiently large for the wants of the people, can be permanently, usefully, and safely maintained.

Is there, then, any other mode in which the necessary provision for the public wants can be made, and the great advantages of a safe and uniform currency secured? I know of none which promises so certain results, and is, at the same time, so unobjectionable as the organization of banking associations, under a general act of Congress, well guarded in its provisions. To such associations the government might furnish circulating notes, on the security of United States bonds deposited in the Treasury. These notes, prepared under the supervision of proper officers, being uniform in appearance and security, and convertible always into coin, would at once protect labor against the evils of a vicious currency, and facilitate commerce by cheap and safe exchanges. A moderate reservation from the interest on the bonds would compensate the United States for the preparation and distribution of the notes, and a general supervision of the system, and would lighten the burden of that part of the public debt employed as securities. The public credit, moreover, would be greatly improved, and the negotiation of new loans greatly facilitated by the steady market demand for government bonds which the adoption of the proposed system would create.

It is an additional recommendation of the measure, of considerable weight, in my judgment, that it would reconcile, as far as possible, all existing interests, by the opportunity offered to existing institutions to reorganize under the act, substituting only the secured uniform national circulation for the local and various circulation, secured and unsecured, now issued by them.

In his annual message of December 8, 1863, he refers to the same subject as follows:

The operations of the Treasury during the last year have been successfully conducted. The enactment by Congress of a national-banking law has proved a valuable support of the public credit; and the general legislation in relation to loans has fully answered the expectations of its favorers. Some amendments may be required to perfect existing laws; but no change in their principles or general scope is believed to be needed. Since these measures have been in operation, all demands on the Treasury, including the pay of the army and navy, have been promptly met and fully satisfied. No considerable body of troops, it is believed, were ever more amply provided, and more liberally and punctually paid; and it may be added that by no people were the burdens incident to a great war ever more cheerfully borne.

In his message of December 6, 1864, he again refers to the subject, and says:

The national-banking system is proving to be acceptable to capitalists and to the people. On the twenty-fifth day of November five hundred and eighty-four national banks had been organized, a considerable number of which were conversions from State banks. Changes from State systems to the national system are rapidly taking place, and it is hoped that, very soon, there will be in the United States no banks of issue not authorized by Congress, and no bank-note circulation not secured by the government. That the government and the people will derive great benefit from this change in the banking systems of the country can hardly be questioned. The national system will create a reliable and permanent influence in support of the national credit, and protect the people against losses in the use of paper money. Whether or not any further legislation is advisable for the suppression of State bank issues, it will be for Congress to determine. It seems quite clear that the Treasury cannot be satisfactorily conducted unless the government can exercise a restraining power over the bank-note circulation of the country.

More than a year before the passage of the national-bank act, Secretary Chase, in referring to the proposed system, said:

Its principal features are, first, a circulation of notes bearing a common impression and authenticated by a common authority; second, the redemption of these notes by the associations and institutions to which they may be delivered for issue; and, third, the security of that redemption by the pledge of United States stocks and an adequate provision of specie. In this plan the people, in their ordinary business, would find the advantages of uniformity in currency; of uniformity in security; of effectual safeguard, if effectual safeguard is possible, against depreciation; and of protection from losses in discounts and exchanges; while in the operations of the government the people would find the further advantage of a large demand for government securities, of increased facilities for obtaining the loans required by the war, and of some alleviation of the burdens on industry, through a diminution in the rate of interest or a participation in the profit of circulation, without risking the perils of a great money monopoly. A further and important advantage to the people may be reasonably expected in the increased security of the Union, springing from the common interest in its preservation, created by the distribution of its stocks to associations throughout the country as the basis of their circulation.

The Secretary entertains the opinion that if a credit circulation in any form be desirable it is most desirable in this. The notes thus issued and secured would, in his judgment, form the safest currency which this country has ever enjoyed, while their receivability for all government dues, except customs, would make them, wherever payable, of equal value as a currency in every part of the Union. The large amount of specie now in the United States will easily support payments of duties in coin, while these payments and ordinary demands will aid in retaining this specie in the country as a solid basis, both of circulation and loans.

The whole circulation of the country, except a limited amount of foreign coin, would, after the lapse of two or three years, bear the impress of the nation, whether in coin or notes; while the amount of the latter, always easily ascertainable and, of course, always generally known, would not be likely to be increased beyond the real wants of business. He expresses an opinion in favor of this plan with the greater confidence, because it has the advantage of recommendation from experience. It is not an untried theory. In the State of New York, and in one or more of the other States, it has been subjected in its most essential parts to the test of experiment, and has been found practicable and useful. The probabilities of success will not be diminished but increased by its adoption under national sanction and for the whole country.

These anticipations have been realized. The national banks have held, almost continually, nearly one-fifth of the bonds of the United States, thus increasing the value of these bonds and the credit of the government, so that, when recently returned to us in large amounts from abroad, they could be taken at home without depreciation, and they have also furnished a currency both safe and uniform. If the banks have received a profit from their circulation, the discounts and exchanges and the rates of interest in most of the States have been reduced, and the people have thus participated in that profit. Their notes are of equal value in every part of the Union, and the whole circulation of the country, both paper and coin, bears the impress of the nation. The amount of coin held by the country is now much larger than then estimated, the amount held by the Treasury Department being 160 millions, and the total coin and bullion in the country being estimated by the Director of the Mint at more than 358 millions. This amount is constantly increasing, and it is to-day "a solid basis" for circulation. Congress has fixed the day for the restoration of the specie standard, and the legislation needed is that which will not overthrow but co-operate with the present well-managed monetary institutions of the country in accomplishing this result. When this is done the present banking system, if then thought desirable, may be modified without danger to the credit or the business and commercial interests of this great nation.

RESUMPTION AND RESERVE.

The law provides that banks in New York City shall hold a cash reserve of 25 per cent. upon their deposits, and that banks in the other principal cities shall hold an equal ratio of reserve, one-half of which must be in bank, while the remainder may be on deposit in New York. All other banks must hold a reserve of 15 per centum upon deposits, two-fifths of which must be on hand in lawful money, and the remainder may be on deposit with banks in the reserve cities. The amount of reserve held on the first day of October last was greater than that required by law, as may be seen by reference to the following table:

Cities.	No. of banks.	Circulation.	Net deposits.	Legal-tender funds.	Due from reserve agents.	Total reserve funds.	Ratio of legal-tender funds to—		Ratio of reserve funds to circulation and deposits.
							Circulation.	Deposits.	
		millions	*millions*	*millions*	*millions*	*millions*	*per cent.*	*per cent.*	*per cent.*
New York	47	20.63	189.79	50.92	....	50.92	254.3	26.8	24.3
Boston	54	25.89	63.71	10.54	9.77	20.31	40.7	16.5	22.7
Albany	7	1.60	7.57	1.14	1.68	2.82	71.0	15.0	30.7
Philadelphia	31	11.73	43.19	10.55	4.83	15.38	89.1	24.4	28.0
Pittsburgh	22	5.72	11.82	2.76	1.71	4.47	48.4	23.4	25.5
Baltimore	14	5.36	13.04	2.74	1.78	4.52	51.1	21.0	24.6
Washington	6	0.80	1.73	0.36	0.30	0.66	44.9	20.8	26.0
New Orleans	7	1.38	5.00	1.44	0.35	1.79	104.0	28.8	28.1
Louisville	8	2.34	3.42	0.63	0.35	0.98	26.8	18.4	17.0
Cincinnati	6	3.10	8.12	2.04	1.08	3.12	65.7	25.1	27.8
Cleveland	6	1.87	5.45	1.39	1.67	3.06	74.4	25.5	41.9
Chicago	9	0.47	21.63	5.18	3.03	8.21	1106.0	24.0	37.1
Detroit	4	1.16	4.53	0.96	1.34	2.30	82.6	21.1	40.3
Milwaukee	3	0.20	2.53	0.37	0.38	0.75	183.1	14.7	27.4
Saint Louis	5	0.35	6.07	1.04	0.74	1.78	295.6	17.2	27.7
San Francisco	2	0.67	1.43	0.87	0.05	0.92	129.8	60.7	43.8
Totals	231	82.67	389.03	92.93	29.06	121.99	112.4	23.9	25.9
Other banks	1,822	219.22	288.30	50.02	56.02	106.04	22.8	17.4	20.9
Aggregates	2,053	301.89	677.33	142.95	85.08	228.03	47.3	21.1	23.3

The amount of legal tender funds held by the banks in New York City on October 1 was $50,921,576, which was 26.8 per cent. upon their deposits and 24.3 per cent. upon circulation and deposits. The amount held by the banks in the principal cities, including New York, was $92,934,123, or 112.4 per cent. upon their circulation, and 23.9 per cent. upon their deposits; and the total cash reserve of all the national banks was $142,955,718, or 47.3 per cent. of the total outstanding circulation of the banks then in operation, and 21.1 per cent. of their deposits. This reserve consisted of $30,688,606 of specie, $97,061,571 of legal-tender notes, and $15,205,541 deposited in the Treasury for the redemption of circulating notes. It is evident that the banks are well prepared to redeem their circulating notes in legal-tender notes, in accordance with law. The national and State banks in New York City and in Boston have already signified their intention to co-operate with the Treasury Department in the resumption of specie payments, which takes place on the 1st day of January next, as provided by law, as may be seen from the late action of the Clearing House Association of that city, which will be found upon another page. It is for the interest not only of the banks with their large assets, but also of the depositors of more than 800 millions of dollars in savings banks, as well as depositors in other banks, to encourage resumption and permanently fix the coin value of their deposits. The legal-tender note will then become a coin certificate payable on demand at the office of the Assistant Treasurer of New York, and will be more convenient and desirable for general use than coin itself.

The Treasury department owns 140 millions of coin, which is equal to more than forty per cent. of the entire issues of the legal-tender notes, and is available for their redemption, while the banks hold nearly one-third of the legal-tender notes. If, therefore, the banks of the country co-operate with the Treasury, it is impossible that resumption shall fail. But even if this co-operation should not be universal, it could not affect the ultimate result; for if any considerable portion of the legal-tender notes be exchanged for coin at the Treasury and withdrawn from use, the notes will become scarce and the coin be forced into circulation to supply the requirements of business and fill the gap. The coin will soon thereafter be returned to the Treasury in payment of customs duties and internal-revenue taxes, and offered in exchange for the greenback coin-certificates, which will be more generally acceptable to the people, for the same reason that the notes of the Bank of England and of the Bank of France are now preferred to coin.

But while it is conceded that both the Treasury and the banks can readily redeem their circulating notes, it is said that it will not be possible for the banks to provide for their deposits. In answer to this statement the Comptroller repeats what has been previously said by him:

Those who take this view proceed on the assumption that the banks will be called upon to pay their deposits in specie. This was not true during any former period of specie payment, and is less likely to be true under the national banking system than it was under any previous system of banking. The banks in this country, from their first organization, have, in times of resumption as well as of suspension, received from their dealers current bank-notes and have paid out the same. This is true to-day in England, Scotland, Germany, and France, in all of which countries the bank-note is preferred, as a rule, to either gold or silver. Only a small portion of the bank circulation of the country, at any period prior to 1863, was either safe or convertible; yet even this circulation, poor as it was, was freely received by the banks outside of the commercial cities, and was paid out by them to their depositors, so closely identified were the interests of the one with the other. The notes which were returned from the commercial centers for redemption were readily paid out and circulated at home, and the demand for specie, wherever it existed, was almost entirely owing either to an excess of currency or to a want of confidence in the institutions which issued it.

The people throughout the country now know that the national-bank notes are safe, and that if these notes are not paid at the counters of the banks which issued them they will be paid at the Treasury Department in lawful money, and that the securities held for their redemption are amply sufficient for that purpose. No reason therefore exists why the people, who, in the last fourteen years, have not lost one dollar through the use of bank-notes, should decline to receive such notes in payment of their deposits. These notes are not only guaranteed by the government, but they are received by it in payment of all taxes and other dues except duties on imports, and are disbursed by it in payment of all demands except interest on the public debt, and in the redemption of national-bank notes.

The national banks hold eight hundred and eighty millions of loans made to the people, and each bank is required, by section 5196 of the Revised Statutes, "to take and receive at par, for any debt or liability to it, any and all notes or bills issued by any lawfully-organized national banking association." There are, therefore, eight hundred and eighty millions of liabilities of the people due to the national banks—a sum largely exceeding the whole amount of deposits—which may be paid in the notes of any or all of the national banks in the country. The national-bank notes are therefore very different in character from the heterogeneous bank-notes formerly issued by authority of the several States. Moreover, the deposits of the banks are largely owned by their own shareholders and by their borrowers; and surely business men, who look to the banks for accommodations, and stockholders, whose profits depend upon their successful management, will be the last to conspire to injure their credit.

Deposits consist chiefly of bank-credits, are derived largely from the discount of commercial paper, and are paid mainly by transfers upon the books—not with either coin or currency. Throughout the country all large payments are made, not with money, but with checks. In the principal cities these payments are accomplished through the operations of clearing-houses. During the last twenty-four years the exchanges of the New York clearing-house were 454 thousand millions, while the balances paid in money were less than 19 thousand millions. The average daily exchanges during this whole period were more than sixty-one millions, while the average daily balances paid in money were but two and one-half millions, or but four and one-fifth cents upon the dollar, as will be seen by a table on another page.

Immediately after resumption in England, in 1821, there was but little demand for gold, and the same was true in France after resumption by the Bank of France in 1850, and in this country in 1838 and 1858. The Bank of France is at present in a state of suspension,* but its notes are preferred by the public to specie, and the bank has found it difficult to reduce the volume of its circulating notes in exchange for coin. All thought of demanding actual payment in specie will vanish as soon as resumption is assured, and those timid bankers who fear that coin will be demanded for every dollar of their deposits can reassure themselves by an agreement with their dealers that their deposits shall be payable, as at the present time, "in current funds," which will then consist of legal-tender notes and the notes of specie-paying banks.

RECENT ACTION OF THE NEW YORK CLEARING-HOUSE IN REFERENCE TO RESUMPTION—ITS EXCHANGES SINCE ORGANIZATION.

The New York Clearing-House Association, which is composed of forty-five national and thirteen State banks, has, during the present month, consummated an arrangement with this department greatly facilitating the payment of drafts and checks which constantly pass between the office of the assistant treasurer and the banks. The basis of this arrangement is as follows:

First. Hereafter, drafts drawn upon any bank represented in the Clearing-House Association in the city of New York, received by the assistant treasurer in that city, may be presented to such bank at the clearing-house for payment.

Second. Hereafter, drafts drawn upon the assistant treasurer at New York may be adjusted by him at the clearing-house, and the balance due from the United States may be paid at his office in United States notes or clearing-house certificates.

---

* Since this was written the Bank of France has resumed, and there has been no special demand for coin, the transition having taken place almost imperceptibly.

Third. After the 1st of January next payment of checks presented to the assistant treasurer by any bank connected with the clearing-house may be made by him in United States notes.

The Association subsequently adopted a report, and the following propositions for the guidance of the banks in the transaction of business after the first day of January, 1879, which propositions have also since been adopted by the Clearing-House in Boston:

1. Decline receiving gold coins as "special deposits," but accept and treat them only as "lawful money."

2. Abolish special exchanges of gold checks at the clearing-house.

3. Pay and receive balances between banks at clearing house either in gold or United States legal tender.

4. Receive silver dollars upon deposit only under special contract to withdraw the same in kind.

5. Prohibit payments of balances at clearing-house in silver certificates or in silver dollars, excepting as subsidiary coin in small sums (say under $10).

6. Discontinue gold special accounts by notice to dealers to terminate them on 1st January next.

The following is an extract from the report referred to:

There are diverse views honestly entertained respecting the relative merits and powers of circulating notes, of banks or of government, as to which will best promote the public interests and meet the requirements of the people. Avoiding all discussion of this subject as not pertinent to the immediate occasion, let us accept the situation as it now exists, and as it will continue until after the day of resumption, and remit all such questions to the test of future experience.

At present there is a marked distinction made in the daily transactions of banks between their deposits of gold and their deposits of currency, by treating the former as a special fund, payable in kind. It must be evident that if this discrimination continues to be made after resumption, it will prolong the idea of the inferiority of circulating notes after they have been declared to be restored to an equality with gold by becoming interchangeable, and will therefore falsify the proclamation of the government. It will not only be a practical denial by the banks of the sincere purpose of the government to maintain its resolution, but, by affording protection and facility to those who draw coin from the Treasury, will place the moral force and power of the banks in direct opposition to the effort of government.

Specie payments will not have been truly accomplished until all distinctions in the use of gold coin and currency as money are obliterated in ordinary commercial transactions.

To make resumption effective, the banks must cordially co-operate by practically treating lawful currency and gold coin as equivalent in value, as they did before the war, declining to receive all deposits of gold as subject to special contract as hitherto, and accepting it only as lawful money. They should also abolish all existing arrangements in which gold coin is preferred, by giving notice that they will expire on the 1st January next, the day of resumption, and terminate all special gold exchanges at the clearing-house.

If the government, also, forbearing all further legislation upon the subject, will discontinue the issue of gold-certificates at the Treasury, and regard gold coin as practically the equivalent of lawful money in all its disbursements, the distinction which has so long existed between coin and currency will rapidly fade away, and natural law will reassert its beneficent dominion over our financial affairs. Resumption of the coin standard being assured, it is entirely safe to leave the circulating notes to find their true place, as their constitutional merits and the demands of trade and the public interest may naturally determine. But resumption of the coin standard can be successfully reached only by the fearless disbursement of gold both by banks and government, and by such unreserved and confident action as will manifest to the public that they are working harmoniously together, and feel the utmost assurance of its practicability and permanence.

The exchanges at the clearing-house in New York City for the year ending October 1, 1878, were nearly twenty thousand millions, and the balances paid in money were about nine hundred and fifty millions. The average daily exchanges were about sixty-five millions, and the average daily balances paid in money were but about three and one-tenth millions, or only 4.8 per cent. of the amount of the settlements.

The New York clearing-house was organized in 1853, and the following table exhibits its transactions, and the amount and ratio of currency required for the payment of daily balances, yearly, for the last twenty-five years:

Years.	No. of banks.	*Capital.	Exchanges.	Balances paid in money.	Average daily exchanges.	Average daily balances paid in money.	Ratios.
							Pr. ct.
1854	50	$47,044,900	$5,750,455,987	$297,411,494	$19,104,505	$988,078	5.2
1855	48	48,884,180	5,362,912,098	289,604,137	17,412,952	940,565	5.4
1856	50	52,883,700	6,906,213,328	334,714,489	22,278,108	1,079,724	4.8
1857	50	64,420,200	8,333,226,718	365,313,902	26,968,371	1,182,246	4.4
1858	46	67,146,018	4,756,664,386	314,238,911	15,393,736	1,016,954	6.6
1859	47	67,921,714	6,448,005,956	363,984,683	20,867,333	1,177,944	5.6
1860	50	69,907,435	7,231,143,057	380,693,438	23,401,757	1,252,018	5.3
1861	50	68,900,605	5,915,742,758	353,383,944	19,269,520	1,151,088	6.0
1862	50	68,375,820	6,871,443,591	415,530,331	22,237,682	1,344,758	6.0
1863	50	68,972,508	14,867,597,849	677,626,483	48,428,658	2,207,252	4.6
1864	49	68,586,763	24,097,196,656	885,719,205	77,984,455	2,866,405	3.7
1865	55	80,363,013	26,032,384,342	1,035,765,108	84,796,040	3,373,828	4.0
1866	58	82,370,200	28,717,146,914	1,066,135,106	93,541,195	3,472,753	3.7
1867	58	81,770,200	28,675,159,472	1,144,963,451	93,101,167	3,717,414	4.0
1868	59	82,270,200	28,484,288,637	1,125,455,237	92,182,164	3,642,250	4.0
1869	59	82,720,200	37,407,028,987	1,120,318,308	121,451,393	3,617,397	3.0
1870	61	83,620,200	27,804,539,406	1,036,484,822	90,274,479	3,365,210	3.7
1871	62	84,420,200	29,300,986,682	1,209,721,029	95,133,074	3,927,666	4.1
1872	61	84,420,200	32,636,997,404	1,213,293,827	105,964,277	3,939,266	3.7
1873	59	83,370,200	33,972,773,943	1,152,372,108	111,022,137	3,765,922	3.4
1874	59	81,635,200	20,850,681,963	971,231,281	68,139,484	3,173,958	4.7
1875	59	80,435,200	23,042,276,858	1,104,346,845	75,301,558	3,608,907	4.8
1876	59	81,731,200	19,874,815,361	1,009,532,637	64,738,812	3,288,381	5.1
1877	58	71,085,500	20,876,555,937	1,015,256,483	68,447,724	3,328,710	4.9
1878	57	63,611,500	19,922,733,947	951,970,454	65,106,974	3,111,015	4.8
		†72,674,670	‡474,138,972,237	‡19,835,157,113	†61,705,866	†2,581,591	4.2

* The capital stock is stated at various dates, the amount at a uniform date in each year not being obtainable.
† Yearly averages for twenty-five years.   ‡ Totals for twenty-five years.

NATIONAL-BANK AND LEGAL-TENDER NOTES, BY DENOMINATIONS.

The subjoined table exhibits, by denominations, the amount of national-bank and legal-tender notes outstanding on November 1, 1878:

Denominations.	Amount of national-bank notes.	Amount of legal-tenders.	Total.
Ones	$4,284,219	$20,368,531	$24,652,750
Twos	2,582,146	20,332,920	22,915,066
Fives	92,539,275	55,576,740	148,116,015
Tens	102,981,440	65,926,631	168,908,071
Twenties	68,219,780	63,565,929	131,785,709
Fifties	20,967,800	26,691,195	47,658,995
One-hundreds	27,104,400	31,227,070	58,331,470
Five-hundreds	657,500	30,501,500	31,159,000
Thousands	304,000	33,490,500	33,794,500
Add for fractions of notes not presented or destroyed.	11,561		11,561
Totals	319,652,121	347,681,016	667,333,137
Deduct for legal-tenders destroyed in Chicago fire		1,000,000	1,000,000
Balances	319,652,121	346,681,016	666,333,137

Section 5175 of the Revised Statutes provides "that not more than one-sixth part of the notes furnished to any association shall be of a less denomination than five dollars, and that after specie payments are resumed, no association shall be furnished with notes of a less denomination than five dollars." In view of this provision, the printing of one and two dollar notes was discontinued on November 1 last, and it is not expected that any notes of these denominations will be issued after the close of the present year. Section 5182 of the Revised Statutes requires that the circulating notes of national banks shall be "signed by the president or vice-president and cashier thereof." The written signature of at least one bank officer is necessary, as a check between this office and the issuing bank; for, if the question of an overissue of notes should arise, the signature of such officer would be a means of determining the genuineness of the note. A number of banks, however, issue their notes with printed signatures, and in some cases with lithographic ones, which are frequently so badly executed as to excite suspicion as to the genuineness of the notes. The Comptroller, in his last report, recommended an amendment of section 5182 of the Revised Statutes, imposing a penalty of twenty dollars for every note issued by a national bank without the written signature of at least one of the officers of the bank, which recommendation is now renewed.

PUBLIC DEBT AT ITS MAXIMUM—CURRENCY AND ITS COIN VALUE.

The public debt reached its maximum on August 31, 1865, when it amounted to $2,845,907,626, composed as follows:

Funded debt	$1,109,568,192
Matured debt	1,503,020
Temporary loans	107,148,713
Certificates of debt	85,093,060
Five per cent. legal-tender notes	33,954,230
Compound-interest legal-tender notes	217,024,160
Seven-thirty notes	830,000,000
United States notes, (legal-tenders)	433,160,569
Fractional currency	26,344,742
Suspended requisitions uncalled for	2,111,000
Total	2,845,907,626

Of these obligations $684,138,959 were a legal tender in the payment of all debts, public and private, except customs duties and interest on the public debt.

The amount of legal-tender notes, demand notes, fractional currency, and national bank notes, outstanding on August 31, 1865, and annually thereafter, from January 1, 1866, to January 1, 1878, and the amounts outstanding November 1, 1878, are shown by the following table, together with the currency price of gold and the gold price of currency at each date:

Date.	United States issues.			Notes of national banks, including gold notes.	Aggregate.	Currency price of $100 gold.	Gold price of $100 currency.
	Legal-tender notes.	Old demand notes.	Fractional currency.				
Aug. 31, 1865	$432,757,604	$402,965	$26,344,742	$176,213,955	$635,719,266	$144 25	$69 32
Jan. 1, 1866	425,839,319	392,670	26,000,420	298,588,419	750,820,228	144 50	69 20
Jan. 1, 1867	380,276,160	221,682	28,732,812	299,816,266	709,076,860	133 00	75 18
Jan. 1, 1868	356,000,000	159,127	31,597,583	299,717,569	687,504,279	133 25	75 04
Jan. 1, 1869	355,892,975	128,098	34,215,715	299,629,322	689,866,110	135 00	74 07
Jan. 1, 1870	356,000,000	113,098	39,762,664	299,904,020	695,779,791	120 00	83 33
Jan. 1, 1871	356,000,000	101,086	39,995,089	306,307,672	702,403,847	110 75	90 29
Jan. 1, 1872	357,500,000	92,804	40,767,877	328,465,431	726,826,109	109 50	91 32
Jan. 1, 1873	358,557,907	81,387	45,722,061	344,582,812	718,947,167	112 00	89 28
Jan. 1, 1874	378,101,702	79,637	48,544,792	350,848,236	777,874,307	110 25	90 70
Jan. 1, 1875	382,000,000	72,317	46,390,598	354,128,250	782,591,165	112 50	88 89
Jan. 1, 1876	371,827,220	69,642	44,147,072	316,179,756	762,523,690	112 75	88 69
Jan. 1, 1877	366,055,084	65,102	26,348,206	321,595,606	714,061,358	107 00	93 46
Jan. 1, 1878	349,943,776	63,532	17,764,109	321,672,505	689,443,922	102 87	97 21
Nov. 1, 1878	346,681,016	62,065	16,211,493	322,490,715	685,414,980	100 25	99 75

NATIONAL-BANK CIRCULATION.

The following table exhibits by States and geographical divisions the number of banks organized and in operation, with their capital, bonds on deposit, and circulation issued, redeemed, and outstanding on the 1st day of November, 1878:

States and Territories.	Banks.			Capital.	Bonds.	Circulation.		
	Organized.	In liquidation.	In operation.	Capital paid in.	Bonds on deposit.	Issued.	Redeemed.	Outstanding.
Maine	74	2	72	$10,660,000	$9,626,250	$20,538,580	$11,738,656	$8,799,924
New Hampshire	47	1	46	5,740,000	5,769,000	12,118,075	6,923,328	5,194,747
Vermont	50	3	47	8,533,000	7,662,500	18,979,600	11,627,166	7,352,434
Massachusetts	242	5	237	95,407,000	72,221,950	166,473,645	102,777,080	63,696,565
Rhode Island	62	1	61	20,009,800	14,254,400	35,026,715	21,976,505	13,050,210
Connecticut	86	4	82	25,504,620	20,323,700	47,555,410	29,564,017	17,991,393
Totals, Eastern States	561	16	545	165,854,420	129,857,800	300,692,025	184,606,752	116,085,273
New York	340	60	280	90,689,691	55,766,300	169,802,715	118,990,888	50,871,827
New Jersey	71	2	69	13,858,350	12,626,350	29,531,520	18,172,195	11,359,325
Pennsylvania	257	22	235	55,909,840	46,677,650	109,208,135	66,960,830	42,247,305
Delaware	14		14	1,764,985	1,549,200	3,432,665	2,000,605	1,432,060
Maryland	34	2	32	12,865,010	7,821,000	22,314,450	14,614,276	7,700,174
Totals, Middle States	716	86	630	175,086,876	124,440,500	334,349,485	220,738,794	113,610,691
Dist. of Col	11	4	7	1,507,000	1,155,000	3,549,600	2,459,001	1,090,599
Virginia	29	11	18	3,285,000	2,529,850	7,226,270	4,865,578	2,360,692
West Virginia	20	5	15	1,756,000	1,458,000	4,941,430	3,393,022	1,548,408
North Carolina	15		15	2,551,000	1,764,000	3,986,200	2,272,720	1,713,480
South Carolina	12		12	2,851,100	1,490,000	3,580,325	2,230,960	1,349,365
Georgia	17	5	12	2,041,000	1,925,000	4,817,790	2,891,381	1,926,409
Florida	2	1	1	50,000	50,000	59,500	15,700	43,800
Alabama	11	1	10	1,658,000	1,621,000	2,990,130	1,511,142	1,478,988
Mississippi	2	2				66,000	65,389	611
Louisiana	11	4	7	3,475,000	1,820,000	6,557,760	4,533,224	2,024,536
Texas	12	1	11	1,100,000	680,000	1,686,420	1,149,415	537,005
Arkansas	3	1	2	205,000	205,000	531,900	280,307	251,593
Kentucky	55	7	48	9,936,500	8,546,350	18,039,495	9,812,155	8,227,340
Tennessee	32	7	25	3,080,300	2,754,500	6,400,280	3,832,947	2,567,333
Missouri	43	21	22	7,175,000	2,000,000	10,947,375	8,602,943	2,344,432
Totals, Southern States	275	70	205	40,670,900	27,998,700	75,380,475	47,915,884	27,464,591
Ohio	196	34	162	26,986,900	23,157,250	56,231,270	34,845,147	21,386,123
Indiana	115	21	94	15,026,530	12,918,500	34,542,755	22,144,156	12,398,599
Illinois	165	26	139	17,194,600	9,988,500	33,574,905	23,659,677	9,915,228
Michigan	90	11	79	9,514,500	6,275,750	16,253,190	10,255,860	5,997,330
Wisconsin	56	18	38	3,315,000	2,094,500	7,165,660	4,878,370	2,287,290
Iowa	99	23	76	5,927,000	4,557,000	12,427,740	8,038,221	4,389,519
Minnesota	39	8	31	4,968,700	2,679,400	7,124,600	4,502,396	2,622,264
Kansas	27	16	11	800,000	740,000	2,813,680	1,891,161	922,519
Nebraska	12	2	10	1,000,000	844,000	1,853,340	1,112,106	741,234
Totals, Western States	799	159	640	84,733,230	63,254,900	171,987,200	111,327,094	60,669,106
Nevada	1	1				131,700	128,587	3,113
Oregon	1		1	250,000	250,000	487,000	263,100	223,900
Colorado	18	5	13	1,235,000	823,000	1,611,920	868,639	743,281
Utah	4	3	1	200,000	50,000	614,930	545,874	69,056
Idaho	1		1	100,000	100,000	197,740	115,739	82,001
Montana	6	3	3	350,000	280,000	544,420	297,871	246,549
Wyoming	2		2	125,000	60,000	116,360	62,300	54,060
New Mexico	2		2	300,000	300,000	591,070	325,510	265,560
Dakota	3		3	175,000	110,000	155,530	56,530	99,000
Washington	1		1	150,000	50,000	45,000		45,000
Totals, Pacific States and Territories	39	12	27	2,885,000	2,023,000	4,495,670	2,664,210	1,831,460
Due for mutilated notes retired								1,339,674
Grand totals	2,390	343	2,046	469,230,426	347,574,900	886,904,855	567,252,724	320,991,795
Add gold banks	10	1	9	4,300,000	1,834,000	3,051,220	1,582,300	1,468,920
Totals for all banks	2,400	344	2,056	473,530,426	349,408,900	889,956,075	568,835,034	322,460,715

The act of February 28, 1863, and the subsequent act of June 3, 1864, authorized the issue of 300 millions of dollars of national-bank circulation, which was increased by the act of July 12, 1870, to 354 millions. The act of June 20, 1874, authorized any national bank desiring to withdraw its circulating notes, in whole or in part, to deposit lawful money with the Treasurer of the United States, in sums of not less than $9,000, and to withdraw a proportionate amount of the bonds held as security for such notes; and the act of January 14, 1875, repealed all provisions restricting the aggregate amount of national-bank circulation, and required the Secretary of the Treasury to retire legal-tender notes to an amount equal to 80 per cent. of the national-bank notes thereafter issued, until the amount of such legal-tender notes outstanding should be $300,000,000, and no more. That portion of the above act which required a reduction of United States legal-tender notes was repealed by the act of May 31, 1878, which provides:

That from and after the passage of this act it shall not be lawful for the Secretary of the Treasury, or other officer under him, to cancel or retire any more of the United States legal-tender notes; and when any of said notes may be redeemed, or be received into the Treasury under any law, from any source whatever, and shall belong to the United States, they shall not be retired, canceled, or destroyed, but they shall be reissued, and paid out again and kept in circulation: *Provided*, That nothing herein shall prohibit the cancellation and destruction of mutilated notes, and the issue of other notes of like denomination in their stead, as now provided by law.

Subsequent to the passage of the act of June 20, 1874, and of that of January 14, 1875, which authorized the retirement and reissue of national-bank notes at the pleasure of the banks, the circulation steadily decreased in volume until the year 1877, the total decrease being $30,869,655, since which time there has been a small increase. This will be seen from the following table, which exhibits the total outstanding circulation, not including mutilated notes in transit, upon the 1st day of November for the last twelve years, and also upon the dates of the acts above named:

November 1, 1867	$299,153,293	June 20, 1874	$349,894,182
November 1, 1868	300,002,234	November 1, 1874	351,927,243
November 1, 1869	293,910,419	January 14, 1875	351,861,410
November 1, 1870	302,607,942	November 1, 1875	345,586,902
November 1, 1871	324,840,696	November 1, 1876	321,170,718
November 1, 1872	341,512,772	November 1, 1877	316,775,111
November 1, 1873	348,382,015	November 1, 1878	320,991,795

Since the passage of the act of June 20, 1874, $79,910,488 of legal-tender notes have been deposited in the Treasury for the purpose of retiring circulation, and $74,095,965 of bank notes have been redeemed, destroyed, and retired. From the date of passage of the act of January 14, 1875, to that of the act of May 31, 1878, which prohibited the further cancellation of legal-tender notes, $44,148,730 of additional circulation was issued, and legal-tender notes equal to 80 per cent. thereof, or $35,318,984, have been retired, leaving $346,681,016 of legal-tender notes outstanding at the latter date. The amount of additional circulation issued for the year ending November 1, 1878, was $16,291,685, of which $1,598,800 was issued to twenty-eight banks organized during the year; while within the same period $12,075,001 of circulation was retired without reissue, the actual increase for the year being $4,216,684.

During the year ending November 1, 1878, lawful money to the amount of $7,502,943 was deposited with the Treasurer to retire circulation, of which amount $3,366,469 was deposited by banks in liquidation. The amount previously deposited under the act of June 20, 1874, was $61,028,049, and by banks in liquidation, $11,379,496; to which is to be added a balance of $3,813,675, remaining from deposits made by liquidating banks prior to the passage of that act. Deducting from the total of the sums named ($83,724,163) the amount of circulating notes redeemed and destroyed, and for which no reissue has been made ($74,095,965), there remained in the hands of the Treasurer on November 1, 1878, $9,628,198 of lawful money for the redemption and retirement of circulation.

The following table exhibits by States the issue and retirement of circulation during the year ending November 1, 1878, and the total amount issued and retired since June 20, 1874:

States and Territories.	Circulation issued.	Circulation retired.		
		Under act of June 20, 1874.	Of liquidating banks.	Total.
Maine	$208, 800	$56, 460	$2, 865	$59, 325
New Hampshire	4, 800		1, 590	1, 590
Vermont	544, 600	427, 944	14, 152	442, 096
Massachusetts	3, 072, 710	478, 262	56, 937	535, 199
Rhode Island	227, 850		11, 120	11, 120
Connecticut	355, 600		13, 700	13, 700
New York	4, 963, 575	2, 509, 780	473, 092	2, 982, 872
New Jersey	290, 730	117, 181	5, 586	122, 767
Pennsylvania	1, 851, 340	801, 339	190, 862	992, 201
Delaware	71, 100			
Maryland	153, 600	329, 887	11, 869	341, 736
District of Columbia	138, 000	74, 515	17, 209	91, 724
Virginia		60, 565	76, 546	137, 111
West Virginia	1, 000	5, 865	56, 559	62, 424
North Carolina	405, 000	179, 860		179, 860
South Carolina	18, 000	64, 425		64, 425
Georgia	113, 410	45, 915	41, 271	87, 186
Alabama	90, 000	78, 400	75	78, 475
Mississippi			915	915
Louisiana	810, 500	292, 356	39, 090	331, 446
Texas		20, 663	3, 865	24, 528
Arkansas	45, 000	27, 752	390	28, 142
Kentucky	305, 100	246, 261	95, 197	341, 458
Tennessee	116, 900	28, 052	38, 029	66, 081
Missouri	94, 580	184, 373	201, 672	386, 045
Ohio	176, 860	518, 318	286, 050	804, 368
Indiana	591, 210	533, 572	186, 694	720, 266
Illinois	370, 890	659, 231	393, 729	1, 052, 960
Michigan	334, 090	141, 110	69, 048	210, 158
Wisconsin	44, 100	90, 399	68, 647	159, 046
Iowa	208, 360	103, 794	100, 251	204, 045
Minnesota	110, 880	116, 537	64, 597	181, 134
Kansas	7, 700	20, 137	107, 786	127, 923
Nebraska	18, 000	60, 231	7, 975	68, 206
Nevada			810	810
Colorado	108, 900	28, 508	27, 214	55, 722
Utah			14, 912	14, 912
Montana	39, 600		4, 120	4, 120
Dakota	54, 000			
Washington	45, 000			
Surrendered to this office and retired				1, 088, 885
Total for year ending November 1, 1878	16, 201, 685	8, 301, 692	2, 684, 424	12, 075, 001
Add totals from June 20, 1874, to November 1, 1877	39, 120, 885	52, 700, 916	10, 408, 933	63, 109, 849
Surrendered to this office between same dates				9, 130, 107
Total issued and retired from June 20, 1874, to November 1, 1878	55, 412, 570	61, 002, 608	13, 093, 357	84, 314, 957

The following table exhibits the monthly issue and retirement of national-bank notes, and the deposit and retirement of legal-tender notes (for the purpose of retiring national-bank notes), from the passage of the act of January 14, 1875, to November 1 of this year; also, the amount of legal-tender notes retired from that date to May 31, 1878 :

Months.	National-bank circulation.		Legal-tender notes.	
	Issued.	Retired.	Deposited.	Retired.
Jan., 1875 (last 17 days)	$537,580	$255,600	$1,323,214	
Feb., "	1,062,440	1,139,204	3,283,100	
Mar., "	1,956,580	583,200	2,875,448	$2,773,100
Apr., "	1,390,200	1,614,400	2,261,463	1,175,140
May, "	1,237,500	1,532,530	1,637,309	987,760
June, "	1,735,525	1,734,900	3,099,626	1,292,420
July, "	1,151,140	2,156,500	1,886,910	1,016,472
Aug., "	626,960	1,847,596	943,246	509,400
Sept., "	520,650	1,803,020	2,167,406	304,584
Oct., "	768,100	1,963,355	3,241,885	704,880
Nov., "	981,010	967,969	1,284,079	764,472
Dec., "	821,220	808,030	2,006,950	644,352
Jan., 1876	702,370	1,986,723	2,629,900	554,080
Feb., "	329,385	1,949,873	3,856,237	329,748
Mar., "	322,380	1,853,549	5,304,627	188,144
Apr., "	225,815	1,622,117	3,001,600	227,372
May, "	476,560	2,087,421	2,085,692	404,208
June, "	485,670	4,744,747	2,612,645	351,384
July, "	144,880	2,831,816	1,232,831	153,056
Aug., "	360,100	4,032,953	1,137,630	284,624
Sept., "	1,045,510	2,330,168	1,776,085	839,864
Oct., "	1,198,780	2,201,606	1,251,609	959,024
Nov., "	780,895	1,900,862	432,600	624,716
Dec., "	1,069,895	1,410,285	870,975	855,916
Jan., 1877	1,337,840	1,447,868	703,240	1,070,272
Feb., "	931,660	2,250,377	818,247	745,328
Mar., "	1,979,100	1,319,728	737,755	1,583,280
Apr., "	1,452,250	1,435,491	675,265	1,161,800
May, "	1,352,280	1,739,105	682,240	1,081,824
June, "	810,310	2,121,440	1,732,690	648,248
July, "	837,640	1,123,854	1,610,079	670,112
Aug., "	1,397,570	1,444,141	1,263,940	1,118,056
Sept., "	1,326,540	595,599	787,325	1,061,232
Oct., "	3,630,050	1,476,581	151,400	2,424,040
Nov., "	3,938,255	1,385,767	261,600	3,150,004
Dec., "	1,745,640	694,833	488,000	1,396,512
Jan., 1878	1,041,690	621,285	660,500	833,352
Feb., "	615,500	653,449	511,662	492,400
Mar., "	961,640	750,617	1,246,780	709,312
April, "	1,450,620	502,655	633,230	1,167,696
May, "	2,007,620	1,140,124	377,490	
June, "	1,400,450	877,271	818,100	
July, "	844,910	1,435,685	853,200	
Aug., "	607,910	914,597	298,000	
Sept., "	630,640	947,743	641,500	
Oct., "	1,037,810	1,062,090	703,881	
National-bank notes surrendered to this office and retired		10,218,992		
Total	50,678,070	81,547,725	68,867,591	35,318,984

The following summary exhibits concisely the operations of the acts of June 20, 1874, and of January 14, 1875, from the dates of their passage to November 1, 1878:

National-bank notes outstanding when act of June 20, 1874, was passed. $349,894,182
Amount of same issued from June 20, 1874, to January 14, 1875 ...... $4,734,500
Amount redeemed and retired between same dates 2,767,232

Increase from June 20, 1874, to January 14, 1875 1,967,268

Total amount notes outstanding January 14, 1875 351,861,450
Amount redeemed and retired from January 14, 1875, to date. 71,328,733
Amount surrendered between same dates 10,218,992

Total redeemed and surrendered 81,547,725
Amount issued between same dates 50,678,070

Decrease from January 14, 1875, to date 30,869,655

National-bank notes outstanding at date............... 320,991,795

Greenbacks on deposit in the Treasury June 20, 1874, to retire notes of
insolvent and liquidating banks... $3,813,675
Deposited from June 20, 1874, to date, to retire national-bank notes..... 79,910,488

Total deposits.. 83,724,163
Circulation redeemed by Treasurer between same dates without reissue.. 74,095,965

Greenbacks on deposit at date.. 9,628,198

Greenbacks retired under act of January 14, 1875........................ 35,318,984

Greenbacks outstanding at date... 346,681,016

The circulation of the nine National Gold Banks located in the State of
California, having a capital of $4,300,000 and a circulation of $1,468,920,
is not included in the above table.

LOST OR UNREDEEMED BANK-NOTES.

The belief is very generally entertained that a considerable proportion of the circulating notes of each national bank will ultimately be lost
or destroyed, and will therefore never be presented for redemption. It
is also frequently stated that the loss of such notes inures to the benefit of the banks. Neither supposition is correct. Section 5222 of the
Revised Statutes requires that all national banks which go into voluntary liquidation shall, within six months thereafter, deposit in the
Treasury an amount of lawful money equal to the amount of their circulating notes outstanding. The law also requires that full provision
shall be made for the redemption of the circulating notes of any insolvent
bank, before a dividend is made to its creditors. Thus it will be seen
that no association can close up its business without first providing for
the payment of all of its circulating notes, and that the amount deposited
for their redemption must remain in the Treasury until the last outstanding note shall have been presented. It is therefore plain that the government, and not the bank, receives all the benefit arising from lost or
unredeemed circulating notes.

In a previous report returns as to unredeemed circulation were given
for 286 State banks organized under the authority of the legislature of
the State of New York. The maximum amount of circulation issued to
them was $50,754,514, and the amount of unredeemed circulation at the
date of the report named was $1,336,337, or 2.63 per cent. of the highest
amount issued. The maximum amount of circulation issued to 30 State
banks in the city of New York, which are still in operation either as national
or State associations, was $7,763,010, while the amount remaining unre-
deemed in October, 1875, was $142,365, or only 1.83 per cent. of the highest
amount issued. The amount of circulation issued to 240 State banks in
Wisconsin was $7,565,409, and the amount unredeemed is $134,747, the
percentage of unredeemed notes being 1.78 only. The maximum issue to
210 State banks in the six New England States was $39,245,380, while
the amount remaining unredeemed is but $792,767, the proportion of
the latter to the former being 2.02 per cent. The returns from 332 State
banks in New York, New Jersey, Delaware and Maryland show their
maximum circulation to have been $65,664,176, while the amount unre-
deemed is $1,707,428, and the percentage 2.60. The percentage of unre-
deemed notes of 25 State banks in Ohio, having a circulation of $2,196,381,
was 2.79. The greatest amount of circulation issued to 707 State banks,
in 12 States, was $114,671,346, the amount outstanding $2,696,282, and
the proportion unredeemed 2.4 per cent.

It is probable that, under the national system of redemption, the proportion of national-bank notes redeemed will be much greater than that of the State-bank notes under the old systems. The highest amount of circulation issued to 15 national banks which failed previous to 1870 was $1,554,400, and the amount outstanding on November 1, 1878, was $13,440.50, the proportion of notes remaining unredeemed being only 0.86 per cent. of the amount issued. The total amount issued to 23 national banks which failed previous to the year 1873 was $3,196,693; and the amount outstanding on November 1, 1878, was $57,074, the proportion of notes remaining unredeemed being but 1.78 per cent. of the amount issued. This is shown in the following table:

Name and location of bank.	Receiver appointed.	Circulation issued.	Circulation outstanding.	Percentage unredeemed.
First National Bank, Attica, N. Y	Apr. 14, 1865	$44,000 00	$348 50	.79
Venango National Bank, Franklin, Pa	May 1, 1866	85,000 00	441 50	.52
Merchants' National Bank, Washington, D. C	May 8, 1866	180,000 00	1,461 00	.81
First National Bank, Medina, N. Y	Mar. 13, 1867	40,000 00	139 00	.35
Tennessee National Bank, Memphis, Tenn	Mar. 21, 1867	90,000 00	611 25	.68
First National Bank, Selma, Ala	Apr. 30, 1867	85,000 00	689 00	.81
First National Bank, New Orleans, La	May 20, 1867	180,000 00	2,130 00	1.18
National Umadilla Bank, Umadilla, N. Y	Aug. 20, 1867	100,000 00	506 00	.51
Farmers and Citizens' National Bank, Brooklyn, N. Y	Sept. 6, 1867	253,900 00	2,164 00	.85
Croton National Bank, New York, N. Y	Oct. 1, 1867	180,000 00	891 00	.49
First National Bank, Bethel, Conn	Feb. 28, 1868	26,300 00	301 00	1.14
First National Bank, Keokuk, Iowa	Mar. 3, 1868	90,000 00	676 00	.75
National Bank, Vicksburg, Miss	Apr. 24, 1868	25,500 00	201 25	.80
First National Bank, Rockford, Ill	Mar. 15, 1869	45,000 00	632 00	1.41
First National Bank of Nevada, Austin, Nev	Oct. 14, 1869	129,700 00	2,249 00	1.73
Totals and average percentage to 1870.		1,554,400 00	13,440 50	.86
Ocean National Bank, New York, N. Y	Dec. 13, 1871	800,000 00	20,418 00	2.55
Union Square National Bank, New York, N. Y	Dec. 15, 1871	50,000 00	984 00	1.97
Eighth National Bank, New York, N. Y	Dec. 15, 1871	243,393 00	5,856 50	2.41
Fourth National Bank, Philadelphia, Pa	Dec. 20, 1871	179,000 00	4,910 00	2.74
Waverly National Bank, Waverly, N. Y	Apr. 23, 1872	71,000 00	2,272 00	3.20
First National Bank, Fort Smith, Ark	May 2, 1872	45,000 00	1,175 00	2.61
Scandinavian National Bank, Chicago, Ill	Dec. 12, 1872	135,000 00	3,874 00	2.87
Wallkill National Bank, Middletown, N. Y	Dec. 31, 1872	118,900 00	4,144 50	3.48
Totals and average percentage to 1873.		3,193,693 00	57,074 50	1.78

Of the circulation of 51 national banks in voluntary liquidation previous to 1870, amounting to $5,832,940, there yet remains outstanding $151,484, or 2.59 per cent. only, of the amount issued; and of the circulation of 75 banks in liquidation prior to 1872, amounting to $8,648,980, there remains outstanding $227,448, which is equal to a percentage of 2.63; and of the circulation of 89 banks in liquidation prior to 1873, in amount $10,764,080, there remains outstanding $303,274, or 2.82 per cent. of the amount issued.

The amount of demand Treasury notes issued from July 17, 1861, to December 31, 1862, was $60,000,000, in denominations of five, ten, and twenty dollars; and the amount remaining outstanding on the 1st of November last was $62,065, the proportion unredeemed being a little more than one-tenth of one per cent., $3,627 having been redeemed within the last two years.

SPECIE IN BANK AND ESTIMATED SPECIE IN THE COUNTRY.

The table below exhibits the amount of specie held by the national banks at the dates of their reports for the last ten years; the coin, coin-certificates, and checks payable in coin, held by the New York City banks being stated separately:

Dates.	Held by national banks in New York City.				Held by other national banks.	Aggregate.
	Coin.	U. S. coin certificates.	Checks payable in coin.	Total.		
Oct. 5, 1868..	$1,698,623 24	$6,390,140	$1,536,353 66	$9,625,116 90	$3,378,596 40	$13,003,713 30
Jan. 4, 1869...	1,902,769,48	18,038,520	2,348,140 49	22,289,429 97	7,337,320 29	29,626,750 26
Apr. 17, 1869..	1,652,575 21	3,720,040	1,469,826 64	6,842,441 85	3,102,090 30	9,944,532 15
June 12, 1869...	2,542,533 96	11,953,680	975,015 82	15,471,229 78	2,983,860 70	18,455,090 48
Oct. 9, 1869..	1,792,740 73	16,897,900	1,013,948 72	19,704,589 45	3,297,816 37	23,002,405 83
Jan. 22, 1870..	6,196,036 29	28,501,460	2,190,644 74	36,888,141 03	11,457,242 69	48,345,383 72
Mar. 24, 1870..	2,647,908 39	21,872,480	1,060,094 30	25,580,482 69	11,507,060 75	37,096,543 44
June 9, 1870..	2,942,400 24	18,660,920	1,163,905 88	22,767,226 12	8,332,211 66	31,099,437 78
Oct. 8, 1870..	1,607,742 91	7,533,900	3,994,006 42	13,135,649 33	5,324,362 14	18,460,011 47
Dec. 28, 1870..	2,268,581 96	14,063,540	3,748,126 87	20,080,248 83	6,227,002 76	26,307,251 59
Mar. 18, 1871..	2,982,155 61	13,099,720	3,829,881 64	19,911,757 25	5,857,409 39	25,769,166 64
Apr. 29, 1871..	2,047,930 71	9,845,080	4,382,107 24	16,275,117 95	6,456,909 07	22,732,027 02
June 10, 1871...;	2,249,408 06	9,161,160	3,680,854 92	15,091,422 98	4,833,532 18	19,924,955 16
Oct. 2, 1871..	1,121,869 40	7,590,260	1,163,628 44	9,875,757 84	3,377,240 33	13,252,998 17
Dec. 16, 1871..	1,454,930 73	17,354,740	4,255,631 39	23,065,302 12	6,529,997 44	29,595,299 56
Feb. 27, 1872..	1,490,417 70	12,341,060	3,117,100 90	16,948,578 60	8,559,246 72	25,507,825 32
Apr. 19, 1872..	1,828,659 74	10,102,400	4,715,364 25	16,646,423 99	7,787,475 47	24,433,899 46
June 10, 1872..	3,782,909 64	11,411,160	4,219,419 52	19,414,489 16	4,842,154 98	24,256,644 14
Oct. 3, 1872...	920,767 37	5,454,580	....	6,375,347 37	3,854,409 42	10,229,756 79
Dec. 27, 1872..	1,306,091 05	12,471,940	....	13,778,031 05	5,269,305 40	19,047,336 45
Feb. 28, 1873..	1,958,769 68	11,539,780	....	13,498,549 86	4,279,123 67	17,777,673 53
April 25, 1873..;	1,344,950 93	11,743,320	....	13,088,250 93	3,780,557 81	16,868,808 74
June 13, 1873..	1,442,097 71	22,139,080	....	23,581,177 71	4,368,909 01	27,950,086 72
Sept. 12, 1873..	1,063,210 55	13,522,600	....	14,585,810 55	5,282,658 90	19,868,469 45
Dec. 26, 1873..	1,376,170 50	18,325,760	....	19,701,930 50	7,205,107 08	26,907,037 58
Feb. 27, 1874..	1,167,820 09	23,518,640	....	24,686,460 09	8,679,403 40	33,365,863 58
May 1, 1874..	1,530,282 10	23,454,660	....	24,984,942 10	7,585,027 16	32,569,969 26
June 26, 1874..	1,842,525 00	13,671,660	....	15,514,185 00	6,812,022 27	22,326,207 27
Oct. 2, 1874...	1,291,786 56	13,114,480	....	14,406,266 56	6,834,678 67	21,240,945 23
Dec. 31, 1874..	1,443,215 42	14,410,940	....	15,854,155 42	6,582,605 62	22,436,761 04
Mar. 1, 1875..	1,084,555 54	10,622,160	....	11,706,715 54	4,960,390 63	16,667,106 17
May 1, 1875..	930,105 76	5,753,220	....	6,683,325 76	3,937,035 88	10,620,361 64
June 30, 1875..	1,023,015 86	12,642,180	....	13,665,195 86	5,294,386 44	18,959,582 30
Oct. 1, 1875..	753,904 90	4,201,720	....	4,955,624 90	3,094,704 83	8,050,329 73
Dec. 17, 1875..	869,436 72	12,532,810	....	13,402,246 72	3,668,659 18	17,070,905 90
Mar. 10, 1876..	3,261,131 36	19,086,920	....	22,348,051 36	6,729,294 49	29,077,345 85
May 12, 1876...	832,313 70	15,183,760	....	16,016,073 70	5,698,520 66	21,714,594 36
June 30, 1876...	1,214,522 92	16,872,780	....	18,087,302 92	7,131,167 00	25,218,469 92
Oct. 2, 1876..	1,129,814 34	13,446,760	....	14,576,574 34	6,785,079 69	21,361,654 03
Dec. 22, 1876..	1,434,701 83	21,602,900	....	23,037,601 83	9,962,046 06	32,999,647 89
Jan. 20, 1877..	1,669,284 94	33,629,660	....	35,298,944 94	14,410,322 61	49,709,267 55
Apr. 14, 1877..	1,930,725 50	13,899,180	....	15,829,905 50	11,240,132 19	27,070,037 78
June 22, 1877..	1,423,258 17	10,324,320	....	11,747,578 17	9,588,417 89	21,335,996 06
Oct. 1, 1877..	1,538,486 47	11,409,920	....	12,948,406 47	9,710,413 84	22,658,820 31
Dec. 28, 1877..	1,955,746 20	19,119,080	....	21,074,826 20	11,832,924 50	32,907,750 70
Mar. 15, 1878..	2,428,797 44	35,003,220	....	37,432,017 44	17,290,040 58	54,722,058 02
May 1, 1878..	2,688,092 06	25,397,640	....	28,085,732 06	17,938,024 00	46,023,756 06
June 29, 1878 .	1,905,705 22	11,954,500	....	13,860,205 22	15,391,264 55	29,251,469 77
Oct. 1, 1878..	1,779,792 43	11,514,810	....	13,294,602 43	17,394,004 16	30,688,606 59

The amount of silver coin held by the national banks on June 30 and October 2, 1876, was $1,627,566 and $2,557,599 respectively. The amount held on October 1, 1877, was $3,709,703, and on October 1, 1878, $5,387,738. The aggregate amount of specie held by the State banks in New England, in New York, New Jersey, Pennsylvania, Maryland, Louisiana, Ohio, and Wisconsin, as shown by their official reports for 1878, was $3,023,429, of which the banks in New York City held $2,629,839. In the returns from California the amount of coin is not given separately.

In my last annual report a statement was given from estimates made by the Director of the Mint, showing that the probable amount of coin and bullion in the country on June 30, 1877, was $242,855,858, of which $50,135,628 was silver. Assuming this estimate to have been substantially correct, the movement of coin and bullion for the year ending June

30, 1878, and the amount in the country at the latter date, is shown, from further estimates of the Director of the Mint, to have been as follows:

Estimated amount of coin and bullion in the country June 30, 1877....	$242,855,858
Estimated product of the mines for the year..................	99,000,000
Importations of gold for the year.............................	13,330,715
Importations of silver for the year	16,490,599

Total..		371,677,172
Deduct exportations of gold	$9,197,555	
Deduct exportations of silver	24,535,670	
Deduct amount used in the arts and manufactures	5,500,000	
		39,233,225

Total estimated amount of coin and bullion in the country on June 30, 1878	332,443,947

Of this amount, $244,353,390 was in gold coin and bullion, and $88,090,557 in silver coin and bullion. The increase for the fiscal year was $89,588,089, of which $51,633,160 was in gold coin and bullion and $37,954,929 in silver coin and bullion. The Director estimates the amount of gold coin and bullion in the country on September 30, 1878, at about $259,353,390, and of silver coin and bullion at about $99,090,557, making a total of $358,443,947.

LOANS AND RATES OF INTEREST OF NEW YORK CITY NATIONAL BANKS.

The following table contains a classification of the loans of the national banks in New York City for the last five years:

Loans and discounts.	October 2, 1874.	October 1, 1875.	October 2, 1876.	October 1, 1877.	October 1, 1878.
	48 banks.	48 banks.	47 banks.	47 banks.	47 banks.
On endorsed paper	$116,719,349	$120,189,537	$95,510,311	$92,618,776	$83,924,333
On single-name paper........	10,959,609	18,555,100	16,634,532	15,800,540	17,297,475
On U. S. bonds on demand....	4,721,638	4,934,674	6,277,492	4,783,448	7,003,085
On other stocks, &c., on demand	51,453,682	50,179,384	58,749,574	48,376,633	51,152,021
On real-estate security........	278,081	868,160	536,802	497,524	786,514
Payable in gold	5,735,138	3,454,276	4,681,570	4,319,014	6,752,181
All other loans	2,909,557	3,908,602	1,852,944	2,786,456	2,670,371
Totals	201,777,054	202,089,733	184,243,225	169,162,391	169,585,980

The average rate of interest in New York City for each of the fiscal years from 1874 to 1878, as ascertained from data derived from the Journal of Commerce and the Financial Chronicle of that city, was as follows:

1874, call loans, 3.8 per cent.; commercial paper, 6.4 per cent.
1875, call loans, 3.0 per cent.; commercial paper, 5.6 per cent.
1876, call loans, 3.3 per cent.; commercial paper, 5.3 per cent.
1877, call loans, 3.0 per cent.; commercial paper, 5.2 per cent.
1878, call loans, 4.4 per cent.; commercial paper, 5.1 per cent.

The average rate of interest of the Bank of England for the same years was as follows:

During the calendar year ending December 31, 1874, 3.69 per cent.
During the calendar year ending December 31, 1875, 3.23 per cent.
During the calendar year ending December 31, 1876, 2.61 per cent.
During the calendar year ending December 31, 1877, 2.91 per cent.
During the fiscal year ending June 30, 1878, 3.07 per cent.

The rate of interest in the city of New York, on November 22 of the present year, as quoted in the Daily Bulletin, was, on call loans, from 3 to 4 per cent., and on commercial paper of the best grade, from 4½ to 5 per cent. The rate of interest of the Bank of England, which, on November 29 of last year, was 4 per cent., had fallen on January 30 following to 2 per cent., from which date to October 14 there were seven changes, and, with a single exception on May 29, a gradual increase. The rate was fixed on the date last named at 6 per cent. and reduced on November 21 to 5 per cent.

SECURITY OF CIRCULATING NOTES.

The following table exhibits the kinds and amounts of United States bonds held by the Treasurer on the 1st day of November, 1878, to secure the redemption of the circulating notes of national banks :

Class of bonds.	Authorizing act.	Rate of interest.	Amount.
Loan of February, 1861 (81s)	February 8, 1861	6 per cent	$2, 276, 000
Loan of July and August, 1861 (81s)	July 17 and August 5, 1861	....do	34, 416, 550
Loan of 1863 (81s)	March 3, 1863	do	19, 790, 900
Consols of 1865	March 3, 1865	do	825, 700
Consols of 1867	....do	do	8, 172, 100
Consols of 1868	....do	do	1, 764, 500
Ten-forties of 1864	March 3, 1864	5 per cent	70, 688, 850
Funded loan of 1881	July 14, 1870, and January 20, 1871.	....do	125, 926, 750
Funded loan of 1891	....do	4½ per cent	49, 397, 250
Funded loan of 1907	....do	4 per cent	30, 566, 300
Pacific Railway bonds	July 1, 1862, and July 2, 1864	6 per cent	5, 584, 000
Total			349, 408, 900

All of these bonds, with the exception of $53,038.50 of 6 per cents, are, by the terms of the acts under which they were issued, payable in coin. Of the latter amount, $36,692,550 consist of sixes of 1881, which were issued prior to the passage of the legal-tender act; $10,762,300 of five-twenties, which were issued under the act of March 3, 1865, which law does not specify the kind of money in which the bonds issued under it shall be paid; and $5,584,000 of Pacific Railroad currency sixes.

On October 1, 1870, the banks held $246,891,300 of 6 per cent. bonds, and $95,942,550 of 5 per cents. Since that time there has been a decrease of $174,061,550 in 6 per cent. bonds, and an increase of $100,673,050 in the 5 per cents.

During the three years ending November 1, 1878, there has been a decrease of $55,673,462 in 6 per cent., and of $42,430,600 in 5 per cent. bonds, while in the same period $49,397,250 of 4½ per cents., and within the last eighteen months $30,566,300 of 4 per cents. have been deposited.

TAXATION, EARNINGS, AND DIVIDENDS.

The Comptroller has in former reports discussed at considerable length the question of bank taxation, and he respectfully repeats at the present time his previous recommendations for the repeal of the law imposing a tax upon capital and deposits.

Special attention is called in this connection to the elaborate tables herewith presented, showing, for a series of years, the amount of national and State taxation paid by the national banks, the amount of losses charged off by them, the number of banks which have been compelled to pass dividends, and the low ratio of their earnings and dividends to capital and surplus. It will be seen that the average rate of taxation upon capital for the past four years has been nearly three and one-half per cent., while in the city of New York it has exceeded five per cent.; that during the last three years the banks have suffered losses amounting to more than sixty-four million dollars; and that the ratio of their earnings to capital and surplus was, in 1877, but 5.62, and in 1878, but 5.14 per cent. No more conclusive proof of the justice of the request for the repeal of the law imposing these taxes can be given than is contained in these various tables.

The national banks pay annually to the government, in semi-annual installments, a duty or tax of one per cent. upon the average amount of their circulating notes outstanding, one-half of one per cent. upon the average amount of their deposits, and a like rate upon the average amount of their capital stock not invested in United States bonds. The following table exhibits the amount of such duties paid by the national banks yearly, from the commencement of the system to July 1 of the present year:

Years.	On circulation.	On deposits.	On capital.	Totals.
1864	$53,096 97	$93,811 25	$18,402 23	$167,310 45
1865	733,247 59	1,087,530 86	133,251 15	1,954,029 60
1866	2,106,785 36	2,633,102 77	406,947 74	5,146,835 81
1867	2,868,636 78	2,650,180 07	321,881 36	5,840,698 21
1868	2,946,343 07	2,564,143 44	306,781 67	5,817,268 18
1869	2,957,416 73	2,614,553 58	312,918 68	5,884,888 99
1870	2,949,744 13	2,614,767 61	375,962 26	5,940,474 00
1871	2,987,021 69	2,802,840 85	385,292 13	6,175,154 67
1872	3,193,570 03	3,120,984 37	389,356 27	6,703,910 67
1873	3,353,186 13	3,196,569 29	454,891 51	7,004,646 93
1874	3,404,483 11	3,209,967 72	468,648 02	7,083,198 85
1875	3,283,405 89	3,514,310 39	507,417 76	7,305,134 04
1876	3,091,795 76	3,505,129 64	632,396 16	7,229,321 56
1877	2,899,637 09	3,445,252 74	654,636 96	6,998,926 79
1878	2,948,047 08	3,273,111 74	560,296 83	6,781,455 65
Aggregates	39,775,817 35	40,328,256 32	5,929,480 73	86,033,554 40

The amounts paid to the Commissioner of Internal Revenue during the same years, by banks and bankers other than national, is shown in the following table:

Years.	On circulation.	On deposits.	On capital.	Totals.
1864	$2,056,996 30	$780,723 52		$2,837,719 82
1865	1,993,661 84	2,043,841 08	$903,367 98	4,940,870 90
1866	990,278 11	2,099,635 83	374,074 11	3,463,988 05
1867	214,298 75	1,355,395 98	476,867 73	2,046,562 46
1868	28,669 88	1,438,512 77	399,562 90	1,866,745 55
1869	16,565 05	1,734,417 63	445,071 49	2,196,054 17
1870	15,419 94	2,177,576 46	827,087 21	3,020,083 61
1871	22,781 92	2,702,196 84	919,262 77	3,644,241 53
1872	8,919 82	3,643,251 71	976,057 61	4,628,229 14
1873	24,778 62	3,009,302 79	736,950 05	3,771,031 46
1874	16,738 26	2,453,544 26	916,878 15	3,387,160 67
1875	22,746 27	2,972,260 27	1,102,241 58	4,097,248 12
1876	17,947 67	2,999,530 75	989,219 61	4,006,698 03
1877	5,430 16	2,806,637 93	927,661 24	3,820,729 33
1878	1,118 72	2,593,687 29	897,225 84	3,492,031 85
Aggregates	5,436,351 31	34,900,515 11	10,891,528 27	51,228,394 69

It will be seen by the above tables that, since 1864, the total taxes collected by the government from the banks and bankers of the country amounts to $137,261,949.09, of which the national banks have paid nearly two-thirds. One object in imposing these taxes upon the national banks was to make the system self-sustaining, so far as cost to the government is concerned; but while the whole expenses of this Office, from its establishment to July 1 of this year, have been but $4,525,022.66, the first of the foregoing tables shows that the national banks have returned to the government in taxes during this period the large sum of $86,033,554, of which $39,775,817 was paid on circulation alone. It is to be further observed that the whole of this amount has been collected without any expense to the government.

From returns made to this office by the national banks in several different years, in response to requests therefor by the Comptroller, the amount of State taxes paid by them for the years 1866, 1867, 1869, 1874, 1875, 1876, and 1877 has been definitely ascertained. No returns were obtained for the missing years in this series; but from the data furnished for the known years, estimates have been made in this Office for the intervening ones, and the whole amount of taxes, State and national, paid by the national banks from the year 1866 to the present time is shown, yearly, in the table below:

Years.	Capital stock.	Amount of taxes.			Ratio of tax to capital.		
		United States.	State.	Total.	United States.	State.	Total.
					Per ct.	*Per ct.*	*Per ct.*
1866	$410,593,435	$7,949,451	$8,069,938	$16,019,389	1.9	2.0	3.9
1867	422,804,666	9,525,607	8,813,127	18,338,734	2.2	2.1	4.3
1868	420,143,491	9,465,652	8,757,656	18,223,308	2.2	2.1	4.3
1869	419,619,860	10,081,244	7,297,096	17,378,340	2.4	1.7	4.1
1870	429,314,041	10,190,682	7,465,675	17,656,357	2.4	1.7	4.1
1871	451,994,133	10,649,895	7,860,078	18,509,973	2.4	1.7	4.1
1872	472,956,958	6,703,910	8,343,772	15,047,682	1.4	1.8	3.2
1873	488,778,418	7,004,646	8,499,748	15,504,394	1.4	1.8	3.2
1874	493,751,679	7,256,083	9,620,326	16,876,409	1.5	2.0	3.5
1875	503,687,911	7,317,531	10,058,122	17,375,653	1.5	2.0	3.5
1876	501,788,079	7,076,087	9,701,732	16,777,819	1.4	2.0	3.4
1877	485,250,694	6,902,573	8,829,304	15,731,877	1.4	1.9	3.3

In the returns of United States taxes prior to the year 1872, in the above table, are included the special or license tax of two dollars on each one thousand dollars of capital, and an income tax on net earnings.

The following table shows, by geographical divisions, the amount and the ratio to capital of the total taxation of the national banks, for the years 1874 to 1877 inclusive:

1874.

Geographical divisions.	Capital.ª	Amount of taxes.			Ratios to capital.		
		U. S.	State.	Total.	U. S.	State.	Total.
					Per ct.	*Per ct.*	*Per ct.*
New England States	$160,517,266	$1,896,533	$2,980,484	$4,877,017	1.2	1.8	3.0
Middle States	190,162,129	3,325,425	3,911,371	7,236,796	1.7	2.1	3.8
Southern States	33,558,483	436,540	517,792	954,332	1.3	1.5	2.8
Western States and Terr's.	109,513,801	1,597,585	2,210,679	3,808,264	1.5	2.0	3.5
United States	493,751,679	7,256,083	9,620,326	16,876,409	1.5	2.0	3.5

1875.

New England States	$164,316,333	$1,937,016	$3,016,537	$4,953,553	1.2	1.8	3.0
Middle States	193,585,507	3,300,498	4,062,459	7,362,957	1.7	2.1	3.8
Southern States	34,485,483	445,018	476,236	921,284	1.3	1.4	2.7
Western States and Terr's.	111,300,588	1,634,969	2,502,890	4,137,859	1.5	2.4	3.9
United States	503,687,911	7,317,531	10,058,122	17,375,653	1.5	2.0	3.5

1876.

New England States	$168,068,379	$1,947,970	$2,914,808	$4,862,778	1.2	1.7	2.8
Middle States	192,163,773	3,190,247	4,025,316	7,215,563	1.7	2.2	3.9
Southern States	33,430,193	423,781	431,164	854,945	1.3	1.3	2.6
Western States and Terr's.	108,116,734	1,514,089	2,330,444	3,844,533	1.4	2.3	3.7
United States	501,788,079	7,076,087	9,701,732	16,777,819	1.4	2.0	3.4

1877.

Geographical divisions.	Capital.[a]	Amount of taxes.			Ratios to capital.		
		U. S.	State.	Total.	U. S.	State.	Total.
					Per ct.	Per ct.	Per ct.
New England States	$167,788,475	$1,907,776	$2,864,119	$4,771,895	1.1	1.7	2.8
Middle States	182,885,562	3,129,990	3,544,862	6,674,852	1.7	1.9	3.6
Southern States	32,212,288	411,486	429,149	840,635	1.3	1.4	2.7
Western States and Terr's	102,364,369	1,453,321	1,991,174	3,444,495	1.4	2.1	3.5
United States	485,250,694	6,902,573	8,829,304	15,731,877	1.4	1.9	3.3

The States in which the ratios of taxation to capital were most excessive during the years 1875, 1876 and 1877, are shown in the table below:

States.	1875.			1876.			1877.		
	U. S.	State.	Total.	U. S.	State.	Total.	U. S.	State.	Total.
	Per cent	Per cent	Per cent	Per cent	Per cent	Per cent	Per cent	Per cent	Per cent
New York	1.8	2.9	4.7	1.8	3.1	4.9	1.9	2.7	4.6
New Jersey	1.5	2.1	3.6	1.4	2.1	3.5	1.4	1.9	3.3
Ohio	1.4	2.4	3.8	1.3	2.7	4.0	1.0	2.4	3.4
Indiana	1.2	2.6	3.8	1.2	2.5	3.7	1.2	2.3	3.5
Illinois	1.8	2.4	4.2	1.8	2.4	4.2	1.6	2.2	3.8
Wisconsin	1.7	2.1	3.8	1.7	2.1	3.8	1.7	2.1	3.8
Kansas	1.4	3.2	4.6	1.5	3.0	4.5	1.7	2.6	4.3
Nebraska	2.2	2.3	4.5	2.2	2.5	4.7	2.3	2.3	4.6
South Carolina	1.1	3.4	4.5	1.0	2.7	3.7	1.0	2.6	3.6
Tennessee	1.4	2.3	3.7	1.4	2.1	3.5	1.6	2.2	3.8

The evil effect of these high rates of taxation may be seen in the reduction of capital and surplus by the banks in the city of New York alone, during the last five years, which has been upon capital $16,435,000, and upon surplus $6,002,981; making a total of $22,437,981. The State banks of the same city are reported to have also reduced their capital $4,794,000, and surplus $1,340,300; making a total reduction for all of the New York city banks, during that period, of $28,572,281.

The inequality in the rate of taxation imposed by State authority upon banking capital in different localities is well illustrated by the following table, which gives the rate of such taxation in the principal cities of the country for the years 1875, 1876, and 1877, the ratio of United States taxation upon deposits, capital, and circulation combined, being also given for purposes of comparison:

Rates of taxation.

Cities.	1875.			1876.			1877.		
	United States.	State.	Total.	United States.	State.	Total.	United States.	State.	Total.
	Per cent	Per cent	Per cent	Per cent	Per cent	Per cent	Per cent	Per cent	Per cent
Boston	1.4	1.9	3.3	1.4	1.6	3.0	1.3	1.6	2.9
New York	2.0	3.1	5.1	1.9	3.5	5.1	2.1	2.9	5.0
Albany	3.0	3.6	6.6	3.2	3.4	6.6	3.0	3.2	6.2
Philadelphia	2.0	0.8	2.8	2.1	0.7	2.8	2.1	0.7	2.8
Pittsburgh	1.4	0.5	1.9	1.4	0.5	1.9	1.4	0.5	1.9
Baltimore	1.3	2.0	3.3	1.2	2.0	3.2	1.2	1.9	3.1
Washington	1.4	0.3	1.7	1.2	1.1	2.3	1.3	0.7	2.0
New Orleans	1.6	0.3	1.9	1.6	0.2	1.8	1.5	0.9	2.4
Louisville	1.3	0.5	1.8	1.4	0.5	1.9	1.4	0.5	1.9
Cincinnati	2.0	2.6	4.6	1.7	2.9	4.6	1.7	2.9	4.6
Cleveland	1.1	2.3	3.4	1.1	2.5	3.6	1.1	2.2	3.3
Chicago	2.3	2.5	4.8	2.2	3.0	5.2	2.2	2.9	5.8
Detroit	1.8	1.3	3.1	1.6	1.5	3.1	1.6	1.7	3.3
Milwaukee	2.5	3.0	5.3	2.2	2.9	5.1	2.4	2.6	5.0
Saint Louis	1.2	2.8	4.0	1.3	2.6	3.9	1.4	2.5	3.9
Saint Paul	1.3	2.2	3.5	1.2	1.8	3.0	1.3	1.7	3.0

The capital of the banks which reported State taxes in 1874 was $476,836,031; in 1875 $493,738,408; in 1876 $488,272,782, and in 1877 $474,667,771.

The following table gives in detail, by States and principal cities, the amount of national and State taxation paid by the national banks for the year 1877, and their ratios to capital:

States and Territories.	Capital.*	Amount of taxes.			Ratios to capital.		
		United States.	State.	Total.	U. S.	State.	Total.
					Per ct.	Per ct.	Per ct.
Maine	$10,689,837	$113,855	$240,442	$354,297	1.1	2.2	3.3
New Hampshire	5,683,750	63,252	100,700	163,952	1.1	1.8	2.9
Vermont	8,568,700	88,659	168,551	257,210	1.0	2.0	3.0
Massachusetts	44,413,464	493,489	828,064	1,321,553	1.1	1.9	3.0
Boston	52,320,080	684,562	830,847	1,515,409	1.3	1.6	2.9
Rhode Island	20,271,650	193,088	273,227	466,315	1.0	1.4	2.4
Connecticut	25,831,904	270,871	422,288	693,159	1.0	1.6	2.6
New England States	167,788,475	1,907,776	2,864,119	4,771,895	1.1	1.7	2.8
New York	34,118,002	498,204	754,951	1,253,155	1.5	2.3	3.8
New York City	60,057,247	1,250,636	1,822,196	3,072,832	2.1	2.9	5.0
Albany	2,000,000	59,870	64,281	124,151	3.0	3.2	6.2
New Jersey	14,278,350	202,678	276,680	479,358	1.4	1.9	3.3
Pennsylvania	28,417,582	409,062	200,841	609,903	1.4	0.7	2.1
Philadelphia	16,985,667	357,311	120,471	477,782	2.1	0.7	2.8
Pittsburgh	10,347,500	139,751	54,335	194,086	1.4	0.5	1.9
Delaware	1,663,985	23,398	6,842	30,240	1.4	0.4	1.8
Maryland	2,302,459	31,818	30,395	62,213	1.4	1.3	2.7
Baltimore	11,233,651	137,075	205,830	342,905	1.2	1.9	3.1
District of Columbia	252,000	4,317	312	4,629	1.8	0.8	2.6
Washington	1,229,119	15,870	7,728	23,598	1.3	0.7	2.0
Middle States	182,885,562	3,129,990	3,544,862	6,674,852	1.7	1.9	3.6
Virginia	3,285,229	49,796	64,684	114,480	1.5	2.0	3.5
West Virginia	1,746,000	21,461	27,737	49,198	1.2	1.6	2.8
North Carolina	2,586,096	30,792	33,945	64,737	1.2	1.4	2.6
South Carolina	2,927,643	28,918	74,027	102,945	1.0	2.6	3.6
Georgia	2,146,305	25,547	42,632	68,179	1.2	2.1	3.3
Florida	50,000	818	1,023	1,841	1.6	2.0	3.6
Alabama	1,658,000	18,653	19,372	38,025	1.1	1.2	2.3
New Orleans	3,300,000	50,099	26,387	76,486	1.5	0.9	2.4
Texas	1,081,782	14,597	20,655	35,252	1.4	2.2	3.6
Arkansas	205,000	2,760	3,601	6,361	1.3	1.8	3.1
Kentucky	7,008,500	77,141	30,636	107,777	1.1	0.4	1.5
Louisville	3,085,500	42,265	15,936	58,201	1.4	0.5	1.9
Tennessee	3,112,251	48,639	68,514	117,153	1.6	2.2	3.8
Southern States	32,212,288	411,486	429,149	840,635	1.3	1.4	2.7
Ohio	19,944,625	269,544	428,902	698,446	1.4	2.3	3.7
Cincinnati	4,400,000	73,817	128,159	201,976	1.7	2.9	4.6
Cleveland	4,416,667	48,139	97,591	145,730	1.1	2.2	3.3
Indiana	16,559,568	202,594	347,744	550,338	1.2	2.3	3.5
Illinois	11,480,927	163,585	223,996	387,581	1.4	2.0	3.4
Chicago	6,472,418	145,367	131,744	277,111	2.2	2.9	5.8
Michigan	7,871,463	94,201	120,716	214,917	1.2	1.7	2.9
Detroit	2,000,000	31,105	34,885	65,990	1.6	1.7	3.3
Wisconsin	2,814,808	43,360	50,969	94,329	1.5	1.9	3.4
Milwaukee	650,000	15,395	16,610	32,005	2.4	2.6	5.0
Iowa	6,090,538	85,085	121,291	206,376	1.4	2.1	3.5
Minnesota	4,519,779	61,429	93,923	155,352	1.4	2.2	3.6
Missouri	2,391,167	34,718	41,243	75,961	1.5	2.6	4.1
Saint Louis	4,015,639	56,812	65,722	122,534	1.4	2.5	3.9
Kansas	1,108,333	18,993	18,855	37,848	1.7	2.6	4.3
Nebraska	938,398	21,485	19,922	41,407	2.3	2.3	4.6
Colorado	976,872	20,544	23,951	44,495	2.1	3.0	5.1
Oregon	250,000	7,224	2,650	9,874	2.9	1.1	4.0
California†	1,579,167	18,416	3,940	22,356	1.2	0.2	1.4
San Francisco†	2,750,000	23,292	535	23,827	0.8	0.0	0.8
New Mexico	300,000	4,192	3,168	7,360	1.4	1.1	2.5
Utah	200,000	2,779	2,750	5,529	1.4	1.4	2.8
Idaho	100,000	1,367	3,184	4,551	1.4	3.2	4.6
Montana	350,000	6,795	6,432	13,227	1.9	3.2	5.1
Wyoming	125,000	1,973	1,599	3,572	1.6	2.1	3.7
Dakota	50,000	1,110	693	1,803	2.2	1.4	3.6
Western States and Territories	102,364,369	1,453,321	1,991,174	3,444,495	1.4	2.1	3.5
Totals	485,250,691	6,902,573	8,829,304	15,731,877	1.4	1.9	3.3

* The capital of the banks that paid State, county, and municipal taxes on stock and real estate is $471,997,771.

† California banks pay no State taxes on capital, except such as is invested in real estate.

Tables similar to the foregoing, for the years 1867 and 1869, and from 1874 to 1876 inclusive, appear in the appendix.

The amount of losses charged off by the banks during the last three years have been tabulated from the semi-annual reports of dividends and earnings made by the banks, and the results appear in the table below, which shows the number of banks which have suffered losses, and the amounts charged off by them, during each of the semi-annual periods ending on March 1 and September 1 of the years named:

Geographical divisions.	Six months ending—				Aggregate losses.
	March 1, 1878.		September 1, 1878.		
	No. of banks.	Losses.	No. of banks.	Losses.	
New England States	327	$3,344,012	399	$4,016,814	$7,360,826
Middle States	417	4,506,813	449	5,502,770	10,009,583
Southern States	124	672,032	140	1,225,602	1,897,634
Western States and Territories	436	2,380,288	442	2,818,469	5,198,757
Totals for 1878	1,304	10,903,145	1,430	13,563,655	24,466,800
Add totals for 1877	980	8,775,961	1,108	11,757,627	19,933,588
Add totals for 1876	806	6,501,170	1,034	13,217,857	19,719,027
Aggregate losses and average number of banks, yearly	1,030	25,580,276	1,191	38,539,139	64,119,415

In his last two reports, the Comptroller gave tables showing the amount of losses thus charged off by the banks in each State and principal city in the Union during the years 1876 and 1877. A similar table is here presented for the present year, which gives the number of banks and amount of losses for each dividend period, to which are added the losses of the years 1876 and 1877:

States and cities.	March 1, 1878.		September 1, 1878.		Total.
	No. of banks.	Losses.	No. of banks.	Losses.	
Maine	39	$82,399 47	42	$133,457 93	$215,857 40
New Hampshire	23	52,704 69	31	86,158 23	138,862 92
Vermont	25	160,026 03	33	218,407 69	378,433 72
Massachusetts	116	606,935 00	146	1,099,369 18	1,706,304 18
Boston	45	1,068,186 86	48	1,422,010 60	2,490,197 46
Rhode Island	23	721,661 20	38	415,073 24	1,136,734 44
Connecticut	56	652,098 23	61	642,337 12	1,294,435 35
New York	120	528,530 28	157	716,514 78	1,245,045 06
New York City	40	2,443,380 83	42	2,703,939 15	5,147,319 98
Albany	7	128,137 72	7	145,251 96	273,389 68
New Jersey	54	235,224 34	54	425,650 62	660,874 96
Pennsylvania	124	702,158 74	121	535,441 55	1,237,600 29
Philadelphia	29	190,045 35	22	371,630 95	561,676 30
Pittsburgh	13	100,208 94	18	318,827 57	419,036 51
Delaware	5	11,212 94	2	12,081 86	23,294 80
Maryland	8	25,101 77	8	9,341 37	34,443 14
Baltimore	12	138,674 34	12	230,241 65	368,915 99
District of Columbia	1	1,000 00	1	3,375 00	4,375 00
Washington	4	3,138 14	5	30,473 39	33,611 53
Virginia	15	88,235 87	16	122,704 26	210,940 13
West Virginia	6	12,809 04	9	22,434 35	35,243 39
North Carolina	12	71,363 73	12	149,901 81	221,265 54
South Carolina	10	70,696 13	10	29,367 83	100,063 96
Georgia	8	26,833 14	9	59,247 73	86,080 87
Florida	1	6,078 48			6,078 48
Alabama	7	28,244 60	9	70,802 41	99,047 01
New Orleans	6	40,557 55	7	297,939 35	338,496 90
Texas	11	32,828 14	9	41,031 60	73,859 74
Arkansas	2	14,402 05	2	11,060 18	25,462 23
Kentucky	21	163,343 81	30	163,171 41	326,515 22
Louisville	7	85,198 52	8	150,327 53	235,526 05
Tennessee	18	91,441 06	19	107,613 07	199,054 13
Ohio	83	358,859 37	94	606,815 54	965,674 91
Cincinnati	4	49,797 47	5	30,233 26	80,030 73
Cleveland	4	70,025 04	4	152,883 00	222,908 04
Indiana	59	257,823 49	56	353,474 40	611,297 89

Losses of the National Banks—Continued.

States and cities.	March 1, 1878.		September 1, 1878.		Total.
	No. of banks.	Losses.	No. of banks.	Losses.	
Illinois	67	$161,741 93	73	$288,720 66	$450,462 59
Chicago	9	394,762 84	9	520,321 30	915,084 14
Michigan	52	205,873 19	48	165,988 78	371,861 97
Detroit	3	91,935 74	3	42,681 27	134,617 01
Wisconsin	18	50,044 39	18	27,715 87	77,760 26
Milwaukee	2	46,141 17	3	28,817 41	74,958 58
Iowa	50	183,032 46	40	92,673 24	275,706 70
Minnesota	23	128,388 05	24	98,568 87	226,956 92
Missouri	18	65,477 18	16	47,822 11	113,299 29
Saint Louis	4	75,838 52	5	95,618 14	171,456 66
Kansas	9	53,597 18	11	113,305 78	166,902 96
Nebraska	5	40,919 54	8	22,978 62	63,898 16
Colorado	10	56,941 34	10	48,430 80	105,372 14
Oregon	1	14,054 46	1	6,805 58	20,860 04
California	4	12,635 37	3	9,834 06	22,469 43
San Francisco	2	38,241 06	2	14,662 85	52,903 91
New Mexico	1	10,160 57	1	12,872 37	23,032 94
Utah	1	1,241 01	1	11,499 00	12,740 01
Montana	5	8,663 39	4	9,082 52	17,745 91
Wyoming	1	3,051 12	2	11,228 05	14,279 17
Dakota	1	1,041 17	1	5,436 00	6,477 17
Totals for 1878	1,304	10,903,145 04	1,430	13,563,654 85	24,466,799 89
Add for 1877	980	8,175,960 56	1,108	11,757,627 43	19,933,587 99
Add for 1876	806	6,501,169 82	1,034	13,217,856 60	19,719,026 42
Aggregate losses for three years		25,580,275 42		38,539,138 88	64,119,414 30

It will be seen from the foregoing tables that the total losses charged off by the banks during the current year were $24,466,799.89; that in 1877 they amounted to $19,933,587.99, and in 1876 to $19,719,026.42; making a grand aggregate of $64,119,414.30 of losses which the banks have sustained during the three years named, and have wiped off from their books by charging them largely to their previously accumulated undivided profit and surplus accounts.

The amount of losses sustained by the banks in the more important cities during the same period is shown in the following table:

Cities.	1876.	1877.	1878.
New York	$6,873,759 97	$4,247,941 66	$5,147,319 98
Boston	1,598,722 68	2,192,053 81	2,490,197 46
Philadelphia	152,976 14	333,248 47	561,676 30
Pittsburgh	333,851 56	289,466 59	419,036 51
Baltimore	876,207 32	200,597 74	368,915 99
New Orleans	519,701 41	286,259 47	338,496 90

In consequence of the losses above shown, many of the banks have been compelled to entirely forego dividends for a longer or shorter period. A tabular statement is given below, showing by geographical divisions the number of banks, with their capital, which passed dividends during each of the semi-annual dividend periods of 1877 and 1878:

Geographical divisions.	Six months ending—							
	March 1, 1877.		September 1, 1877.		March 1, 1878.		September 1, 1878.	
	No.	Capital.	No.	Capital.	No.	Capital.	No.	Capital.
New England States	25	$8,150,000	35	$9,085,000	37	$9,389,500	51	$14,870,000
Middle States	73	12,742,000	92	15,573,200	95	17,244,400	114	22,454,850
Southern States	27	3,720,000	30	4,236,000	36	5,266,000	44	6,867,000
Western States	106	11,090,000	118	10,737,000	144	15,013,000	132	12,870,100
Pacific States and Territories	14	1,750,000	13	1,535,000	16	1,885,000	16	1,675,000
Totals	245	40,452,000	288	41,166,200	328	48,797,900	357	58,736,950

The number of banks passing dividends in the first dividend period of 1876 was 235, with a capital of $34,290,320; and in the second period the number was 273, and the capital represented was $44,057,725. It will be seen that during the last three years, an average amount of $44,583,516 of capital of the national banks has paid no dividends whatever to its owners.

But the foregoing table of the number of banks which have passed dividends during the last three years does not fully represent the effect of the great losses suffered by them, nor the diminution of their profits in later years. For, in addition to what is here shown, very many of the banks which have declared dividends have been compelled to reduce them to rates which cannot be considered a fair compensation for the use of the capital employed. This additional effect is shown in the following table, which exhibits the amount of capital, surplus, dividends, and total earnings of all the national banks, for each half year, from March 1, 1869, to September 1, 1878, together with the ratios of such dividends and earnings to capital and surplus:

						RATIOS.		
Period of six months ending—	No. of banks.	Capital.	Surplus.	Total dividends.	Total net earnings.	Dividends to capital.	Dividends to capital and surplus.	Earnings to capital and surplus.
						Per ct.	*Per ct.*	*Per ct.*
Sept. 1, 1869	1,481	$401,650,802	$82,105,848	$21,767,831	$29,221,184	5.42	4.50	6.04
Mar. 1, 1870	1,571	416,366,991	86,118,210	21,479,005	28,996,934	5.16	4.27	5.77
Sept. 1, 1870	1,601	425,317,104	91,630,620	21,080,343	26,813,885	4.96	4.08	5.19
Mar. 1, 1871	1,605	428,699,165	94,672,401	22,205,150	27,243,162	5.18	4.24	5.21
Sept. 1, 1871	1,693	445,999,264	98,286,591	22,125,279	27,315,311	4.96	4.07	5.02
Mar. 1, 1872	1,750	450,693,706	99,431,243	22,859,826	27,502,539	5.07	4.16	5.00
Sept. 1, 1872	1,852	465,676,023	105,181,942	23,827,289	30,572,891	5.12	4.17	5.36
Mar. 1, 1873	1,912	475,918,683	114,257,288	24,826,061	31,926,478	5.22	4.21	5.41
Sept. 1, 1873	1,955	488,100,951	118,113,848	21,823,029	33,122,000	5.09	4.09	5.46
Mar. 1, 1874	1,967	489,510,323	123,469,859	21,529,998	29,544,120	4.81	3.84	4.82
Sept. 1, 1874	1,971	489,938,284	128,364,639	24,929,307	30,036,811	5.09	4.03	4.86
Mar. 1, 1875	2,007	493,568,831	131,560,637	24,750,816	29,136,007	5.01	3.96	4.46
Sept. 1, 1875	2,047	497,864,833	134,123,619	24,317,785	28,890,217	4.88	3.85	4.56
Mar. 1, 1876	2,076	504,209,491	134,467,595	24,811,581	23,097,921	4.92	3.88	3.62
Sept. 1, 1876	2,081	500,482,271	132,251,078	22,503,829	20,540,231	4.50	3.57	3.25
Mar. 1, 1877	2,080	496,651,580	130,872,165	21,803,969	19,592,962	4.39	3.47	3.12
Sept. 1, 1877	2,072	486,324,860	124,349,254	22,117,116	15,274,028	4.54	3.62	2.50
Mar. 1, 1878	2,074	475,609,751	122,373,561	18,982,390	16,916,696	3.99	3.17	2.83
Sept. 1, 1878	2,047	470,231,896	118,687,134	17,959,223	13,658,893	3.81	3.04	2.31

This table shows a gradual and steady decline in the ratio, not only of dividends but of earnings, from 1870 to the present time. The ratio of dividends to capital has declined from 10.12 per cent. in 1870 to 7.80 per cent. in the present year; the ratio of dividends to capital and surplus, which in 1870 was 8.35, is this year but 6.21; while the ratio of total net earnings to capital and surplus has receded during the same period from 10.96 to 5.14. The latter fact shows how largely the dividends of late years have been drawn from the accumulated earnings of former periods, and that even the diminished dividends of to-day much exceed the actual current earnings of the banks.

A table is given in the appendix which shows concisely the ratio of dividends to capital, and to capital and surplus, and of total net earnings to capital and surplus, of each State and principal city in the Union, for each half year from March 1, 1874, to September 1, 1878.

4 C C

The following table exhibits by geographical divisions ratios similar to those on the foregoing page, for the years 1876 1877, and 1878:

Geographical divisions.	1876.				1877.			1878.		
	Dividends to capital.	Dividends to capital and surplus.	Earnings to capital and surplus.	Dividends to capital.	Dividends to capital and surplus.	Earnings to capital and surplus.	Dividends to capital.	Dividends to capital and surplus.	Earnings to capital and surplus.
	Per ct.	Per ct.	Per ct.	Per ct.	Per ct.	Per ct.	Per ct.	Per ct.	Per ct.
New England States	8.4	6.7	6.5	7.6	6.0	4.7	6.9	5.5	4.3
Middle States	9.8	7.7	5.5	8.5	6.6	5.4	7.9	6.1	4.9
Southern States	8.8	7.6	9.6	8.3	7.1	7.1	7.3	6.2	5.7
Western States and Territories	10.3	8.1	9.9	12.2	9.6	7.2	9.6	7.8	6.9
United States	9.4	7.5	6.9	8.9	7.1	5.6	7.8	6.2	5.1

REDEMPTION.

The following table exhibits the amount of national-bank notes received for redemption monthly by the Comptroller of the Currency for the year ending November 1, 1878, and the amount received for the same period at the redemption-agency of the Treasury, together with the total amount received since the passage of the act of June 20, 1874:

Months.	Received by Comptroller.					Received at the redemption-agency.
	From national banks for re-issue or surrender.	From redemption-agency for reissue.	Notes of national banks in liquidation.	Under act of June 20, 1874.	Total.	
November, 1877	$11,680	$3,107,800	$166,546	$1,432,017	$4,718,043	$17,340,759
December, 1877	17,590	3,101,900	137,500	529,692	3,786,682	17,222,396
January, 1878	15,400	4,323,100	258,189	577,010	5,173,699	18,040,569
February, 1878	30,900	3,720,600	203,750	524,397	4,479,647	13,538,278
March, 1878	18,000	3,534,800	129,420	392,760	4,074,980	12,025,805
April, 1878	106,500	4,001,700	211,458	721,178	5,040,836	15,766,848
May, 1878	68,700	6,086,500	326,315	1,096,429	7,577,944	24,076,684
June, 1878	66,073	5,909,800	402,043	1,017,166	7,485,082	23,615,670
July, 1878	346,750	4,635,100	183,127	690,264	5,855,241	22,785,473
August, 1878	115,405	3,435,400	308,585	625,507	4,484,897	16,418,603
September, 1878	37,600	2,997,500	177,911	327,069	3,540,080	13,292,206
October, 1878	161,159	2,995,000	89,580	283,063	3,528,802	8,376,449
Total	995,757	47,849,200	2,684,424	8,216,552	59,745,933	202,499,740
Received from June 20,1874, to November 1, 1877	10,974,288	273,670,855	10,283,941	52,805,216	347,734,300	664,794,553
Grand total	11,970,045	321,520,055	12,968,365	61,021,768	407,480,233	867,294,293

During the year ending November 1, 1878, there was received at the redemption-agency of the Treasury $202,499,740 of national-bank notes, of which amount $65,847,000, or about 32½ per cent., was received from the banks in New York City, and $75,396,000, or about 37½ per cent., from Boston. The amount received from Philadelphia was $10,756,000; from Baltimore, $1,215,000; Pittsburgh, $1,026,000; Cincinnati, $2,223,000; Chicago, $2,866,000; Saint Louis, $814,000; Providence, $4,945,000. The amount of circulating notes, fit for circulation, returned by the agency to the banks during the year was $151,683,200. The total amount received by the Comptroller for destruction, from the redemption-agency and from the national banks direct, was $57,061,509. Of this amount $5,830,516 were issues of the banks in the city of New York; $4,447,325 of Boston; $1,811,160 of Philadelphia; $1,107,323 of Baltimore; $1,087,470 of Pittsburgh; $435,200 of Cincinnati; $444,398 of Chicago; $169,673 of Saint Louis; $360,281 of New Orleans; $351,800 of Albany; and $359,490 of Cleveland.

There were, on November 1, $282,991,768 of national-bank notes outstanding upon which the charter number had been printed, and $36,660,353 not having that imprint.

The following table exhibits the number and amount of national-bank notes of each denomination which have been issued and redeemed since the organization of the system, and the number and amount outstanding on November 1, 1878:

Denominations.	Number.			Amount.		
	Issued.	Redeemed.	Outstanding.	Issued.	Redeemed.	Outstanding.
Ones	22,478,415	18,194,196	4,284,219	$22,478,415	$18,194,196	$4,284,219
Twos	7,517,765	6,226,692	1,291,073	15,035,530	12,453,384	2,582,146
Fives	61,191,288	42,683,433	18,507,855	305,956,440	213,417,165	92,539,275
Tens	24,157,293	13,859,149	10,298,144	241,572,930	138,591,490	102,981,440
Twenties	7,344,167	3,933,178	3,410,989	146,883,340	78,663,560	68,219,780
Fifties	1,147,578	728,222	419,356	57,378,900	36,411,100	20,967,800
One-hundreds	812,903	541,859	271,044	81,290,300	54,185,900	27,104,400
Five-hundreds	20,210	18,895	1,315	10,105,000	9,447,500	657,500
Thousands	6,204	5,900	304	6,204,000	5,900,000	304,000
					*—11,562	*+11,562
Totals	124,675,823	86,191,524	38,484,299	886,904,855	567,252,733	319,652,122

A table showing the number and denominations of national-bank notes issued and redeemed, and the number of each denomination outstanding on November 1 for the last eleven years, will be found in the appendix.

The following table shows the amount of national-bank notes received at this Office and destroyed yearly since the establishment of the system:

Prior to November 1, 1865... 175,490
During the year ending October 31, 1866......................... 1,050,382
During the year ending October 31, 1867......................... 3,401,423
During the year ending October 31, 1868......................... 4,602,825
During the year ending October 31, 1869......................... 8,603,729
During the year ending October 31, 1870......................... 14,305,689
During the year ending October 31, 1871......................... 24,344,047
During the year ending October 31, 1872......................... 30,211,720
During the year ending October 31, 1873......................... 36,433,171
During the year ending October 31, 1874......................... 49,939,741
During the year ending October 31, 1875......................... 137,697,696
During the year ending October 31, 1876......................... 98,672,716
During the year ending October 31, 1877......................... 76,918,963
During the year ending October 31, 1878......................... 57,381,249
Additional amount destroyed of notes of banks in liquidation............ 23,524,492

Total.. 567,263,333

INSOLVENT BANKS.

Since November 1, 1877, receivers have been appointed for banks in operation at that date, as follows:

Capital.
Third National Bank of Chicago, Ill...................................... $750,000
Central National Bank of Chicago, Ill.................................... 200,000
First National Bank of Kansas City, Mo................................. 500,000
Commercial National Bank of Kansas City, Mo.......................... 100,000
First National Bank of Tarrytown, N. Y................................. 100,000
Washington County National Bank of Greenwich, N. Y................. 200,000

* Subtract or add for portions of notes lost or destroyed.

Capital.

First National Bank of Dallas, Tex $50, 000
People's National Bank of Helena, Mont 100, 000
First National Bank of Bozeman, Mont 50, 000
Farmers' National Bank of Platte City, Mo 50, 000

2,100, 000

Receivers have also been appointed, since the date named, for the following banks which had previously gone into voluntary liquidation: First National Bank of Ashland, Pa.; First National Bank of Allentown, Pa.; First National Bank of Waynesburg, Pa.; Citizens' National Bank of Charlottesville, Va.; and Merchants' National Bank of Fort Scott, Kans. The receivers for the five last-mentioned banks were appointed under authority of an act "authorizing the appointment of receivers of national banks, and for other purposes," approved June 30, 1876. This action was rendered necessary by the complaints of creditors that the affairs of the several banks were not being properly or efficiently settled by the officers or agents having them in charge.

Dividends have been paid to the creditors of six of the banks that have failed during the year, as follows:

Third National Bank of Chicago, Ill .... 70 per cent.
Central National Bank of Chicago, Ill .... 40 per cent.
First National Bank of Kansas City, Mo .... 30 per cent.
Commercial National Bank of Kansas City, Mo .... 100 per cent.
First National Bank of Tarrytown, N. Y .... 70 per cent.
Washington County National Bank of Greenwich, N. Y .... 50 per cent.

The aggregate amount of these dividends is $1,309,167; the average rate being 53.8 per cent.

Dividends have also been paid during the year to creditors of banks which failed previous to November 1, 1877, as follows:

Merchants' National Bank of Washington, D. C. 14$\frac{7}{10}$ per cent.; total, 24$\frac{7}{10}$ per cent.
First National Bank of Selma, Ala 7   per cent.; total, 42   per cent.
Ocean National Bank, New York, N. Y 5   per cent.; total, 95   per cent.
Wallkill National Bank, Middletown, N. Y 15   per cent.; total, 100   per cent.
Crescent City National Bank, New Orleans, La.. 15   per cent.; total, 75   per cent.
Atlantic National Bank, New York, N. Y 15   per cent.; total, 85   per cent.
New Orleans National Banking Association, La . 20   per cent.; total, 50   per cent.
First National Bank of Carlisle, Pa 32   per cent.; total, 72   per cent.
First National Bank of Topeka, Kans .... 13$\frac{3}{10}$ per cent.; total, 58$\frac{3}{10}$ per cent.
First National Bank of Norfolk, Va 10   per cent.; total, 45   per cent.
First National Bank of Tiffin, Ohio 10   per cent.; total, 37   per cent.
Charlottesville National Bank, Va 10   per cent.; total, 30   per cent.
Miners' National Bank, Georgetown, Colo 25   per cent.; total, 35   per cent.
Fourth National Bank of Chicago, Ill 10   per cent.; total, 50   per cent.
First National Bank of Bedford, Iowa .... 12$\frac{1}{2}$ per cent.; total, 12$\frac{1}{2}$ per cent.
First National Bank of Osceola, Iowa 75   per cent.; total, 100   per cent.
First National Bank of Duluth, Minn 27   per cent.; total, 72   per cent.
First National Bank of La Crosse, Wis 15   per cent.; total, 35   per cent.
City National Bank of Chicago, Ill 10   per cent.; total, 45   per cent.
Watkins National Bank, Watkins, N. Y .... 12$\frac{1}{2}$ per cent.; total, 100   per cent.
First National Bank, Wichita, Kans 25   per cent.; total, 60   per cent.
Northumberland County Nat. B'k, Shamokin, Pa. 25   per cent.; total, 50   per cent.
First National Bank of Winchester, Ill 30   per cent.; total, 50   per cent.
National Exchange Bank, Minneapolis, Minn 15   per cent.; total, 65   per cent.
National Bank of the State of Missouri, Saint
    Louis, Mo 10   per cent.; total, 35   per cent.
First National Bank of Delphi, Ind 25   per cent.; total, 50   per cent.
Lock Haven National Bank, Lock Haven, Pa.... 30   per cent.; total, 30   per cent.

The total amount of dividends disbursed by the Comptroller to creditors of insolvent banks during the year ending November 1, 1878, was $2,856,851. The total dividends paid since the organization of the system is $14,010,313, upon proved claims amounting to $23,147,393, or 60.53 per cent. of the amount of the claims.

Assessments amounting to $5,703,500 have been made upon the shareholders of thirty-four insolvent banks for the purpose of enforcing their individual liability, of which $1,458,834 has been collected.

A table showing the national banks which have been placed in the hands of receivers, the date of appointment of receivers, the amount of capital and of claims proved, and the rates of dividends paid; and also one showing the amount of circulation of such banks, issued, redeemed, and outstanding, on November 1, 1878, will be found in the appendix.

STATE BANKS AND SAVINGS BANKS.

The laws of the United States require returns of capital and deposits to be made to the Commissioner of Internal Revenue, for purposes of taxation, by all State banks, savings-banks, and private bankers. The data for the following table were obtained from the Commissioner and compiled in this Office. This table exhibits, by geographical divisions, the number of State banks and trust companies, private bankers, and savings-banks, and their average capital and deposits for the six months ending May 31, 1878:

STATE BANKS AND TRUST COMPANIES.

Geographical divisions.	Number of banks.	Capital.	Deposits.
New England States	42	$8,189,517	$15,062,430
Middle States	217	42,446,037	122,908,847
Southern States	233	27,378,751	30,667,577
Western States	296	20,247,869	38,877,287
Pacific States and Territories	65	26,085,088	22,776,484
United States	853	124,347,262	229,482,625

PRIVATE BANKERS.

	Number of banks.	Capital.	Deposits.
New England States	71	$2,858,688	$3,228,297
Middle States	916	34,482,781	61,922,908
Southern States	280	7,298,396	13,683,874
Western States	1,450	26,917,565	75,167,656
Pacific States and Territories	139	6,240,798	29,830,230
United States	2,856	77,798,228	183,832,965

SAVINGS-BANKS WITH CAPITAL.

	Number of banks.	Capital.	Deposits.
New England States	1	$68,400	$1,139,916
Middle States	3	160,000	1,373,145
Southern States	4	881,882	1,278,900
Western States	11	304,852	1,931,700
Pacific States and Territories	4	1,822,208	20,456,307
United States	23	3,237,342	26,179,968

SAVINGS-BANKS WITHOUT CAPITAL.

	Number of banks.	Capital.	Deposits.
New England States	441	....	$403,427,083
Middle States	190	....	358,680,633
Southern States	3	....	2,143,723
Western States	25	....	10,308,123
Pacific States and Territories	9	....	28,739,783
United States	668	....	803,299,345

SUMMARY.

	Number of banks.	Capital.	Deposits.
New England States	555	$11,116,605	$422,857,726
Middle States	1,326	77,088,818	544,075,533
Southern States	520	35,559,029	47,774,074
Western States	1,782	47,470,286	126,284,766
Pacific States and Territories	217	34,148,094	101,802,804
United States	4,400	205,382,832	1,242,794,903

The following table exhibits by States, cities, and geographical divisions, the average capital and deposits of the same banks and bankers, and the taxes thereon for the same period:

States and Territories.	No. of banks.	Capital.	Deposits.	Tax. On capital.	On deposits.	Total.
Maine	69	$92,108	$28,957,428	$188 08	$1,253 21	$1,442 19
New Hampshire	71	64,000	28,300,624	152 50	4,270 50	4,423 00
Vermont	21	344,167	8,140,383	820 33	4,096 57	4,925 90
Massachusetts	170	834,666	157,816,812	1,429 33	5,085 19	6,514 52
Boston	59	3,061,397	70,746,941	3,826 47	17,694 04	21,520 51
Rhode Island	58	3,883,267	50,028,328	8,188 16	39,301 63	47,489 79
Connecticut	107	2,840,000	78,858,210	5,604 82	31,271 53	36,876 35
New England States...	555	11,116,605	422,857,726	20,219 59	102,972 67	123,192 26
New York	328	10,427,448	148,258,669	20,290 36	100,972 62	121,262 98
New York City	443	40,700,289	247,964,314	56,276 58	214,356 85	270,633 43
Albany	14	642,000	12,153,189	706 47	4,039 36	4,745 83
New Jersey	59	1,741,071	19,326,498	3,536 29	14,587 16	18,123 45
Pennsylvania	313	10,807,358	20,970,015	25,172 82	74,851 74	100,024 56
Philadelphia	59	2,113,756	42,552,729	4,648 68	61,604 26	66,252 94
Pittsburgh	37	4,657,547	13,727,252	10,284 93	22,599 96	32,884 89
Delaware	9	712,578	1,798,521	1,667 97	2,031 54	3,699 51
Maryland	13	627,513	559,703	962 01	913 51	1,875 52
Baltimore	41	4,162,516	24,604,030	8,795 49	15,740 49	24,535 98
Washington	10	496,742	3,151,613	513 18	6,469 94	6,983 12
Middle States	1,326	77,088,818	544,075,533	132,854 78	518,167 43	651,022 21
Virginia	77	3,281,067	6,499,580	7,753 69	15,421 29	23,174 98
West Virginia	22	1,496,792	3,927,737	3,608 37	9,819 28	13,487 65
North Carolina	13	588,290	978,018	1,470 72	2,445 03	3,915 75
South Carolina	18	911,523	1,004,868	2,278 77	2,428 28	4,707 05
Georgia	67	4,317,817	3,948,488	10,711 40	9,190 49	19,901 89
Florida	6	89,483	233,405	223 70	583 48	807 18
Alabama	22	993,276	1,813,605	2,420 69	4,533 93	6,954 62
Mississippi	32	1,289,573	1,732,597	2,535 64	4,331 42	6,867 06
Louisiana	3	116,000	48,110	177 50	120 28	297 78
New Orleans	21	4,473,905	7,994,123	10,726 42	15,184 95	25,911 37
Texas	102	3,707,957	4,626,420	8,744 54	11,565 63	20,310 17
Arkansas	15	225,576	298,605	514 24	746 48	1,260 72
Kentucky	74	7,010,103	6,287,202	16,656 29	15,718 26	32,374 55
Louisville	17	5,288,296	5,650,057	12,971 68	14,125 04	27,096 72
Tennessee	31	1,760,671	2,731,199	4,233 85	6,828 00	11,061 85
Southern States	520	35,550,029	47,774,074	85,087 50	113,041 84	198,129 34
Ohio	255	6,042,364	15,952,258	12,959 68	38,776 39	51,736 07
Cincinnati	21	2,022,360	7,361,629	3,388 23	17,295 38	20,683 61
Cleveland	9	898,623	12,244,967	1,590 98	17,403 31	18,994 29
Indiana	150	5,081,175	10,224,039	11,724 36	21,838 78	33,563 14
Illinois	319	4,509,738	12,472,557	10,153 55	29,981 71	40,135 26
Chicago	31	3,612,908	6,832,759	4,892 45	17,043 45	21,935 90
Michigan	153	2,636,707	4,737,722	6,454 25	11,844 11	18,298 36
Detroit	15	1,108,368	5,179,000	1,800 91	11,038 32	12,839 23
Wisconsin	89	1,386,425	3,714,069	3,026 20	9,284 96	12,311 16
Milwaukee	11	729,853	5,747,509	1,669 66	14,368 72	16,038 38
Iowa	287	5,255,013	8,224,785	12,711 94	20,377 82	33,089 76
Minnesota	77	1,510,502	3,233,603	3,662 47	7,950 50	11,612 97
Missouri	176	4,124,269	10,184,792	9,811 03	25,461 50	35,272 53
Saint Louis	32	6,576,033	16,387,002	14,540 48	40,967 45	55,507 93
Kansas	109	1,472,344	2,508,746	3,441 85	6,496 55	9,938 40
Nebraska	48	503,595	1,189,250	1,203 76	2,972 96	4,176 72
Western States	1,782	47,470,286	126,284,766	103,634 80	293,101 91	396,133 71
Oregon	10	643,225	1,480,547	1,499 49	3,602 45	5,101 94
California	84	9,945,129	17,422,175	24,733 99	37,946 00	62,679 99
San Francisco	33	21,787,036	78,070,629	46,256 46	132,601 59	178,858 05
Colorado	28	526,190	934,915	1,315 46	2,336 38	3,651 84
Nevada	18	412,268	1,914,583	1,030 66	4,786 37	5,817 03
Utah	8	190,000	714,535	475 00	1,786 37	2,261 37
New Mexico	4	5,000	61,180	12 50	152 95	165 45
Wyoming	3	82,794	148,682	198 69	371 70	570 39
Idaho	2	54,000	16,358	135 00	40 88	175 88
Dakota	12	78,030	277,927	195 10	694 80	889 90
Montana	8	133,413	188,918	333 53	472 28	805 81
Washington	3	208,000	537,450	520 00	1,343 62	1,863 62
Arizona	4	85,000	25,885	212 50	64 70	277 20
Pacific States and Territories	217	34,148,094	101,802,804	76,918 38	186,200 09	263,118 47
Totals	4,400	205,382,832	1,242,794,903	418,112 05	1,213,483 94	1,631,595 99

Tables giving similar information for previous years will be found in the appendix.

Section 333 of the Revised Statutes requires the Comptroller to report to Congress the resources and liabilities of banks other than national, so far as such information can be obtained by him. Statements showing the condition of the State and savings banks of New York and New England are readily obtained for this purpose from the State authorities. A summary of these, and of returns showing the condition of the State banks of New Jersey, Pennsylvania, Maryland, Ohio, Louisiana, Kentucky, Michigan, Wisconsin, Minnesota, Kansas, and California, are given in the appendix. Complete returns are also given showing the condition of the savings-banks of New England, New York, New Jersey, Ohio, and California. It will be seen that complete returns of State banks have been received from seventeen States only, of savings-banks from but ten States, and of trust and loan companies from five only. The laws of fourteen States do not require returns to be made by banking associations to any State official. The tables referred to do not therefore present a satisfactory exhibit of the condition of the resources and liabilities of the State banks and savings-banks of the country.

SUMMARY OF THE PRINCIPAL RESTRICTIONS AND REQUIREMENTS OF THE NATIONAL BANK ACT.

1. The corporate powers possessed by the national banking associations, and which they cannot exceed, are limited by the organic act which governs them, and are very carefully enumerated therein. They are, briefly, as follows:

First. To adopt and use a corporate seal.

Second. To have succession for twenty years, unless sooner voluntarily dissolved, or their franchise becomes forfeited by some violation of law.

Third. To make contracts.

Fourth. To sue and be sued, as fully as natural persons.

Fifth. To elect or appoint directors, and by the directors to appoint a president, cashier, and other officers, and define their duties.

Sixth. To adopt all necessary by-laws, not inconsistent with law.

Seventh. To exercise by their boards of directors, or officers, *subject to law,* such incidental powers as are necessary to carry on the business of banking; by discounting and negotiating promissory notes and other evidences of debt; by receiving deposits; by buying and selling exchange, coin, and bullion; by loaning money on personal security; and by obtaining and issuing circulating notes.

These are the entire powers possessed by the national banks, and it has been judicially held that all powers not here enumerated are withheld. These enumerated powers, therefore, operate also as restrictions upon the banks.

2. One of the provisions appearing in the above grant of powers is that the national banks may loan money upon personal security only—that is, real estate may not be taken by them, directly or indirectly, as *original* security for any loan; the effect of which is to make them commercial institutions, and to discourage the loaning of money upon securities not readily convertible.

3. Mortgages on real estate may be taken, or real estate be conveyed to them, by way of security for or in satisfaction of debts previously contracted in good faith; or they may purchase the same at sales under judgments, decrees, or mortgages held by them. But all possession by them of such real estate, whether under mortgage, by purchase, or otherwise, is limited to five years.

4. They are required to have a paid-up capital of not less than $100,000 each, and in cities of 50,000 inhabitants their capital must be not less than $200,000 each. In the discretion of the Secretary of the Treasury, however, banks with not less than $50,000 capital may be organized in places having less than 6,000 inhabitants. The design and effect of these provisions is to prevent, as far as possible, the establishment of feeble organizations, unequal to the wants of the communities in which they are located.

5. At least one-half of the authorized capital must be paid in before commencing business, and the remaining portion must be paid in at the rate of not less than one-fifth monthly from the time the association is authorized to commence business. Proper provision is made for enforcing payment of installments of capital stock subscribed, or for making good any impairment of capital which may occur in the course of business.

6. The Comptroller is also authorized and required, before issuing his certificate of authority to any association to commence business, to ascertain if such association has in good faith complied with all the requirements of law preliminary to its organization, and he may appoint a special commission for this purpose if thought necessary. He must also obtain a sworn statement of the president and cashier and of a majority of the directors of the proposed association, setting forth all the facts properly bearing on this inquiry.

7. No increase or reduction of the authorized capital of an association can be made without the approval of the Comptroller being first obtained, and no increase is valid until the whole amount is actually paid in and certified to under oath.

8. Every director must be a citizen of the United States, and three-fourths of the directors of any association must be residents of the State, Territory, or District in which it is located. Each director must also, during his whole continuance in office, be the bona-fide owner of not less than ten shares of the capital stock of the association of which he is a director, which shares must not be hypothecated or in any way pledged as security for any loan or debt. To all of which he must make oath.

9. Every director must also, immediately upon his election or appointment, make and transmit to the Comptroller an oath that he will faithfully administer the affairs of his association, and will not knowingly violate, or permit to be violated, any of the provisions of the national-bank act.

10. The shareholders of every national bank are each made individually responsible, equally and ratably, and not one for another, for all contracts, debts, and engagements of such association, to the extent of their stock therein, at its par value, *in addition* to the amount invested in such shares; thus giving a double security to the general creditors of these associations.

11. Each national bank, before it is authorized to commence business, must have first deposited with the Treasurer of the United States an amount of interest-bearing, registered United States bonds, not less in any case than $30.000, nor less than one-third of the paid-in capital of the bank, except that, by a late act, the maximum deposit of bonds required for any bank is $50,000. These bonds are primarily held as security for the redemption of the circulating notes of the bank; but as the amount of circulation issued equals ninety per cent. only of the par value of the bonds deposited, any excess in the value of the bonds above the amount of circulation to be redeemed becomes an added security, in the possession of the government, applicable to the payment

of claims of the general creditors of the association depositing them, should it become insolvent.

12. National banks are forbidden to make transfers or assignments of any of their assets or credits after an act of insolvency, or in contemplation thereof, with a view to the preference of one creditor to another; and any transfer or assignment so made is null and void.

13. Every association in the national system is required to receive at par, for any debt or liability to it, the circulating notes of any and all other banks in the system, and these notes are also receivable by the government for all taxes or other dues, except duties on imports, and are payable for all debts or demands owing by the government, except interest on the public debt. These features give to the notes an additional value beyond that which they possess through a deposit of United States bonds.

14. One of the most invaluable features of the national banking system is that requiring each association to have at all times on hand an available cash reserve of specified proportions as compared with its deposits and circulation. The proportion required for banks located in the financial centers of the country is 25 per cent. of their deposits. For all other banks the required proportion is 15 per cent. of their deposits. The proportion of reserve to circulation is the same for all banks, namely, five per cent., which amount is to be at all times on deposit with the Treasurer of the United States, to be held and used by him in the redemption of their notes. This sum is also permitted to be counted as part of the required reserve on deposits. Most stringent means are placed at the disposal of the Comptroller for enforcing compliance by the banks with the requirements of the law relating to the maintenance of a cash reserve.

15. Equal in importance with the requirements as to a cash reserve are the provisions which compel the accumulation by each national bank of a surplus fund, to be set apart by it from time to time out of the profits of its business, and which fund may not be used by the bank for any purpose other than to meet and charge off losses in excess of its current earnings. These provisions require that each association shall, before making any dividend, carry to its surplus fund one-tenth part of its net profits since its last preceding dividend, until the same shall amount to 20 per cent. of its capital stock. It is further provided that no dividend shall ever be declared by any association to an amount greater than its undivided profits (not surplus) then on hand, deducting therefrom its losses and bad debts, and that if such losses shall equal or exceed its profits on hand other than surplus, no dividend shall be made. Careful provision is thus made for the steady growth of the surplus fund of each national bank, until its sum shall equal one-fifth of the capital of the association, thereby establishing a reserve fund against which it may charge any excess of losses over and above its other profits on hand, and thus preserve its capital stock unimpaired. Under these provisions the amount of surplus accumulated by all the banks now in operation is $116,897,800, against an aggregate capital of $466,147,436.

16. Another very important feature of the law is the requirement that detailed statements of the condition of each national bank, verified by the oath of its president or cashier, and attested by not less than three of its directors, shall, not less than five times in each year, be made to the Comptroller, and also be published in the city or town where the bank is established; and to guard against the possibility of any bank fortifying itself, in advance of a known day for making a report, so as to make a good showing on that particular day, it is further provided that each report shall be for some *past* day, to be specified by the Comptroller.

This Office, also, under the law, makes annually a report to Congress, containing a great number and variety of statistical tables compiled from the various reports of the banks, through the wide distribution of which full information concerning the banks and the working of the system is annually placed before the public.

17. The national banks are also required to make semi-annual reports to the Comptroller of their dividends declared, and the amount of their profits in excess of such dividends, which returns are also tabulated by him and the results presented to Congress and the country in his annual reports. Full means are provided for enforcing compliance by the banks with the provisions of law concerning both classes of reports here named, by authorizing a severe penalty for any failure or neglect to make and transmit the same.

18. In addition to the means for acquiring a knowledge of the condition of the banks furnished by the reports already mentioned, the law provides for their examination periodically by disinterested persons to be appointed by the Comptroller. These persons visit the banks, inspect their books of account, securities, and assets and liabilities generally, have power to examine their officers and directors under oath and inquire into all matters necessary to a full understanding of their actual, existing condition, and then make immediate and full report in writing of the results of such examination. This feature of the law is an invaluable one, operating not only as a restraint against irregular practices by any banks so disposed, but as a means of detecting them and preventing their recurrence. These examinations may be as frequent as is thought necessary, and their expense is borne by the banks themselves.

19. All necessary publicity as to the ownership of shares in any national banking association is secured by a provision requiring that a list of the names and residences of all its shareholders, and the number of shares held by each, shall be kept in the office where its business is transacted, and shall, during business hours, be subject to the inspection of any shareholder or creditor of the association, and of the officers authorized to assess taxes under State authority. A copy of such list, verified by oath, must also be transmitted to the Comptroller annually.

20. The national banks serve a very useful purpose, both to the government and the public, more especially in localities where there is not a subtreasury, by acting, when so authorized by the Secretary of the Treasury, as depositories of public moneys and financial agents of the United States. For their services in this regard they receive no direct compensation, and are, moreover, required to give satisfactory security for the faithful performance of their duties and the safe custody and prompt payment of all public moneys intrusted to them, by a deposit with the Treasurer of a sufficient amount of United States bonds.

21. The national banks are prohibited from loaning to any person, company, corporation or firm, an amount exceeding one-tenth part of their capital; and in estimating the liabilities of a company or firm the liabilities of its several members are to be included. They are thus, by law, made conservative in their management, and restrained from granting excessive loans, which would at least lessen their general usefulness to the communities in which they are situated and perhaps impair their safety.

22. They are further prohibited from making any loan or discount whatever on the security of the shares of their own capital stock, or from purchasing or holding the same unless to prevent loss upon a debt previously contracted in good faith. And, even in the latter case, they are not permitted permanently to hold or to cancel shares so obtained, but

must, within six months from the date of their acquirement, sell or dispose of them at public or private sale.

23. They are also prohibited from becoming indebted or in any way liable to an amount exceeding that of their capital stock actually paid in, except on account (1) of their circulating notes; (2) their deposits or collections; (3) bills of exchange or drafts drawn against money actually on deposit to their credit or due to them; and (4) liabilities to their own stockholders for reserved profits. The purpose and effect of these provisions are to make the national banks lenders and not borrowers of money.

24. They are further forbidden, either directly or indirectly to pledge or hypothecate any of their circulating notes for the purpose of procuring money with which to pay in or increase their capital stock, or for use in their banking operations, or otherwise. This restriction effectually precludes the practice, which was common in some former State systems, of employing the circulating notes of an association in the increase of its own capital, or in furnishing capital for a new association, which practice has at times been carried to an extreme limit.

25. The national banks are restricted in the rate of interest which they may take, receive, or reserve, to the rate allowed by the laws of the State, Territory, or District in which they are located.

26. A system of redemption of the circulating notes of the national banks is provided, whereby not only may they be readily converted into lawful money, but the mass of the circulation may be kept clean through the retirement of such portion as becomes worn or mutilated and the issue of new notes by the Comptroller, in their stead. This redemption is accomplished and compelled by requiring, first, that each national bank shall redeem its circulating notes at its own counter, at par, in lawful money on demand; second, that the notes of all closed banks shall be redeemed by the Treasurer; third, that all worn, mutilated, or defaced national-bank notes which are received by any assistant treasurer or designated depository of the United States shall be forwarded to the Treasury for redemption; and, fourth, by providing that when the notes of any associations, assorted or unassorted, are presented in sums of $1,000, or any multiple thereof, to the Treasurer they shall be redeemed by that officer. The government is indemnified for all redemptions made by it, either by the bonds which it holds, as in the case of insolvent banks, or by a deposit of lawful money which is required to be previously made by all other banks.

27. If a national bank fails to pay its circulating notes, the Comptroller is authorized to sell its bonds and provide for their payment. The government is indemnified against any possible loss from its guaranty of the payment of such circulating notes, by having reserved to it by law a paramount lien upon all the assets of any association which defaults in the redemption of its notes, to make good any deficiency arising from the sale of its bonds.

28. The destruction of all mutilated notes and of notes of closed banks, redeemed by the Treasurer, is regulated by instructions of the Secretary, given in pursuance of law. All notes destroyed are previously counted by separate agents or representatives of the Secretary, the Treasurer, the Comptroller of the Currency, and the banks which issued the notes; they are effectually mutilated by clipping and punching, to prevent their possible circulation should they by any remote chance pass out of the possession of the Treasury before destruction; they are, in the presence of each of the agents mentioned, placed in a triple-locked macerating machine, where they are immediately ground

into pulp; and their destruction is certified to by all the agents, both upon proper books in the Treasury department and in certificates sent to the banks of issue.

29. The banks are prohibited, under a severe penalty, from certifying any check drawn upon them, unless the person or company drawing the check has at the time on deposit with them an amount of money equal to that specified in the check.

30. They are also prohibited from making any loan on the security of United States or national-bank notes, or from agreeing for a consideration to withhold the same from use, the purpose of the prohibition being to prevent the "locking up" of money by the national-banks, in the interests of speculators.

31. The officers of national banks are required to make returns under oath to the Treasurer of the United States and to pay to him in semi-annual installments an annual duty of one per cent. upon the average amount of their circulating notes, one-half of one per cent. upon the average amount of their deposits, and a like rate upon the average amount of their capital stock beyond the amount invested in United States bonds. This duty is in lieu of all other *government* taxes.

32. The payment to the United States of the duties named does not, however, relieve the national banks from any liability to taxation by other than government authority, as it is expressly provided that nothing in the act shall prevent the shares of these associations from being taxed by the States as is other similar property, or shall exempt their real property from State, county, or municipal taxation, to the same extent as other real property.

33. Should the capital stock of any association become impaired in the course of business, by losses or otherwise, it must, within three months after the association shall have received notice from the Comptroller, be made good by assessment upon the shareholders *pro rata* for the amount of stock held by them; and during such impairment the Treasurer is required, upon notification from the Comptroller, to withhold the interest on all bonds held by him in trust for such association. The authorized capital of the banks is thus by law compelled to be kept always intact, for the protection of their creditors.

34. When a national bank goes into voluntary liquidation, it must, within six months thereafter, deposit in the Treasury an amount of lawful money equal to its entire outstanding circulation, which circulation is thereafter redeemed by the Treasurer. Thus the banks, under existing law, derive no benefit from the accidental loss or destruction of any portion of their notes, such benefit inuring solely to the government.

35. Should any bank become insolvent, the most ample powers are possessed by the Comptroller to take possession of such association, through a receiver to be appointed by him, and to proceed to collect its assets, and pay off, by dividends from time to time, the claims of its creditors. The note-holders are in such cases as secure as though the bank had remained solvent, the notes being protected by the bonds held by the government; while the other creditors have as a protection, in addition to the assets of the bank, the individual liability of the shareholders before mentioned, together with the capital paid in, no part of which can be returned to the shareholders until all approved claims against the association shall have been paid.

36. Mention has several times been made herein of the ample means provided in the national-bank act for enforcing compliance with its provisions, by the infliction of penalties for their violation or non-observ-

ance. All of these penalties are severe, and many of them summary, the principal ones being here enumerated:

I. For charging or exacting a usurious rate of interest, the whole interest agreed to be paid is forfeited; or, if actually paid, twice its amount may be recovered back by the person paying the same.

II. For certifying any check, unless the person by whom the check is drawn has on deposit with the association an amount of money equal to that represented by the check, the bank may be immediately closed by the appointment of a receiver.

III. For every day, after five days, in which a national bank shall fail to make and transmit to the Comptroller any report of its condition called for by him, and for similar delay in transmitting to him the required proof of publication of such report, and also for every day, after ten days, in which a bank shall fail to transmit its semi-annual report of dividends and earnings, a penalty of one hundred dollars is imposed. And if any association fails or refuses to pay the amount of such penalty when assessed and demanded, the Treasurer of the United States is authorized to retain it, upon the order of the Comptroller, out of the interest, as it may become due to the association, upon the bonds deposited to secure its circulation.

IV. For failure of the president or cashier of any association to report to the Treasurer semi-annually, for purposes of taxation, the average amount of its notes in circulation, deposits, and capital stock not invested in United States bonds, a penalty of $200 is imposed, which may be collected as in the preceding paragraph. The Treasurer may also, in such cases, assess the association upon the highest amount of its circulation, deposits, and capital stock, to be ascertained in such manner as he may deem best.

V. If an association fails to pay the duties assessed upon its circulation, deposits, and capital, such duties also may be reserved by the Treasurer out of the interest falling due upon its bonds.

VI. The making of any loan upon the security of United States or national-bank notes, or agreeing for a consideration to withhold the same from use—in other words, the "locking up" of money—is made a misdemeanor, punishable by a fine of $1,000 and a further sum of one-third of the money so loaned; and the officers making the loan are subject to the further penalty of one-quarter of the money loaned.

VII. Embezzlement of the funds of an association by any of its officers, directors or agents, or any false entry by any of them, in any book, statement or report, with intent to injure or defraud the association or any other company or person, is punishable by imprisonment of not less than five nor more than ten years.

VIII. If any officer or agent of an association whose charter has expired knowingly reissues or puts into circulation any note, draft, check, or other security of such association, he is punishable by a fine of $10,000, or by imprisonment of from one to five years, or by both such fine and imprisonment.

IX. If the capital stock of any national bank falls below the minimum amount required by law, through the failure of any shareholder to pay the whole or any part of the amount of his subscription for such stock, and the deficiency in capital shall not be made good within thirty days thereafter, a receiver may be appointed to close up the affairs of the association.

X. Whenever the lawful money reserve of a national bank falls below the limit required by law, and remains below such limit for thirty days after receiving notice from the Comptroller to make its reserve good, a receiver may be appointed and the bank closed.

XI. A receiver may also be appointed for any association which fails to redeem its circulating notes at its own counter or at the Treasury, at par, on demand.

XII. If an association which accepts any shares of its own capital stock in order to prevent a loss upon a debt previously contracted in good faith (which is the only way in which such stock can be legally acquired by it), shall fail to sell such stock, at public or private sale, within six months thereafter, it may be closed by the appointment of a receiver.

XIII. Whenever an association fails to pay up its capital stock as required by law, or an impairment of its capital occurs by losses or otherwise, and it shall not, within three months after receiving notice from the Comptroller, make good the deficiency by an assessment upon its shareholders, it may, unless it consents to go into liquidation, be placed in possession of a receiver and its business closed.

37. Finally, if the directors of any national banking association knowingly violate, or knowingly permit any of its officers, agents or servants to violate, *any* of the provisions of the national-bank act, all the rights, privileges, and franchises of the association become thereby forfeited; in addition to which, every director who participates in or assents to such violation is held personally and individually responsible for all damages sustained by any person in consequence thereof.

SYNOPSIS OF JUDICIAL DECISIONS.

The synopsis of decisions of the Supreme Court of the United States, and other inferior tribunals as heretofore prepared, is reproduced in this report, but it is not deemed expedient at present to extend it. Within the past year several important cases have been adjudicated in circuit courts which will probably be taken to the Supreme Court and there affirmed or reversed. It is best to await such final results.

In this connection it is proper, however, to note that the case of *Casey, receiver*, vs. *La Societé de Crédit Mobilier et al.*, cited in the synopsis from 2 Woods, 77, under the head of "*Transfers of Assets*," and two other cases in which similar rulings upon similar facts had been pronounced, were reversed by the Supreme Court at its last term; the latter tribunal holding that the attempted pledges on the part of the bank were invalid as against the general creditors. The cases are fully reported in 96th U. S. (6 Otto), pp. 467–496, and are not only important because of the amount involved, but are of interest to bankers and the business public generally, on account of the legal question involved and settled.

ABATEMENT.
  1. An action brought by a creditor of a national bank is abated by a decree of a district or circuit court dissolving the corporation and forfeiting its franchises. (*National Bank of Selma* vs. *Colby*, 21 *Wallace, p.* 609.)
  II. Suit by the receiver of the *New Orleans National Banking Association* (formerly a State organization called the Bank of New Orleans) against a shareholder to enforce his personal liability. Plea in abatement that "at the date of the appointment of said receiver there was not, nor has there since been, nor is there now, any such corporation as said New Orleans National Association, because said Bank of New Orleans had no power by its charter, nor authority otherwise from the State of Louisiana, to change its organization to that of a national association under the laws of the United States."
      On general demurrer this plea was held bad, because no authority from the State was necessary to enable the bank to make such change. The option to do so was given by the forty-fourth section of the banking act of Congress, 13 Statutes, 112. "The power there conferred was ample, and its validity cannot be doubted." (*Casey, receiver, &c.,* vs. *Galli*, 4 *Otto, p.* 673.)

ABATEMENT—Continued.

This plea was also held bad upon the additional ground that "where a shareholder of a corporation is called upon to respond to a liability as such, and where a party has contracted with a corporation, and is sued on his contract, neither is permitted to deny the existence and legal validity of such corporation." (*Ibid.*)

"To hold otherwise," says Mr. Justice Swayne (p. 680), "would be contrary to the plainest principles of reason and good faith, and involve a mockery of justice. Parties must take the consequences of the positions they assume." "They are estopped to deny the reality of the state of things which they have made to appear to exist, and upon which others have been led to rely. Sound ethics require that the apparent, in its effects and consequences, should be as if it were real, and the law properly so regards it."

ACCOMMODATION INDORSEMENTS.

I. Where bills, indorsed by a national bank for accommodation only, had been negotiated by the bank through its usual channels of communication with its correspondents as its own bills, and the proceeds thereof had been placed to the credit of the bank, which thereupon gave the same credit to the parties for whom it had thus indorsed, and received no benefit therefrom—

Held, That although an accommodation indorsement by a national bank, in such cases, was void in the hands of holders against whom notice of the character of the indorsement could be concluded, yet that the bank was liable for the same to holders, for value, without notice. (*Blair vs. First National Bank, Mansfield, Ohio. United States circuit court for Ohio, at Cleveland, November term, 1875, Emmons, J.*)

Query, whether, under the provisions of section 5202 of the Revised Statutes of the United States, any indorsement by a national bank is not *ultra vires.*

ACTIONS.

I. A national bank may be sued in proper State court. (*Bank of Bethel vs. Pahquioque Bank,* 14 *Wall.,* 383, *p.* 395.)

II. Such banks may sue in Federal courts. The word "by" was omitted in section 57 of act of 1864 by mistake. (*Kennedy vs. Gibson,* 8 *Wall., pp.* 506–7.)
Receivers may also sue in United States courts. (*Ibid., pp.* 506–7.)

III. When the full personal liability of shareholders is to be enforced the action *must* be at law. (*Kennedy vs. Gibson,* 8 *Wall., p.* 505; see also *Casey, &c., vs. Galli, supra.*)

IV. But, if contribution only is sought, the proceedings may be in *equity,* joining all the shareholders within the jurisdiction of the court. (*Ibid., pp.* 505–6.)
See, also, title "SHAREHOLDERS, INDIVIDUAL LIABILITIES OF," VI, *post.* Judge Swayne says "may," and Nelson, J., says that *"we may sue at law."*

ATTACHMENT OF ASSETS.

I. When a creditor attaches the property of an insolvent national bank, he cannot hold such property against the claim of a receiver appointed after the attachment suit was commenced. Such creditor must share *pro rata* with all others. (*National Bank of Selma vs. Colby,* 21 *Wall., p.* 609.)
See, also, title "JURISDICTION," II, *post.*

ATTORNEYS.

I. Section 56 of currency act is directory only, and it cannot be objected by defense that a suit is brought by private attorney instead of the United States district attorney. (*Kennedy vs. Gibson,* 8 *Wall., p.* 504.)

BY-LAWS.

I. A national bank cannot by its by-laws create a lien on the shares of a stockholder who is a debtor of the association. (*Bullard vs. National Bank, &c.,* 18 *Wall., p.* 589.)
See, also, case of *Bank vs. Lanier,* 11 *Wall., p.* 369, cited under "LOANS ON SHARES," *post.*

[NOTE.—In *Young vs. Vaugh,* 23 *N. J. Equity R., p.* 325, it was held that a national bank could by its by-laws prohibit the transfer of shares by a shareholder while indebted to the bank, and that transfers in violation of such by-laws were void. As it is held by the Supreme Court of the United States that such by-laws can create no lien or indebtedness, it would seem that a regulation prohibiting such transfers can be of little practical use, even if the power exists.]

CHECKS.

I. The holder of a check on a national bank cannot sue the bank for refusing payment, in the absence of proof that it was accepted by the bank. (*National Bank of the Republic* vs. *Millard*, 10 *Wall.*, *p.* 152.)

II. The relation of banker and customer is that of debtor and creditor. Receiving deposits is an important part of the business of banking, but the moment they are received they become the moneys of the bank, may be loaned as a part of its general fund, and the check of the depositor gives no lien upon them. (*Ibid.*, *per Davis, J., p.* 155.)

III. Perhaps, on proof that check had been charged to the drawer, and that the bank had settled with him on that basis, the holder or payee could recover on a count for "*money had and received.*" (*Ibid.*, *pp.* 155–6.)

IV. The facts that the bank was a United States depository and the check was drawn by a United States officer to a United States creditor do not vary the rule. (*Ibid.*, *pp.* 155–6.)

V. Where a bank pays a check drawn on it, in favor of a party whose indorsement thereon is forged, and the same has passed through several hands, only reasonable diligence is required to be exercised in giving notice to prior holders of the forgery, after its discovery, in order to hold them liable. (*Schroeder* vs. *Harvey*, 75 *Ill.*, *p.* 638.)

VI. A clerk of plaintiffs' received from their debtors checks, payable to their (plaintiffs') order, in payment of sums due. The clerk, wrongfully and without authority, indorsed the names of the plaintiffs on these checks and transferred them to other persons, appropriating the proceeds to his own use. Subsequently these checks were deposited with a bank which in good faith collected them and paid over the proceeds to the depositors. In a suit by plaintiffs against the bank, to recover the amounts so collected by it: *Held*, that the bank was liable. (*Johnson* vs. *First National Bank*, 13 *N. Y. Sup. Court*, *p.* 121.)

VII. The act of Congress of March 3, 1869, making it unlawful for a national bank to certify checks unless the drawer has at the time funds on deposit to an amount equal to the amount specified in the check, does not invalidate a conditional acceptance of a check by such bank, having no funds of the drawer in its hands at the time, but engaging to pay the same when a draft left with it for collection by the drawer shall have been paid. (*National Bank* vs. *National Bank*, *West Va. St.*, *p.* 544.)

CITIZENSHIP.

I. National banks are *citizens* of the State in which they are organized and located, and when sued by national banks of other States have a right to demand a removal of the suit from a State to the proper Federal court. (*Chatham National Bank* vs. *Merchants' National Bank*, 4 *Thomp. & C.* (*Thompson & Cook*) *N. Y. Sup. C., p.* 196, *and* 1 *Hunter N. Y., p.* 702.)

COLLECTIONS.

I. A collection agent who receives from his principal a bill of lading of merchandise, deliverable to order, and attached to it a *time* draft, may, in the absence of special instructions, deliver the bill of lading to the drawee of the draft, upon the latter's acceptance of the draft. It is not the duty of the agent to hold the bill after such acceptance. (*National Bank of Commerce* vs. *Merchants' National Bank*, 1 *Otto*, *p.* 92.)

II. *Wooten & Co.*, bankers at Indianapolis, sent to defendant, a bank at Buffalo, a draft on one Bugbee; also bills of lading for sundry car-loads of lumber. The remittance was by letter, which merely stated that the draft and bills were sent to defendant for collection and remittance of proceeds to plaintiffs, *Wooten & Co.* The draft was drawn by, and to the order of, *Coder & Co.*, indorsed by them, by Mayhew, and the plaintiffs. By the terms of draft the drawer, indorsers, and acceptor waived presentment for payment and notice of protest and non-payment. It was payable fifteen days after its date, and it was admitted that by ordinary course of *transit* the lumber would reach its destination eight days prior to the maturity of the draft. There had been no business transactions between plaintiffs and defendants, save one collection similar to this. Defendants presented the draft to Bugbee for acceptance, and, upon such acceptance, delivered to him the bills of lading. Bugbee failed before the draft matured, and plaintiffs sued defendants for delivering the bills of lading to Bugbee before payment of the draft. It was conceded that the draft was drawn for the price or value of the lumber: *Held*, *per Wallace, J.*, that, the draft being on time, it must be presumed that it was the intent of parties that Bugbee should realize from sale of the lumber the funds to meet the draft at maturity. Therefore, upon his acceptance of

COLLECTIONS—Continued.

the draft, he was entitled to the bills of lading, and defendants were not liable for thus delivering them, but if the draft had not been upon time, a different rule might have prevailed. (*Woolen & Webb* vs. *N. Y. and Erie Bank*, 12 *Blatchf.*, *p.* 359.)

III. The *Corn Exchange National Bank of Chicago* sent defendant, the *Dawson Bank* at Wilmington, N. C., a draft drawn upon one *Wiswall*, living at Washington, N. C., for collection. Defendant by letter acknowledged the receipt of the draft, stating that it had been credited to the Corn Exchange Bank, and entered for collection. Thereupon defendant sent draft to *Burbank & Gallagher*, bankers at Washington, N. C., for collection. The latter house collected the draft, but failed and passed into bankruptcy before remitting. In a suit brought by the assignee of the Corn Exchange National Bank against the Dawson Bank to recover the proceeds of the draft: *Held, per Wallace, J.*, that the latter bank was liable for the amount. (*Kent, Assignee, &c.*, vs. *The Dawson Bank*, 13 *Blatchf.*, *p.* 237.)

  [NOTE.—The court concedes that the authorities are conflicting upon the point involved in this case. In *New York, Ohio*, and in *England*, the decisions sustain the conclusion of Judge Wallace, while in *Connecticut, Massachusetts, Illinois*, and *Pennsylvania*. precisely the contrary rule prevails. The point was made in this case that the law of Illinois should control the rights of parties, but it was held otherwise.]

IV. In an action by G against a bank it appeared that a note was made to G's order, indorsed by him and sent through the house of B, a banker, for collection, and by B indorsed to the defendant bank, "for collection and credit": *Held*, that B, by the indorsement, did not become the owner of the note, and had no right to pledge it, or direct its proceeds to be credited to him in payment of his indebtedness to the defendant bank. (*First National Bank* vs. *Gregg*, 79 *Pa. St.*, *p.* 384.)

V. In such case if the defendant bank had made advances, or given new credit to B on the faith of the note, it would have been entitled to retain the amount out of the proceeds. (*Ibid.*)

VI. A bank holding a customer's demand-note has a lien upon the proceeds of drafts delivered to it for collection, after the giving of the note, though collected after the filing of a petition in bankruptcy, and can apply such proceeds upon the notes. (*Re Farnsworth*, 5 *Biss.*, *p.* 223.)

COMPROMISES.

I. In adjusting and compromising contested claims against it, growing out of a legitimate banking transaction, a national bank may pay a larger sum than would have been exacted in satisfaction of them, so as to thereby obtain a transfer of stocks of railroad and other corporations, in the honest belief that by turning them into money under more favorable circumstances than then existed, a loss, which it would otherwise suffer from the transaction, might be averted or diminished. (*First National Bank* vs. *National Exchange Bank*, 2 *Otto*, *p.* 122.)

II. So, also, it may accept stocks in satisfaction of a doubtful debt, with a view to their subsequent conversion into money, in order to make good or reduce an anticipated loss. (*Ibid.*)

See, also, ESTATE, REAL, I, *post.*

COMPTROLLER.

I. The Comptroller appoints the *receiver*, and can therefore remove him. (*Kennedy* vs. *Gibson*, 8 *Wall.*, *p.* 498.)

II. The Comptroller's certificate, reciting the existence of the facts of which he is required to be satisfied, to justify the appointment of a receiver, under section 50 of the national-bank act, is sufficient evidence of the validity of such appointment, in an action brought by such receiver. (*Platt* vs. *Bebee*, 57 *N. Y.*, *p.* 339.)

III. The Comptroller must authorize any increase of the capital stock of a national bank; and such increase must be certified by him as prescribed by sec. 13 of the act of Congress providing for the organization of national banks. (R. S., sec. 5142. *Charleston* vs. *People's National Bank*, 5 *S. C.*, *p.* 103.)

IV. The Comptroller cannot subject the United States Government to the jurisdiction of a court, though he appears and answers to the suit. (*Case* vs. *Terrill*, 11 *Wall.*, *p.* 199.)

CURRENCY ACT.

I. The purpose of the currency act was, in part, to provide a currency for the whole country, and, in part, *to create a market for the government loans.* (*Per Strong, J.*, in *Tiffany* vs. *Missouri*, 18 *Wall.*, *p.* 413.)

5 C C

CURRENCY ACT—Continued.

II. National banks organized under the act of Congress of June 3, 1864, are the instruments designed to be used to aid the government in the administration of an important branch of the public service; and Congress, which is the sole judge of the necessity for their creation, having brought them into existence, the States can exercise no control over them, nor in any wise affect their operation, except so far as Congress may see proper to permit. (*Per Swayne, J.*, in *Farmers and Mechanics' National Bank* vs. *Dearing*, 1st *Otto*, *p.* 29.)

III. The constitutionality of the act of June 3, 1864, is unquestioned. It rests on the same principle as the act creating the second Bank of the United States. The reasoning of Secretary Hamilton, and of this court in *McCulloch* vs. *Maryland*, 4 *Wheat.*, *p.* 316, and in *Osborne* vs. *Bank U. S.*, 7 *Wheat.*, *p.* 708, therefore applies.

IV. The power to create carries with it the power to preserve. The latter is a corollary of the former. (*Ibid., per Swayne, J.*, pp. 33–34.)

DEBTORS OF NATIONAL BANKS.

I. Debtors of an insolvent national bank, when sued by the receiver, cannot object that pleadings do not show a compliance with all the steps prescribed by statutes as preliminary to the appointment of such receiver. (*Cadle, Receiver, &c.*, vs. *Baker & Co.*, 20 *Wall.*, *p.* 650.)

II. Such ordinary debtors may be sued by receiver without previous order of the Comptroller. (*Bank* vs. *Kennedy*, 17 *Wall.*, *p.* 19.)

DEPOSITS, GENERAL.

I. The relation between a bank and its depositors is that of debtor and creditor only, and is not fiduciary. Thus, a note deposited for collection, if passed to the credit of the depositor in his general account, then overdrawn, becomes the property of the bank, which becomes indebted to him for the proceeds. Upon the bankruptcy of the bank, the proceeds are assets available to the general creditors. And the fact that the account was made good by other deposits, before collection of the note, makes no difference. (*In re Bank of Madison*, 5 *Bissell*, *p.* 515.)

II. A deposit is general, unless the depositor makes it special, or deposits it expressly in some particular capacity. And in case of a general deposit of money with a banker, a previous demand by the depositor, or some other person by his order, is indispensable to the maintenance of an action for the deposit, unless circumstances are shown which amount to a legal excuse. (*Brahm* vs. *Adkins*, 77 *Ill.*, *p.* 263.)

DEPOSITS, CERTIFICATES OF.

I. A certificate of deposit was issued by a bank for a certain sum, subject to the order of the depositor at a certain date, payable on the return of the certificate:

Held, in an action on said certificate against the bank, brought by an assignee, that there could be no recovery without proof of an actual demand and refusal of payment. (*Brown* vs. *McElroy*, 52 *Ind.*, *p.* 404.)

II. In a suit against the bank, upon a stolen certificate of deposit given by the defendant to the plaintiff, reciting that he had deposited in the bank a certain number of dollars, payable to his order *in current funds*, on the return of the certificate properly indorsed:

Held, first, that the instrument should be regarded as the promissory note of the bank, assignable under the statute (of Indiana), but that it was not negotiable as an inland bill of exchange, being made payable, not in money, but "in current funds"; second, that the payee could recover on said stolen certificate without giving a bond against a subsequent claim thereunder by another person. (*National State Bank* vs. *Ringel*, 51 *Ind.*, *p* 393.)

III. Where a bank issues a certificate of deposit, payable on its return properly indorsed, it is liable thereon to a *bona-fide* holder, to whom it was transferred *seven* years after it was issued, notwithstanding the payment thereof to the original holder. Such certificate is not dishonored until presented. (*National Bank Fort Edward* vs. *Washington Co. National Bank*, 5 *Hun.*, *N. Y. Sup. Court*, *p.* 605.)

DEPOSITS, SPECIAL.

I. The taking of special deposits to keep, merely for the accommodation of the depositor, is not within the authorized business of national banks; and the cashiers of such banks have no power to bind them on any express contract accompanying, or any implied contract arising out of, such taking. (*Wiley* vs. *First National Bank*, 47 *Vt.*, *p.* 546.)

DEPOSITS, SPECIAL.—Continued,

II. If a banking association, under the national-currency act, has power to assume the duties and obligations of a naked bailee of property, either gratuitously or for hire (as to which point the court does not decide, though apparently inclined to deny such power), it is clearly outside its ordinary business; and it is not within the scope of the general powers or general authority of its executive or ministerial offices to bind such corporation by a contract for such bailment. Therefore, in the absence of proof of special authority for that purpose, delegated by the board of directors, or evidence that such powers have been exercised by their knowledge and sanction, or that such has been the habit and custom of the bank, it is not responsible for property thus received by its cashier. (*First National Bank Lyons* vs. *Ocean National Bank*, 60 *N. Y.*, *p.* 278.)

III. A circular issued by such corporation, inviting the correspondence of other banks, and offering to buy and sell securities for them, is no evidence of a consent, on its part, to become a general bailee and depository of such securities for its correspondents. (*Ibid.*)

IV. The corporations formed under the national-currency act are banks of deposit, as well as circulation. They are authorized to issue their own notes, and receive from others their money and circulate it. Money so received is termed a deposit, although it has none of the qualifications of a bailment, thus named. There is no trust or promise to redeliver the same money. By the deposit the money becomes the property of the bank, and only the relation of debtor and creditor is created. (*Ibid., per Allen, J., p.* 288.)

[NOTE.—In the last cited case the cashier of the Ocean National Bank had, at sundry times, received United States bonds belonging to the Lyons bank. Some of these bonds had been purchased by said cashier and the assistant cashier for the Lyons bank. Two or three times, by the order of the latter bank, the coupons of these bonds had been cut off by said cashier and proceeds credited to the Lyons bank. But there was no proof that these transactions were done, or that said bonds were kept in the vault of said Ocean Bank, with the knowledge of the directors. While said bonds were thus kept, burglars broke in and stole them. The court held, and the opinion was unanimous, that there was no difference under the currency act between such a deposit of United States bonds and a deposit of other valuable property, such as plate, diamonds, or jewelry, for safe-keeping, gratuitously. It was a naked bailment of deposit, without reward, and such an act of the cashier as did not bind the bank.]

For definition of the bailment called "deposit," and the liabilities of such a bailee, see *Story on Bailments, section* 4, and *sections* 61 *to* 135.

As to special deposits of money with a bank, see *Story on Bailments, section* 88; also *Smith* vs. *First National Bank*, 99 *Mass., p.* 605. In this last case there had been a special deposit of gold coin, to be returned when called for. The cashier embezzled the funds: *Held*, that the bank was not liable, as there was no gross negligence on the part of the corporation.

DIRECTORS OF NATIONAL BANKS.

I. Directors of a national bank may remove the president, both under the law of Congress and the articles of association, where the latter so provide. The power exists if the bank has adopted no by-laws. (*Taylor* vs. *Hutton*, 43 *Barb., N. Y. Sup. Court, p.* 195; *S. C., 18 Abb. Pr. R., p.* 16.)

ESTATE, REAL.

I. The want of power of a bank, or of its trustee (receiver) in insolvency, to purchase and hold real estate, does not render void an arrangement whereby land subject to a lien in favor of the bank, and to other liens, is discharged of those other liens by funds from the assets of the bank, the land being then sold, and the entire proceeds of such sale realized to the bank assets, provided the title does not pass through the bank or its trustee. (*Zantzingers* vs. *Gunton*, 19 *Wall., p.* 32.)

INTEREST.

I. Under section 30, act of 1864, a national bank in any State may take as high rate of interest as by the laws of such State a natural person may stipulate for, although State banks of issue are restricted to a less rate. (*Tiffany* vs. *National Bank of Missouri*, 18 *Wall., p.* 409.)

[NOTE.—In Missouri, natural persons may take ten per cent., but State banks are restricted to eight per cent. In this case the national bank had taken nine per cent.: *Held*, legal.]

INTEREST—Continued.

II. *Held*, also, that as the action was virtually brought tor recover the penalty for *usury*, the statute (section 30) must receive a strict construction. (*Ibid.*, *p.* 409.)

See also Title "USURY," *post.*

INTEREST ON CLAIMS OF CREDITORS.

I. Where a national bank is put in charge of a receiver, under section 50 of the original currency act (R. S., sec. 5234), and a sufficient sum is realized from its assets to pay all claims against it and leave a surplus, the Comptroller ought to allow interest on the claims during the period of administration, before appropriating the surplus to the stockholders of the bank. An action of assumpsit by the holder of such a claim will not lie against the Comptroller, nor against the receiver, but will lie against the bank. (*Chemical National Bank* vs. *Bailey*, 12 *Blatchf.*, *p.* 480.)

II. In such action interest is recoverable on all demands originating in contract conditioned for the payment of interest, and on all demands for money due and unpaid, by way of damages for non-payment after such demands became due. And interest is recoverable on a balance due a depositor in such bank, although he has made no formal demand of payment. (*Ibid.*) But, as to this last point, see the ruling of the Supreme Court.

III. In the case of *National Bank of the Commonwealth* vs. *Mechanics' National Bank*, 4 *Otto*, *p.* 437, the Supreme Court United States, at its last term, decided that a depositor in a national bank, when it suspends payment and a receiver is appointed, is entitled from the date of his demand to interest upon the deposit; that the claims of depositors in such bank at date of suspension for the amount of their deposits are, when proved to the satisfaction of the Comptroller of the Currency, placed upon the same footing as if reduced to judgments; that is to say, they draw interest from the time of such proof and allowance.

It was also decided that, such interest being a liquidated sum at the time of the payment of the deposit, an action lies to recover it, *and interest thereon.*

JUDGMENTS.

I. A judgment against a national bank in the hands of a receiver, upon a claim, only establishes the validity of such claim; the plaintiff can have no execution on such judgment, but must await *pro rata* distribution. (*Bank of Bethel* vs. *Pahquioque Bank*, 14 *Wall.*, *p.* 383. *Clifford, J.*, *p.* 402.)

JURISDICTION.

I. A United States district court has jurisdiction to authorize a receiver of an insolvent national bank to compromise a debt. (*Matter of Platt*, 1 *Ben.*, *p.* 534.)

II. A resident (citizen) of Kentucky was a creditor of a national bank located in Alabama, and commenced a suit on his claim against said bank in the supreme court of the State of New York, at the same time attaching certain moneys belonging to said bank, in the hands of the National Park Bank, in New York. Subsequently the receiver of the Alabama bank (which had failed) was, on his own motion, made party defendant to the action pending in the New York supreme court, and pleaded "*want of jurisdiction*," and other defenses. The supreme court overruled his plea to the jurisdiction, rendered judgment against the receiver on the merits, and ordered satisfaction to be made from the moneys attached. Thereupon the receiver filed his bill in chancery in the *United States circuit court* for the proper circuit, praying an injunction to restrain the collection of the judgment rendered by said supreme court, and that the moneys attached be paid to him as receiver.

Held, that, by the provisions of the currency act, the State court was deprived of jurisdiction of the attachment proceedings; that the receiver was not estopped by the proceedings in said State court from asserting his rights in said circuit court, and that he was entitled to the relief prayed for in his bill. (*Cadle, receiver, &c.*, vs. *Tracy*, 11 *Blatchf.*, *p.* 101.)

(*Vide* Title "RECEIVERS, VII," *post.*)

LOANS ON SHARES.

I. National banks are governed by the act of 1864, which repealed the act of 1863, and cannot, therefore, make loans on the security of their own shares, unless to secure a pre-existing debt, contracted in good faith. (*Bank, &c.*, vs. *Lanier*, 11 *Wall.*, *p.* 369.)

II. The placing of funds by one bank on permanent deposit with another bank is a loan within the spirit of section 35 of act of 1864. (*Ibid.*, *p.* 369.)

III. Loans by such banks to their shareholders do not create a lien on the shares of such borrowers. (*Ibid.*, *p.* 369. See also *Bullard* vs. *Bank*, 18 *Wall.*, *p.* 580; and "BY-LAWS," *supra.*)

LOANS IN EXCESS.

I. A loan by a national bank in excess of the restriction of section 29 of the act of 1864 (Revised Statutes, section 5200), which provides that the total liabilities of any person (borrower) shall not exceed ten per centum of the capital stock, &c., is not void on that account. The loan may be enforced, though the bank may be liable to proceedings for forfeiture of its privileges, &c., for making it. (*Stewart* vs. *National Union Bank of Maryland*, 2 *Abb.*, *United States*, *p.* 424. See also *O'Hare* vs. *Second National Bank*, 77 *Pa. St.*, *p.* 96.)

In *Samuel M. Shoemaker* vs. *The National Mechanics' Bank*, and *The Same* vs. *The National Union Bank*, application for injunction, &c., United States circuit court, Baltimore, Md., Judge Giles held * * * "As to the first charge in this bill against the defendant, in reference to the amount loaned to Bayne & Co., in violation of the twenty-ninth section of the act of June 3, 1864, I would only say that the loan made under such circumstances is not void; it can be enforced as any other loan made by the bank." * * *

LOCATION.

1. Under sections 6, 8, 10, 15, 18, and 44 of the original currency act (13 Stat. at Large, 101), respecting the location of banking associations, a national bank is to be regarded as located at the place specified in its organization-certificate. If such place is in a State, the association is located in that State. (*Manufacturers' National Bank* vs. *Baack*, 8 *Blatchf.*, *p.* 137.)

OFFICERS.

I. It is the duty of directors of a bank to use ordinary diligence in acquiring knowledge of its business. They cannot be heard, when sued, to say that they were not apprised of facts, the existence of which is shown by the books, accounts, and correspondence of the bank. They should control the subordinate officers of the bank in all important transactions. Therefore, under the circumstances proved in this particular case, they were held liable for the abstraction and sale of special deposit by the latter. (*United Society, &c.*, vs. *Underwood*, 9 *Bush*, *Ky.*, *p.* 609.)

II. The cashier of a national bank, who had executed no bond, embezzled its funds, discovery whereof might have been effected by use of slight diligence on the part of the directory. They, however, published, according to law, a statement of the condition of the bank, which showed that its affairs were being prudently and honestly administered, and from which the public had a right to believe that he was trustworthy. Afterward, persons who had seen this report became sureties on the official bond of the cashier, and for his subsequent embezzlements were sought to be held liable thereon : *Held*, that such sureties, being misled by the statement, were released. They had a right to believe that the directors, before publishing it, investigated the condition of the bank. (*Graves* vs. *Lebanon National Bank*, 10 *Bush*, *Ky.*, *p.* 23.)

III. A guaranty against loss for signing as sureties, given by a bank president, without authority from the directors, to those whom he had solicited thus to sign a note, given to the bank to retire a prior note held by it against their principal, is held to be the individual contract of the president, and not binding upon the bank. (*First National Bank* vs. *Bennett*, 33 *Mich.*, *p.* 520.)

IV. A cashier, who has made sale of corporate property, and holds a balance in his hands, is the agent of the board of directors, and not of the respective stockholders, and cannot be charged by an individual stockholder as holding such balance for his benefit. (*Brown* vs. *Adams*, 5 *Biss.*, *p.* 181.)

V. A cashier, without special authority, cannot bind his bank by an official indorsement of his individual note, and the *onus* is on the payee to show such authority. (*West Saint Louis Savings Bank* vs. *Shawnee Co. Bank*, 3 *Dill.*, *p.* 403.)

VI. Although the cashier of a bank may, in the ordinary course of business, without the action of the directors, dispose of the negotiable securities of the bank, he has not the power to pledge its assets for the payment of an antecedent debt. (*State of Tennessee* vs. *Davis*, 50 *How.* (*N. Y.*), *p.* 447.)

RECEIVERS.

I. The receiver of a national bank is the instrument of the Comptroller, and may be removed by him. (*Kennedy* vs. *Gibson*, 8 *Wall.*, *p.* 505.)

II. Such receiver is the statutory assignee of the assets of the bank, and may sue to collect the same in his own name, or in the name of the bank, *for his use*. (*Ibid.*, *p.* 506.)

III. In such suit it is not necessary to make the bank or creditors parties. (*Ibid.*, *p.* 506.)

IV. The receiver of a national bank represents such bank and its creditors, *but he in no sense represents the United States Government*, and cannot subject the government to the jurisdiction of any court. (*Case* vs. *Terrill*, 11 *Wall.*, *p.* 199.)

RECEIVERS—Continued.

V. The decision of a receiver, rejecting a claim against his bank, is not final. Claimant may still sue. (*Bank of Bethel* vs. *Pahquioque Bank*, 14 *Wall, p.* 383.)

VI. The clause of section 50, act of 1864, which prescribes that the receiver shall be "*under the direction* of the Comptroller," means only that he shall be *subject* to his direction, not that he shall not act without orders. He may and must collect the assets. That is what he is appointed for. (*Bradley, J., in Bank* vs. *Kennedy*, 17 *Wall., pp.* 22–3.)

VII. Receivers of national banks are officers of the United States, within the meaning of the act of Congress of March 3, 1815, giving United States courts jurisdiction of actions by United States officers, and may sue in such courts. (*Platt, receiver, &c.,* vs. *Beach,* 2 *Ben., p.* 303.)

[NOTE.—The judge places stress upon the provision of section 31 of the act of 1864, which requires (in that particular instance) that the Secretary of the Treasury shall concur in the appointment of the receiver.]

SET-OFF.

I. In an action brought to enforce the individual liability of a shareholder of an insolvent bank, such shareholder cannot set off against such liability the amount due to him as a creditor of the bank. (*Garrison* vs. *Howe,* 17 *N. Y., p.* 458; *In re Empire City Bank,* 18 *N. Y., p.* 199.)

[NOTE.—Though these cases were decided by a State tribunal (New York court of appeals), and the rulings were based upon provisions of a State constitution and a State statute, yet the principle they enunciate is recognized and fully affirmed in *Sawyer* vs. *Hoag,* 17 *Wall., p.* 610, and *Scammon* vs. *Kimball,* 2 *Otto, p.* 362.]

SHAREHOLDERS, INDIVIDUAL LIABILITY OF.

I. Comptroller must decide *when and for what amount* the personal liability of the shareholders of an insolvent national bank shall be enforced. (*Kennedy* vs. *Gibson,* 8 *Wall., p.* 505.)

II. His decision as to this is conclusive. Shareholders cannot controvert it. (*Ibid., p.* 505.)

III. In any suit brought to enforce such personal liability, such decision of the Comptroller must be averred by the plaintiff, and, if put in issue, must be proved. (*Ibid., p.* 505.)

IV. The liability of shareholders is several, and not joint. (*Ibid., p.* 505.)

V. The limit of such liabilities is the par value of the stock held by each one. (*Ibid., p.* 505.)

VI. Where the whole amount is sought to be recovered, the proceeding must be at law; where less is required the proceeding may be in equity, and in such case an interlocutory decree may be taken for contribution, and the case may stand over for the further action of the court, if such action should subsequently prove to be necessary, until the full amount of the liability is exhausted. (*Ibid., p.* 505.)

But in *Bailey, receiver, &c.,* vs. *First National Bank Duluth, U. S. circuit court for Minnesota, Nelson, J.,* held that even where less than the par value was assessed the suit *might* be at law; and this would seem to be the true theory. *Vide* Bankers' Magazine, April 1877, p. 793.

VII. In such equity suit, all shareholders within the jurisdiction of the court should be made parties defendants; but it is no defense that those not within the jurisdiction are not joined. (*Ibid., p.* 506.)

VIII. Suits to enforce personal liability of shareholders may properly be brought before other assets are exhausted. (*Ibid., pp.* 505–6.)

SHAREHOLDER, LIABILITY OF TRANSFEREE.

I. The transferee of shares, when such transfer is absolute on the books of the bank, is liable to creditors to the amount of such shares, although in fact he holds them as collateral security for a loan to the shareholder who transferred them. (*Hale* vs. *Walker,* 31 *Iowa, p.* 344.)

[NOTE.—This also is a State court adjudication, but it is believed to be in harmony with the rulings of other high and eminent State tribunals upon the same question.] (*Adderly* vs. *Storm,* 6 *Hill, p.* 624, and *Worrall* vs. *Johnson,* 5 *Barb., p.* 210.)

[In the Bankers' Magazine for January, 1875, is a notice of the case of *Mann, receiver,* vs. *Dr. Cheeseman,* decided by Blatchford, J., in the United States circuit court, in New York, in which the judge held that until there was a transfer of shares *on the books of the bank* the shareholder whose name there appeared was liable for the debts of the bank; that an actual sale and the signing the ordinary power of attorney on the back of the certificate will not relieve the

SHAREHOLDER, LIABILITY OF TRANSFEREE—Continued.

seller. The learned judge also held that such shareholder could not question the action of the Comptroller as to the necessity of suing the shareholder.] (See also SET-OFF, *supra*.)

In the case of *Bowden* vs. *Farmers and Merchants' National Bank of Baltimore*, decided by Judge Giles in the United States circuit court, Maryland district, April, 1877, it was held that the defendant was liable, though the shares had originally been transferred to it as security for a loan, which loan had been paid, and though, upon such payment, defendant delivered the certificate of stock to the original owner, with a power of attorney authorizing him to re-transfer the stock to himself.

SHARES OF STOCK.

    I. A national bank whose certificates of stock specify that the shares are transferable on the books of the bank on surrender of the certificates, *and not otherwise*, and which suffers a shareholder to transfer without such surrender, is liable to a *bona fide* transferee, for value of same stock, who produces such certificate with usual power of attorney to transfer; and this is so though no notice had been given to the bank of the transfer. (*Bank* vs. *Lanier*, 11 *Wall., p.* 369.)

   II. Shares *quasi* negotiable. (*Ibid., p.* 369.)

TAXATION OF SHARES.

    I. The act of 1864, rightly construed, subjects the shares of the association in the hands of shareholders to taxation by the States, under certain limitations set forth in section 41, without regard to the fact that part or the whole of the capital of such association is invested in national securities which are declared by law exempt from State taxation. (*Van Allen* vs. *Assessors*, 3 *Wall., p.* 573.) (Chase, C. J., and other judges dissented.)

   II. Act thus construed is constitutional. (*Ibid., p.* 573.)

  III. A certain statute of New York, which taxed *shares* of national-bank stock, declared void, because *shares* of State banks were not taxed, although their capital was; the act of Congress prescribing that shares of national banks shall be taxed only as *shares* of State banks are. (*Ibid., p.* 573.)

     The ruling as to taxing shares of stock reaffirmed in *Bradley* vs. *People*, 4 *Wall., p.* 459; *National Bank* vs. *Commonwealth*, 9 *Wall., p.* 353.

     In last case, *held* that a State law requiring the cashier to pay the tax was valid. *Held*, also, that a certain State tax law virtually taxed "*shares* of moneyed corporations," &c. (*Ibid., p.* 353.)

  IV. Shares of stock in national banks are personal property, and though in one sense incorporeal, the law which created them could separate them from the person of their owner, for taxation, and give them a *situs* of their own. (*Tappan, collector*, vs. *Bank*, 19 *Wall., p.* 490.)

   V. Sec. 41 did thus separate them and give them a *situs* of their own. (*Ibid., p.* 490.)

  VI. This provision of the national-currency act became a law of the property (in shares), and every State in which a bank was located acquired jurisdiction, for taxation, of all the shares, whether owned by residents or non-residents, and power to legislate accordingly. (*Ibid., p.* 490.)

 VII. Under the act of Congress of February 10, 1868, enacting that each State legislature may direct the manner of taxing all shares of stock of national banks located within the State, subject to the restriction that the taxation shall not be greater than the rate assessed *upon other moneyed capital* in the hands of individual citizens of such State, and of a certain act of the legislature of Pennsylvania which provided that such shares shall be assessed for school, municipal, and local purposes at the same rate as is now or may hereafter be assessed and imposed upon other moneyed capital in the hands of individual citizens of the State; *held*, that shares of national-bank stock may be valued for taxation, for county, school, municipal, and local purposes, *at an amount above their par value*. (*Hepburn* vs. *School Directors of the Borough of Carlisle*, 23 *Wall., p.* 480.)

    [NOTE.—In this case it appeared that Hepburn owned several thousand dollars of national-bank stock, the par value of which was $100 per share, and that it was valued for taxation, for a school tax, at $150 per share. This assessment was held valid, notwithstanding that by a certain act of the State legislature, applicable to the county of Cumberland, in which the borough of Carlisle was situated, certain specified kinds of moneyed obligations were exempt from taxation, except for State purposes.]

TAXATION OF SHARES—Continued.

See also *Saint Louis National Bank, National Bank of Missouri, Third National Bank, Valley National Bank*, and *Merchants' National Bank of Saint Louis* vs. *Papin*, in United States circuit court, eastern district of Missouri, September term, 1876. Also, *Gallatin National Bank of New York* vs. *Commissioners of Taxes*, supreme court of New York, first department, general term, November, 1876. These latter cases are published in the Bankers' Magazine for December, 1876.

TAXATION OF INTEREST AND DIVIDENDS.

I. Under the internal-revenue act of July, 1870, interest paid and dividends declared during the last five months of 1870 are taxable, as well as those declared during the year 1871. (*Blake* vs. *National Banks*, 23 *Wall.*, p. 307.)

LICENSE TAX.

I. The District of Columbia imposed a *license tax* on all the national banks in the District, the rate being 50 cents annually on each $1,000 of the capital invested. The *Citizens' National Bank* refused to pay this assessment, and a test case was made in the District criminal court, Mr. *Justice Mac Arthur* presiding. This court, after full argument, held the tax illegal and void, as being contrary to the mode of taxation prescribed by Congress, which mode was held to be exclusive.

TRANSFERS OF ASSETS.

I. *When binding.* The receiver of a national bank cannot repudiate a pledge of its assets made by the bank for advances to it, either on the ground that the pledge was not formally executed, or that the transfer was void because not authorized by the charter of the bank, so long as he retains, as assets, the advances, to secure repayment of which the pledge was given. (*Casey* vs. *Le Société de Crédit Mobilier*, 2 *Woods*, p. 77.)

A preference of one creditor to another, within the meaning of section 5242, Revised Statutes, is a preference given by the bank to secure or pay a pre-existing debt. Where a person, knowing that a national bank is embarrassed, makes to it a loan, taking as security therefor a pledge of part of the assets of the bank, this transfer does not give him the preference prohibited by the statute. (*Ibid.*)

II. *When not binding.* Under said section 5242, which declares void transfers of its property by a national bank, made in contemplation of insolvency, and with a view to give a preference to one creditor over another, or with a view to prevent the application of the assets of the bank in the manner prescribed by law, such a transfer is void if the insolvency is in the contemplation of the bank making the transfer, although the party to whom it is made does not know or contemplate the insolvency of the bank. (*Case, receiver*, vs. *Citizens' Bank*, 2 *Woods*, p. 23.)

ULTRA VIRES, WHAT IS.

I. National banks cannot sell railroad bonds for third parties on commission, or engage in business of that character. (*Susan Welcker* vs. *First National Bank of Hagerstown*, Court of Appeals of Maryland, 43 Md., p. 581.)

II. In an action of deceit against a national bank, for alleged false representations of its teller in the sale to plaintiff of certain railroad bonds:
Held, That the selling of such bonds on commission was not within the authorized business of a national bank, and being thus beyond the scope of its corporate powers, the defense of *ultra vires* was open to it, and it was not responsible for the deceit of its teller. (*Ibid.*)

III. The national-bank act confers no power on a national bank to take a deed of trust of real estate as security for a contemporaneous loan; and such bank has no power not conferred by Congress. A sale under such a deed enjoined. (*Matthews* vs. *Skinner*, 62 Mo., p. 329. See also DEPOSITS, SPECIAL, I, II, III, IV.)

ULTRA VIRES, WHAT IS NOT.

IV. A national bank took a lien upon real estate to secure a pre-existing debt. Afterward, the bank paid $500 to discharge a prior lien upon the land, taking a note and mortgage on land in Kansas to secure this advance. Lien and mortgage held valid and warranted by law. (*Oram* vs. *National Bank*, 16 *Kans.*, p. 341.)

V. A *chattel mortgage* taken by a national bank to secure a pre-existing debt is valid, and will be enforced. (*Spafford* vs. *First National Bank*, 37 *Iowa*, p. 181.)

Usury.

I. State laws relative to usury do not apply to national banks. (*Farmers and Mechanics' National Bank* vs. *Dearing*, 1 *Otto, p.* 29.)

II. The only forfeiture declared by the 30th section of the act of June 3, 1864 (Revised Statutes, section 5198), is of the *entire interest* which the note or bill carries with it, or which has been agreed to be paid thereon, when the rate knowingly received, reserved, or charged by a national bank is in excess of that allowed by that section; and no loss of the entire debt is incurred by such bank, as a penalty or otherwise, by reason of the provision of the usury law of a State. (*Ibid.*)

To same effect are *National Exchange Bank* vs. *Moore*, 2 *Bond, p.* 170, and several State decisions.

(The *New York court of appeals* had decided the other way.)

APPENDIX.

On the following page will be found a complete index of the numerous tables contained in the report and appendix, and an alphabetical index of the cities and villages in which the national banks whose detailed reports are printed herewith are located appears at the end of the volume.

In concluding, the Comptroller deems it but just that he should gratefully acknowledge the zealous and efficient co-operation of the officers and clerks associated with him in the performance of official duties.

JOHN JAY KNOX,
Comptroller of the Currency.

Hon. SAMUEL J. RANDALL,
Speaker of the House of Representatives.

TABLES CONTAINED IN REPORT AND APPENDIX.

[In the full volume, of which this report and appendix form a part, statements of the assets and liabilities of each of the 2,053 national banks in operation on October 1, 1878, appear.]

REPORT.

APPENDIX.

Names and compensation of officers and clerks in the office of the Comptroller of the Currency.

Name.	Grade.	Salary.
John Jay Knox	Comptroller	$5,000
John S. Langworthy	Deputy Comptroller	2,800
J. Franklin Bates	Chief of division	2,200
John W. Magruder	do	2,200
John D. Patten, jr	do	2,200
Edward Wolcott	do	2,200
Edward S. Peck	Superintendent	2,000
Watson W. Eldridge	Teller	2,000
Frank A. Miller	Principal bookkeeper	2,000
Theodore O. Ebaugh	Assistant bookkeeper	2,000
F. A. Simkins	Stenographer	1,800
Fernando C. Cate	Fourth class	1,800
Nathaniel O. Chapman	do	1,800
William Elder	do	1,800
William B. Greene	do	1,800
John W. Griffin	do	1,800
George W. Martin	do	1,800
Charles H. Norton	do	1,800
William Sinclair	do	1,800
George H. Wood	do	1,800
Charles E Brayton	Third class	1,600
James C. Brown	do	1,600
Charles H. Cherry	do	1,600
William H. Glascott	do	1,600
John A. Hebrew	do	1,600
John A. Kayser	do	1,600
George T. May	do	1,600
Washington R. McCoy	do	1,600
Edward Myers	do	1,600
Charles Scott	do	1,600
William D. Swan	do	1,600
Edgar C. Beaman	Second class	1,400
David B. Bremner	do	1,400
Isaac C. Miller	do	1,400
Edward W. Moore	do	1,400
Edmund E. Schreiner	do	1,400
Charles J. Stoddard	do	1,400
Walter Taylor	do	1,400
William H. Walton	do	1,400
Frederick Widdows	do	1,400
Noah Hayes	First class	1,200
Edward McCauley	do	1,200
John J. Patton	do	1,200
Arthur M. Wheeler	do	1,200
Julia R. Donoho	do	1,200
Sarah F. Fitzgerald	do	1,200
Mary L. McCormick	do	1,200
Margaret L. Simpson	do	1,200
Philo Burr	Messenger	840
J. Eddie De Saules	do	840
Charles McC. Taylor	do	840
Zachariah E. Thomas	do	840
Silas Holmes	Watchman	720
William H. Romaine	do	720
Charles B. Hinckley	Laborer	720
Thomas Jackson	do	720
R. Le Roy Livingston	do	720

Names and compensation of officers and clerks, &c.—Continued.

Name.	Grade.	Salary.
Eliza M. Barker	Female clerk	$900
Eveline C. Bates	do	900
Harriet M. Black	do	900
Margaret L. Browne	do	900
Louisa Campbell	do	900
Virginia Clarke	do	900
Mary L. Conrad	do	900
May Crosby	do	900
Cornelia M. Davidson	do	900
Margaret F. Dewar	do	900
Jane A. Dorr	do	900
Annabella H. Finlay	do	900
Flora M. Fleming	do	900
Margaret E. Gooding	do	900
Lizzie S. Henry	do	900
Eliza R. Hyde	do	900
Elizabeth Hutchinson	do	900
Mary E. Kammerer	do	900
Alice M. Kennedy	do	900
Louisa W. Knowlton	do	900
Emma Lafayette	do	900
Julia R. Marvin	do	900
Lillian D. Massey	do	900
Maggie B. Miller	do	900
Emma F. Morrill	do	900
Mary E. Oliver	do	900
Carrie L. Pennock	do	900
Eliza Peters	do	900
Etha E. Poole	do	900
Annie E. Ranney	do	900
Emily H. Reed	do	900
Maria Richardson	do	900
Eliza A. Saunders	do	900
Fayette C. Snead	do	900
Amelia P. Stockdale	do	900
Marie L. Sturgus	do	900
Maria A. Summers	do	900
Sarah A. W. Tiffey	do	900
Julia C. Townsend	do	900
Martha A. Walker	do	900

Expenses of the office of the Comptroller of the Currency for the fiscal year ending June 30, 1878.

For special dies, plates, printing, &c $121, 932 32
For salaries 104, 820 00

226, 752 32

The contingent expenses of the office are not paid by the Comptroller, but from the general appropriation for contingent expenses of the Treasury Department ; and, as separate accounts are not kept for the different bureaus, the amount cannot be stated.

Amount and rate of taxation (United States and State) of the national banks for the year 1867.

States and Territories.	Capital stock.	Amount of taxes.			Rate of taxation.		
		United States.	State.	Total.	United States.	State.	Total.
					Per ct.	Pr. ct.	Pr. ct.
Maine	$9,085,000	$180,119	$141,226	$321,345	2.0	1.5	3.5
New Hampshire	4,735,000	88,773	93,179	181,952	1.9	1.9	3.8
Vermont	6,510,012	122,214	144,164	266,377	1.9	2.2	4.1
Massachusetts	79,932,000	1,616,825	1,562,128	3,178,953	2.0	2.0	4.0
Rhode Island	20,364,800	324,844	195,355	520,200	1.5	1.0	2.5
Connecticut	24,584,220	434,440	387,146	821,587	1.7	1.6	3.3
New York	116,494,941	3,022,662	4,058,706	7,081,368	2.6	3.5	6.1
New Jersey	11,333,350	253,350	223,106	476,465	2.2	2.0	4.2
Pennsylvania	50,277,795	1,242,037	278,268	1,520,305	2.5	0.5	3.0
Delaware	1,428,185	32,621	1,261	33,881	2.3	0.1	2.4
Maryland	12,590,203	260,261	166,054	426,315	2.1	1.3	3.4
District of Columbia	1,350,000	15,330	3,286	18,615	1.3	0.3	1.6
Virginia	2,500,000	48,345	13,926	62,270	1.9	0.6	2.5
West Virginia	2,216,400	46,966	51,457	98,424	2.1	2.3	4.4
North Carolina	583,300	9,049	5,144	14,193	1.5	0.9	2.4
Georgia	1,700,000	40,845	6,050	46,895	2.5	0.4	2.9
Alabama	500,000	8,763	3,830	12,592	1.7	1.0	2.7
Louisiana	1,300,000	35,894	20,042	55,936	2.8	1.5	4.3
Texas	576,450	6,865	2,149	9,015	1.2	0.4	1.6
Arkansas	200,000	5,745	1,351	7,096	2.9	0.7	3.6
Kentucky	2,885,000	59,816	17,467	77,283	2.1	0.6	2.7
Tennessee	2,100,000	52,460	27,975	80,435	2.7	1.4	4.1
Ohio	22,404,700	514,681	520,951	1,035,633	2.3	2.3	4.6
Indiana	12,867,000	278,798	200,372	479,170	2.2	1.5	3.7
Illinois	11,620,000	321,406	231,917	553,323	2.8	2.0	4.8
Michigan	5,070,010	111,790	68,061	179,851	2.2	1.3	3.5
Wisconsin	2,935,000	76,583	62,012	138,595	2.6	2.1	4.7
Iowa	3,992,000	106,340	88,281	194,631	2.7	2.2	4.9
Minnesota	1,660,000	39,132	29,522	68,655	2.0	1.3	3.3
Missouri	7,559,300	133,142	189,248	322,389	1.4	2.0	3.4
Kansas	400,000	10,229	7,801	18,030	2.5	2.0	4.5
Nebraska	250,000	10,735	7,014	17,749	4.3	2.8	7.1
Oregon	100,000	1,624		1,624	2.4		2.4
Colorado	350,000	9,702	1,615	11,317	2.8	0.4	3.2
Utah	150,000	1,887	1,097	2,984	1.3	0.7	2.0
Idaho	100,000	479	1,405	1,884	0.5	1.4	1.9
Montana	100,000	837	560	1,397	0.8	0.6	1.4
Total	422,804,666	9,525,607	8,813,126	18,338,734	2.2	2.1	4.3

6 C C

Amount and rate of taxation (United States and State) of the national banks for the year 1869.

| States and Territories. | Capital stock. | Amount of taxes. | | | Rate of taxation. | | |
		United States.	State.	Total.	United States.	State.	Total.
					Per ct.	*Per ct.*	*Per ct.*
Maine	$9, 185, 000	$101, 779	$164, 150	$355, 929	2. 1	1. 8	3. 9
New Hampshire	4, 835, 000	97, 245	102, 812	200, 057	2. 0	2. 1	4. 1
Vermont	6, 385, 012	129, 059	117, 107	246, 166	2. 0	1. 8	3. 8
Massachusetts	81, 282, 000	1, 691, 620	1, 329, 018	3, 020, 638	2. 1	1. 6	3. 7
Rhode Island	20, 164, 800	344, 687	175, 466	520, 153	1. 7	0. 9	2. 6
Connecticut	24, 606, 820	476, 244	366, 457	842, 701	1. 9	1. 5	3. 4
New York	112, 267, 841	2, 958, 089	2, 980, 104	5, 938, 193	2. 6	2. 7	5. 3
New Jersey	11, 465, 350	279, 410	200, 121	479, 531	2. 4	1. 8	4. 2
Pennsylvania	49, 560, 390	1, 312, 419	266, 186	1, 578, 605	2. 7	0. 5	3. 2
Delaware	1, 428, 185	30, 907	3, 265	34, 172	2. 2	0. 2	2. 4
Maryland	12, 790, 293	277, 590	147, 854	425, 444	2. 2	1. 1	3. 3
District of Columbia	1, 050, 000	23, 814	1, 850	25, 664	2. 2	0. 2	2. 4
Virginia	2, 221, 860	59, 281	8, 882	68, 163	2. 7	0. 4	3. 1
West Virginia	2, 116, 400	51, 979	37, 053	89, 032	2. 3	1. 7	4. 0
North Carolina	683, 400	15, 712	2, 455	18, 167	2. 3	0. 4	2. 7
South Carolina	823, 500	19, 763	7, 952	27, 715	2. 4	1. 0	3. 4
Georgia	1, 500, 000	45, 824	8, 254	54, 078	3. 0	0. 6	3. 6
Alabama	400, 000	5, 926	490	6, 416	1. 5	0. 1	1. 6
Louisiana	1, 300, 000	27, 455	7, 107	34, 562	2. 1	0. 6	2. 7
Texas	525, 000	11, 184	4, 375	15, 559	2. 2	0. 8	3. 0
Arkansas	200, 000	4, 284	6, 908	11, 282	2. 1	3. 5	5. 6
Kentucky	2, 835, 000	62, 836	10, 236	73, 072	2. 2	0. 4	2. 6
Tennessee	1, 987, 400	47, 164	6, 570	53, 734	2. 4	0. 3	2. 7
Ohio	21, 917, 399	635, 935	573, 576	1, 209, 511	2. 9	2. 6	5. 5
Indiana	12, 752, 000	298, 336	218, 888	517, 224	2. 4	1. 7	4. 1
Illinois	12, 370, 000	369, 742	217, 652	587, 394	3. 0	1. 8	4. 8
Michigan	5, 510, 000	143, 649	34, 384	178, 033	2. 6	0. 6	3. 2
Wisconsin	2, 710, 000	80, 963	50, 663	131, 626	3. 0	1. 9	4. 9
Iowa	3, 717, 000	122, 162	53, 621	175, 783	3. 3	1. 4	4. 7
Minnesota	1, 770, 000	45, 223	29, 873	75, 096	2. 5	1. 7	4. 2
Missouri	7, 810, 300	171, 198	120, 720	291, 918	2. 2	1. 5	3. 7
Kansas	400, 000	17, 443	16, 009	33, 452	4. 4	4. 0	8. 4
Nebraska	400, 000	14, 593	10, 838	25, 431	3. 7	2. 7	6. 4
Oregon	100, 000	2, 917		2, 917	2. 9		2. 9
Colorado	350, 000	11, 902	11, 286	23, 188	3. 4	3. 2	6. 6
Idaho	100, 000	1, 179	2, 541	3, 720	1. 2	2. 5	3. 7
Montana	100, 000	1, 731	2, 283	4, 014	1. 7	2. 3	4. 0
Totals	419, 619, 860	10, 081, 244	7, 297, 096	17, 378, 340	2. 4	1. 7	4. 1

Amount and rate of taxation (United States and State) of the national banks for the year 1874.

States and Territories.	Capital stock.	Amount of taxes.			Rate of taxation.		
		United States.	State.	Total.	United States.	State.	Total.
					Per ct.	Per ct.	Per ct.
Maine	$9,654,019	$111,403	$192,290	$303,693	1.2	2.0	3.2
New Hampshire	5,317,037	60,002	106,587	166,589	1.1	2.1	3.2
Vermont	7,862,712	88,152	139,297	227,449	1.1	1.8	2.9
Massachusetts	91,754,078	1,163,858	1,878,368	3,042,226	1.3	2.1	3.4
Rhode Island	20,504,800	201,317	224,540	425,857	1.0	1.1	2.1
Connecticut	25,424,620	271,801	439,402	711,203	1.1	1.8	2.9
New York	106,599,708	2,026,960	3,044,565	5,071,525	1.9	2.9	4.8
New Jersey	13,830,466	205,451	282,645	488,096	1.5	2.1	3.6
Pennsylvania	53,178,261	871,220	377,546	1,248,766	1.6	0.7	2.3
Delaware	1,523,185	20,798	6,630	27,428	1.4	0.4	1.8
Maryland	13,720,897	181,249	194,697	375,946	1.3	1.5	2.8
District of Columbia	1,309,512	19,747	5,288	25,035	1.5	0.4	1.9
Virginia	3,580,913	54,957	52,207	107,164	1.5	1.6	3.1
West Virginia	2,375,216	33,484	34,507	67,991	1.4	1.8	3.2
North Carolina	2,175,338	30,837	38,601	69,438	1.4	1.9	3.3
South Carolina	3,156,250	34,421	111,654	146,075	1.1	3.6	4.7
Georgia	2,843,962	31,656	53,872	85,528	1.1	1.9	3.0
Alabama	1,634,883	18,746	25,289	44,035	1.2	1.7	2.9
Louisiana	4,000,000	61,642	52,270	113,912	1.5	1.4	2.9
Texas	1,054,897	14,384	22,863	37,247	1.4	2.3	3.7
Arkansas	205,000	2,488	8,030	10,518	1.2	3.9	5.1
Kentucky	9,076,127	103,635	47,655	151,290	1.1	0.5	1.6
Tennessee	3,457,897	50,290	70,844	121,134	1.5	2.2	3.7
Ohio	29,112,642	403,697	642,054	1,045,751	1.4	2.2	3.6
Indiana	17,936,404	214,977	429,585	644,562	1.2	2.6	3.8
Illinois	20,507,963	367,718	420,461	788,179	1.8	2.2	4.0
Michigan	10,098,162	134,052	149,720	283,772	1.3	1.5	2.8
Wisconsin	3,704,032	67,485	76,330	143,815	1.8	2.3	4.1
Iowa	6,048,562	98,421	117,115	215,536	1.6	2.1	3.7
Minnesota	4,268,026	63,224	76,876	140,100	1.5	2.0	3.5
Missouri	9,308,198	112,525	190,140	302,665	1.2	2.1	3.3
Kansas	1,783,235	26,182	41,867	68,049	1.5	3.3	4.8
Nebraska	1,025,000	20,883	34,282	55,165	2.0	3.3	5.3
Oregon	250,000	5,808	3,488	9,296	2.3	1.4	3.7
California	3,358,594	46,044	....	46,044	1.4	....	1.4
Colorado	748,581	16,983	10,750	27,733	2.3	2.1	4.4
Utah	439,402	5,387	4,137	9,524	1.2	1.4	2.6
New Mexico	300,000	3,718	3,150	6,868	1.2	1.1	2.3
Wyoming	125,000	1,697	1,180	2,877	1.4	2.5	3.9
Idaho	100,000	1,393	129	1,522	1.4	0.1	1.5
Dakota	50,000	614	1,225	1,839	1.2	2.5	3.7
Montana	350,000	6,777	8,190	14,967	1.9	2.3	4.2
Totals	*493,751,679	7,256,083	9,620,326	16,876,409	1.5	2.0	3.5

* Including capital of banks from which returns of the amount of State taxation were not received.

Amount and rate of taxation (United States and State) of the national banks for the year 1875.

States and Territories.	Capital.	Amount of taxes.			Ratios to capital.		
		United States.	State.	Total.	United States.	State.	Total.
					Per ct.	*Per ct.*	*Per ct.*
Maine	$9,790,104	$112,652	$215,981	$328,633	1.2	2.2	3.4
New Hampshire	5,482,514	61,006	103,949	164,955	1.1	1.9	3.0
Vermont	8,216,467	89,360	169,044	258,404	1.1	2.2	3.3
Massachusetts	43,063,374	491,157	865,198	1,356,355	1.1	2.0	3.1
Boston	51,362,454	703,218	957,283	1,660,501	1.4	1.9	3.3
Rhode Island	20,548,433	201,639	269,402	471,041	1.0	1.3	2.3
Connecticut	25,852,987	277,984	435,680	713,664	1.1	1.7	2.8
New York	35,471,333	529,804	962,982	1,492,786	1.5	2.7	4.2
New York City	68,466,576	1,376,541	2,093,143	3,469,684	2.0	3.1	5.1
Albany	2,088,462	62,215	71,740	133,955	3.0	3.6	6.6
New Jersey	14,072,520	208,559	300,894	509,453	1.5	2.1	3.6
Pennsylvania	29,655,994	410,928	175,059	585,987	1.4	0.6	2.0
Philadelphia	17,019,239	346,950	128,996	475,946	2.0	0.8	2.8
Pittsburgh	10,059,641	141,545	56,246	197,791	1.4	0.5	1.9
Delaware	1,523,185	22,025	7,952	29,977	1.5	0.5	2.0
Maryland	2,268,238	30,468	31,355	61,823	1.3	1.4	2.7
Baltimore	11,469,355	150,003	230,368	380,371	1.3	2.0	3.3
District of Columbia	252,000	4,555	262	4,817	1.8	0.1	1.9
Washington	1,239,564	16,905	3,462	20,367	1.4	0.3	1.7
Virginia	3,535,719	54,132	70,710	124,842	1.5	2.0	3.5
West Virginia	1,971,000	25,775	30,102	55,877	1.3	1.7	3.0
North Carolina	2,232,150	31,406	34,584	65,990	1.4	1.6	3.0
South Carolina	3,135,000	34,747	106,760	141,507	1.1	3.4	4.5
Georgia	2,716,974	29,023	45,790	74,813	1.1	1.6	2.7
Florida	50,000	854	1,056	1,910	1.7	2.1	3.8
Alabama	1,638,866	18,865	22,204	41,069	1.2	1.4	2.6
New Orleans	3,706,667	59,314	9,870	69,184	1.6	0.3	1.9
Texas	1,205,350	15,819	20,844	36,663	1.3	1.7	3.0
Arkansas	205,000	1,983	3,288	5,271	1.0	1.6	2.6
Tennessee	3,468,992	47,341	78,427	125,768	1.4	2.3	3.7
Kentucky	7,201,765	80,777	36,311	117,088	1.1	0.5	1.6
Louisville	3,358,000	45,012	16,290	61,302	1.3	0.5	1.8
Ohio	21,110,393	292,900	507,231	800,131	1.4	2.4	3.8
Cincinnati	4,000,000	80,198	105,199	185,397	2.0	2.6	4.6
Cleveland	4,550,000	51,011	104,872	155,883	1.1	2.3	3.4
Indiana	18,588,189	229,606	470,836	700,442	1.2	2.6	3.8
Illinois	11,873,363	186,188	271,636	457,824	1.6	2.3	3.9
Chicago	7,073,757	173,506	188,524	362,030	2.3	2.5	4.8
Michigan	8,568,270	105,676	146,993	252,669	1.2	1.7	2.9
Detroit	1,900,000	33,331	24,744	58,075	1.8	1.3	3.1
Wisconsin	2,974,651	47,584	55,156	102,740	1.6	1.9	3.5
Milwaukee	700,000	16,263	19,229	35,492	2.3	3.0	5.3
Minnesota	4,391,068	60,781	93,736	154,517	1.4	2.3	3.7
Iowa	6,416,607	104,667	126,088	230,755	1.6	2.0	3.6
Missouri	2,742,199	36,361	93,467	129,828	1.3	3.5	4.8
Saint Louis	6,360,300	75,135	177,464	252,599	1.2	2.8	4.0
Kansas	1,588,821	22,901	45,548	68,449	1.4	3.2	4.6
Nebraska	994,758	22,277	21,689	43,966	2.2	2.3	4.5
Oregon	250,000	5,654	3,037	8,691	2.3	1.2	3.5
California	1,552,622	17,186		17,186	1.1		
San Francisco	2,917,112	35,780		35,780	1.2		
New Mexico	300,000	4,228	3,250	7,478	1.4	1.1	2.5
Colorado	923,478	18,997	25,714	44,711	2.1	3.3	5.4
Utah	300,000	3,472	2,550	6,022	1.2	1.3	2.5
Idaho	100,000	1,429	2,367	3,796	1.4	2.4	3.8
Montana	350,000	7,047	9,137	16,184	2.0	2.6	4.6
Wyoming	125,000	2,049	3,523	5,572	1.6	2.8	4.4
Dakota	50,000	742	900	1,642	1.5	1.8	3.3
Totals	503,687,911	7,317,531	10,058,122	17,375,653	1.5	2.0	3.5

Amount and rate of taxation (United States and State) of the national banks for the year 1876.

States and Territories.	Capital.*	Amount of taxes.			Ratios to capital.		
		United States.	State.	Total.	United States.	State.	Total.
					Per ct.	Per ct.	Per ct.
Maine	$10, 635, 819	$115, 272	$237, 792	$353, 064	1.1	2.2	3.3
New Hampshire	5, 615, 000	62, 627	97, 255	159, 882	1.1	1.7	2.8
Vermont	8, 722, 369	91, 777	179, 876	271, 653	1.1	2.1	3.2
Massachusetts	44, 290, 557	497, 228	825, 685	1, 322, 913	1.1	1.9	3.0
Boston	52, 200, 000	704, 655	855, 446	1, 560, 101	1.4	1.6	3.0
Rhode Island	20, 579, 800	290, 420	279, 765	480, 185	1.0	1.3	2.3
Connecticut	26, 015, 834	275, 991	438, 980	714, 980	1.0	1.7	2.7
New York	35, 326, 077	512, 233	826, 929	1, 339, 162	1.5	2.4	3.9
New York City	66, 607, 325	1, 278, 956	2, 197, 681	3, 476, 637	1.9	3.5	5.4
Albany	2, 000, 000	63, 650	67, 972	131, 622	3.2	3.4	6.6
New Jersey	14, 238, 634	204, 512	292, 024	496, 536	1.4	2.1	3.5
Pennsylvania	29, 354, 981	417, 324	182, 003	599, 327	1.4	0.6	2.0
Philadelphia	17, 189, 489	356, 204	119, 655	475, 859	2.1	0.7	2.8
Pittsburgh	10, 531, 592	142, 232	56, 620	198, 852	1.4	0.5	1.9
Delaware	1, 571, 730	22, 030	6, 900	28, 930	1.4	0.4	1.8
Maryland	2, 299, 960	31, 280	28, 046	59, 326	1.4	1.3	2.7
Baltimore	11, 491, 085	142, 102	229, 484	371, 586	1.2	2.0	3.2
District of Columbia	252, 000	4, 478	3, 906	8, 384	1.8	1.2	3.0
Washington	1, 300, 000	15, 246	14, 096	29, 342	1.2	1.1	2.3
Virginia	3, 339, 307	51, 297	71, 827	123, 124	1.5	2.1	3.6
West Virginia	1, 746, 000	21, 783	28, 878	50, 661	1.2	1.7	2.9
North Carolina	2, 499, 499	31, 021	39, 933	70, 954	1.2	1.6	2.8
South Carolina	3, 172, 500	31, 793	84, 863	116, 656	1.0	2.7	3.7
Georgia	2, 504, 317	26, 265	41, 764	68, 029	1.0	2.0	3.0
Florida	50, 000	941	948	1, 889	1.9	1.9	3.8
Alabama	1, 690, 412	19, 184	16, 888	36, 072	1.1	1.0	2.1
New Orleans	3, 436, 786	53, 388	6, 534	59, 922	1.6	0.2	1.8
Texas	1, 038, 782	14, 518	19, 057	33, 575	1.4	1.9	3.3
Arkansas	205, 000	2, 055	2, 830	4, 885	1.0	1.4	2.4
Kentucky	7, 259, 641	79, 609	32, 587	112, 196	1.1	0.5	1.6
Louisville	3, 095, 500	42, 676	14, 576	57, 252	1.4	0.5	1.9
Tennessee	3, 401, 449	49, 251	70, 479	119, 730	1.4	2.1	3.5
Ohio	20, 757, 903	274, 814	550, 498	834, 312	1.3	2.8	4.1
Cincinnati	4, 373, 680	74, 720	128, 087	202, 807	1.7	2.9	4.6
Cleveland	4, 550, 000	49, 454	114, 072	163, 526	1.1	2.5	3.6
Indiana	17, 781, 910	210, 769	424, 904	635, 673	1.2	2.5	3.7
Illinois	11, 728, 823	173, 495	231, 693	405, 188	1.5	2.0	3.5
Chicago	6, 950, 123	154, 246	200, 866	355, 112	2.2	3.0	5.2
Michigan	8, 238, 890	100, 414	128, 446	228, 860	1.2	1.6	2.8
Detroit	1, 900, 000	31, 078	28, 633	59, 711	1.6	1.5	3.1
Wisconsin	2, 827, 322	43, 783	53, 499	97, 282	1.5	1.9	3.4
Milwaukee	650, 000	14, 207	18, 606	32, 813	2.2	2.9	5.1
Iowa	6, 430, 308	91, 667	122, 519	214, 186	1.4	2.0	3.4
Minnesota	4, 455, 478	60, 336	86, 923	147, 259	1.4	2.0	3.4
Missouri	2, 574, 000	35, 824	53, 580	89, 404	1.4	2.2	3.6
Saint Louis	5, 742, 500	73, 344	76, 071	149, 415	1.3	2.6	3.9
Kansas	1, 369, 167	20, 722	34, 518	55, 240	1.5	3.0	4.5
Nebraska	975, 000	21, 839	23, 274	45, 113	2.2	2.5	4.7
Oregon	237, 500	6, 319	2, 550	8, 869	2.7	1.0	3.7
California†	1, 700, 000	17, 484	3, 463	20, 947	1.0	0.2	1.2
San Francisco†	2, 875, 000	23, 526	705	24, 231	0.8	....	0.8
New Mexico	300, 000	3, 976	3, 513	7, 489	1.3	1.2	2.5
Colorado	824, 025	18, 276	16, 465	34, 741	2.2	2.2	4.4
Utah	250, 000	2, 840	2, 625	5, 465	1.1	1.3	2.4
Idaho	100, 000	1, 278	2, 370	3, 648	1.3	2.4	3.7
Montana	350, 000	6, 811	9, 561	16, 372	1.9	2.7	4.6
Wyoming	125, 000	1, 976	3, 367	5, 343	1.6	2.7	4.3
Dakota	50, 000	891	636	1, 527	1.8	1.3	3.1
Total	501, 788, 079	7, 076, 087	9, 701, 732	16, 777, 819	1.4	2.0	3.4

* The capital of the banks that paid State, county, and municipal taxes on stock and real estate is $488,272,782.

† California banks pay no State taxes on capital, except such as is invested in real estate.

Dividends and earnings of the national banks, arranged by geographical divisions, for semi-annual periods from September 1, 1869, to September 1, 1878.

Geographical divisions.	Number of banks.	Capital.	Surplus.	Dividends.	Net earnings.	Ratios.		
						Dividends to capital.	Dividends to capital and surplus.	Earnings to capital and surplus.
Sept., 1869, to March, 1870:						*Pr. ct.*	*Pr. ct.*	*Pr. ct.*
New England States....	488	$148,466,032	$27,335,824	$7,503,307	$10,148,574	5.0	4.3	5.8
Middle States	577	187,741,859	43,043,795	9,550,034	12,352,534	5.1	4.1	5.3
Southern States	76	12,850,100	1,419,995	804,972	1,035,938	6.3	5.6	7.3
Western States	430	67,309,000	14,318,596	3,620,782	5,459,888	5.4	4.4	6.7
Totals	1,571	416,366,991	86,118,210	21,479,095	28,996,934	5.2	4.3	5.8
March, 1870, to Sept., 1870:								
New England States....	491	152,700,033	29,268,791	7,554,081	9,609,814	4.9	4.1	5.3
Middle States	584	188,131,868	43,455,429	9,250,780	11,244,110	4.9	4.0	4.8
Southern States	81	14,441,203	1,586,312	809,439	1,153,852	5.6	5.0	7.2
Western States	444	70,044,000	15,320,088	3,466,043	4,806,109	4.9	4.1	5.6
Totals	1,600	425,317,104	91,630,620	21,080,343	26,813,885	5.0	4.1	5.2
Sept., 1870, to March, 1871:								
New England States....	492	153,419,032	30,647,742	7,747,077	9,547,922	5.0	4.2	5.2
Middle States	585	189,066,550	46,418,681	9,494,432	11,146,367	5.0	4.0	4.7
Southern States	83	15,221,574	1,733,167	924,477	1,138,066	6.1	5.4	6.7
Western States	445	70,992,000	15,872,811	4,039,164	5,410,807	5.7	4.6	6.2
Totals	1,605	428,699,165	94,672,401	22,205,150	27,243,162	5.2	4.2	5.2
March, 1871, to Sept., 1871:								
New England States....	493	154,151,032	31,938,761	7,619,422	9,259,127	4.9	4.1	5.0
Middle States	591	190,676,860	47,776,315	9,274,773	11,207,080	4.9	3.9	4.7
Southern States	113	22,153,463	1,885,311	1,148,638	1,317,419	5.2	4.8	5.5
Western States	496	79,017,900	16,686,204	4,082,446	5,531,085	5.2	4.3	5.8
Totals	1,693	445,999,264	98,286,591	22,125,279	27,315,311	5.0	4.1	5.0
Sept., 1871, to March, 1872:								
New England States....	494	154,869,032	33,163,949	7,713,428	9,152,734	5.0	4.1	4.9
Middle States	589	190,985,969	48,754,556	9,674,512	10,988,549	5.1	4.0	4.6
Southern States	129	26,182,281	2,118,475	1,317,525	1,700,043	5.0	4.7	6.0
Western States	538	78,656,424	15,394,263	4,154,361	5,060,613	5.3	4.4	6.0
Totals	1,750	450,693,706	99,431,243	22,859,826	27,502,539	5.1	4.2	5.0
March, 1872, to Sept., 1872:								
New England States....	497	155,220,568	34,113,635	7,025,549	9,721,465	4.9	4.0	5.1
Middle States	594	191,776,118	50,328,781	9,432,709	12,009,457	4.9	3.9	5.0
Southern States	141	29,513,235	2,353,213	1,552,664	1,967,089	5.3	4.9	6.2
Western States	620	89,166,102	18,386,313	5,216,367	6,784,880	5.8	4.8	6.5
Totals	1,852	465,676,023	105,181,942	23,827,289	30,572,891	5.1	4.2	5.4
Sept., 1872, to March, 1873:								
New England States....	495	155,650,232	36,858,324	7,938,341	10,324,340	5.1	4.1	5.4
Middle States	594	192,845,669	53,303,503	9,766,087	11,642,716	5.1	4.0	4.7
Southern States	147	31,328,787	3,207,788	1,612,680	2,170,179	5.1	4.7	6.3
Western States	676	100,684,995	20,887,673	5,508,953	7,789,243	5.5	4.5	6.4
Totals	1,912	480,518,683	114,257,288	24,826,061	31,926,478	5.2	4.2	5.4
March, 1873, to Sept., 1873:								
New England States....	496	157,014,832	38,303,887	7,941,687	10,103,736	5.1	4.1	5.2
Middle States	591	192,234,009	53,431,089	9,575,193	12,565,331	5.0	3.9	5.1
Southern States	161	33,259,530	3,600,607	1,544,046	2,246,024	4.6	4.2	6.1
Western States	707	105,592,580	22,778,265	5,762,103	8,206,909	5.5	4.5	6.4
Totals	1,955	488,100,951	118,113,848	24,823,029	33,122,000	5.1	4.1	5.5
Sept., 1873, to March, 1874:								
New England States ...	503	159,041,832	39,714,859	7,627,811	9,682,704	4.8	3.8	4.9
Middle States	588	190,368,609	55,931,654	9,164,682	10,983,048	4.8	3.7	4.5
Southern States	159	32,605,522	3,865,491	1,415,933	1,750,914	4.3	3.9	4.8
Western States	717	107,494,300	23,957,855	5,321,571	7,127,454	4.9	4.0	5.4
Totals	1,967	489,510,323	123,469,859	23,529,997	29,544,120	4.8	3.8	4.8

Dividends and earnings of the national banks, &c.—Continued.

Geographical divisions.	Number of banks.	Capital.	Surplus.	Dividends.	Net earnings.	Ratios.		
						Dividends to capital.	Dividends to capital and surplus.	Earnings to capital and surplus.
March, 1874, to Sept., 1874:						*Pr. ct.*	*Pr. ct.*	*Pr. ct.*
New England States ...	506	$159,531,832	$41,978,153	$7,838,007	$9,603,512	4.9	3.9	4.8
Middle States	586	189,385,019	37,176,298	9,463,707	11,214,753	5.0	3.8	4.5
Southern States	159	33,138,800	4,121,405	1,594,208	1,871,502	4.8	4.3	5.0
Western States	720	107,882,633	25,088,183	6,033,384	7,346,984	5.6	4.5	5.5
Totals.............	1,971	489,938,284	128,364,039	24,929,306	30,036,811	5.1	4.0	4.9
Sept., 1874, to March, 1875:								
New England States ...	510	160,461,832	43,020,505	7,785,166	9,031,409	4.8	3.8	4.4
Middle States	589	189,619,519	57,749,497	9,537,118	10,361,652	5.0	3.9	4.2
Southern States	169	33,681,310	4,646,468	1,463,170	1,861,758	4.3	3.8	4.9
Western States	739	109,786,170	26,144,167	5,965,362	7,881,188	5.4	4.4	5.8
Totals.............	2,007	493,568,831	131,560,637	24,750,816	29,136,007	5.0	4.0	4.7
March, 1875, to Sept., 1875:								
New England States ...	512	161,928,732	43,563,385	7,758,400	8,767,978	4.8	3.8	4.3
Middle States	603	190,775,569	57,826,444	9,151,653	9,985,736	4.8	3.7	4.0
Southern States	175	34,640,100	4,965,170	1,539,234	1,956,203	4.4	3.9	4.9
Western States	757	110,520,432	27,768,650	5,868,438	8,090,300	5.3	4.2	5.8
Totals.............	2,047	497,864,833	134,123,649	24,317,785	28,800,217	4.9	3.8	4.6
Sept., 1875, to March, 1876:								
New England States ...	531	166,396,620	43,739,079	7,371,060	7,548,855	4.4	3.5	3.6
Middle States	625	190,834,271	56,319,205	10,174,655	5,770,198	5.2	4.1	2.3
Southern States	174	33,390,100	5,348,175	1,509,125	2,211,357	4.5	3.9	5.7
Western States	746	110,588,500	29,061,135	5,756,741	7,567,511	5.2	4.1	5.4
Totals.............	2,076	504,209,491	134,467,594	24,811,581	23,097,921	4.9	3.9	3.6
March, 1876, to Sept., 1876:								
New England States ...	539	167,902,820	43,319,060	6,770,149	6,098,661	4.0	3.2	2.9
Middle States	626	190,926,351	54,527,758	8,818,572	6,751,345	4.6	3.6	3.2
Southern States	179	33,392,600	5,486,630	1,432,194	1,498,873	4.3	3.7	3.9
Western States	737	108,258,500	28,917,630	5,542,914	6,191,353	5.1	4.0	4.5
Totals.............	2,081	500,482,271	132,251,078	22,563,829	20,540,232	4.5	3.6	3.3
Sept., 1876, to March, 1877:								
New England States ...	542	168,178,520	43,109,865	6,501,179	6,128,206	3.9	3.1	2.9
Middle States	631	190,272,820	53,430,368	8,328,761	6,787,978	4.4	3.4	2.8
Southern States	175	32,120,440	5,678,226	1,387,478	1,470,475	4.3	3.7	3.9
Western States	732	106,079,800	28,653,706	5,586,551	5,206,303	5.3	4.1	3.9
Totals.............	2,080	496,651,580	130,872,165	21,803,969	19,592,962	4.4	3.5	3.1
March, 1877, to Sept., 1877:								
New England States ...	511	167,237,820	41,370,408	6,147,573	3,744,799	3.7	2.9	1.8
Middle States	631	185,468,951	51,871,038	7,686,267	6,185,157	4.1	3.2	2.6
Southern States	175	32,166,800	5,571,362	1,299,476	1,207,343	4.0	3.4	3.2
Western States	725	101,018,100	25,536,446	6,983,800	4,136,729	6.9	5.5	3.3
Totals.............	2,072	486,324,860	124,349,254	22,117,116	15,274,028	4.5	3.6	2.5
Sept., 1877, to March, 1878:								
New England States ...	544	166,546,320	40,560,405	5,903,213	4,985,926	3.5	2.9	2.4
Middle States	631	178,149,931	51,551,601	7,261,608	6,283,445	4.1	3.2	2.7
Southern States	176	32,166,800	5,482,012	1,217,880	1,174,220	3.8	3.2	3.1
Western States	722	98,746,700	24,779,543	4,599,689	4,503,105	4.7	3.7	3.7
Totals.............	2,074	475,609,751	122,373,561	18,982,390	16,946,696	4.0	3.2	2.8
March, 1878, to Sept., 1878:								
New England States ...	543	166,587,820	38,956,874	5,459,786	3,846,183	3.3	2.7	1.9
Middle States	629	176,040,576	50,182,622	6,674,618	4,999,505	3.8	2.9	2.2
Southern States	176	31,491,800	5,684,035	1,115,865	931,995	3.5	3.0	2.6
Western States	699	95,457,700	23,863,603	4,708,954	3,861,210	4.9	4.0	3.2
Totals.............	2,047	470,231,896	118,087,134	17,959,223	13,658,893	3.8	3.0	2.3
General averages ..	1,909	472,542,445	116,011,728	22,721,782	25,562,283	4.8	3.9	4.3

Table, by States and reserve cities, of the ratios to capital, and to capital and surplus, of

States, Territories, and reserve cities.	Ratio of dividends to capital for six months ending—										Ratios of	
	1874.		1875.		1876.		1877.		1878.		1874.	
	Mar. 1.	Sept. 1.	Mar. 1.	Sept. 1.	Mar. 1.	Sept. 1.	Mar. 1.	Sept. 1.	Mar. 1.	Sept. 1.	Mar. 1.	Sept. 1.
1 Maine	6.1	5.4	5.3	5.4	5.0	4.8	4.8	5.1	4.5	4.4	5.1	4.4
2 New Hampshire	4.8	4.9	5.0	4.9	4.6	4.3	4.3	4.1	3.9	3.8	4.1	4.1
3 Vermont	4.7	4.6	4.7	4.6	3.9	4.0	4.0	4.0	4.0	3.6	3.9	3.8
4 Massachusetts	5.1	5.2	5.2	5.3	4.6	4.3	4.1	4.0	3.9	3.4	3.9	4.0
5 Boston	4.4	4.7	4.4	4.1	3.9	3.1	3.1	3.0	2.9	2.3	3.5	3.7
6 Rhode Island	4.2	4.3	4.6	4.5	4.2	4.1	3.5	3.3	3.3	3.4	3.6	3.6
7 Connecticut	5.1	5.2	5.2	5.4	5.1	5.0	4.7	4.0	3.0	4.2	4.0	4.1
8 New York	4.7	4.5	5.0	4.6	4.8	5.1	4.4	4.3	4.2	3.8	3.8	3.7
9 New York City	4.6	4.8	4.8	4.5	6.0	4.2	4.1	3.7	3.7	3.6	3.5	3.6
10 Albany	5.2	5.0	5.6	4.7	5.6	5.1	5.4	5.0	5.2	4.7	3.5	3.3
11 New Jersey	4.9	5.1	4.9	4.8	4.7	4.7	4.4	4.3	4.7	4.0	3.9	4.0
12 Pennsylvania	4.8	5.1	4.9	5.0	4.7	4.7	4.4	4.1	3.9	3.6	3.8	4.0
13 Philadelphia	5.7	5.7	5.8	5.5	5.4	5.4	5.4	5.0	5.1	4.6	4.0	4.0
14 Pittsburgh	5.1	5.4	5.2	4.8	4.4	4.2	4.0	4.0	3.8	3.6	3.8	4.1
15 Delaware	5.1	5.1	5.2	5.2	5.2	5.2	4.9	4.9	4.7	4.7	4.0	4.0
16 Maryland	5.1	5.2	5.5	5.4	5.4	5.4	4.8	5.1	4.8	4.2	4.2	
17 Baltimore	4.9	5.7	5.1	5.1	4.8	4.2	4.4	4.1	3.9	3.3	4.1	4.7
18 District of Columbia	4.0	4.0	4.0	4.0	4.0	4.0	4.0	4.0	4.0	4.0	3.6	3.5
19 Washington	2.4	8.0	4.7	4.7	4.8	4.8	4.1	8.0	2.3	2.6	1.9	6.2
20 Virginia	4.7	4.3	4.6	4.6	4.1	4.0	3.9	3.6	3.2	3.5	4.0	3.7
21 West Virginia	4.5	4.3	5.0	5.1	5.3	4.7	4.4	4.6	4.1	4.2	3.9	3.7
22 North Carolina	4.6	4.7	4.3	4.2	4.0	3.7	4.3	2.7	2.5	2.3	4.3	4.3
23 South Carolina	4.1	4.3	4.8	4.4	4.4	4.2	4.0	3.8	3.5	2.3	3.1	3.8
24 Georgia	5.4	5.3	5.1	3.7	4.7	3.5	3.2	4.8	3.4	3.5	4.7	4.6
25 Florida					10.0	5.0	5.0	4.0	3.0	3.0		
26 Alabama	4.7	5.8	4.2	3.9	2.9	3.5	3.4	2.9	2.3	2.7	4.3	5.3
27 New Orleans	2.5	3.6	2.9	4.1	3.7	4.0	3.5	4.6	4.3	6.2	2.3	3.4
28 Texas	5.8	9.3	3.4	2.6	8.5	4.7	9.0	3.2	8.4	4.5	4.8	7.6
29 Arkansas	3.7	3.3		7.1		9.3		1.3		1.6	3.3	3.0
30 Kentucky	4.6	4.8	4.1	4.5	4.7	4.3	4.3	4.1	3.9	3.7	4.2	4.3
31 Louisville	3.7	5.0	5.0	4.7	4.9	4.7	4.5	3.8	3.5	1.6	3.4	4.5
32 Tennessee	4.7	5.4	4.9	5.3	4.5	4.9	5.5	5.2	4.8	4.6	4.1	4.8
33 Ohio	5.0	5.3	5.3	5.5	5.1	5.4	4.9	5.5	4.6	4.4	4.1	4.3
34 Cincinnati	4.9	5.5	4.9	5.5	4.9	4.9	4.5	5.9	4.4	4.5	4.0	4.5
35 Cleveland	3.7	4.9	4.9	5.0	5.0	5.4	4.0	5.3	3.4	4.1	3.3	4.3
36 Indiana	4.8	5.6	5.0	5.3	5.3	5.1	5.5	4.9	4.5	5.0	3.8	4.4
37 Illinois	5.7	7.0	5.8	6.0	5.9	5.3	5.7	5.8	5.5	4.8	4.6	5.6
38 Chicago	4.0	3.7	3.5	4.4	4.0	2.9	9.4	31.0	1.8	6.6	3.0	2.7
39 Michigan	5.5	4.8	5.6	5.4	5.2	6.0	5.4	4.5	5.7	4.5	4.5	3.9
40 Detroit	5.8	5.5	5.8	5.5	5.8	5.5	5.5	5.5	5.3	17.2	4.3	4.0
41 Wisconsin	7.1	5.0	6.9	6.1	6.0	5.1	6.9	5.1	5.5	5.0	5.7	4.8
42 Milwaukee	4.6	4.9	4.9	5.3	5.6	20.7	5.6	5.6	4.7	2.9	3.3	3.5
43 Iowa	5.3	6.9	5.5	5.9	5.8	5.6	5.1	5.2	5.5	4.7	4.3	5.7
44 Minnesota	6.4	5.8	6.2	3.8	5.6	5.2	5.2	4.6	5.5	5.3	5.5	5.0
45 Missouri	3.7	3.9	4.6	4.6	5.5	4.3	4.5	4.0	3.8	5.3	3.2	3.3
46 Saint Louis	3.3	3.7	3.9	3.7	1.6	3.5	1.1	3.9	3.6	2.0	2.9	3.3
47 Kansas	3.2	5.7	4.1	4.5	7.6	1.7	5.3	4.4	3.8	4.9	2.8	4.9
48 Nebraska	4.8	17.2	5.1	7.6	7.6	5.5	6.2	7.6	6.8	5.4	4.1	15.2
49 Oregon	6.0	6.0	6.0	6.0	12.0	12.0	12.0	37.0	12.0	12.0	5.0	5.0
50 California	5.6	6.6	6.5	6.3	6.7	5.7	5.6	5.1	9.9	3.7	5.4	6.3
51 San Francisco	6.4	6.6	6.6	6.5	4.8	3.3	3.6	3.6	2.9	4.1	5.9	6.1
52 Colorado	2.8	17.9	13.1	7.2	12.2	6.7	4.8	3.8	2.1	2.4	2.1	13.2
53 New Mexico	6.5	6.5	6.5	6.5	6.5	3.5	6.5	6.5	4.0	2.5	6.1	6.0
54 Utah	4.4	2.7	4.0	4.0	4.0	6.0	6.0	6.0	6.0	6.0	4.0	2.3
55 Wyoming												
56 Idaho	23.0	20.0	20.0	20.0		20.0	25.0	15.0	18.0	10.0	19.7	16.8
57 Montana	3.4	11.8	12.5	3.6	12.2	11.4	4.1	5.7	5.5	1.5	2.9	9.9
58 Dakota	6.0	4.5		5.0	5.0	5.0	5.0	4.0	5.8	4.3		
Averages	4.8	5.1	5.0	4.9	4.9	4.5	4.4	4.5	4.0	3.8	3.8	4.0

the dividends and earnings of national banks, from March 1, 1874, to September 1, 1878.

dividends to capital and surplus for six months ending—								Ratio of earnings to capital and surplus for six months ending—										
1875.		1876.		1877.		1878.		1874.		1875.		1876.		1877.		1878.		
Mar. 1.	Sept. 1.	Mar. 1.	Sept. 1.	Mar. 1.	Sept. 1.	Mar. 1.	Sept. 1.	Mar. 1.	Sept. 1.	Mar. 1.	Sept. 1.	Mar. 1.	Sept. 1.	Mar. 1.	Sept. 1.	Mar. 1.	Sept. 1.	
Pr. ct.	*Pr. ct.*	*Pr. ct.*	*Pr. ct.*	*Pr. ct.*	*Pr. ct.*	*Pr. ct.*	*Pr. ct.*	*Pr. ct.*	*Pr. ct.*	*Pr. ct.*	*Pr. ct.*	*Pr. ct.*	*Pr. ct.*	*Pr. ct.*	*Pr. ct.*	*Pr. ct.*	*Pr. ct.*	
4.3	4.4	4.2	3.9	3.9	4.1	3.7	3.6	5.9	5.4	5.7	5.3	3.8	4.6	4.0	3.1	4.2	3.2	1
4.1	4.1	3.9	3.6	3.7	3.5	3.3	3.2	6.3	4.5	4.8	4.2	3.7	2.4	4.7	3.7	3.9	2.9	2
3.8	3.7	3.2	3.3	3.2	3.2	2.9		5.2	5.1	5.1	4.8	4.7	3.1	4.6	4.3	2.9	2.2	3
4.0	4.0	3.6	3.3	3.2	3.1	3.0	2.6	4.7	5.1	4.5	4.7	3.7	3.1	3.1	2.9	2.6	1.9	4
3.5	3.3	3.1	2.5	2.5	2.4	2.4	1.9	4.4	4.4	4.1	3.8	3.2	1.7	1.9	1.4	1.2	0.9	5
3.8	3.7	3.5	3.4	2.9	2.7	2.8	2.9	5.5	4.7	4.3	4.4	3.1	3.6	2.8	0.3	1.9	2.0	6
4.0	4.1	3.9	3.9	3.7	3.2	3.1	3.3	4.9	4.7	4.3	4.6	4.2	3.6	3.2	0.1	3.7	2.7	7
4.1	3.7	3.9	4.1	3.5	3.5	3.4	3.1	4.5	4.3	4.3	4.4	3.7	2.8	3.5	2.9	2.8	2.7	8
3.6	3.4	4.6	3.2	3.2	2.9	2.8	2.8	4.1	4.8	3.8	3.6	....	1.7	1.4	1.5	2.0	2.0	9
3.5	2.7	3.2	2.9	3.1	2.9	3.0	2.7	5.3	3.9	3.4	3.3	3.3	3.0	3.9	2.5	1.1	0.7	10
3.9	3.8	3.7	3.7	3.5	3.4	3.7	3.2	4.8	5.1	4.8	3.7	4.1	3.2	3.6	3.4	3.4	1.9	11
3.0	3.9	3.7	3.7	3.4	3.2	3.1	2.8	5.0	4.6	4.3	4.1	4.3	3.5	3.8	2.8	3.1	2.5	12
4.1	3.8	3.7	3.7	3.7	3.5	3.5	3.2	4.3	4.5	4.2	3.9	4.2	4.2	3.6	3.2	3.8	2.3	13
3.9	3.7	3.4	3.3	3.1	3.1	2.9	2.8	4.4	5.0	4.4	4.3	3.9	3.4	3.0	3.2	3.4	1.2	14
4.0	4.0	4.0	4.0	3.9	3.9	3.7	3.7	4.2	4.5	4.3	4.0	4.6	4.7	4.3	4.0	3.9	3.4	15
4.4	4.3	4.2	4.2	4.2	3.7	4.0	3.7	5.2	5.4	4.7	5.1	5.3	4.2	4.4	4.4	3.5	4.1	16
4.2	4.3	3.9	3.5	3.7	4.4	3.3	2.7	5.4	4.7	4.8	4.2	3.0	1.2	3.2	4.2	2.8	2.2	17
3.5	3.5	3.4	3.4	3.4	3.3	3.3	3.3	5.7	5.1	5.8	2.4	4.8	4.6	4.7	4.8	4.5	3.9	18
3.9	3.9	3.0	3.0	3.4	6.3	2.0	2.1	4.9	4.7	6.2	5.0	6.6	0.6	5.6	5.5	3.7	1.2	19
3.8	3.9	3.3	3.2	3.1	2.9	2.6	2.8	5.0	4.6	4.6	5.8	5.5	3.1	3.3	3.2	1.6	1.6	20
4.2	4.2	4.3	3.8	3.5	3.6	3.3	3.4	4.7	4.2	5.5	5.8	5.8	4.8	3.7	2.3	3.4	3.2	21
3.9	3.9	3.6	3.4	3.9	2.4	2.2	2.1	5.8	5.5	5.5	5.2	5.6	4.7	4.2	4.0	2.3	**0.1**	22
4.2	3.8	3.8	3.6	3.3	3.0		2.0	4.9	2.9	6.2	4.3	5.0	2.7	5.2	2.9	2.4	2.2	23
5.1	3.0	4.0	2.9	2.7	4.1	2.0	2.6	4.2	4.7	4.0	3.0	4.8	0.9	3.2	1.8	2.8	3.1	24
....	....	9.9	4.9	4.8	3.9	2.8	2.9	....	....	0.1	5.9	7.2	7.0	4.0	3.2	3.8	4.0	25
3.8	3.6	2.6	3.2	3.1	2.7	2.1	2.5	3.9	5.8	4.4	4.6	2.9	2.1	3.5	3.4	2.5	0.9	26
2.7	3.8	3.2	3.4	3.1	3.0	3.7	5.1	3.3	4.8	2.6	3.7	8.0	3.6	2.2	3.8	4.5	9.8	27
2.8	2.1	6.9	3.7	7.2	2.5	6.6	3.5	6.9	8.8	5.7	6.0	0.6	5.6	5.5	3.7	4.7	2.7	28
....	6.3	....	8.1	....	1.2	....	1.4	3.4	3.8	5.2	1.2	3.6	2.3	3.6	1.0	3.5	0.5	29
3.6	4.0	4.1	3.7	3.7	3.3	3.3	3.2	5.5	5.3	5.1	5.6	6.0	4.4	4.0	3.9	3.4	2.2	30
4.6	4.3	4.5	4.0	4.1	3.4	3.1	1.5	5.0	5.8	5.2	5.2	5.4	4.9	4.6	3.8	2.7	**0.2**	31
4.3	4.7	3.9	4.5	4.7	4.4	4.1	4.0	4.7	5.8	5.3	5.2	5.9	4.9	4.6	3.5	4.2	2.5	32
4.3	4.4	4.2	4.4	4.0	4.6	3.8	3.7	5.4	5.1	4.8	5.0	4.9	3.9	4.2	2.1	4.0	3.1	33
4.0	4.5	4.0	4.0	3.9	3.7	3.7		5.5	5.2	5.7	5.9	4.9	4.2	3.6	1.0	3.8	3.8	34
4.3	4.3	4.3	4.6	3.4	4.5	2.9	3.5	4.6	4.9	4.7	4.9	4.7	3.2	4.6	3.9	3.5	0.4	35
4.7	4.2	4.2	4.0	4.3	3.9	3.5	3.9	5.2	5.4	6.0	4.3	4.8	4.3	4.0	3.5	3.7	2.6	36
4.6	4.7	4.5	4.4	4.3	4.3	4.1	3.6	5.9	6.4	6.4	6.5	6.5	5.1	5.2	4.0	4.1	3.1	37
2.5	2.9	2.5	1.8	5.5	21.8	1.3	4.5	5.7	4.5	6.0	9.4	6.6	6.4	1.5	2.2	**1.6**	4.8	38
4.6	4.4	4.1	4.7	4.3	3.5	4.5	3.5	5.5	5.4	5.3	6.3	5.7	4.8	3.2	3.9	4.3	3.9	39
4.2	4.0	3.9	3.7	3.7	3.7	12.8	6.5	6.8	6.2	6.5	5.3	4.5	4.7	5.4	5.1	4.5	4.0	40
5.5	4.8	4.7	4.0	5.4	4.1	4.3	3.9	6.1	6.1	6.1	5.6	5.6	5.9	5.3	5.3	4.2	4.2	41
3.4	3.5	3.7	15.1	4.1	4.1	3.5	2.2	5.1	4.5	6.6	4.2	6.4	6.1	2.8	4.2	1.0	1.1	42
4.5	4.8	4.8	4.6	4.1	4.2	4.4	3.7	6.1	5.9	5.8	6.6	6.6	5.3	5.5	3.7	3.4	3.1	43
5.2	3.2	4.1	4.1	4.3	3.0	4.0	4.5	6.5	7.2	8.0	5.2	6.5	3.6	5.1	2.9	4.5	4.2	44
3.8	3.8	4.6	3.5	3.8	3.3	3.2	4.3		5.2	2.8	5.4	4.3	5.3	3.5	4.4	2.6	4.4	45
3.4	3.2	1.4	3.0	1.0	3.3	3.9	1.6	3.6	3.9	4.0	1.8	3.2	1.5	0.5	1.0	2.0	1.6	46
3.5	3.8	6.2	1.5	4.4	3.5	3.1	4.1	5.2	5.1	5.3	4.2	5.6	3.4	3.9	4.5	3.9	**6.3**	47
4.5	6.6	6.5	4.6	5.2	6.3	5.8	4.3	6.4	9.6	6.5	7.4	6.4	4.4	7.4	5.7	6.7	7.3	48
5.0	5.0	10.0	10.0	10.0	30.8	10.0	10.0	11.7	10.1	13.5	14.9	18.1	15.7	11.0	11.1	12.6	14.9	49
6.3	6.1	6.5	5.4	5.3	4.7	6.8	3.4	10.0	8.7	6.1	8.2	6.2	6.4	7.1	5.9	6.4	5.6	50
5.9	5.8	4.3	3.1	3.5	3.5	2.8	3.9	7.1	6.6	9.2	8.7	1.5	6.6	1.8	3.9	3.6	3.8	51
9.7	5.5	9.4	5.5	3.6	3.3	2.0	2.6	13.2	10.3	11.0	9.2	7.8	2.9	1.2	0.9	3.5	0.6	52
5.9	5.8	5.8	3.1	5.9	3.6	2.2		7.8	7.4	7.9	6.8	7.3	6.4	6.3	....	4.8	4.4	53
3.2	3.0	3.0	5.1	5.0	5.0	5.0	4.5	5.7	11.2	6.3	5.9	6.4	6.9	5.5	7.3	3.6		54
16.5	16.3	....	16.6	20.7	12.4	15.0	8.3	21.5	18.3	18.6	18.1	11.7	6.1	18.3	13.1	12.9	7.7	56
10.2	3.0	10.0	9.4	3.4	4.6	4.4	1.2	11.6	9.9	8.4	7.1	13.1	4.5	7.3	4.0	10.8	4.3	57
....	....	4.2	4.2	4.2	4.2	4.2	3.3	7.6	5.1	6.6	5.1	5.7	5.9	3.4	0.8	6.1	**1.6**	58
3.9	3.8	3.9	3.6	3.5	3.6	3.2	3.0	4.8	4.9	4.7	4.6	3.6	3.2	3.1	2.5	2.8	2.3	

NOTE.—Figures printed in bold-face type in column for 1878 signify percentage of loss.

Abstract of dividends and earnings of national banks in the United States from September 1877, to March, 1878.

States and Territories.	Number of banks.	Capital.	Surplus.	Dividends.	Net earnings.	Ratios. Dividends to capital.	Dividends to capital and surplus.	Earnings to capital and surplus.
						Pr. ct.	*Pr. ct.*	*Pr. ct.*
Maine	72	$10,760,000	$2,396,346 52	$481,144 75	$549,713 19	4.47	3.66	4.18
New Hampshire	46	5,740,000	1,024,246 59	224,200 00	263,054 34	3.91	3.31	3.88
Vermont	46	8,568,700	2,130,217 21	342,615 00	306,253 35	4.00	3.20	2.86
Massachusetts	183	44,347,000	13,281,867 59	1,709,654 49	1,482,728 43	3.85	2.97	2.57
Boston	54	51,600,000	11,712,464 07	1,486,804 72	743,384 91	2.88	2.35	1.17
Rhode Island	62	20,079,800	3,608,485 76	662,878 75	454,982 97	3.30	2.80	1.92
Connecticut	81	25,450,820	6,406,777 31	995,915 20	1,185,808 86	3.91	3.13	3.72
New York	225	33,522,691	7,810,445 19	1,402,516 24	1,173,233 70	4.18	3.39	2.84
New York City	47	56,450,000	16,509,656 82	2,062,453 40	1,440,428 02	3.65	2.83	1.97
Albany	7	2,000,000	1,470,000 00	103,500 00	39,619 56	5.18	2.98	1.14
New Jersey	69	14,183,350	3,863,627 83	660,284 00	621,570 75	4.66	3.66	3.44
Pennsylvania	179	28,506,220	7,724,983 56	1,118,753 70	1,018,071 19	3.92	3.09	3.06
Philadelphia	31	16,843,000	7,454,739 83	855,140 00	918,132 01	5.07	3.52	3.78
Pittsburgh	22	10,350,000	3,082,310 91	394,000 00	454,862 04	3.81	2.93	3.39
Delaware	13	1,663,985	449,800 21	78,733 35	83,063 68	4.73	3.72	3.93
Maryland	18	2,306,700	669,102 49	118,043 00	105,339 92	5.12	3.97	3.54
Baltimore	14	10,891,985	2,175,934 79	428,604 65	369,922 61	3.93	3.28	2.75
Dist. of Columbia.	1	252,000	52,000 00	10,080 00	13,795 48	4.00	3.31	4.54
Washington	5	1,180,000	289,000 00	29,500 00	45,405 64	2.25	2.01	3.02
Virginia	19	3,485,000	810,409 32	111,150 00	68,541 83	3.19	2.59	1.60
West Virginia	15	1,746,000	408,676 11	71,400 00	74,193 79	4.09	3.31	3.44
North Carolina	15	2,576,000	310,332 86	63,500 00	65,329 03	2.47	2.20	2.26
South Carolina	12	2,854,000	427,582 93	99,750 00	78,907 15	3.50	3.04	2.40
Georgia	12	2,141,000	357,391 43	72,110 00	68,849 61	3.37	2.89	2.70
Florida	1	50,000	1,810 00	1,500 00	1,985 11	3.00	2.81	3.83
Alabama	10	1,668,000	194,042 38	38,400 00	45,572 36	2.30	2.06	2.45
New Orleans	7	3,300,000	518,504 20	142,000 00	171,560 62	4.33	3.72	4.49
Texas	12	1,125,000	302,859 27	94,250 00	68,239 47	8.38	6.60	4.71
Arkansas	2	205,000	30,375 00		8,185 40			3.48
Kentucky	38	6,941,000	1,233,630 11	272,260 00	278,501 42	3.92	3.33	3.41
Louisville	8	2,995,500	351,852 17	103,380 00	91,831 22	3.45	3.09	2.74
Tennessee	25	3,080,300	535,146 22	148,180 00	152,433 10	4.81	4.10	4.22
Ohio	153	19,591,900	4,152,975 61	895,531 83	961,045 06	4.57	3.77	4.05
Cincinnati	6	4,400,000	872,400 00	195,000 00	197,517 26	4.43	3.70	3.75
Cleveland	6	4,350,000	734,045 90	147,500 00	179,466 56	3.39	2.90	3.53
Indiana	99	16,248,500	4,495,040 45	730,035 00	763,826 97	4.49	3.52	3.68
Illinois	132	11,427,100	3,851,639 48	623,500 00	627,291 08	5.46	4.08	4.11
Chicago	10	5,150,000	2,290,000 00	95,000 00	116,969 68	1.80	1.28	1.57
Michigan	76	7,767,200	2,034,303 65	444,832 89	419,023 05	5.73	4.54	4.28
Detroit	4	2,100,000	925,000 00	112,000 00	155,631 07	5.33	3.70	5.14
Wisconsin	37	2,750,000	740,393 14	150,859 63	147,458 28	5.49	4.32	4.22
Milwaukee	3	650,000	230,000 00	30,500 00	8,704 62	4.69	3.47	0.99
Iowa	78	6,057,000	1,508,571 65	331,180 00	200,113 85	5.47	4.38	3.44
Minnesota	30	4,330,000	792,104 84	236,900 00	228,992 59	5.47	4.62	4.47
Missouri	24	2,425,000	482,163 23	92,750 00	74,125 10	3.82	3.19	2.55
Saint Louis	6	2,850,000	570,788 33	101,500 00	67,514 98	3.56	2.97	1.97
Kansas	14	1,015,000	240,914 42	38,800 00	49,590 52	3.82	3.09	3.95
Nebraska	10	950,000	175,200 00	65,000 00	74,899 82	6.84	5.78	6.66
Colorado	13	1,010,000	163,340 15	21,000 00	41,035 23	2.08	1.97	3.53
Oregon	1	250,000	50,000 00	30,000 00	37,912 21	12.00	10.00	12.64
California	7	1,550,000	131,355 92	114,000 00	106,718 35	9.91	6.78	6.35
San Francisco	2	2,750,000	123,081 77	80,000 00	102,128 10	2.91	2.78	3.55
New Mexico	2	300,000	33,724 12	12,000 00	16,062 67	4.00	3.60	4.80
Utah	1	200,000	40,000 00	12,000 00	17,521 95	6.00	5.00	7.30
Idaho	1	100,000	20,000 00	18,000 00	15,477 36	18.00	15.00	12.89
Montana	5	350,000	88,500 00	19,299 43	47,504 19	5.51	4.40	10.81
Wyoming	2	125,000	25,000 00		16,869 79			11.25
Dakota	1	50,000	10,000 00	2,500 00	3,643 56	5.00	4.17	6.07
Totals	2,074	475,609,751	122,373,561 34	18,982,390 03	16,946,695 90	3.99	3.17	2.83

NOTE.—Figures in bold-faced type signify loss.

*Abstract of dividends and earnings of national banks in the United States from March, 1878'
to September, 1878.*

States and Territories.	Number of banks.	Capital.	Surplus.	Dividends.	Net earnings.	Dividends to capital.	Dividends to capital and surplus.	Earnings to capital and surplus.
						Perct.	Perct.	Perct.
Maine	72	$10,760,000	$2,383,258 74	$470,150 00	$418,506 40	4.36	3.57	3.18
New Hampshire	46	5,740,000	1,632,383 17	217,350 00	197,386 19	3.78	3.20	2.91
Vermont	46	8,558,700	2,061,979 95	311,115 00	233,119 51	3.63	2.92	2.19
Massachusetts	182	44,197,000	12,897,351 63	1,510,305 17	1,116,277 05	3.41	2.64	1.95
Boston	54	51,825,000	10,842,945 14	1,208,982 00	546,151 10	2.33	1.92	0.87
Rhode Island	62	20,079,800	3,502,726 85	683,043 75	478,427 51	3.40	2.90	2.02
Connecticut	81	25,427,320	6,236,228 72	1,058,840 20	856,315 21	4.16	3.34	2.70
New York	223	33,169,291	7,678,101 55	1,279,890 30	1,114,547 59	3.85	3.13	2.72
New York City	47	55,800,000	16,030,230 13	1,994,750 00	1,415,450 36	3.57	2.77	1.97
Albany	7	2,000,000	1,445,000 00	94,750 00	25,847 79	4.73	2.75	0.75
New Jersey	69	14,183,350	3,310,732 61	569,234 00	327,909 46	4.01	3.25	1.87
Pennsylvania	178	28,262,940	7,532,387 11	1,008,793 20	885,110 27	3.56	2.81	2.47
Philadelphia	31	16,843,000	7,286,545 71	774,560 00	562,161 64	4.60	3.21	2.32
Pittsburgh	22	10,350,000	3,631,918 04	373,500 00	163,654 52	3.60	2.79	1.22
Delaware	13	1,663,985	454,135 75	78,559 35	71,300 32	4.72	3.70	3.36
Maryland	18	2,281,700	675,237 07	108,767 50	120,491 09	4.76	3.67	4.07
Baltimore	14	10,683,310	2,395,934 26	348,974 60	281,853 45	3.28	2.67	2.16
Dist. of Columbia	1	252,000	53,000 00	10,080 00	11,814 77	4.00	3.30	3.87
Washington	6	1,255,000	289,400 00	32,750 00	19,363 74	2.60	2.12	1.25
Virginia	19	3,285,000	811,959 32	115,650 00	63,940 91	3.52	2.82	1.56
West Virginia	15	1,746,000	407,074 20	72,770 00	70,119 17	4.16	3.37	3.25
North Carolina	15	2,551,000	274,945 82	58,500 00	2,343 76	2.29	2.07	0.08
South Carolina	12	2,854,000	433,267 68	66,750 00	73,268 42	2.33	2.03	2.22
Georgia	12	2,091,000	713,561 09	74,110 00	88,475 19	3.54	2.64	3.15
Florida	1	50,000	1,980 00	1,500 00	2,103 37	3.00	2.88	4.04
Alabama	10	1,668,000	160,850 87	46,000 00	16,603 86	2.75	2.51	0.90
New Orleans	7	2,875,000	573,268 44	177,250 00	338,531 90	6.16	5.14	9.81
Texas	11	1,050,000	297,183 50	47,500 00	37,104 10	4.52	3.52	2.75
Arkansas	2	205,000	31,750 00	3,300 00	1,091 37	1.60	1.39	0.46
Kentucky	39	7,941,000	1,779,728 27	260,510 00	179,086 81	3.70	3.16	2.17
Louisville	8	2,993,500	323,247 34	49,545 00	6,880 32	1.65	1.49	0.20
Tennessee	25	3,080,300	475,218 51	142,480 00	96,893 67	4.62	4.00	2.55
Ohio	150	18,706,900	3,961,050 14	830,337 50	701,631 79	4.43	3.66	3.10
Cincinnati	6	4,300,000	878,300 00	192,000 00	197,400 64	4.46	3.70	3.81
Cleveland	6	4,350,000	652,418 39	177,500 00	20,332 78	4.08	3.54	0.40
Indiana	95	15,326,000	4,313,934 37	764,020 00	515,424 20	4.98	3.89	2.62
Illinois	128	11,624,600	3,792,362 94	554,575 00	481,426 73	4.77	3.59	3.12
Chicago	10	4,650,000	2,215,000 00	307,500 00	332,380 01	6.61	4.47	4.84
Michigan	74	7,508,200	2,044,887 33	339,411 86	375,708 76	4.52	3.55	3.93
Detroit	4	2,100,000	715,000 00	362,000 00	126,629 67	17.23	12.85	4.50
Wisconsin	36	2,665,000	743,834 40	133,100 00	145,046 75	4.99	3.90	4.25
Milwaukee	3	650,000	215,000 00	18,750 00	9,784 43	2.88	2.16	1.13
Iowa	77	6,057,000	1,483,176 22	282,699 98	237,804 86	4.66	3.74	3.15
Minnesota	30	4,720,000	777,883 93	294,400 00	231,880 00	5.28	4.53	4.21
Missouri	19	1,665,000	392,535 53	88,500 00	90,866 80	5.31	4.30	4.41
Saint Louis	5	2,650,000	555,149 68	52,000 00	51,990 46	1.96	1.62	1.62
Kansas	12	900,000	181,374 00	44,400 00	68,299 73	4.93	4.10	6.31
Nebraska	10	950,000	222,775 00	51,000 00	86,242 21	5.36	4.34	7.35
Colorado	12	960,000	165,700 00	23,250 00	7,187 29	2.42	2.06	0.63
Oregon	1	250,000	50,000 00	30,000 00	44,755 90	12.00	10.00	14.91
California	7	1,550,000	142,274 76	58,000 00	94,251 93	3.74	3.42	5.56
San Francisco	2	2,750,000	137,775 57	113,750 00	100,293 18	4.13	3.93	3.78
New Mexico	2	300,000	37,670 20	7,500 00	15,007 81	2.50	2.22	4.44
Utah	1	200,000	40,000 00	12,000 00	8,587 96	6.00	5.00	3.57
Idaho	1	100,000	20,000 00	9,288 02	10.00	8.33	7.74	
Montana	5	350,000	90,500 00	5,259 65	21,103 80	1.50	1.19	4.79
Wyoming	2	125,000	25,000 00		16,447 81			10.96
Dakota	1	50,000	10,000 00	2,000 00	963 77	4.00	3.33	1.60
Totals	2,047	470,231,896	118,687,133 93	17,959,223 06	13,658,892 95	3.81	3.04	2.31

NOTE.—Figures in bold-faced type signify loss.

Table of the state of the lawful-money reserve of the national banks,

STATES AND

	Dates.	No. of banks.	Circulation and deposits.	Reserve required.	Reserve held.	
					Amount.	Ratio to liabilities.
						Per cent.
1	Oct. 3, 1872	1,689	$509,415,295	$76,435,968	$97,765,876	19.2
2	Dec. 27, 1872	1,707	503,568,806	75,535,321	102,069,282	20.3
3	Feb. 28, 1873	1,717	521,394,885	78,209,233	108,246,881	20.6
4	Apr. 25, 1873	1,732	522,649,052	78,428,804	105,693,322	20.2
5	June 13, 1873	1,737	527,741,608	79,204,426	108,935,374	20.6
6	Sept. 12, 1873	1,747	536,925,203	80,593,659	110,456,096	20.6
7	Dec. 26, 1873	1,749	486,180,869	72,985,967	101,120,726	20.8
8	Feb. 27, 1874	1,748	510,946,655	76,700,872	115,577,200	22.6
9	May 1, 1874	1,751	521,953,283	78,351,858	112,637,640	21.6
10	June 26, 1874	1,755	522,874,575	43,173,243	111,464,693	38.8
11	Oct. 2, 1874	1,774	527,506,306	44,077,914	100,641,694	34.3
12	Dec. 31, 1874	1,797	535,679,077	45,487,042	103,592,165	34.2
13	Mar. 1, 1875	1,801	536,289,193	46,018,207	106,826,053	34.9
14	May 1, 1875	1,815	536,716,262	46,020,096	100,091,135	32.9
15	June 30, 1875	1,845	541,385,844	46,996,069	105,154,553	33.6
16	Oct. 1, 1875	1,851	537,418,449	46,304,791	100,128,907	32.5
17	Dec. 17, 1875	1,850	525,303,754	44,647,985	97,855,940	32.9
18	Mar. 10, 1876	1,853	527,361,413	45,535,811	108,547,092	35.8
19	May 12, 1876	1,853	521,137,335	44,990,757	104,514,789	34.9
20	June 30, 1876	1,855	517,605,821	44,996,205	103,832,286	34.7
21	Oct. 2, 1876	1,853	509,793,743	43,862,907	99,985,627	34.3
22	Dec. 22, 1876	1,848	506,146,248	43,416,361	101,429,543	35.1
23	Jan. 20, 1877	1,849	510,509,339	44,978,935	108,706,493	36.3
24	Apr. 14, 1877	1,839	511,110,102	44,203,308	103,945,584	35.3
25	June 22, 1877	1,844	505,411,087	43,814,051	101,962,783	35.0
26	Oct. 1, 1877	1,845	505,863,456	43,594,978	95,379,331	32.9
27	Dec. 28, 1877	1,834	508,016,893	43,616,668	101,866,983	35.1
28	Mar. 15, 1878	1,831	504,088,183	42,990,670	108,782,223	38.0
29	May 1, 1878	1,827	501,295,836	42,476,500	99,320,989	35.1
30	June 29, 1878	1,824	500,160,076	42,539,987	102,308,371	36.1
31	Oct. 1, 1878	1,822	507,520,794	43,437,474	106,045,159	36.7

NOTE.—Prior to June 20, 1874, the required reserve in States and Territories was 15 per

RESERVE

	Dates.	No.	Circulation and deposits.	Reserve required.	Amount.	Per cent.
1	Oct. 3, 1872	230	$443,845,782	$110,961,445	$112,152,056	25.3
2	Dec. 27, 1872	233	462,035,037	115,508,759	123,136,887	26.7
3	Feb. 28, 1873	230	478,040,388	119,510,097	122,710,780	25.3
4	Apr. 25, 1873	230	465,796,482	116,449,120	119,676,330	25.7
5	June 13, 1873	231	502,959,230	125,739,807	145,209,534	28.9
6	Sept. 12, 1873	229	475,521,916	118,880,480	118,679,153	25.0
7	Dec. 26, 1873	227	453,081,026	113,270,257	127,402,586	28.1
8	Feb. 27, 1874	227	518,570,014	129,642,504	158,040,175	30.6
9	May 1, 1874	227	523,075,980	130,768,995	155,563,677	29.5
10	June 26, 1874	228	528,619,121	106,380,827	159,275,638	37.4
11	Oct. 2, 1874	230	521,561,727	106,136,122	144,307,907	34.0
12	Dec. 31, 1874	230	509,411,623	103,317,529	132,348,803	32.0
13	Mar. 1, 1875	228	514,896,921	105,569,158	132,217,368	31.3
14	May 1, 1875	231	507,208,290	104,199,595	129,803,941	31.1
15	June 30, 1875	231	532,175,922	111,317,435	154,560,093	34.7
16	Oct. 1, 1875	236	512,848,868	106,542,005	134,976,509	31.7
17	Dec. 17, 1875	236	468,689,930	95,863,466	118,201,125	30.8
18	Mar. 10, 1876	238	499,853,392	104,535,425	142,753,190	34.1
19	May 12, 1876	236	472,260,505	98,776,747	126,170,248	31.9
20	June 30, 1876	236	490,357,058	103,860,841	142,906,797	34.4
21	Oct. 2, 1876	236	487,415,795	103,721,942	136,821,941	34.2
22	Dec. 22, 1876	234	470,362,089	99,237,733	122,270,996	30.8
23	Jan. 20, 1877	234	495,143,120	105,461,207	142,409,114	33.8
24	Apr. 14, 1877	234	478,473,129	100,522,583	127,205,252	29.0
25	June 22, 1877	234	552,836,716	119,511,586	138,499,197	31.6
26	Oct. 1, 1877	235	453,740,223	94,748,175	115,329,428	30.5
27	Dec. 28, 1877	233	452,799,150	93,174,248	119,041,848	31.9
28	Mar. 15, 1878	232	466,473,764	96,235,626	131,607,266	34.2
29	May 1, 1878	233	455,737,410	93,408,789	121,342,350	32.5
30	June 29, 1878	232	476,710,381	98,898,369	129,369,019	32.7
31	Oct. 1, 1878	231	471,702,867	97,257,896	121,993,977	31.3

NOTE.—Prior to June 20, 1874, the required reserve in reserve cities was 25 per *as shown by their reports from October 3, 1872, to October 1, 1878.*

TERRITORIES.

			Classification of reserve held.					
Specie.	Legal tenders.	U. S. certificates of deposit.	Clearing-house certificates.	Three per cent. certificates.	Due from reserve agents.	Redemption fund with Treasurer.	
$1,950,142	$42,717,294	$220,000	....	$335,000	$52,543,440	....	1
1,978,383	43,228,892	350,000	....	185,000	56,327,007	....	2
1,779,651	41,605,799	1,485,000	....	90,000	63,286,431	....	3
1,567,149	43,202,852	1,895,000	....	10,000	59,018,321	....	4
1,715,293	42,800,960	2,125,000	....	10,000	62,284,121	....	5
2,071,686	42,279,728	2,250,000	....	....	63,854,682	....	6
2,286,734	43,904,389	2,015,000	....	....	50,914,603	....	7
2,475,202	44,017,327	2,270,000	....	....	66,814,671	....	8
2,431,605	47,003,805	2,490,000	....	....	60,112,230	....	9
2,256,951	44,663,155	2,585,000	....	....	61,978,337	$11,250	10
2,375,290	32,885,197	775,000	....	....	52,714,793	11,891,414	11
1,992,383	34,952,061	820,000	....	....	53,935,013	11,892,708	12
1,652,694	33,493,083	845,000	....	....	59,021,623	11,813,653	13
1,511,483	34,414,616	790,000	....	....	52,061,059	11,913,977	14
1,600,028	34,610,241	890,000	....	....	58,439,613	11,614,671	15
1,555,034	32,783,502	900,000	....	....	53,322,152	11,568,219	16
1,452,639	32,075,246	805,000	....	....	52,073,208	11,451,847	17
1,800,017	32,141,468	1,180,000	....	....	62,102,613	11,322,904	18
1,912,171	33,630,711	1,285,000	....	....	56,654,608	11,032,239	19
2,469,391	31,920,120	1,280,000	....	....	57,268,334	10,894,441	20
2,763,198	29,723,138	1,280,000	....	....	56,362,468	10,856,823	21
3,427,133	30,714,772	1,280,000	....	....	55,244,747	10,762,881	22
3,941,358	32,707,525	1,245,000	....	....	60,110,702	10,701,848	23
4,166,989	31,948,207	1,180,000	....	....	55,904,422	10,745,584	24
4,208,317	30,879,163	1,250,000	....	*............	55,012,171	10,613,132	25
4,155,631	30,316,538	1,315,000	....	....	48,885,195	10,706,697	26
4,486,185	32,730,224	1,225,000	....	....	52,587,886	10,837,688	27
6,305,680	31,528,169	1,115,000	....	....	58,950,369	10,883,005	28
7,007,260	32,024,586	1,035,000	....	....	48,325,035	10,929,108	29
7,049,274	29,390,198	1,040,000	....	....	54,033,882	10,795,017	30
7,988,990	30,064,665	995,000	....	....	56,023,564	10,972,940	31

centum of circulation and deposits; since that date, 15 per centum of deposits only.

CITIES.

$8,279,613	$59,356,810	$6,490,000	$8,632,000	$1,220,000	$28,173,633	....	1
17,068,954	57,358,477	12,300,000	5,600,000	775,000	30,074,456	....	2
15,998,022	54,816,110	16,975,000	2,115,000	320,000	32,486,648	....	3
15,301,659	56,732,435	16,475,000	1,370,000	....	29,797,236	....	4
26,234,795	63,205,531	20,525,000	385,000	....	34,859,208	....	5
17,796,781	50,067,935	18,360,000	175,000	....	32,279,437	....	6
24,620,304	58,943,716	21,695,000	....	....	21,843,566	....	7
30,890,661	58,620,606	34,065,000	....	....	34,463,818	....	8
30,138,364	54,062,598	37,645,000	....	....	33,717,715	....	9
20,069,256	58,423,307	45,195,000	....	....	35,508,075	$80,000	10
18,865,654	47,082,343	42,055,000	....	....	31,142,306	5,162,694	11
20,444,378	47,458,251	38,850,000	....	....	26,553,818	5,042,356	12
15,014,411	44,952,897	36,555,000	....	....	30,967,551	4,927,509	13
9,108,878	49,462,643	37,825,000	....	....	28,559,818	4,347,602	14
17,359,554	54,756,083	46,420,000	....	....	31,291,415	4,732,441	15
6,495,294	43,583,429	47,910,000	....	....	32,322,812	4,664,974	16
15,618,267	38,563,571	30,200,000	....	....	29,389,472	4,519,815	17
27,277,329	44,603,748	29,605,000	....	....	36,905,578	4,301,565	18
19,802,423	46,171,398	26,095,000	....	....	30,114,214	3,996,213	19
22,749,078	58,852,046	26,675,000	....	....	30,710,768	3,910,905	20
18,598,456	54,488,445	27,890,000	....	....	31,981,905	3,863,045	21
29,572,511	35,466,510	24,815,000	....	....	28,544,429	3,881,546	22
45,767,909	39,908,797	24,225,000	....	....	26,587,547	3,919,861	23
22,903,049	40,330,831	30,920,000	....	....	29,638,296	4,013,076	24
17,127,679	47,072,388	43,180,000	....	....	27,119,929	3,999,201	25
18,503,189	36,544,635	32,095,000	....	....	24,398,938	3,787,666	26
28,421,566	37,767,429	25,290,000	....	....	23,372,201	4,190,652	27
48,416,378	32,422,675	19,490,000	....	....	27,066,622	4,211,591	28
39,016,496	35,463,963	19,960,000	....	....	23,906,184	4,195,707	29
22,202,196	42,209,909	35,865,000	....	....	24,841,174	4,250,740	30
22,699,616	34,306,906	31,695,000	....	....	29,050,854	4,232,601	31

centum of circulation and deposits; since that date, 25 per centum of deposits only.

Lawful money reserve of the national banks, as shown by the reports

STATES AND

States and Territories.	No. of banks.	Deposits.	Reserve required.
Maine	72	$6, 033, 118	$904, 968
New Hampshire	46	3, 338, 031	500, 705
Vermont	46	3, 642, 838	546, 426
Massachusetts	182	26, 596, 515	3, 989, 477
Rhode Island	61	8, 432, 644	1, 264, 897
Connecticut	81	16, 152, 973	2, 422, 946
New York	225	47, 218, 546	7, 082, 782
New Jersey	69	18, 051, 484	2, 707, 723
Pennsylvania	180	30, 718, 323	4, 607, 748
Delaware	14	2, 036, 583	305, 487
Maryland	18	2, 563, 660	384, 549
District of Columbia	1	473, 404	71, 011
Virginia	19	5, 664, 179	849, 627
West Virginia	15	1, 233, 718	185, 058
North Carolina	15	2, 614, 634	392, 195
South Carolina	12	2, 047, 279	307, 092
Georgia	12	1, 642, 420	246, 363
Florida	1	83, 233	12, 485
Alabama	10	1, 090, 893	163, 634
Texas	11	1, 782, 530	267, 379
Arkansas	2	378, 428	56, 764
Kentucky	39	3, 889, 220	583, 383
Tennessee	25	5, 954, 242	893, 136
Ohio	151	18, 607, 389	2, 791, 108
Indiana	95	13, 288, 645	1, 993, 297
Illinois	128	16, 551, 268	2, 482, 690
Michigan	75	7, 123, 880	1, 068, 582
Wisconsin	36	4, 208, 224	631, 233
Iowa	77	7, 857, 238	1, 178, 586
Minnesota	31	6, 890, 530	1, 033, 579
Missouri	19	2, 401, 784	360, 267
Kansas	12	1, 971, 367	295, 705
Nebraska	10	3, 332, 824	499, 924
Oregon	1	1, 007, 573	151, 136
Colorado	12	3, 031, 045	454, 657
New Mexico	2	449, 750	67, 462
Utah	1	328, 791	49, 319
Idaho	1	137, 013	20, 552
Montana	5	1, 154, 285	173, 143
Wyoming	2	301, 446	45, 217
Dakota	2	242, 551	36, 383
Washington	1	81, 789	12, 268
	1, 817	280, 606, 287	42, 090, 943
California	7	*2, 494, 949	449, 044
Totals	1, 824	283, 101, 236	42, 539, 987

* Includes $748,015 of circulating notes, of
NOTE.—Prior to June 20, 1874, the required reserve in States and Territories was 15

RESERVE

Boston	54	$64, 634, 781	$16, 158, 695
Albany	7	7, 569, 474	1, 892, 368
Philadelphia	31	43, 207, 060	10, 801, 765
Pittsburgh	22	11, 313, 055	2, 828, 264
Baltimore	14	13, 438, 505	3, 359, 626
Washington	6	1, 732, 916	433, 229
New Orleans	7	6, 293, 444	1, 573, 361
Louisville	8	3, 271, 338	817, 835
Cincinnati	6	7, 341, 554	1, 835, 389
Cleveland	6	4, 023, 449	1, 005, 862
Chicago	10	21, 529, 577	5, 382, 394
Detroit	4	3, 982, 580	995, 645
Milwaukee	3	2, 597, 828	649, 457
Saint Louis	5	6, 150, 542	1, 537, 636
	183	197, 086, 103	49, 271, 526
New York	47	196, 562, 991	49, 140, 748
San Francisco	2	*1, 824, 383	456, 095

* Includes $667,400 of circulating notes, of
NOTE.—Prior to June 20, 1874, the required reserve in reserve cities was 25 per

of their condition at the close of business on June 29, 1878.

TERRITORIES.

Reserve held.	Ratio of reserve.	Classification of reserve held.				
		Specie.	Legal tenders.	United States certificates of deposit.	Due from reserve agents.	Redemption fund with Treasurer.
	Per cent.					
$2,795,580	46.3	$120,487	$428,745	$5,000	$1,822,615	$418,733
1,582,632	47.4	65,758	134,850	....	1,128,049	253,975
1,674,285	46.0	58,793	315,063	....	947,051	353,378
11,236,567	42.2	655,282	1,444,827	290,000	7,052,454	1,794,004
3,556,375	42.2	170,430	409,371	....	2,370,896	605,678
7,483,047	46.3	416,575	1,195,057	30,000	4,971,195	870,220
14,085,538	29.8	731,585	3,379,842	380,000	8,297,756	1,296,355
8,072,888	44.7	441,214	1,647,739	110,000	5,298,710	575,225
9,579,182	31.2	701,638	3,490,604	105,000	4,144,244	1,137,696
682,461	31.1	41,429	148,354	40,000	331,884	70,794
751,125	20.3	62,628	271,355	10,000	316,170	90,972
265,708	56.1	9,330	79,500	30,000	135,628	11,250
1,609,700	28.4	51,359	500,056	....	953,662	104,413
470,087	38.1	32,901	191,196	....	179,832	66,158
582,837	22.3	62,224	311,993	....	140,166	68,454
636,995	31.1	79,021	163,790	....	341,911	61,273
674,384	41.1	87,364	351,063	....	142,583	93,374
20,652	24.8	672	10,000	....	7,730	2,250
439,547	40.3	61,691	169,024	....	147,587	61,245
619,898	34.8	132,245	407,043	....	51,410	29,200
80,761	21.3	5,985	35,350	....	30,951	8,475
1,546,618	39.8	61,090	565,789	5,000	647,316	267,423
2,334,608	39.2	145,523	1,058,629	....	1,010,804	119,562
6,176,686	33.2	391,162	2,638,377	....	2,432,927	714,240
5,254,551	39.5	352,620	2,228,453	15,000	2,116,913	541,565
6,602,075	39.9	409,304	2,418,475	20,000	3,388,580	365,716
2,346,462	32.9	246,597	880,916	....	1,001,334	208,615
1,267,129	30.1	131,607	491,438	....	557,981	86,103
3,039,858	38.7	251,096	1,325,447	....	1,268,246	195,060
1,772,924	25.7	72,088	858,752	....	727,139	114,945
873,053	36.4	47,342	303,481	....	462,330	59,900
627,533	31.8	46,455	254,323	....	296,806	29,949
1,193,810	35.8	125,922	387,254	....	646,413	34,221
226,052	22.4	71,778	57,520	....	85,504	11,250
742,989	24.4	44,424	375,133	....	291,495	31,937
104,636	23.1	14,249	44,442	....	31,845	13,500
171,073	52.0	27,943	137,918	....	2,962	2,250
28,888	21.1	9,050	15,338	....	....	4,500
214,018	18.5	21,937	130,500	....	39,981	12,600
102,318	33.9	18,254	67,456	....	13,908	2,700
62,746	25.9	4,960	10,335	....	34,851	3,600
71,218	87.1	40,392	27,520	....	1,056	2,250
101,608,954	36.2	6,513,404	29,390,198	1,040,000	53,870,335	10,795,017
699,417	28.0	535,870	....	....	163,547	....
102,308,371	36.1	7,049,274	29,390,198	1,040,000	54,033,882	10,795,017

which the reserve required is 25 per cent.
per centum of circulation and deposits; since that date, 15 per centum of deposits only.

CITIES.

$18,755,947	29.0	$2,814,103	$3,730,582	$2,830,000	$8,048,855	$1,332,407
2,906,649	38.4	166,556	434,015	470,000	1,763,909	72,169
16,244,976	37.6	2,018,094	4,863,700	4,800,000	3,966,378	596,804
3,544,865	31.3	244,875	1,704,234	....	1,315,426	280,330
4,957,203	36.9	318,393	1,658,042	1,515,000	1,805,676	280,092
619,618	35.8	52,462	215,552	35,000	277,904	38,700
3,103,289	40.3	230,097	1,933,097	....	803,605	76,500
932,587	28.5	62,235	388,200	....	363,141	119,011
2,503,455	35.3	63,370	609,158	420,000	1,274,427	166,500
1,689,368	42.0	109,193	820,000	5,000	661,796	93,379
8,616,748	40.0	1,292,631	2,949,500	1,560,000	2,771,867	42,750
1,723,132	43.3	128,869	681,326	....	853,537	59,400
949,173	36.5	78,125	420,087	....	438,436	12,525
1,003,847	31.0	86,067	934,000	400,000	465,330	18,450
68,540,857	34.8	7,665,060	20,841,493	12,035,000	24,810,287	3,189,017
60,120,344	30.6	13,860,205	21,368,416	23,830,000	....	1,061,723
707,818	38.8	676,931	....	....	30,887	....

which the reserve required is 25 per centum.
centum of circulation and deposits; since that date, 25 per centum of deposits only.

Table of the liabilities of the national banks, and of the reserve required and held, at three dates in each year, from 1874 to 1878.

STATES AND TERRITORIES, EXCLUSIVE OF RESERVE CITIES.

Dates.	Number of banks.	Net deposits.	Reserve req'red.	Reserve held.		Classification of reserve.			
				Amount	Ratio to deposits.	Specie.	Other lawful money.	Due from agents.	Redemption fund.
		Millions	*Millions*	*Millions*	*Per cent*	*Millions*	*Millions*	*Millions*	*Millions*
October 2, 1874	1,774	293.4	44.1	100.6	34.3	2.4	33.6	52.7	11.9
May 1, 1875	1,815	306.2	46.0	100.7	32.9	1.5	35.2	52.1	11.9
June 30, 1875	1,845	312.6	47.0	105.1	33.6	1.6	33.5	58.4	11.6
October 1, 1875	1,851	307.9	46.3	100.1	32.5	1.6	33.7	53.3	11.5
May 12, 1876	1,853	299.4	45.0	104.5	34.9	1.9	34.9	56.7	11.0
June 30, 1876	1,855	299.5	45.0	103.8	34.7	2.5	33.2	57.2	10.9
October 2, 1876	1,853	201.7	43.8	99.9	34.3	2.7	31.0	55.4	10.8
April 14, 1877	1,839	294.2	44.2	103.9	35.3	4.2	33.1	55.9	10.7
June 22, 1877	1,844	290.6	43.8	101.9	35.0	4.2	32.1	55.0	10.6
October 1, 1877	1,845	290.1	43.6	95.4	32.9	4.2	31.6	48.9	10.7
May 1, 1878	1,827	282.7	42.5	99.3	35.1	7.0	33.1	48.3	10.9
June 29, 1878	1,824	283.1	42.5	102.3	36.1	7.1	30.4	54.0	10.8
October 1, 1878	1,822	289.1	43.4	106.1	36.7	8.0	31.1	56.0	11.0

NEW YORK CITY.

Dates.	Num.	*Millions*	*Millions*	*Millions*	*Per cent*	*Millions*	*Millions*	*Millions*	*Millions*
October 2, 1874	48	204.6	51.2	68.3	33.4	14.4	52.4		1.5
May 1, 1875	48	197.5	49.4	57.8	29.2	6.7	49.9		1.2
June 30, 1875	48	218.4	54.6	76.6	35.1	13.7	61.8		1.1
October 1, 1875	48	202.3	50.6	60.5	29.9	5.0	54.4		1.1
May 12, 1876	47	180.5	45.1	53.4	29.6	16.0	36.5		0.9
June 30, 1876	47	195.8	49.0	65.1	33.2	18.1	46.2		0.8
October 2, 1876	47	197.9	49.5	60.7	30.7	14.6	45.3		0.8
April 14, 1877	47	191.9	48.0	54.9	28.6	15.8	38.2		0.9
June 22, 1877	47	243.7	60.9	61.3	25.1	11.7	48.7		0.9
October 1, 1877	47	174.9	43.7	48.1	27.5	13.0	34.3		0.8
May 1, 1878	47	182.0	45.5	56.9	31.3	28.1	27.7		1.1
June 29, 1878	47	196.6	49.1	60.1	30.6	13.9	45.1		1.1
October 1, 1878	47	189.8	47.4	50.9	26.8	13.3	36.5		1.1

OTHER RESERVE CITIES.

Dates.	Num.	*Millions*	*Millions*	*Millions*	*Per cent*	*Millions*	*Millions*	*Millions*	*Millions*
October 2, 1874	182	221.4	55.3	76.0	34.3	4.5	36.7	31.1	3.7
May 1, 1875	183	219.3	54.8	72.1	32.9	2.4	37.4	28.6	3.6
June 30, 1875	183	226.0	56.7	77.9	34.4	3.7	39.3	31.3	3.6
October 1, 1875	188	223.9	56.0	74.5	33.3	1.5	37.1	32.3	3.6
May 12, 1876	180	214.6	53.6	72.8	33.9	3.8	35.7	30.1	3.2
June 30, 1876	180	219.6	54.9	77.8	35.4	4.7	39.4	30.7	3.0
October 2, 1876	180	217.0	54.2	76.1	35.1	4.0	37.1	32.0	3.0
April 14, 1877	187	210.2	52.5	72.3	34.4	7.1	33.1	29.1	3.0
June 22, 1877	187	234.3	58.6	77.2	32.9	5.4	41.6	27.1	3.1
October 1, 1877	188	204.1	51.0	67.3	33.0	5.6	34.3	24.4	3.0
May 1, 1878	185	191.9	48.0	64.4	33.6	10.9	27.4	23.0	3.1
June 20, 1878	185	198.9	49.7	69.2	34.8	8.3	32.9	24.8	3.2
October 1, 1878	184	199.9	50.0	71.1	35.6	9.4	29.4	20.1	3.2

SUMMARY.

Dates.	Num.	*Millions*	*Millions*	*Millions*	*Per cent*	*Millions*	*Millions*	*Millions*	*Millions*
October 2, 1874	2,004	719.4	150.6	244.9	34.0	21.3	122.7	83.8	17.1
May 1, 1875	2,046	723.0	150.2	230.6	31.9	10.6	122.5	80.7	16.7
June 30, 1875	2,076	757.9	158.3	259.6	34.3	10.0	134.6	89.7	16.3
October 1, 1875	2,087	734.1	152.2	235.1	32.0	8.1	125.2	85.6	16.2
May 12, 1876	2,080	694.5	143.7	230.7	33.2	21.7	107.1	86.8	15.1
June 30, 1876	2,091	714.9	148.9	246.7	34.5	25.3	118.8	87.9	14.7
October 2, 1876	2,089	706.6	147.5	236.7	33.5	21.3	113.4	87.4	14.6
April 14, 1877	2,073	696.3	144.7	231.1	33.2	27.1	104.4	85.0	14.6
June 22, 1877	2,078	770.6	163.3	240.4	31.2	21.3	122.4	82.1	14.6
October 1, 1877	2,080	669.1	138.3	210.8	31.5	22.8	100.2	73.3	14.5
May 1, 1878	2,050	656.6	136.0	220.6	33.6	46.0	88.2	71.3	15.1
June 20, 1878	2,056	678.6	141.3	231.6	34.1	29.3	108.4	78.8	15.1
October 1, 1878	2,053	678.8	140.8	228.1	33.6	30.7	97.0	85.1	15.3

Average weekly deposits, circulation, and reserve of the national banks in New York City, as reported to the New York clearing-house, for the months of September and October in each year from 1871 to 1878.

| Week ending— | Liabilities. | | | Reserve. | | | |
	Circulation.	Net deposits.	Total.	Specie.	Legal-tenders.	Total.	Ratio to liabilities.
	Dollars.	*Dollars.*	*Dollars.*	*Dollars.*	*Dollars.*	*Dollars.*	*Percent.*
Sept. 2, 1871..	29,835,300	212,534,300	242,369,600	10,196,600	60,957,800	71,154,400	29.36
Sept. 9, 1871..	30,087,200	213,442,100	243,529,300	9,193,400	60,106,800	69,300,200	28.21
Sept. 16, 1871..	30,071,600	211,537,700	241,609,300	9,050,100	56,847,200	65,897,300	27.27
Sept. 23, 1871..	29,944,100	203,048,400	232,992,500	8,291,700	53,275,600	61,567,300	26.42
Sept. 30, 1871..	29,992,800	193,601,500	223,684,300	11,554,000	49,933,900	61,487,900	27.49
Oct. 7, 1871..	30,199,100	189,277,300	219,476,400	9,153,400	49,589,300	58,742,700	26.76
Oct. 14, 1871..	30,273,000	183,192,100	213,465,100	8,025,300	45,835,200	53,860,500	25.23
Oct. 21, 1871..	30,233,400	172,343,800	202,577,200	8,647,600	44,079,000	52,726,600	26.63
Oct. 28, 1871..	30,431,800	171,737,300	202,169,100	9,249,700	43,694,700	52,944,400	26.19
Sept. 7, 1872..	27,487,200	183,510,100	210,997,300	11,619,600	43,866,500	55,486,100	26.30
Sept. 14, 1872..	27,580,600	179,765,800	207,346,400	11,130,700	42,993,300	54,124,000	26.10
Sept. 21, 1872..	27,622,300	171,742,500	199,364,800	16,851,600	39,419,300	56,270,900	28.22
Sept. 28, 1872..	27,689,400	165,721,900	193,411,300	10,045,900	39,651,700	49,697,600	25.18
Oct. 5, 1872..	27,551,100	158,849,300	186,399,400	8,469,700	37,998,500	46,468,200	24.93
Oct. 12, 1872..	27,692,900	161,816,200	189,509,100	10,070,200	40,675,100	50,745,300	26.77
Oct. 19, 1872..	27,661,300	171,115,000	198,776,300	10,657,400	46,260,100	56,917,500	28.63
Oct. 26, 1872..	27,641,000	174,086,400	201,727,400	9,234,300	46,885,000	56,119,300	27.82
Sept. 6, 1873..	27,323,300	182,775,700	210,099,000	19,935,900	33,993,600	53,929,500	25.66
Sept. 13, 1873..	26,351,200	177,850,500	204,201,700	17,655,500	32,500,800	50,156,300	24.56
Sept. 20, 1873..	27,382,600	168,877,100	196,259,100	16,135,200	30,083,800	46,219,000	23.55
Sept. 27, 1873..	27,295,400	150,171,300	177,366,700	11,448,100	17,883,300	29,331,400	16.54
Oct. 4, 1873..	27,393,700	131,855,500	159,249,200	9,240,300	9,251,900	18,492,200	11.61
Oct. 11, 1873..	27,419,400	131,958,900	159,378,300	10,506,600	8,049,300	18,556,200	11.64
Oct. 18, 1873..	27,421,200	129,575,800	156,997,000	11,650,100	5,179,800	16,829,900	10.72
Oct. 25, 1873..	27,390,100	125,671,300	153,061,400	11,433,500	7,187,300	18,620,800	12.16
Sept. 5, 1874..	25,630,500	202,918,100	228,548,600	16,807,500	54,878,100	71,785,600	31.41
Sept. 12, 1874..	27,701,700	205,166,500	232,868,200	17,589,200	54,715,700	72,304,900	31.05
Sept. 19, 1874..	25,595,700	204,285,600	229,881,300	17,453,200	55,017,300	72,470,500	31.52
Sept. 26, 1874..	25,593,900	187,139,700	212,733,600	16,799,500	53,977,900	70,777,400	33.27
Oct. 3, 1874..	25,387,700	202,605,300	227,993,000	15,373,400	53,297,600	68,671,000	30.01
Oct. 10, 1874..	25,083,900	200,054,500	225,138,400	14,517,700	52,152,000	66,669,700	29.61
Oct. 17, 1874..	25,028,600	197,261,900	222,290,500	12,691,400	51,855,500	64,546,500	29.04
Oct. 24, 1874..	24,981,600	193,514,600	218,496,200	11,457,900	49,893,900	61,351,800	28.82
Oct. 31, 1874..	25,025,100	193,611,700	218,636,800	10,324,900	50,773,000	61,097,900	27.94
Sept. 4, 1875..	18,093,700	210,397,200	228,490,900	9,155,700	58,810,600	67,966,300	29.75
Sept. 11, 1875..	17,725,000	209,802,100	227,527,100	8,494,500	57,828,300	66,322,800	29.15
Sept. 18, 1875..	17,223,200	206,816,800	224,040,000	6,537,800	57,856,600	64,394,800	28.67
Sept. 25, 1875..	17,902,600	205,483,200	223,385,800	6,432,400	56,348,400	62,780,800	28.10
Oct. 2, 1875..	17,894,100	201,303,700	219,303,800	5,438,900	56,581,500	62,020,400	28.10
Oct. 9, 1875..	17,820,700	197,555,800	215,376,500	5,716,200	51,342,300	57,058,500	26.49
Oct. 16, 1875..	17,781,200	195,192,400	212,973,600	5,528,500	48,582,700	54,111,200	25.41
Oct. 23, 1875..	17,841,600	191,468,500	209,313,100	5,735,600	47,300,900	53,035,900	25.34
Oct. 30, 1875..	17,900,100	189,068,800	206,968,900	8,975,600	45,762,800	54,738,400	26.45
Sept. 2, 1876..	14,577,300	197,992,100	212,569,700	19,017,600	48,238,000	67,855,600	31.92
Sept. 9, 1876..	14,339,700	200,754,700	215,091,400	20,202,700	48,699,700	68,902,400	32.03
Sept. 16, 1876..	14,403,500	202,734,500	217,138,000	20,068,900	49,338,200	69,407,100	31.96
Sept. 23, 1876..	14,100,800	200,794,800	215,195,600	16,907,800	48,625,500	65,533,300	30.45
Sept. 30, 1876..	14,615,700	196,591,400	211,206,102	14,751,200	47,538,900	62,290,100	29.49
Oct. 7, 1876..	11,897,040	195,115,700	207,012,700	17,682,600	45,535,900	63,218,200	30.53
Oct. 14, 1876..	14,693,300	190,689,600	205,392,900	16,233,600	43,001,600	59,238,200	28.84
Oct. 21, 1876..	14,809,200	190,019,900	201,829,100	15,577,900	41,421,700	56,999,600	27.83
Oct. 28, 1876..	15,059,600	183,810,200	198,869,800	14,011,600	41,645,600	55,657,200	27.99
Sept. 1, 1877..	15,357,900	181,741,500	197,099,400	13,993,800	41,460,400	55,454,200	28.14
Sept. 8, 1877..	15,513,000	182,679,400	198,192,100	17,411,000	38,439,900	55,850,800	28.63
Sept. 15, 1877..	15,551,700	181,584,100	197,135,800	17,451,000	38,429,900	55,880,900	28.35
Sept. 22, 1877..	15,570,700	180,635,700	196,201,400	16,945,100	37,113,200	54,058,300	27.55
Sept. 29, 1877..	15,699,000	175,036,800	190,735,800	14,682,100	36,978,900	51,661,000	27.09
Oct. 6, 1877..	15,961,900	172,106,600	188,070,300	14,685,600	36,853,900	50,833,900	27.03
Oct. 13, 1877..	16,055,600	171,058,500	187,111,100	14,726,500	35,178,900	49,905,400	26.67
Oct. 20, 1877..	16,205,000	169,670,500	185,875,500	11,087,400	35,101,500	49,189,100	26.46
Oct. 27, 1877..	16,600,700	168,373,800	184,974,500	15,209,000	34,367,800	49,576,800	26.80
Sept. 7, 1878..	19,037,000	191,650,200	210,687,200	14,583,200	43,260,300	57,813,500	27.45
Sept. 14, 1878..	19,453,000	191,090,500	210,543,500	15,929,600	41,673,400	57,602,700	27.36
Sept. 21, 1878..	19,591,000	190,268,100	209,859,100	15,590,400	41,894,700	57,485,100	27.40
Sept. 28, 1878..	19,592,500	189,832,700	209,425,200	15,373,300	39,762,000	55,135,300	26.33
Oct. 5, 1878..	19,552,200	187,568,400	207,120,600	14,995,800	38,304,900	53,300,700	25.73
Oct. 12, 1878..	19,567,800	181,825,100	201,393,200	12,184,600	37,685,100	49,869,700	24.40
Oct. 19, 1878..	19,575,900	183,627,600	203,203,500	13,531,100	36,576,000	50,107,400	21.66
Oct. 26, 1878..	19,861,400	186,082,100	205,916,500	17,384,200	35,690,500	53,074,700	25.77

Table showing the number of State banks, savings-banks, trust companies, and private bankers, their average capital and deposits, and the tax thereon, for the six months ending November 30, 1876.

States, &c.	Number.	Capital.	Deposits.	Tax On capital	Tax On deposits	Total.
Maine	66	$177,658	$27,017,950	$403	$5,837	$6,240
New Hampshire	78	151,000	30,937,358	314	12,757	13,071
Vermont	21	302,500	8,123,983	650	4,348	4,998
Massachusetts	168	855,000	163,436,726	1,569	6,546	8,115
Boston	67	3,108,788	84,686,258	4,442	18,732	23,174
Rhode Island	58	3,923,222	52,888,125	8,482	45,724	54,206
Connecticut	112	3,027,892	82,818,889	5,815	50,228	56,043
New England States	570	11,546,060	449,909,289	21,675	144,172	165,847
New York	340	10,850,325	151,986,519	23,044	111,326	134,370
New York City	472	48,518,475	278,634,125	78,635	271,833	350,468
Albany	15	579,500	12,754,583	452	10,177	10,629
New Jersey	67	2,418,120	36,110,777	5,243	28,120	33,363
Pennsylvania	344	12,475,573	41,393,026	29,125	102,767	131,892
Philadelphia	66	2,502,021	47,415,908	5,845	78,369	84,214
Pittsburgh	43	5,137,193	13,937,144	11,863	24,939	36,802
Delaware	10	708,596	1,684,846	1,687	2,000	3,687
Maryland	17	631,885	543,171	1,293	875	2,168
Baltimore	40	4,066,837	24,876,500	8,591	18,217	26,808
District of Columbia	1	20,000	28,452	50	71	121
Washington	11	595,102	3,618,467	412	7,973	8,385
Middle States	1,426	88,503,627	612,983,558	166,240	656,667	822,907
Virginia	77	3,563,878	7,188,428	8,723	16,925	25,648
West Virginia	25	1,426,858	3,939,744	3,553	9,849	13,402
North Carolina	15	576,602	885,795	1,442	2,214	3,656
South Carolina	18	1,006,452	1,008,634	2,516	2,341	4,857
Georgia	69	4,823,597	3,383,964	12,059	8,264	20,323
Florida	3	39,000	240,821	97	602	699
Alabama	18	1,095,900	1,501,305	2,650	3,753	6,403
Mississippi	29	1,251,577	1,196,752	2,423	2,992	5,415
Louisiana	2	54,000	40,508	135	101	236
New Orleans	24	3,611,584	6,290,194	9,029	11,796	20,825
Texas	98	3,400,041	4,302,285	7,559	10,756	18,315
Arkansas	13	225,167	264,300	561	661	1,222
Kentucky	72	7,488,271	6,086,657	18,132	15,216	33,348
Louisville	18	5,592,382	5,976,005	13,838	14,940	28,778
Tennessee	31	1,723,291	2,775,023	4,172	6,938	11,110
Southern States	512	35,878,660	45,079,815	86,889	107,348	194,237
Ohio	262	6,327,007	16,069,106	14,181	38,794	52,975
Cincinnati	21	1,963,150	8,955,100	3,454	20,312	23,766
Cleveland	10	802,819	11,859,737	1,863	16,446	18,309
Indiana	149	6,033,563	10,533,776	12,847	22,287	35,134
Illinois	315	5,452,244	17,518,220	12,205	41,892	54,097
Chicago	41	4,918,350	14,913,501	9,538	20,172	29,710
Michigan	140	2,597,657	4,935,755	6,391	12,339	18,730
Detroit	14	1,172,902	6,148,749	2,292	15,372	17,664
Wisconsin	87	1,328,635	3,645,026	2,927	9,112	12,039
Milwaukee	12	677,522	6,236,008	1,415	15,590	17,005
Iowa	266	4,832,196	8,738,362	11,691	21,846	33,537
Minnesota	68	1,158,438	2,539,637	2,732	6,306	9,038
Missouri	165	3,467,093	9,921,909	7,597	24,865	32,462
Saint Louis	54	7,928,799	24,723,031	18,496	60,801	79,297
Kansas	109	1,638,143	2,800,868	3,887	7,002	10,889
Nebraska	35	407,354	1,250,342	1,011	3,126	4,137
Western States	1,748	50,705,272	150,789,217	112,527	336,142	448,669
Oregon	7	546,985	1,200,830	1,266	3,024	4,290
California	84	9,917,377	16,928,318	24,739	35,258	59,997
San Francisco	49	23,728,485	96,733,616	57,129	166,926	224,055
Colorado	29	549,540	1,007,576	1,374	2,519	3,893
Nevada	17	299,438	1,690,357	749	4,226	4,975
Utah	6	151,000	588,283	377	1,471	1,848
New Mexico	3	2,000	33,743	5	84	89
Wyoming	3	38,372	54,368	96	136	232
Idaho	3	57,417	25,990	143	65	208
Dakota	7	24,000	137,911	60	345	405
Montana	6	97,431	66,863	244	175	419
Washington	4	222,947	272,450	557	681	1,238
Arizona	1	8,333	4,167	21	10	31
Pacific States and Territories	219	35,643,325	118,756,472	86,760	214,920	301,680
Totals	4,475	222,276,944	1,377,518,351	474,091	1,459,249	1,933,340

Table showing the number of State banks, savings-banks, trust companies, and private bankers, their average capital and deposits, and the tax thereon, for the six months ending May 31, 1877.

States and Territories.	No. of banks.	Capital.	Deposits.	Tax. On capital.	On deposits.	Total.
Maine	66	$173,905	$26,499,218	$393	$4,412	$4,805
New Hampshire	72	52,333	30,896,234	124	6,900	7,024
Vermont	21	335,000	8,107,445	714	4,198	4,912
Massachusetts	167	819,333	162,477,183	1,473	6,514	7,987
Boston	64	3,127,387	88,716,005	3,516	18,490	22,006
Rhode Island	58	3,894,673	53,031,370	8,340	45,213	53,553
Connecticut	109	2,869,642	82,893,262	5,593	47,952	53,545
New England States	557	11,272,273	452,620,717	20,153	133,679	153,832
New York	336	11,061,720	148,889,703	22,840	106,653	129,493
New York City	466	45,785,796	271,948,412	69,121	258,215	327,336
Albany	14	657,000	12,529,737	713	9,362	10,075
New Jersey	65	2,170,838	35,457,184	4,482	26,330	30,812
Pennsylvania	346	12,216,780	39,203,675	28,753	97,282	126,035
Philadelphia	60	2,091,742	31,884,459	4,798	68,671	73,469
Pittsburgh	41	5,918,826	14,676,683	11,405	24,481	35,886
Delaware	10	717,411	1,780,859	1,709	2,116	3,825
Maryland	15	623,378	566,984	1,196	899	2,095
Baltimore	40	4,104,063	25,023,652	8,709	18,051	26,760
District of Columbia	1	5,917	7,008	15	18	33
Washington	10	595,359	3,657,830	362	8,144	8,506
" Middle States	1,404	85,028,770	585,566,186	154,103	620,222	774,325
Virginia	78	3,407,110	6,809,858	8,182	16,138	24,320
West Virginia	24	1,455,900	3,917,534	3,632	9,794	13,426
North Carolina	14	574,451	872,287	1,436	2,181	3,617
South Carolina	19	1,003,105	1,095,859	2,508	2,597	5,105
Georgia	66	4,392,147	4,363,519	10,980	10,718	21,608
Florida	5	47,000	271,057	92	678	770
Alabama	20	1,034,733	1,747,031	2,458	4,368	6,826
Mississippi	28	1,264,396	1,413,033	2,274	3,532	5,806
Louisiana	2	51,000	49,915	135	125	260
New Orleans	23	3,558,192	7,310,099	8,640	14,303	22,943
Texas	107	3,494,002	4,891,428	8,235	12,228	20,463
Arkansas	15	258,333	376,619	558	942	1,500
Kentucky	73	7,279,957	6,026,535	17,478	16,566	34,044
Louisville	17	5,404,361	6,041,633	13,373	15,103	28,476
Tennessee	33	1,768,147	3,019,790	3,983	7,549	11,532
Southern States	524	34,995,834	48,805,597	83,964	116,822	200,786
Ohio	257	6,334,477	16,640,560	14,051	40,293	54,314
Cincinnati	23	2,008,549	9,016,478	3,436	20,231	23,667
Cleveland	9	836,290	12,767,959	1,653	17,940	19,593
Indiana	146	5,626,955	11,128,830	13,051	23,336	36,387
Illinois	319	5,483,644	17,299,692	12,270	41,303	53,573
Chicago	42	4,826,153	15,136,791	9,508	23,426	32,994
Michigan	145	2,605,763	4,914,596	6,367	12,286	18,653
Detroit	18	1,240,932	5,870,285	2,250	14,676	16,926
Wisconsin	90	1,389,348	3,705,813	3,190	9,414	12,604
Milwaukee	12	672,065	6,328,969	1,406	15,822	17,228
Iowa	279	5,178,613	8,730,477	12,545	21,661	34,206
Minnesota	71	1,168,965	2,508,685	2,757	6,135	8,892
Missouri	180	3,806,229	11,223,423	8,448	28,058	36,506
Saint Louis	46	7,530,583	22,691,281	16,947	56,281	73,228
Kansas	114	1,725,221	3,116,289	4,039	7,791	11,830
Nebraska	39	465,664	1,184,932	1,114	2,962	4,076
Western States	1,790	50,909,184	152,325,060	113,092	341,615	454,707
Oregon	8	610,721	1,319,112	1,418	3,373	4,791
California	91	12,110,922	41,522,335	30,113	68,587	98,700
San Francisco	38	26,902,567	65,805,076	61,308	123,034	184,342
Colorado	30	588,858	971,936	1,472	2,430	3,902
Nevada	19	417,639	1,545,409	1,043	3,864	4,907
Utah	8	179,521	587,894	449	1,470	1,919
New Mexico	4	5,367	36,342	14	91	105
Wyoming	4	55,489	98,987	139	247	386
Idaho	3	50,507	16,182	141	40	181
Dakota	8	31,167	140,321	85	351	436
Montana	8	103,637	93,800	258	234	492
Washington	4	222,312	317,636	556	791	1,350
Arizona	1	10,000	5,000	25	13	38
Pacific States and Territories	226	41,296,810	112,550,090	97,021	204,528	301,549
Totals	4,501	223,503,171	1,351,867,650	468,333	1,416,866	1,885,199

Table, by geographical divisions, of the number, capital, and deposits of State banks and private bankers, savings-banks, and trust and loan companies, for the six months ending November 30, 1875.

Geographical divisions.	State banks and private bankers.			Savings-banks with capital.			Savings-banks without capital.		Total.		
	No.	Capital.	Depos-its.	No.	Capital.	Depos-its.	No.	Depos-its.	No.	Capital.	Depos-its.
		Mill'ns.	*Mill'ns.*		*Mill'ns.*	*Mill'ns.*		*Mill'ns.*		*Mill'ns.*	*Mill'ns.*
New England States	126	11.6	24.0	2	0.3	5.2	436	413.9	564	11.9	443.1
Middle States	1,270	90.8	232.4	3	0.2	0.8	218	382.8	1,491	91.0	616.0
Southern States	517	36.0	42.6	3	0.4	0.5	3	1.9	523	36.4	45.0
Western States and Territories	1,853	70.9	188.0	19	4.1	32.6	38	47.0	1,910	75.0	267.6
United States	3,766	209.3	487.0	27	5.0	39.1	695	845.6	4,488	214.3	1,371.7

Table, by geographical divisions, of the number, capital, and deposits of State banks and private bankers, savings-banks, and trust and loan companies, for the six months ending May 31, 1876.

Geographical divisions.	State banks and private bankers.			Savings-banks with capital.			Savings-banks without capital.		Total.		
	No.	Capital.	Depos-its.	No.	Capital.	Depos-its.	No.	Depos-its.	No.	Capital.	Depos-its.
		Mill'ns.	*Mill'ns.*		*Mill'ns.*	*Mill'ns.*		*Mill'ns.*		*Mill'ns.*	*Mill'ns.*
New England States	135	11.7	23.6	1	0.2	4.4	436	415.1	572	11.9	443.1
Middle States	1,256	89.2	223.4	3	0.3	1.2	212	382.5	1,471	89.5	607.1
Southern States	516	35.7	44.9	3	0.4	0.6	4	2.0	523	36.1	47.5
Western States and Territories	1,896	77.4	188.1	19	4.1	31.0	39	45.0	1,954	81.5	264.1
United States	3,803	214.0	480.0	26	5.0	37.2	691	844.6	4,520	219.0	1,361.8

Table, by geographical divisions, of the number, capital, and deposits of State banks and private bankers, savings-banks, and trust and loan companies, for the six months ending November 30, 1876.

Geographical divisions.	State banks and private bankers.			Savings-banks with capital.			Savings-banks without capital.		Total.		
	No.	Capital.	Depos-its.	No.	Capital.	Depos-its.	No.	Depos-its.	No.	Capital.	Depos-its.
		Mill'ns.	*Mill'ns.*		*Mill'ns.*	*Mill'ns.*		*Mill'ns.*		*Mill'ns.*	*Mill'ns.*
New England States	131	11.34	22.76	1	0.20	4.15	438	422.99	570	11.54	449.90
Middle States	1,213	88.34	226.40	2	0.16	0.77	211	385.82	1,426	88.50	612.99
Southern States	505	35.40	42.40	4	0.48	0.64	3	2.04	512	35.88	45.08
Western States and Territories	1,915	82.14	192.49	17	4.21	32.38	35	44.68	1,967	86.35	269.55
United States	3,764	217.22	484.05	24	5.05	37.94	687	855.53	4,475	222.27	1,377.52

Table, by geographical divisions, of the number, capital, and deposits of State banks and private bankers, savings-banks, and trust and loan companies, for the six months ending May 31, 1877.

Geographical divisions.	State banks and private bankers.			Savings-banks with capital.			Savings-banks without capital.		Total.		
	No.	Capital.	Deposits.	No.	Capital.	Deposits.	No.	Deposits.	No.	Capital.	Deposits.
		Mill'ns.	*Mill'ns.*		*Mill'ns.*	*Mill'ns*		*Mill'ns.*		*Mill'ns.*	*Mill'ns.*
New England States	117	11.07	19.99	1	0.20	3.94	439	428.69	557	11.27	452.62
Middle States	1,202	84.87	215.87	2	0.16	0.88	200	368.81	1,404	85.03	585.56
Southern States	517	34.58	46.17	3	0.42	0.52	4	2.12	524	35.00	48.81
Western States and Territories	1,963	88.11	188.51	20	4.09	32.83	33	43.54	2,016	92.20	264.88
United States	3,799	218.63	470.54	26	4.87	38.17	676	843.16	4,501	223.50	1,351.87

Resources and liabilities of State banks at the dates named.

RESOURCES.	Maine, Aug. 4, 1877.	New Hampshire, Mar. 8, 1878.	Vermont, June 30, '78.	Rhode Island, Nov. 30, 1877.	Connecticut, Oct. 1, 1877.	New York, Sept. 21, '78.
	1 bank.	1 bank.	5 banks.	15 banks.	4 banks.	52 banks.
Loans and discounts	$84,385	$67,458	$1,269,729	$4,631,790	$1,906,832	$20,185,043
Overdrafts					8,511	74,921
United States bonds			64,270		395,118	
Other stocks, bonds, &c		14,992	290,476	266,478	103,455	4,154,646
Due from banks	22,508		42,997	192,162	601,890	3,928,782
Real estate		1,854	5,872	116,397	137,489	769,330
Other investments			22,760	4,861	14,581	97,912
Expenses				4,803		155,548
Cash items	5,468				72,629	315,582
Specie				21,057	7,469	114,695
Legal-tenders, bank-notes, &c	5,869	1,619	15,092	186,070	68,641	933,263
Totals	118,230	85,923	1,711,205	4,823,618	3,316,615	29,829,722
LIABILITIES.						
Capital stock	75,000	50,000	342,500	3,227,850	1,450,000	8,293,000
Circulation	1,594	1,130		16,466	28,271	26,289
Surplus fund		14,194	44,063		188,029	1,639,556
Undivided profits	11,016			242,631		1,648,892
Dividends unpaid		2,747		11,636	2,213	
Deposits	25,859	10,778	1,306,760	1,138,598	1,293,330	16,121,675
Due to banks	4,761			174,052	354,772	1,676,442
Other liabilities		7,074	17,882	12,385		1,023,868
Totals	118,230	85,923	1,711,205	4,823,618	3,316,615	29,829,722

Resources and liabilities of State banks at the dates named—Continued.

RESOURCES.	New York City, Sept. 21, 1878.	New Jersey, Jan. 1, 1878.	Pennsylvania, Nov., 1877.	Maryland, Sept., 1878.	Louisiana, Jan., 1878.	Kentucky Oct., 1878.
	23 banks.	10 banks.	106 banks.	14 banks.	10 banks.	51 banks.
Loans and discounts	$31,440,986	$2,440,131	$22,335,156	$4,496,739	$7,047,289	$15,843,557
Overdrafts	27,648	274		81	1,046	2,926
United States bonds		302,443	847,406	155,759		161,106
Other stocks, bonds, &c	4,659,126	59,004	1,304,035	709,485	1,499,769	1,626,355
Due from banks	2,756,207	580,210	2,851,979	347,834	558,050	2,140,699
Real estate	1,487,735	231,451	1,885,484	671,195	808,668	835,962
Other investments	50,590	46,534	741,263	108,150	191,768	284,270
Expenses	154,370	11,568	273,304	41,018	32,210	12,978
Cash items	6,405,263	766		37,493	9,038	
Specie	2,629,839	4,063	32,355	9,493	104,821	
Legal-tenders, bank-notes, &c	7,214,164	182,889	1,991,889	659,376	2,114,411	1,579,347
Totals	56,825,948	3,868,333	32,262,871	7,236,623	12,367,070	22,487,200
LIABILITIES.						
Capital stock	12,275,200	1,350,300	9,187,882	3,429,433	4,353,055	10,968,668
Circulation	25,282	3,293	493	8,692	8,762	266,623
Surplus fund	2,919,653	92,118	1,318,054	123,253	144,102	833,101
Undivided profits	1,622,151	48,209	654,175	256,321	103,859	694,538
Dividends unpaid		915		23,844	47,968	229,287
Deposits	34,418,946	2,226,416	19,477,173	3,232,563	6,082,800	8,823,277
Due to banks	5,134,675	104,923	531,571	154,140	1,328,816	593,732
Other liabilities	430,041	42,159	1,092,623	8,377	297,708	77,974
Totals	56,825,948	3,868,333	32,262,871	7,236,623	12,367,070	22,487,200

RESOURCES.	Ohio, Oct. 7, 1878.	Michigan, July, 1878.	Wisconsin, July 1, 1878.	Minnesota, Oct., 1878.	Kansas, July, 1878.	California, July 1, 1878.
	36 banks.	26 banks.	28 banks.	14 banks.	23 banks.	56 banks.
Loans and discounts	$4,120,802	$6,890,062	$5,278,826	$2,527,334	$1,133,624	$38,291,684
Overdrafts	58,506	22,817	75,647	20,431	27,151	
United States bonds	209,450				15,328	
Other stocks, bonds, &c	130,407	93,399	1,441,238	76,957	18,317	2,950,088
Due from banks	415,960	968,506	2,235,504	322,941	213,539	7,818,381
Real estate	258,713	325,674	223,220	108,820	188,682	3,035,552
Other investments	103,040		8,322	41,261	54,863	8,924,206
Expenses	86,501	64,392	20,319	37,076	20,639	
Cash items	145,594		316,249	12,763		
Specie	21,187		78,450	18,247		
Legal-tenders, bank-notes, &c	373,102	1,010,172	591,979	251,905	256,510	11,044,076
Totals	5,923,322	9,375,022	10,269,754	3,417,735	1,928,453	72,064,187
LIABILITIES.						
Capital stock	1,921,725	1,907,500	1,420,281	1,091,450	669,313	33,180,135
Circulation			1,403			
Surplus fund	196,407	287,868	72,657	72,362	37,079	
Undivided profits	136,257	162,377		93,877	62,045	6,556,716
Dividends unpaid	3,544			1,898	124	
Deposits	3,203,185	6,860,722	6,977,550	2,008,398	1,071,079	28,485,382
Due to banks	95,595	118,770		39,010	37,652	
Other liabilities	366,609	37,785	1,797,863	110,740	50,561	3,841,954
Totals	5,923,322	9,375,022	10,269,754	3,417,735	1,928,453	72,064,187

Aggregate resources and liabilities of State banks from 1874 to 1878.

RESOURCES.	1873-'74.	1874-'75.	1875-'76.	1876-'77.	1877-'78.
	— banks.	551 banks.	633 banks.	592 banks.	475 banks.
Loans and discounts	$154,377,672	$176,308,949	$178,983,496	$266,585,314	$160,391,427
Overdrafts	212,772	377,297	348,604	516,565	319,950
United States bonds	1,961,447	344,984	860,144	929,260	2,150,880
Other stocks, bonds, &c	16,437,815	23,667,950	19,364,450	23,209,670	19,308,287
Due from banks	19,050,046	19,851,146	23,696,812	25,201,782	25,407,149
Real estate	5,372,186	9,005,657	8,561,224	12,609,160	11,092,118
Other investments	1,164,909	4,909,190	6,863,083	6,442,710	10,604,390
Expenses	1,284,344	1,353,066	1,559,404	1,211,416	914,726
Cash items	10,434,018	8,624,086	9,059,547	9,816,456	7,320,845
Specie	1,980,083	1,156,456	1,926,100	2,319,659	3,041,676
Legal-tenders, bank-notes, &c	25,126,706	26,740,215	27,623,988	34,415,712	28,480,374
Totals	237,402,088	272,338,996	278,255,852	383,257,704	277,911,831
LIABILITIES.					
Capital stock	59,305,532	60,084,980	80,425,634	110,949,515	95,193,292
Circulation	153,432	177,653	388,397	387,661	388,298
Surplus fund	2,942,707	6,797,167	7,027,817	5,665,854	7,983,906
Undivided profits	12,363,205	9,002,133	10,457,346	18,283,567	11,693,064
Dividends unpaid	337,290	83,722	393,419	335,904	324,176
Deposits	137,594,961	165,871,439	157,928,658	226,654,538	142,764,491
Due to banks	14,241,604	10,530,844	13,307,398	9,412,876	10,348,911
Other liabilities	10,463,357	19,791,058	8,327,183	11,567,789	9,215,603
Totals	237,402,088	272,338,996	278,255,852	383,257,704	277,911,831

Resources and liabilities of trust and loan companies at the dates named.

RESOURCES.	Massachusetts, Nov. 1877.	Rhode Island, Nov. 30, 1877.	Connecticut, Oct. 1, 1877.	New York, Dec., 1877.	New Jersey, Jan. 1, 1878.	Pennsylvania, Oct., 1878.
	6 banks.	1 bank.	11 banks.	10 banks.	1 bank.	6 banks.
Loans and discounts	$6,400,604	$4,183,403	$3,614,312	$32,233,892	$453,870	$13,417,246
Overdrafts			11,565			
United States bonds	1,427,809			15,002,671	3,745	3,011,235
Other stocks, bonds, &c	584,145	2,891,226	708,580	6,201,624	42,440	6,871,222
Due from banks	1,524,765		466,721	2,343,652	26,078	1,375,038
Real estate			498,364	1,483,171	20,700	1,698,140
Other investments	222,200	226,215	5,242	*1,524,521	9,937	424,404
Expenses	33,294		166,271			75,346
Cash items			40,304			2,911
Specie						369,831
Legal-tenders, bank-notes, &c	297,106	210,251	75,138	116,591	19,936	1,729,987
Totals	10,287,223	6,511,095	5,586,497	58,906,122	577,306	28,975,360
LIABILITIES.						
Capital stock	2,250,000	500,000	2,562,361	9,999,250	100,000	6,675,000
Circulation						
Surplus fund	206,439	125,000	545,295	5,427,811	28,259	1,502,496
Undivided profits	45,813	114,593				531,245
Dividends unpaid	4,017		2,637		64	4,543
Deposits	7,510,567	3,266,630	2,184,778	10,909,699	448,983	18,815,921
Due to banks			291,426	230,000		
Other liabilities	270,387	2,504,872		2,339,359		1,356,155
Totals	10,287,223	6,511,095	5,586,497	58,906,122	577,306	28,975,360

* Includes $799,979 excess of liabilities over assets.

Aggregate resources and liabilities of trust and loan companies, 1875, 1876, 1877, and 1878.

RESOURCES.	1874-'75.	1875-'76.	1876-'77.	1877-'78.
	35 banks.	38 banks.	39 banks.	35 banks.
Loans and discounts	$65,900,174	$76,608,647	$67,946,390	$59,303,327
Overdrafts	16,883	24,886	13,948	11,565
United States bonds	2,086,842	16,491,646	19,805,685	19,445,460
Other stocks, bonds, &c	37,323,062	18,847,238	17,960,260	17,296,237
Due from banks	1,837,605	5,672,637	8,028,415	5,536,854
Real estate	3,733,357	4,733,647	3,544,221	3,700,375
Other investments	2,880,342	2,090,265	3,410,232	2,412,519
Expenses	92,894	178,231	105,157	274,911
Cash items	5,186,004	54,833	59,393	43,215
Specie		234,321	22,952	369,831
Legal-tenders, bank-notes, &c	3,833,012	2,709,828	2,715,846	2,449,309
Totals	122,890,175	127,646,179	123,612,490	110,843,603
LIABILITIES.				
Capital stock	21,854,020	21,535,490	22,347,440	22,086,611
Circulation				
Surplus fund	6,967,693	8,288,825	7,164,673	7,925,303
Undivided profits	582,867	534,375	1,239,539	691,651
Dividends unpaid	18,021	254,522	387,764	11,261
Deposits	85,025,371	87,817,902	84,215,849	73,136,578
Due to banks	121,441	151,766	333,180	521,426
Other liabilities	8,319,802	9,063,209	7,924,045	6,470,773
Totals	122,890,175	127,646,179	123,612,499	110,843,603

Resources and liabilities of savings banks organized under State laws at the dates named.

RESOURCES.	Maine, Nov. 5, 1877.	New Hampshire, Mar., 1878.	Vermont, June 30, 1878.	Massachusetts, Nov. 1877.	Rhode Island, Nov. 30, 1877.
	60 banks.	66 banks.	16 banks.	179 banks.	37 banks.
Loans on real estate	$7,406,442	$9,237,847	$3,787,335	$116,241,038	$28,240,627
Loans on personal and collateral security	3,158,395	6,874,360	1,026,567	46,912,033	7,054,794
United States bonds	981,809	1,342,927	866,923	16,246,152	2,244,120
State, municipal, and other bonds and stocks	8,941,023	5,881,959	593,977	10,983,439	6,422,064
Railroad bonds and stocks	3,058,639	3,745,931	26,849	9,076,156	1,212,700
Bank stock	1,018,049	1,128,985	89,632	26,154,389	2,392,453
Real estate	805,010		117,253	7,932,582	925,022
Other investments	775,917	1,258,816	141,301	2,135,180	285,888
Expenses					
Due from banks			294,352	6,950,800	
Cash	663,088	747,386	105,141	1,521,295	698,870
Totals	26,898,432	30,218,211	7,079,420	250,153,064	49,486,138
LIABILITIES.					
Deposits	25,708,472	28,789,549	6,722,691	244,596,614	48,103,119
Surplus fund	466,937	889,007	339,451	5,182,570	
Undivided profits	660,888				1,295,891
Other liabilities	62,135	539,655	17,278	373,880	87,128
Totals	26,898,432	30,218,211	7,079,420	250,153,064	49,486,138

Resources and liabilities of savings banks, &c—Continued.

RESOURCES.	Connecticut, Oct. 1, 1877.	New York, Jan. 1, 1878.	New Jersey, Jan. 1878.	Pennsylvania, Oct. 1878.	Maryland, Oct. 1878.
	86 banks.	136 banks.	37 banks.	4 banks.	8 banks.
Loans on real estate	$52,337,213	$107,973,299	$9,875,256	$7,182,286	$3,481,713
Loans on personal and collateral security	4,514,247	5,200,677	889,671	733,850	3,158,941
United States bonds	7,129,260	85,691,300	2,061,249	4,951,723	6,778,104
State, municipal, and other bonds and stocks	7,057,744	106,522,397	3,377,043	3,220,230	4,676,524
Railroad bonds and stocks	902,596			2,243,148	1,461,631
Bank stock	3,801,940				117,808
Real estate	2,208,474	11,215,402	778,750	166,487	210,806
Other investments	313,103	11,741,475	529,546	121,934	84,839
Expenses				96,188	98,974
Due from banks		12,915,208	658,892		2,194
Cash	2,009,361	5,466,444	202,777	1,405,401	669,300
Totals	80,273,938	346,726,202	18,373,184	20,121,247	20,740,834
LIABILITIES.					
Deposits	77,214,372	312,823,058	16,353,275	17,923,825	19,739,206
Surplus fund	2,649,702	32,050,550	778,489	1,405,052	70,745
Undivided profits				732,370	661,762
Other liabilities	409,864	1,852,594	1,241,420		269,121
Totals	80,273,938	346,726,202	18,373,184	20,121,247	20,740,834

RESOURCES.	District of Columbia, Oct. 1, 1878.	Louisiana, Jan. 1878.	Ohio, Oct. 7, 1878.	California, July 1, 1878.
	1 bank.	1 bank.	4 banks.	28 banks.
Loans on real estate	$159,199	$420,610	$3,627,352	$58,852,375
Loans on personal and collateral security	32,320	611,968	673,898	7,350,616
United States bonds	1,700		1,067,563	
State, municipal, and other bonds and stocks	113,875	201,084	2,916,397	3,247,320
Railroad bonds and stocks		25,000		
Bank stock				
Real estate	74,973	520,194	142,330	4,824,611
Other investments	7,135		2,144	772,495
Expenses	1,366		20,162	
Due from banks	553		703,123	1,026,086
Cash	6,948	183,887	89,351	3,699,836
Totals	398,069	1,962,752	9,242,320	79,773,339
LIABILITIES.				
Deposits	382,905	1,932,330	8,623,245	*70,984,764
Surplus fund				
Undivided profits	10,164	30,422	600,964	2,971,716
Other liabilities	5,000		18,111	5,816,859
Totals	398,069	1,962,752	9,242,320	79,773,339

* The total amount of capital of State banks and savings banks in the State of California on July 1, 1877, was reported and published in the report for 1877 as $44,256,800, and deposits $129,100,600. The capital of these banks on July 1, 1878, is reported as $37,609,598, and deposits $99,470,146. The difference in capital is $6,647,202 and the difference in deposits $29,630,454. This large difference in deposits is accounted for by a correspondent in San Francisco, who says: "The falling off in deposits, to which you call attention, is chiefly due to the different manner of making reports adopted by the foreign incorporated banks at the request of the commissioners. A year ago there were five of these banks doing business here, now there are four. A year ago the reports included the business of all the branches, now they include only the branch in this city. This change in the system of reporting makes a vast difference in the totals, as will be seen by the following comparison of the deposits reported by the four incorporated banks now and a year ago:

Deposits June 30, 1877 ... $31,307,200
Deposits June 30, 1878 ... 4,218,900

Total decrease ... 27,178,300 "
† Includes $4,129,463 capital stock.

Aggregate resources and liabilities of savings-banks from 1874 to 1878.

RESOURCES.	1873-'74.	1874-'75.	1875-'76.	1876-'77.	1877-'78.
	— banks.	674 banks.	686 banks.	675 banks.	663 banks.
Loans on real estate	$315,288,088	$351,336,551	$373,501,243	$369,770,878	$408,921,601
Loans on other securities	168,308,332	181,143,206	164,024,477	114,474,163	88,192,337
United States bonds	66,414,629	83,296,272	108,162,624	115,389,880	129,362,890
State and other stocks and bonds	148,456,231	161,334,436	169,801,399	184,116,602	170,155,076
Railroad bonds and stocks	17,981,807	20,690,901	23,902,313	24,586,503	21,752,650
Bank stock	29,545,071	30,508,752	33,267,494	34,571,531	34,703,256
Real estate	11,378,364	14,136,748	15,540,384	21,037,426	29,952,494
Other investments	8,780,263	11,354,781	20,730,050	18,135,673	18,169,863
Expenses	931,959	1,248,688	866,013	1,029,238	216,690
Due from banks	18,431,846	23,378,937	23,011,142	23,522,572	22,551,208
Cash	15,715,134	17,858,182	18,456,405	16,160,096	17,469,085
Totals	801,231,724	896,197,454	951,353,544	922,794,562	941,447,150
LIABILITIES.					
Deposits	759,946,632	849,581,633	891,459,890	866,498,452	879,897,425
Surplus fund	12,500,196	16,499,595	51,321,033	43,845,885	43,892,503
Undivided profits	26,623,850	29,072,493	5,497,503	9,200,778	6,964,177
Other liabilities	2,071,046	1,043,763	3,075,118	3,259,447	10,693,045
Totals	801,231,724	896,197,454	951,353,544	922,794,562	941,447,150

Table, by States, of the aggregate deposits of savings-banks, with the number of their depositors and the average amount due to each, in 1877 and 1878.

States.	1876-'77.			1877-'78.		
	Number of depositors.	Amount of deposits.	Average to each depositor.	Number of depositors.	Amount of deposits.	Average to each depositor.
Maine	90,621	$26,602,150	$294 21	88,661	$25,708,472	$303 00
New Hampshire	98,683	30,963,047	313 76	94,967	28,789,549	303 19
Vermont	25,671	6,815,829	265 50	27,690	6,722,691	242 78
Massachusetts	739,289	243,340,643	329 15	739,757	244,396,614	330 64
Rhode Island	99,865	50,542,272	506 10	89,475	48,103,149	537 61
Connecticut	203,514	78,524,172	385 84	204,575	77,214,372	377 43
New York	861,603	319,716,864	371 07	844,550	312,823,058	370 40
New Jersey	*84,026	29,318,543	348 92	63,447	16,353,275	257 74
Pennsylvania	*67,660	17,577,468	259 79	*68,000	17,923,825	263 59
Maryland	*50,197	19,543,967	389 34	*50,450	19,739,206	391 26
District of Columbia				3,928	382,905	97 48
Louisiana				5,978	1,932,330	323 24
Ohio	26,037	10,041,726	385 67	*22,340	8,623,245	386 00
Indiana	*5,548	1,986,025	358 00			
California	*42,600	31,185,600	732 05	*96,967	70,984,764	732 05
Totals	2,395,314	866,218,306	361 63	2,400,785	879,897,425	366 50

* Estimated.

REPORT OF THE COMPTROLLER OF THE CURRENCY. 107

Number and denominations of national-bank notes issued and redeemed, and the number of each denomination outstanding, on November 1 in each year from 1868 to 1878.

	Ones.	Twos.	Fives.	Tens.	Twenties.	Fifties.	One hundreds.	Five hundreds.	One thousands.
1868.									
Issued	8,896,576	2,978,160	23,106,728	7,915,914	2,219,322	355,181	267,350	13,486	4,746
Redeemed	254,754	73,176	482,132	142,359	36,355	17,256	15,583	1,759	1,846
Outstanding	8,641,822	2,904,984	22,624,596	7,773,555	2,182,967	337,925	251,767	11,727	2,900
1869.									
Issued	9,589,160	3,209,388	23,676,760	8,094,645	2,260,764	363,523	274,799	13,668	4,769
Redeemed	904,013	232,224	985,940	272,495	71,655	22,859	25,968	2,585	2,415
Outstanding	8,685,147	2,977,164	22,690,820	7,821,150	2,198,109	334,664	248,831	11,083	2,354
1870.									
Issued	10,729,327	3,590,157	24,636,720	8,413,244	2,370,056	378,482	284,460	13,926	4,779
Redeemed	2,568,703	667,733	1,747,983	484,135	129,185	47,845	43,599	3,952	3,263
Outstanding	8,160,624	2,922,424	22,808,737	7,929,109	2,240,871	330,637	240,861	9,974	1,516
1871.									
Issued	12,537,657	4,195,791	28,174,940	9,728,375	2,779,392	433,426	321,163	14,642	4,843
Redeemed	5,276,057	1,493,326	3,276,374	933,445	245,361	82,972	76,287	6,017	4,005
Outstanding	7,261,600	2,702,465	24,898,566	8,794,930	2,534,031	350,454	244,876	8,625	838
1872.									
Issued	14,297,360	4,782,628	31,933,348	11,253,452	3,225,688	497,199	367,797	15,621	4,933
Redeemed	7,919,389	2,408,389	5,960,667	1,699,702	438,852	126,180	110,989	7,867	4,315
Outstanding	6,377,971	2,374,239	25,972,681	9,553,750	2,786,836	371,019	256,808	7,754	618
1873.									
Issued	15,524,189	5,105,111	34,804,456	12,560,399	3,608,219	559,722	416,590	16,496	5,148
Redeemed	9,891,606	3,120,723	9,141,963	2,573,070	653,071	168,976	144,057	9,658	4,530
Outstanding	5,632,583	2,074,388	25,752,493	9,987,329	2,955,148	390,746	272,533	6,838	618
1874.									
Issued	16,548,259	5,539,113	39,243,136	13,337,076	3,962,109	666,950	492,482	17,344	5,240
Redeemed	11,143,606	3,755,019	13,041,605	3,912,707	971,608	231,556	196,572	11,676	4,683
Outstanding	5,404,653	1,784,094	26,201,531	9,424,369	2,990,501	435,394	295,910	5,668	557
1875.									
Issued	18,046,176	6,039,752	47,055,184	17,410,507	5,296,064	884,165	645,818	18,476	5,530
Redeemed	14,092,126	4,816,623	24,926,771	7,608,532	2,064,464	381,037	299,428	14,471	5,048
Outstanding	3,954,050	1,223,129	22,128,413	9,801,975	3,201,600	503,128	346,418	4,005	482
1876.									
Issued	18,849,264	6,307,448	51,783,528	20,908,652	6,086,402	985,615	710,900	18,721	5,539
Redeemed	15,556,708	5,324,546	32,382,056	10,369,214	2,852,216	515,784	395,785	16,217	5,272
Outstanding	3,292,556	982,902	19,401,472	9,639,438	3,234,216	469,831	315,115	2,504	267
1877.									
Issued	20,616,924	6,896,968	55,816,818	22,266,464	6,776,253	1,079,781	767,317	20,022	5,608
Redeemed	16,815,568	5,755,526	38,115,868	12,434,779	3,503,528	634,679	479,317	17,615	5,411
Outstanding	3,800,456	1,141,442	18,700,980	9,831,285	3,272,725	445,102	288,000	2,407	257
1878.									
Issued	22,478,415	7,517,765	61,191,288	24,157,293	7,344,167	1,147,578	812,903	20,210	6,204
Redeemed	18,194,196	6,226,692	42,683,433	13,859,149	3,933,178	728,222	541,859	18,895	5,900
Outstanding	4,284,219	1,291,073	18,507,855	10,298,144	3,410,989	419,356	271,044	1,315	304

National banks that have gone into voluntary liquidation under the provisions of sections 5220 and 5221 of the Revised Statutes of the United States, with the dates of liquidation, the amount of their capital, circulation issued and retired, and circulation outstanding November 1, 1878.

Name and location of bank.	Date of liqui-dation.	Capital.	Circulation.		
			Issued.	Retired.	Outstand-ing.
First National Bank, Penn Yan, N. Y.*	Apr. 6, 1864				
First National Bank, Norwich, Conn.*†	May 2, 1864				
Second National Bank, Ottumwa, Iowa*	May 2, 1864				
Second National Bank, Canton, Ohio*	Oct. 3, 1864				
First National Bank, Lansing, Mich.*	Dec. 5, 1864				
First National Bank, Columbia, Mo.	Sept. 19, 1864	$100,000	$90,000	$89,775	$225
First National Bank, Carondelet, Mo	Mar. 15, 1865	30,000	25,500	25,309	191
First National Bank, Utica, N. Y.*†	June 9, 1865				
Pittston National Bank, Pittston, Pa	Sept. 16, 1865	200,000			
Fourth National Bank, Indianapolis, Ind	Nov. 30, 1865	100,000	100,000	98,005	1,995
Berkshire National Bank, Adams, Mass..	Dec. 8, 1865	100,000			
National Union Bank, Rochester, N. Y	Apr. 26, 1866	400,000	192,500	189,323	3,177
First National Bank, Leonardsville, N. Y.	July 11, 1866	50,000	45,000	43,635	1,365
Farmers' National Bank, Richmond, Va	Oct. 22, 1866	100,000	85,000	81,828	3,172
Farmers' National Bank, Waukesha, Wis	Nov. 25, 1866	100,000	90,000	89,090	910
National Bank of the Metropolis, Washington, D. C	Nov. 28, 1866	200,000	180,000	174,073	5,927
First National Bank, Providence, Pa	Mar. 1, 1867	100,000	90,000	85,090	4,910
First National Bank Newton, Newtonville, Mass	Mar. 11, 1867	150,000	130,000	125,507	4,493
National State Bank, Dubuque, Iowa.	Mar. 9, 1867	150,000	127,000	124,194	2,806
First National Bank, New Ulm, Minn	Apr. 18, 1867	60,000	54,000	52,405	1,595
National Bank of Crawford County, Meadville, Pa	Apr. 19, 1867	300,000	No issue		
Kittanning National Bank, Kittanning, Pa.	Apr. 29, 1867	200,000	No issue		
City National Bank, Savannah, Ga.	May 28, 1867	100,000	No issue		
Ohio National Bank, Cincinnati, Ohio†	July 3, 1867	500,000	450,000	437,860	12,140
First National Bank, Kingston, N. Y.†	Sept. 26, 1867	200,000	180,000	172,114	7,886
First National Bank, Bluffton, Ind	Dec. 5, 1867	50,000	45,000	44,046	954
National Exchange Bank, Richmond, Va.	Dec. 5, 1867	200,000	180,000	176,610	3,390
First National Bank, Skaneateles, N. Y.	Dec. 21, 1867	150,000	135,000	132,347	2,653
First National Bank, Jackson, Miss	Dec. 26, 1867	100,000	40,500	40,195	305
First National Bank, Downingtown, Pa	Jan. 14, 1868	100,000	90,000	86,618	3,382
First National Bank, Titusville, Pa.	Jan. 15, 1868	100,000	86,750	83,632	3,118
Appleton National Bank, Appleton, Wis.	Jan. 21, 1868	50,000	45,000	43,980	1,020
National Bank, Whitestown, N. Y.	Feb. 11, 1868	120,000	44,500	44,368	132
First National Bank, New Brunswick, N. J.	Feb. 26, 1868	100,000	90,000	86,293	3,707
First National Bank, Cuyahoga Falls, Ohio.	Mar. 4, 1868	50,000	45,000	44,074	926
First National Bank, Cedarburg, Wis	Mar. 23, 1868	100,000	90,000	88,447	1,553
Commercial National Bank, Cincinnati, Ohio	Apr. 28, 1868	500,000	345,950	338,665	7,285
Second National Bank, Watertown, N. Y	July 21, 1868	100,000	90,000	82,470	7,530
First National Bank, South Worcester, N. Y	Aug. 4, 1868	175,500	157,400	154,546	2,854
National Mechanics and Farmers' Bank, Albany, N. Y	Aug. 4, 1868	350,000	314,950	308,810	6,140
Second National Bank, Des Moines, Iowa.	Aug. 5, 1868	50,000	42,500	41,782	718
First National Bank, Steubenville, Ohio	Aug. 8, 1868	150,000	135,000	124,872	10,128
First National Bank, Plumer, Pa.	Aug. 25, 1868	100,000	87,500	82,027	5,473
First National Bank, Danville, Va	Sept. 30, 1868	50,000	45,000	43,885	1,115
First National Bank, Dorchester, Mass.†	Nov. 23, 1868	150,000	132,500	126,085	6,415
First National Bank, Oskaloosa, Iowa	Dec. 17, 1868	75,000	67,500	66,628	872
Merchants and Mechanics' National Bank, Troy, N. Y	Dec. 31, 1868	300,000	184,750	181,619	3,131
National Savings Bank, Wheeling, W. Va.	Jan. 7, 1869	100,000	90,000	88,255	1,745
First National Bank, Marion, Ohio	Jan. 12, 1869	125,000	109,850	107,695	2,155
First National Insurance Bank, Detroit, Mich..	Feb. 26, 1869	200,010	85,000	84,394	606
National Bank, Lansingburg, N. Y	Mar. 6, 1869	150,000	135,000	132,434	2,566
National Bank of North America, New York, N. Y.	Apr. 15, 1869	1,000,000	333,000	327,294	5,706
First National Bank, Hallowell, Me.	Apr. 19, 1869	60,000	53,350	52,428	922
First National Bank, Clyde, N. Y.	Apr. 23, 1869	50,000	44,000	41,700	2,300
Pacific National Bank, New York, N. Y.	May 10, 1869	422,700	134,990	132,632	2,358
Grocers' National Bank, New York, N. Y.	June 7, 1869	390,000	85,250	84,301	949
Savannah National Bank, Savannah, Ga.	June 22, 1869	100,000	85,000	83,350	1,650
First National Bank, Frostburg, Md	July 30, 1869	50,000	45,000	44,353	647
First National Bank, La Salle, Ill.	Aug. 30, 1869	50,000	45,000	44,145	855
National Bank of Commerce, Georgetown, D. C	Oct. 28, 1869	100,000	90,000	87,885	2,115

* Banks that never completed their organization. † A new bank organized with same title.
‡ Consolidated with another bank.

Table of liquidating banks—Continued.

Name and location of bank.	Date of liquidation.	Capital.	Circulation.		
			Issued.	Retired.	Outstanding.
Miners' National Bank, Salt Lake City. Utah*	Dec. 2, 1869	$150,000	$135,000	$132,209	$2,791
First National Bank, Vinton, Iowa	Dec. 13, 1869	50,000	42,500	41,974	526
National Exchange Bank, Philadelphia, Pa.*	Jan. 8, 1870	300,000	175,750	168,186	7,564
First National Bank, Decatur, Ill	Jan. 10, 1870	100,000	85,250	83,723	1,527
National Union Bank, Owego, N. Y.*	Jan. 11, 1870	100,000	88,250	82,847	5,403
First National Bank, Berlin, Wis	Jan. 25, 1870	50,000	44,000	43,355	645
Central National Bank, Cincinnati, Ohio	Mar. 31, 1870	500,000	425,000	415,145	9,855
First National Bank, Dayton, Ohio	Apr. 9, 1870	150,000	135,000	132,251	2,749
National Bank of Chemung, Elmira, N. Y.	June 10, 1870	100,000	90,000	88,333	1,667
Merchants' National Bank, Milwaukee, Wis	June 14, 1870	100,000	90,000	87,700	2,300
First National Bank, Saint Louis, Mo	July 16, 1870	200,000	176,990	176,537	3,453
Chemung Canal National Bank, Elmira, N. Y.	Aug. 3, 1870	100,000	90,000	89,838	162
Central National Bank, Omaha, Nebr	Sept. 23, 1870	100,000	No issue		
First National Bank, Clarksville, Va.	Oct. 13, 1870	50,000	27,000	26,405	595
First National Bank, Burlington, Vt.*	Oct. 15, 1870	300,000	270,000	255,493	14,507
First National Bank, Lebanon, Ohio	Oct. 24, 1870	100,000	85,000	83,129	1,871
National Exchange Bank, Lansingburg, N. Y.	Dec. 27, 1870	100,000	90,000	86,615	3,385
Muskingum National Bank, Zanesville. Ohio*	Jan. 7, 1871	100,000	90,000	87,430	2,570
United National Bank, Winona, Minn	Feb. 15, 1871	50,000	45,000	44,050	950
First National Bank, Des Moines, Iowa	Mar. 25, 1871	100,000	90,000	87,944	2,056
State National Bank, Saint-Joseph, Mo	Mar. 31, 1871	100,000	90,000	88,916	1,084
Saratoga County National Bank, Waterford, N. Y.	Mar. 28, 1871	150,000	135,000	132,305	2,695
First National Bank, Fenton, Mich	May 2, 1871	100,000	49,500	48,628	872
First National Bank, Wellsburg, W. Va	June 24, 1871	100,000	90,000	87,918	2,082
Clarke National Bank, Rochester, N. Y.*.	Aug. 11, 1871	200,000	180,000	176,056	3,944
Commercial National Bank, Oshkosh, Wis	Nov. 22, 1871	100,000	90,000	87,847	2,153
Fort Madison National Bank, Fort Madison, Iowa	Dec. 26, 1871	75,000	67,500	65,625	1,875
National Bank, Maysville, Ky	Jan. 6, 1872	300,000	270,000	262,923	7,077
Fourth National Bank, Syracuse, N. Y.	Jan. 9, 1872	105,500	91,700	89,321	2,379
American National Bank, New York, N. Y.	May 10, 1872	500,000	450,000	427,334	22,666
Carroll County National Bank, Sandwich, N. H	May 24, 1872	50,000	45,000	42,020	2,980
Second National Bank, Portland, Me.*	June 24, 1872	100,000	81,000	75,964	5,036
Atlantic National Bank, Brooklyn, N. Y.	July 15, 1872	200,000	165,000	160,330	4,670
Merchants and Farmers' National Bank, Quincy, Ill	Aug. 8, 1872	150,000	135,000	131,120	3,880
First National Bank, Rochester, N. Y.	Aug. 9, 1872	400,000	206,100	200,095	6,005
Lawrenceburgh National Bank, Lawrenceburgh, Ind	Sept. 10, 1872	200,000	180,000	174,558	5,442
Jewett City National Bank, Jewett City, Conn	Oct. 4, 1872	60,000	48,750	46,447	2,303
First National Bank, Knoxville, Tenn	Oct. 22, 1872	100,000	80,910	77,118	3,792
First National Bank, Goshen, Ind	Nov. 7, 1872	115,000	103,500	99,338	4,162
Kidder National Gold Bank, Boston, Mass	Nov. 8, 1872	300,000	120,000	120,000	
Second National Bank, Zanesville, Ohio	Nov. 16, 1872	154,700	138,140	132,708	5,432
Orange County National Bank, Chelsea, Vt.*	Jan. 14, 1873	200,000	180,000	166,107	13,893
Second National Bank, Syracuse, N. Y.	Feb. 18, 1873	100,000	90,000	86,712	3,288
Richmond National Bank, Richmond, Ind.†	Feb. 28, 1873	230,000	207,000	207,000	
First National Bank, Adams, N. Y.	Mar. 7, 1873	75,000	66,900	62,755	4,145
Mechanics' National Bank, Syracuse, N. Y.	Mar. 11, 1873	140,000	93,800	90,470	3,330
Farmers and Mechanics' National Bank, Rochester, N. Y.	Apr. 15, 1873	100,000	83,250	79,678	3,572
Montana National Bank, Helena, Mont	Apr. 15, 1873	100,000	31,500	30,070	1,430
First National Bank, Havana, N. Y.*	June 3, 1873	50,000	45,000	41,105	3,895
Merchants and Farmers' National Bank, Ithaca, N. Y.	June 30, 1873	50,000	45,000	41,991	3,009
National Bank, Cazenovia, N. Y.	July 15, 1873	150,000	116,770	111,250	5,520
Merchants' National Bank, Memphis, Tenn	Aug. 30, 1873	250,000	225,000	211,903	13,097
Second National Bank, Chicago, Ill	Sept. 25, 1873	100,000	97,500	89,096	8,404
Manufacturers' National Bank, Chicago, Ill	Sept. 25, 1873	500,000	450,000	400,824 •	49,176
Merchants' National Bank, Dubuque, Iowa	Sept. 30, 1873	200,000	180,000	159,587	20,413
Beloit National Bank, Beloit, Wis	Oct. 2, 1873	50,000	45,000	40,858	4,142
Union National Bank, Saint Louis, Mo.	Oct. 22, 1873	500,000	150,300	135,703	14,597

*Consolidated with another bank. † A new bank organized with same title.

Table of liquidating banks—Continued.

Name and location of bank.	Date of liqui-dation.	Capital.	Circulation.		
			Issued.	Retired.	Outstand-ing.
City National Bank, Green Bay, Wis	Nov. 29, 1873	$50,000	$45,000	$39,229	$5,771
First National Bank, Shelbina, Mo.	Jan. 1, 1874	100,000	90,000	80,056	9,944
Second National Bank, Nashville, Tenn ..	Jan. 8, 1874	125,000	92,920	83,445	9,475
First National Bank, Oneida, N. Y.	Jan. 13, 1874	125,000	110,500	100,541	9,959
Merchants' National Bank, Hastings, Minn*	Feb. 7, 1874	100,000	90,000	33,953	56,047
National Bank, Tecumseh, Mich	Mar. 3, 1874	50,000	45,000	40,960	4,040
Gallatin National Bank, Shawneetown, Ill	Mar. 7, 1874	250,000	225,000	191,744	33,256
First National Bank, Brookville, Pa......	Mar. 26, 1874	100,000	90,000	73,720	16,280
Citizens' National Bank, Sioux City, Iowa	Apr 14, 1874	50,000	45,000	39,905	5,095
Farmers' National Bank, Warren, Ill......	Apr. 28, 1874	50,000	45,000	38,817	6,183
First National Bank, Medina, Ohio.......	May 6, 1874	75,000	45,000	43,882	1,118
Croton River National Bank, South East, N. Y......................	May 25, 1874	200,000	166,550	154,400	12,150
Merchants' National Bank of West Virginia, Wheeling, W. Va............	July 7, 1874	500,000	450,000	378,333	71,667
Central National Bank, Baltimore, Md....	July 15, 1874	200,000	180,000	146,703	33,297
Second National Bank, Leavenworth, Kans.	July 22, 1874	100,000	90,000	76,873	13,127
Teutonia National Bank, New Orleans, La	Sept. 2, 1874	300,000	270,000	221,965	48,035
City National Bank, Chattanooga, Tenn	Sept. 10, 1874	170,000	153,000	127,991	25,009
First National Bank, Cairo, Ill	Oct. 10, 1874	100,000	90,000	72,952	17,048
First National Bank, Olathe, Kans........	Nov. 9, 1874	50,000	45,000	37,517	7,483
First National Bank, Beverly, Ohio......	Nov. 10, 1874	102,000	90,000	73,435	16,565
Union National Bank, Lafayette, Ind...	Dec. 4, 1874	250,000	224,095	163,675	60,420
Ambler National Bank, Jacksonville, Fla.	Dec. 7, 1874	42,500	No issue.	....	....
Mechanics' National Bank, Chicago, Ill...	Dec. 30, 1874	250,000	144,900	107,040	37,860
First National Bank, Evansville, Wis....	Jan. 9, 1875	55,000	45,000	38,744	6,256
First National Bank, Baxter Springs, Kans	Jan. 12, 1875	50,000	36,000	29,069	6,931
People's National Bank, Pueblo, Cal.......	Jan. 12, 1875	50,000	27,000	22,023	4,977
National Bank of Commerce, Green Bay, Wis......................	Jan. 12, 1875	100,000	90,000	74,450	15,550
First National Bank, Millersburg, Ohio	Jan. 12, 1875	100,000	72,000	62,843	9,157
First National Bank, Staunton, Va.*	Jan. 23, 1875	100,000	90,000	63,825	26,175
National City Bank, Milwaukee, Wis.....	Feb. 24, 1875	100,000	76,500	67,385	9,115
Irasburg National Bank, Orleans, Irasburg, Vt......................	Mar. 17, 1875	75,000	67,500	51,882	15,618
First National Bank, Pekin, Ill	Mar. 25, 1875	100,000	90,000	73,471	16,529
Merchants and Planters' National Bank, Augusta, Ga......................	Mar. 30, 1877	200,000	180,000	150,630	29,370
Monticello National Bank, Monticello, Iowa......................	Mar. 30, 1875	100,000	45,000	33,757	11,243
Iowa City National Bank, Iowa City, Iowa.	Apr. 14, 1875	125,000	112,500	80,087	32,413
First National Bank, Wheeling, W. Va. ..	Apr. 22, 1875	250,000	225,000	176,460	48,540
First National Bank, Mount Clemens, Mich......................	May 20, 1875	50,000	27,000	19,690	7,310
First National Bank, Knobnoster, Mo....	May 29, 1875	50,000	45,000	30,008	14,992
First National Bank, Brodhead, Wis.....	June 24, 1875	50,000	45,000	33,381	11,619
Auburn City National Bank, Auburn, N. Y*	June 26, 1875	200,000	141,300	118,020	23,280
First National Bank, El Dorado, Kans ...	June 30, 1875	50,000	45,000	34,949	10,051
First National Bank, Junction City, Kans	July 1, 1875	50,000	45,000	35,980	9,020
First National Bank, Chetopa, Kans	July 19, 1875	50,000	36,000	27,615	8,385
First National Bank, Golden, Colo .!......	Aug. 25, 1875	50,200	27,000	19,395	7,605
National Bank, Jefferson, Wis............	Aug. 26, 1875	60,000	54,000	39,025	14,975
Green Lane National Bank, Green Lane, Pa.	Sept. 9, 1875	100,000	90,000	73,144	16,856
State National Bank, Topeka, Kans	Sept. 15, 1875	60,500	30,000	22,697	7,303
Farmers' National Bank, Marshalltown, Iowa......................	Sept. 18, 1875	50,000	27,000	19,540	7,460
Richland National Bank, Mansfield, Ohio.	Sept. 25, 1875	150,000	135,000	99,357	35,643
Planters' National Bank, Louisville, Ky..	Sept. 30, 1875	350,000	315,000	226,113	88,887
First National Bank, Gallatin, Tenn	Oct. 1, 1875	75,000	45,000	33,230	11,770
First National Bank, Charleston, W. Va.	Oct. 2, 1875	100,000	90,000	66,411	23,589
People's National Bank, Winchester, Ill	Oct. 4, 1875	75,000	67,500	47,646	19,854
First National Bank, New Lexington, Ohio	Oct. 12, 1875	50,000	45,000	35,886	9,114
First National Bank, Ishpeming, Mich....	Oct. 20, 1875	50,000	45,000	32,423	12,577
Fayette County National Bank of Washington, Washington, Ohio	Oct. 26, 1875	100,000	90,000	69,886	20,114
Merchants' National Bank, Fort Wayne, Ind......................	Nov. 8, 1875	100,000	90,000	79,635	10,365
Kansas City National Bank, Kansas City, Mo......................	Nov. 13, 1875	100,000	90,000	72,575	17,425
First National Bank, Schoolcraft, Mich...	Nov. 17, 1875	50,000	45,000	34,095	10,905
First National Bank, Curwensville, Pa...	Dec. 17, 1875	100,000	90,000	62,575	27,425
National Marine Bank, Saint Paul, Minn..	Dec. 28, 1875	100,000	90,000	72,343	17,657
First National Bank, Rochester, Ind......	Jan. 11, 1876	50,000	45,000	31,186	13,814
First National Bank, Lodi, Ohio.........	Jan. 11, 1876	100,000	90,000	60,529	29,471
Iron National Bank, Portsmouth, Ohio ..	Jan. 11, 1876	100,000	90,000	67,832	22,168
First National Bank, Ashland, Nebr......	Jan. 26, 1876	50,000	45,000	29,855	15,145

*Consolidated with another bank.

Table of liquidating banks—Continued.

Name and location of bank.	Date of liqui-dation.	Capital.	Circulation. Issued.	Circulation. Retired.	Circulation. Outstand-ing.
First National Bank, Paxton, Ill	Jan. 28, 1876	$50, 000	$45, 000	$32, 985	$12, 015
First National Bank, Bloomfield, Iowa	Feb. 5, 1876	55, 000	49, 500	33, 220	16, 280
Marietta National Bank, Marietta, Ohio	Feb. 16, 1876	150, 000	135, 000	108, 194	26, 806
Salt Lake City National Bank of Utah, Salt Lake City, Utah	Feb. 21, 1876	100, 000	90, 000	75, 955	14, 045
First National Bank, La Grange, Mo	Feb. 24, 1876	50, 000	45, 000	29, 304	15, 696
First National Bank, Atlantic, Iowa	7, 1876	50, 000	45, 000	27, 929	17, 071
First National Bank, Spencer, Ind	11, 1876	70, 000	63, 000	40, 884	22, 116
National Currency Bank, New York, N. Y.	23, 1876	100, 000	90, 000	79, 460	10, 540
Caverna National Bank, Caverna, Ky	May 13, 1876	52, 000	45, 000	25, 205	19, 795
City National Bank, Pittsburgh, Pa	May 25, 1876	200, 000	90, 000	60, 170	29, 830
National State Bank, Des Moines, Iowa	June 21, 1876	100, 000	90, 000	69, 965	20, 035
First National Bank, Trenton, Mo	June 22, 1876	50, 000	45, 000	24, 150	20, 850
First National Bank, Bristol, Tenn	July 10, 1876	50, 000	45, 000	27, 938	17, 062
First National Bank, Leon, Iowa	July 11, 1876	60, 000	45, 000	31, 082	13, 918
Anderson County National Bank, Law-renceburg, Ind	July 29, 1876	100, 000	45, 000	21, 040	23, 960
First National Bank, Newport, Ind	Aug. 7, 1876	60, 000	45, 000	24, 208	20, 792
First National Bank, De Pere, Wis	Aug. 17, 1876	50, 000	31, 500	18, 693	12, 807
Second National Bank, Lawrence, Kans	Aug. 23, 1876	100, 000	90, 000	46, 495	43, 505
Commercial National Bank, Versailles, Ky	Aug. 26, 1876	170, 000	153, 000	105, 311	47, 689
State National Bank, Atlanta, Ga	Aug. 31, 1876	200, 000	135, 000	105, 615	29, 385
Syracuse National Bank, Syracuse, N. Y.	Sept. 25, 1876	200, 000	180, 000	135, 762	44, 238
First National Bank, Northumberland, Pa	Oct. 6, 1876	100, 000	90, 000	61, 804	28, 196
First National Bank, Lancaster, Mo	Nov. 14, 1876	50, 000	27, 000	14, 620	12, 380
First National Bank, Council Grove, Kans	Nov. 28, 1876	50, 000	26, 500	13, 367	13, 133
National Bank of Commerce, Chicago, Ill	Dec. 2, 1876	250, 000	166, 500	135, 468	31, 032
First National Bank, Palmyra, Mo	Dec. 12, 1876	100, 000	90, 000	69, 584	20, 416
First National Bank, Newton, Iowa	Dec. 16, 1876	50, 000	45, 000	19, 326	25, 674
National Southern Kentucky Bank, Bowl-ing Green, Ky	Dec. 23, 1876	100, 000	27, 000	15, 201	11, 799
First National Bank, Monroe, Iowa	Jan. 1, 1877	60, 000	45, 000	26, 369	18, 631
First National Bank, New London, Conn	Jan. 9, 1877	100, 000	91, 000	72, 585	18, 415
Winona Deposit National Bank, Winona, Minn	Jan. 28, 1877	100, 000	90, 000	55, 457	34, 543
First National Bank, South Charleston, Ohio	Feb. 24, 1877	100, 000	90, 000	44, 397	45, 603
Lake Ontario National Bank, Oswego, N. Y.	Feb. 24, 1877	275, 000	238, 150	209, 909	28, 241
First National Bank, Sidney, Ohio	Feb. 26, 1877	52, 000	46, 200	20, 930	25, 270
Chillicothe National Bank, Chillicothe, Ohio	Apr. 9, 1877	100, 000	89, 990	61, 635	28, 355
First National Bank, Manhattan, Kans	Apr. 13, 1877	50, 000	44, 200	19, 218	24, 982
National Bank, Monticello, Ky	Apr. 23, 1877	60, 000	49, 500	16, 385	33, 115
First National Bank, Rockville, Ind	Apr. 25, 1877	200, 000	173, 090	68, 260	164, 830
Georgia National Bank, Atlanta, Ga	May 31, 1877	100, 000	90, 000	67, 021	22, 979
First National Bank, Adrian, Mich	June 11, 1877	100, 000	88, 500	59, 595	28, 905
First National Bank, Napoleon, Ohio	June 30, 1877	50, 000	90, 000	63, 086	26, 914
First National Bank, Lancaster, Ohio	Aug. 1, 1877	60, 000	54, 000	18, 733	35, 267
First National Bank, Minerva, Ohio	Aug. 24, 1877	50, 000	45, 000	16, 246	28, 754
Kinney National Bank, Portsmouth, Ohio	Aug. 24, 1877	100, 000	89, 000	31, 000	56, 000
First National Bank, Green Bay, Wis	Oct. 19, 1877	50, 000	45, 000	12, 356	32, 644
National Exchange Bank, Wakefield, R. I	Oct. 27, 1877	70, 000	34, 650	11, 120	23, 530
First National Bank, Union City, Ind	Nov. 10, 1877	50, 000	45, 000	13, 860	31, 140
First National Bank, Negaunee, Mich	Nov. 13, 1877	50, 000	45, 000	13, 028	31, 972
Tenth National Bank, New York, N. Y.	Nov. 23, 1877	500, 000	441, 000	49, 078	391, 922
First National Bank, Paola, Kans	Dec. 1, 1877	50, 000	44, 350	10, 594	33, 756
German National Bank, Chicago, Ill	Dec. 5, 1877	500, 000	61, 000	16, 405	44, 595
National Exchange Bank, Troy, N. Y.	Dec. 6, 1877	100, 000	90, 000	38, 966	51, 034
Second National Bank, La Fayette, Ind	Dec. 20, 1877	200, 000	52, 167	15, 899	36, 268
State National Bank, Minneapolis, Minn	Dec. 31, 1877	100, 000	82, 500	11, 731	70, 769
Second National Bank, Saint Louis, Mo	Jan. 8, 1878	200, 000	53, 055	13, 675	39, 380
First National Bank, Sullivan, Ind	Jan. 8, 1878	50, 000	45, 000	12, 610	32, 390
Rockland County National Bank, Nyack, N. Y.	Jan. 10, 1878	100, 000	89, 000	34, 722	54, 278
First National Bank, Boone, Iowa	Jan. 22, 1878	50, 000	32, 400	8, 045	24, 355
First National Bank, Wyandotte, Kans	Jan. 19, 1878	50, 000	44, 500	9, 860	34, 640
First National Bank, Pleasant Hill, Mo	Feb. 7, 1878	50, 000	45, 000	10, 142	34, 858
National Bank, Gloversville, N. Y.	Feb. 28, 1878	100, 000	61, 750	21, 441	43, 309
First National Bank, Independence, Mo	Mar. 1, 1878	50, 000	27, 000	4, 810	22, 190
National State Bank, Linn, Ind	Mar. 2, 1878	100, 000	33, 471	780	32, 691
First National Bank, Tell City, Ind	Mar. 4, 1878	50, 000	44, 500	9, 295	35, 205
First National Bank, Pomeroy, Ohio	Mar. 5, 1878	200, 000	75, 713	17, 229	58, 484
Eleventh Ward National Bank, Boston, Mass	Mar. 14, 1878	200, 000	89, 400	37, 255	52, 145
First National Bank, Prophetstown, Ill	Mar. 19, 1878	50, 000	45, 000	23, 352	21, 648
First National Bank, Jackson, Mich	Mar. 26, 1878	100, 000	88, 400	15, 935	72, 465
First National Bank, Eau Claire, Wis	Mar. 30, 1878	60, 000	38, 461	6, 125	32, 336
First National Bank, Washington, Ohio	Apr. 5, 1878	200, 000	69, 750	14, 532	55, 218

Table of liquidating banks—Continued.

Name and location of bank.	Date of liqui- dation.	Capital.	Circulation.		
			Issued.	Retired.	Outstand- ing.
First National Bank, Middleport, Ohio.....	Apr. 20, 1878	$80,000	$31,500	$6,955	$24,545
First National Bank, Streator, Ill..........	Apr. 24, 1878	50,000	40,500	7,585	32,915
First National Bank, Muir, Mich	Apr. 25, 1878	50,000	44,200	7,566	36,634
Kane County National Bank, Saint Charles, Ill......................................	May 31, 1878	50,000	26,300	3,570	22,730
First National Bank, Carthage, Mo	June 1, 1878	50,000	44,500	3,790	40,710
Security National Bank, Worcester, Mass	June 5, 1878	100,000	49,000	14,720	34,280
Second National Bank, Scranton, Pa	June 12, 1878	200,000	118,820	18,310	100,510
First National Bank, Lake City, Colo	June 15, 1878	50,000	25,300	2,450	22,850
People's National Bank, Norfolk, Va......	July 31, 1878	100,000	85,705	7,130	78,575
Topeka National Bank, Topeka, Kans	Aug. 7, 1878	100,000	89,300	3,740	85,560
First National Bank, Saint Joseph, Mo ...	Aug. 13, 1878	100,000	67,110	420	66,690
First National Bank, Winchester, Ind	Aug. 24, 1878	60,000	52,700	None.	52,700
Muscatine National Bank, Muscatine, Iowa	Sept. 2, 1878	100,000	44,200	500	43,700
Traders' National Bank, Chicago, Ill......	Sept. 4, 1878	200,000	43,700	None.	43,700
Union National Bank, Rahway, N. J......	Sept. 10, 1878	100,000	89,200	3,920	85,280
First National Bank, Sparta, Wis	Sept. 14, 1878	50,000	45,000	1,180	43,820
Herkimer County National Bank, Little Falls, N. Y	Oct. 11, 1878	200,000	178,300	None.	178,300
Totals.................................		34,620,610	25,363,397	20,033,142	5,330,255

National banks that have been placed in the hands of receivers, together with their capital, circulation issued, lawful money deposited with the Treasurer to redeem circulation, the amount redeemed, and the amount outstanding November 1, 1878.

Name and location of bank.	Capital stock.	Lawful money de- posited.	Circulation.		
			Issued.	Redeemed.	Outstand- ing.
First National Bank, Attica, N. Y	$50,000	$44,000 00	$44,000	$43,651	$349
Venango National Bank, Franklin, Pa.....	300,000	85,000 00	85,000	84,558	442
Merchants' National Bank, Washington, D. C...............................	200,000	180,000 00	180,000	178,539	1,461
First National Bank, Medina, N. Y ......'	50,000	40,000 00	40,000	39,861	139
Tennessee National Bank, Memphis, Tenn	100,000	90,000 00	90,000	80,389	611
First National Bank, Selma, Ala...........	100,000	85,000 00	85,000	84,311	689
First National Bank, New Orleans, La.....	500,000	180,000 00	180,000	177,870	2,130
National Unadilla Bank, Unadilla, N. Y...	120,000	100,000 00	100,000	99,494	506
Farmers and Citizens' National Bank, Brooklyn, N. Y	300,000	253,900 00	253,900	251,739	2,161
Croton National Bank, New York, N. Y....	200,000	180,000 00	180,000	179,109	891
First National Bank, Bethel, Conn........	60,000	26,300 00	26,300	25,999	301
First National Bank, Keokuk, Iowa.......	100,000	90,000 00	90,000	89,324	676
National Bank of Vicksburg, Miss........	50,000	25,500 00	25,500	25,299	201
First National Bank, Rockford, Ill........	50,000	45,000 00	45,000	44,368	632
First National Bank of Nevada, Austin, Nev	250,000	129,700 00	129,700	127,351	2,349
Ocean National Bank, New York, N. Y....	1,000,000	800,000 00	800,000	779,587	20,413
Union Square National Bank, New York, N. Y	200,000	50,000 00	50,000	49,016	984
Eighth National Bank, New York, N. Y...	250,000	243,393 00	243,393	237,536	5,857
Fourth National Bank, Philadelphia, Pa ...	200,000	179,000 00	179,000	174,090	4,910
Waverly National Bank, Waverly, N. Y ...	106,100	71,000 00	71,000	68,728	2,272
First National Bank, Fort Smith, Ark.....	50,000	45,000 00	45,000	43,825	1,175
Scandinavian National Bank, Chicago, Ill..	250,000	135,000 00	135,000	131,126	3,874
Wallkill National Bank, Middletown, N. Y	175,000	118,900 00	118,900	114,755	4,145
Crescent City National Bank, New Orleans, La	500,000	450,000 00	450,000	426,130	23,870
Atlantic National Bank, New York, N. Y..	300,000	100,000 00	100,000	96,439	3,561
First National Bank, Washington, D. C....	500,000	450,000 00	450,000	414,669	35,331
National Bank of the Commonwealth, New York. N. Y	750,000	217,062 50	234,000	215,919	18,081
Merchants' National Bank, Petersburg, Va.	400,000	360,000 00	360,000	317,245	42,755
First National Bank, Petersburg, Va	200,000	179,200 00	179,200	158,320	20,880
First National Bank, Mansfield, Ohio......	100,000	90,000 00	90,000	81,701	8,299
New Orleans National Banking Associa- tion, New Orleans, La	600,000	339,337 50	360,000	331,500	28,500
First National Bank, Carlisle, Pa	50,000	45,000 00	45,000	41,205	3,795
First National Bank, Anderson, Ind........	50,000	45,000 00	45,000	41,061	3,939
First National Bank, Topeka, Kans........	100,000	90,000 00	90,000	81,005	8,995
First National Bank, Norfolk, Va.........'	100,000	95,000 00	95,000	84,285	10,715

National banks that have been placed in the hands of receivers, &c.—Continued.

Name and location of bank.	Capital stock.	Lawful money deposited.	Circulation.		
			Issued.	Redeemed.	Outstanding.
Gibson County National Bank, Princeton, Ind	$50,000	$43,800 00	$43,800	$36,075	$7,725
First National Bank of Utah, Salt Lake City, Utah	150,000	134,991 00	134,991	122,111	12,880
Cook County National Bank, Chicago, Ill	500,000	280,900 00	315,900	276,598	39,302
First National Bank, Tiffin, Ohio	100,000	60,850 00	68,850	60,000	8,850
Charlottesville National Bank, Charlottesville, Va	200,000	120,500 00	157,500	120,700	36,800
Miners' National Bank, Georgetown, Colo	150,000	30,857 75	45,000	30,145	14,855
Fourth National Bank, Chicago, Ill	200,000	180,000 00	180,000	156,999	23,001
First National Bank, Bedford, Iowa	30,000	14,512 50	27,000	14,540	12,450
First National Bank, Osceola, Iowa	50,000	45,000 00	45,000	30,260	14,740
First National Bank, Duluth, Minn	100,000	90,000 00	90,000	81,116	8,884
First National Bank, La Crosse, Wis	50,000	45,000 00	45,000	31,040	13,960
City National Bank, Chicago, Ill	250,000	225,000 00	225,000	180,373	44,627
Watkins National Bank, Watkins, N. Y	75,000	67,500 00	67,500	46,342	21,158
First National Bank, Wichita, Kans	60,000	52,200 00	52,200	34,054	18,146
First National Bank, Greenfield, Ohio	50,000	50,000 00	50,000	36,860	13,140
National Bank of Fishkill, N. Y	200,000	111,200 00	177,200	111,686	65,514
First National Bank, Franklin, Ind	132,000	85,992 00	130,992	81,015	49,977
Northumberland County National Bank, Shamokin, Pa	67,000	34,500 00	60,300	33,705	26,595
First National Bank, Winchester, Ill	50,000	21,300 00	45,000	20,839	24,161
National Exchange Bank, Minneapolis, Minn	100,000	37,000 00	90,000	35,525	54,475
National Bank of the State of Missouri, Saint Louis, Mo	2,500,000	1,648,800 00	1,693,660	1,520,009	173,651
First National Bank, Delphi, Ind	50,000	63,600 00	90,000	63,879	26,121
First National Bank, Georgetown, Colo	75,000	18,000 00	45,000	16,710	28,290
Lock Haven National Bank, Lock Haven, Pa	120,000	25,000 00	71,200	27,088	44,112
Third National Bank, Chicago, Ill	750,000	156,500 00	597,840	162,739	435,101
Central National Bank, Chicago, Ill	200,000	15,000 00	45,000	14,480	30,520
First National Bank, Kansas City, Mo	500,000	15,000 00	44,940	10,740	34,200
Commercial National Bank, Kansas City, Mo	100,000	44,500 00	44,500	11,541	32,959
First National Bank, Ashland, Pa	112,500	88,000 00	88,000	27,048	60,952
First National Bank, Tarrytown, N. Y	100,000	27,000 00	89,200	26,955	62,245
First National Bank, Allentown, Pa	250,000	78,641 00	78,641	17,349	61,292
First National Bank, Waynesburg, Pa	100,000	69,345 00	69,345	63,378	5,967
Washington County National Bank, Greenwich, N. Y	200,000	114,220 00	114,220	29,462	84,758
First National Bank, Dallas, Tex	50,000	4,000 00	29,800	3,865	25,935
People's National Bank, Helena, Mont	100,000	None	89,300	2,710	86,590
First National Bank, Bozeman, Mont	50,000	2,000 00	44,400	600	43,800
Citizens' National Bank, Charlottesville, Va	100,000	90,000 00	90,000	79,884	10,116
Merchants' National Bank, Fort Scott, Kans	50,000	45,000 00	45,000	9,482	35,518
Farmers' National Bank, Platte City, Mo	50,000	None	27,000	None	27,000
Totals	16,332,600	9,893,002 25	11,143,172	9,056,906	2,086,266

8 C C

Insolvent national banks, with date of appointment of receivers, amount of capital stock and claims proved, and rate of dividends paid to creditors.

Name and location of bank.	Receiver appointed—	Capital stock.	Claims proved.	Dividends paid.	Remarks.
				Pr. ct.	
First National Bank of Attica, N. Y.	Apr. 14, 1865	$50,000	$122,089	58	Finally closed.
Venango National Bank, Franklin, Pa.	May 1, 1866	300,000	424,116	15	
Merchants' National Bank, Washington, D. C.	May 8, 1866	200,000	669,513	24 $\frac{7}{10}$	Do.
First National Bank of Medina, N. Y.	Mar. 13, 1867	50,000	82,338	38$\frac{3}{4}$	Do.
Tennessee National Bank, Memphis, Tenn.	Mar. 21, 1867	100,000	376,932	17$\frac{1}{2}$	Do.
First National Bank of Selma, Ala	Apr. 30, 1867	100,000	289,467	42	7 per cent. since last report.
First National Bank of New Orleans, La.	May 20, 1867	500,000	1,119,313	63	
National Unadilla Bank, Unadilla, N. Y.	Aug. 29, 1867	120,000	127,801	45$\frac{6}{10}$	Finally closed.
Farmers and Citizens' National Bank of Brooklyn, N. Y.	Sept. 6, 1867	300,000	1,191,500	96$\frac{1}{2}$	Do.
Croton National Bank of New York, N. Y.	Oct. 1, 1867	200,000	170,752	88$\frac{1}{4}$	Do.
First National Bank of Bethel, Conn.	Feb. 28, 1868	60,000	68,986	98	
First National Bank of Keokuk, Iowa.	Mar. 3, 1868	100,000	205,256	68$\frac{1}{2}$	Do.
National Bank of Vicksburg, Vicksburg, Miss.	Apr. 24, 1868	50,000	33,562	35	
First National Bank of Rockford, Ill	Mar. 15, 1869	50,000	69,874	41$\frac{6}{10}$	Do.
First National Bank of Nevada, Austin, Nev.	Oct. 13, 1869	250,000	170,012	00	
Ocean National Bank of New York, N. Y.	Dec. 13, 1871	1,000,000	1,280,328	93	5 per cent. since last report.
Union Square National Bank, New York, N. Y.	Dec. 15, 1871	200,000	157,120	100	10 per cent. paid to stockholders.
Eighth National Bank of New York. N. Y.	Dec. 15, 1871	250,000	378,772	100	Finally closed.
Fourth National Bank of Philadelphia, Pa.	Dec. 20, 1871	200,000	645,558	100	Do.
Waverly National Bank, Waverly, N. Y.	Apr. 23, 1872	106,100	79,864	100	32$\frac{1}{2}$ per cent. paid to stockholders, and finally closed.
First National Bank of Fort Smith, Ark.	May 2, 1872	50,000	15,142	100	13 per cent. paid stockholders, and finally closed.
Scandinavian National Bank of Chicago, Ill.	Dec. 12, 1872	250,000	249,174	40	
Wallkill National Bank, Middletown, N. Y.	Dec. 31, 1872	175,000	171,468	100	15 per cent. since last report.
Crescent City National Bank, New Orleans, La.	Mar. 18, 1873	500,000	642,881	75	10 per cent. since last report.
Atlantic National Bank, New York, N. Y.	Apr. 28, 1873	300,000	520,920	85	15 per cent. since last report.
First National Bank of Washington, D. C.	Sept. 19, 1873	500,000	1,619,965	100	Finally closed.
National Bank of the Commonwealth, New York, N. Y.	Sept. 22, 1873	750,000	796,995	100	35 per cent. paid stockholders.
Merchants' National Bank, Petersburg, Va.	Sept. 25, 1873	400,000	902,636	34	Finally closed.
First National Bank of Petersburg, Va.	Sept. 25, 1873	200,000	167,285	76	Do.
First National Bank of Mansfield, Ohio.	Oct. 18, 1873	100,000	175,068	45	
New Orleans National Banking Association, New Orleans, La.	Oct. 23, 1873	600,000	1,219,361	50	20 per cent. since last report.
First National Bank of Carlisle, Pa	Oct. 24, 1873	50,000	60,280	72	32 per cent. since last report.
First National Bank of Anderson, Ind.	Nov. 23, 1873	50,000	143,534	25	
First National Bank of Topeka, Kans.	Dec. 16, 1873	100,000	55,372	58$\frac{5}{10}$	13$\frac{3}{10}$ per cent. since last report, and finally closed.
First National Bank of Norfolk, Va.	June 3, 1874	100,000	176,330	45	10 per cent. since last report.
Gibson County National Bank, Princeton, Ind.	Nov. 28, 1874	50,000	62,646	100	Finally closed.
First National Bank of Utah, Salt Lake City, Utah.	Dec. 10, 1874	150,000	89,200	15	
Cook County National Bank, Chicago, Ill.	Feb. 1, 1875	500,000	889,643	8	

Insolvent national banks, &c.—Continued.

Name and location of bank.	Receiver appointed—	Capital stock.	Claims proved.	Dividends paid.	Remarks.
First National Bank of Tiffin, Ohio	Oct. 22, 1875	$100,000	$237,824	47	20 per cent. since last report.
Charlottesville National Bank, Charlottesville, Va.	Oct. 28, 1875	200,000	342,794	30	10 per cent. since last report.
Miners' National Bank, Georgetown, Colo.	Jan. 24, 1876	150,000	92,624	35	25 per cent. since last report.
Fourth National Bank, Chicago, Ill*	Feb. 1, 1876	200,000	33,609	50	10 per cent. since last report.
First National Bank of Bedford, Iowa.	Feb. 1, 1876	30,000	50,686	12½	
First National Bank of Osceola, Iowa.	Feb. 25, 1876	50,000	34,535	100	75 per cent. since last report; finally closed.
First Nat⁰ᵃᵉⁱ Bank of Duluth, Minn.	Mar. 13, 1876	100,000	89,837	72	27 per cent. since last report.
First National Bank of La Crosse, Wis.	Apr. 11, 1876	50,000	134,445	35	15 per cent. since last report.
City National Bank of Chicago, Ill	May 17, 1876	250,000	703,497	45	10 per cent. since last report.
Watkins National Bank, Watkins, N. Y.	July 12, 1876	75,000	59,144	100	12½ per cent. since last report.
First National Bank of Wichita, Kans.	Sept. 23, 1876	60,000	97,452	60	25 per cent. since last report.
First National Bank of Greenfield, Ohio.	Dec. 12, 1876	50,000	....	......	
National Bank of Fishkill, Fishkill, N. Y.	Jan. 27, 1877	200,000	216,797	45	
First National Bank of Franklin, Ind.	Feb. 13, 1877	132,000	166,240	45	
Northumberland County National Bank, Shamokin, Pa.	Mar. 12, 1877	67,000	165,435	50	25 per cent. since last report.
First National Bank of Winchester, Ill.	Mar. 16, 1877	50,000	140,568	50	30 per cent. since last report.
National Exchange Bank of Minneapolis, Minn.	May 24, 1877	100,000	223,592	65	15 per cent. since last report.
National Bank of the State of Missouri, Saint Louis, Mo.	June 23, 1877	2,500,000	1,911,492	35	10 per cent. since last report.
First National Bank of Delphi, Ind	July 20, 1877	50,000	133,112	50	25 per cent. since last report.
First National Bank of Georgetown, Colo.	Aug. 18, 1877	75,000	85,512	......	
Lock Haven National Bank, Lock Haven, Pa.	Aug. 20, 1877	120,000	251,047	30	Since last report.
Third National Bank of Chicago, Ill	Nov. 24, 1877	750,000	994,759	70	
Central National Bank, Chicago, Ill	Dec. 1, 1877	200,000	282,642	40	
First National Bank of Kansas City, Mo.	Feb. 11, 1878	500,000	698,151	30	
Commercial National Bank, Kansas City, Mo.	Feb. 11, 1878	100,000	73,452	100	15 per cent. paid to shareholders.
First National Bank of Ashland, Pa.*	Feb. 28, 1878	112,500	44,516	......	
First National Bank of Tarrytown, N. Y.	Mar. 23, 1878	100,000	118,832	70	
First National Bank of Allentown, Pa.²	Apr. 15, 1878	250,000	63,825	......	
First National Bank of Waynesburg, Pa.	May 15, 1878	100,000	22,119	......	
Washington County National Bank, Greenwich, N. Y.	June 8, 1878	200,000	261,697	50	
First National Bank of Dallas, Tex	June 8, 1878	50,000	60,331	......	
People's National Bank of Helena, Mont.	Sept. 13, 1878	100,000	....		
First National Bank of Bozeman, Mont.	Sept. 14, 1878	50,000	....		
Citizens' National Bank of Charlottesville, Va.³	Sept. 14, 1878	100,000	....		
Merchants' National Bank of Fort Scott, Kans.²	Sept. 25, 1878	50,000	....		
Farmers' National Bank of Platte City, Mo.	Oct. 1, 1878	50,000	....		
Total		16,332,600	23,501,628		

* Formerly in voluntary liquidation.

AGGREGATE RESOURCES AND LIABILITIES

OF

THE NATIONAL BANKS

FROM

OCTOBER, 1863, TO OCTOBER, 1878.

Aggregate resources and liabilities of the National

1 8 6 3.

Resources.	JANUARY.	APRIL.	JULY.	OCTOBER 5.
				66 banks.
Loans and discounts.........	....	....	....	$5, 466, 088 33
U. S. bonds and securities....	....	....	....	5, 662, 600 00
Other items................	....	....	....	106, 009 12
Due from nat'l and other b'ks.	....	....	....	2, 625, 597 05
Real estate, furniture, &c	....	....	....	177, 565 60
Current expenses	....	....	....	53, 808 92
Premiums paid	....	....	....	2, 503 69
Checks and other cash items..	....	....	....	492, 138 58
Bills of nat'l and other banks	....	....	....	764, 725 00
Specie and other lawful mon'y.	....	....	....	1, 446, 607 62
Total	....	....	....	16, 797, 644 00

1 8 6 4.

	JANUARY 4.	APRIL 4.	JULY 4.	OCTOBER 3.
	139 banks.	307 banks.	467 banks.	508 banks.
Loans and discounts.........	$10, 666, 095 60	$31, 593, 943 43	$70, 746, 513 33	$93, 238, 657 92
U. S. bonds and securities....	15, 112, 250 00	41, 175, 150 00	92, 530, 500 00	108, 064, 400 00
Other items................	74, 571 48	432, 059 95	842, 017 73	1, 434, 739 76
Due from national banks	....	4, 699, 479 56	15, 935, 730 13	19, 965, 720 47
Due from other b'ks and b'k'rs	*4, 786, 124 58	8, 537, 908 94	17, 337, 558 66	14, 051, 396 31
Real estate, furniture, &c....	381, 144 00	755, 696 41	1, 694, 049 46	2, 202, 318 20
Current expenses	118, 854 43	352, 720 77	502, 341 31	1, 021, 569 02
Checks and other cash items..	577, 507 92	2, 651, 916 96	5, 057, 122 90	7, 640, 109 14
Bills of nat'l and other banks.	895, 521 00	1, 660, 000 00	5, 344, 572 00	4, 687, 727 00
Specie and other lawful mon'y.	5, 018, 622 57	22, 961, 411 64	42, 283, 798 23	44, 801, 497 48
Total	37, 630. 691 58	114, 820, 287 66	252, 273, 803 75	297, 108, 195 30

1 8 6 5.

	JANUARY 2.	APRIL 3.	JULY 3.	OCTOBER 2.
	638 banks.	907 banks.	1,294 banks.	1,513 banks.
Loans and discounts.........	$166, 448, 718 00	$252, 404, 208 07	$362, 442, 743 08	$487, 170, 136 29
U. S. bonds and securities....	176, 578, 750 00	277, 619, 900 00	391, 744, 850 00	427, 731, 300 00
Other items................	3, 294, 883 27	4, 275, 769 51	12, 569, 120 38	19, 048, 513 15
Due from national banks	30, 820, 175 44	40, 963, 243 47	76, 977, 539 59	89, 978, 980 55
Due from other b'ks and b'k'rs	19, 836, 072 83	22, 554, 636 57	26, 078, 028 01	17, 393, 232 25
Real estate, furniture, &c....	4, 083, 226 12	6, 525, 118 80	11, 231, 237 28	14, 703, 281 77
Current expenses	1, 053, 725 34	2, 298, 025 65	2, 338, 775 56	4, 539, 525 11
Premiums paid	1, 323, 023 56	1, 823, 291 84	2, 243, 210 31	2, 585, 501 06
Checks and other cash items..	17, 837, 496 77	29, 681, 394 13	41, 314, 904 50	72, 309, 854 44
Bills of nat'l and other banks.	14, 275, 153 00	13, 710, 370 00	21, 651, 826 00	16, 247, 241 00
Specie.......................	4, 481, 937 68	6, 659, 660 47	9, 437, 060 40	18, 072, 012 59
Legal tenders and fract'l cur'y	72, 535, 504 67	112, 999, 320 59	168, 426, 166 55	189, 988, 496 28
Total	512, 568, 666 68	771, 514, 939 10	1, 126, 455, 481 66	1, 359, 768, 074 49

* Including amount due from national banks.

Banks from October, 1863, to October, 1878.

1 8 6 3.

Liabilities.	JANUARY.	APRIL.	JULY.	OCTOBER 5. 66 banks.
Capital stock...............				$7,188,393 00
Undivided profits..........				128,030 06
Individual and other deposits.				8,497,681 84
Due to nat'l and other banks*.				981,178 59
Other items...............				2,360 51
Total...............				16,797,644 00

1 8 6 4.

	JANUARY 4. 139 banks.	APRIL 4. 307 banks.	JULY 4. 467 banks.	OCTOBER 3. 508 banks.
Capital stock..................	$14,740,522 00	$42,204,474 00	$75,213,945 00	$86,782,802 00
Surplus fund...................			1,129,910 22	2,010,286 10
Undivided profits.............	432,827 81	1,625,656 87	3,094,330 11	5,982,392 22
National b'k notes outstanding	30,155 00	9,797,975 00	25,825,665 00	45,260,504 00
Individual and other deposits.	19,450,492 53	51,274,914 01	119,414,239 03	122,166,536 40
Due to nat'l and other banks*.	2,153,779 38	6,814,930 40	27,382,006 37	34,862,384 81
Other items...................	822,914 86	3,102,337 38	213,708 02	43,289 77
Total...................	37,630,691 58	114,820,287 66	252,273,803 75	297,108,195 30

1 8 6 5.

	JANUARY 2. 638 banks.	APRIL 3. 907 banks.	JULY 3. 1,294 banks.	OCTOBER 2. 1,513 banks.
Capital stock..................	$135,618,874 00	$215,326,023 00	$325,834,558 00	$393,157,206 00
Surplus fund..................	8,663,311 22	17,318,942 65	31,303,565 64	38,713,380 72
Undivided profits.............	12,283,812 65	17,809,307 14	23,159,408 17	32,350,278 19
National b'k notes outstanding	66,769,375 00	98,806,488 00	131,452,158 00	171,321,903 00
Individual and other deposits.	183,479,636 98	262,961,473 13	398,357,559 59	500,910,873 22
United States deposits........	37,764,729 77	57,630,141 01	58,632,720 67	48,170,381 31
Due to national banks........	30,619,175 57	41,301,031 16	78,261,045 64	90,044,837 08
Due to other b'ks and bankers.	37,104,130 62	59,692,581 64	79,591,594 93	84,155,161 27
Other items..................	265,620 87	578,951 37	462,871 02	944,053 70
Total..................	512,568,666 68	771,511,939 10	1,126,455,481 66	1,359,768,074 49

* Including State bank circulation outstanding.

Aggregate resources and liabilities of the National

1 8 6 6.

Resources.	JANUARY 1. 1,582 banks.	APRIL 2. 1,612 banks.	JULY 2. 1,634 banks.	OCTOBER 1. 1,644 banks.
Loans and discounts	$500,650,109 19	$528,080,526 70	$550,353,094 17	$603,314,704 83
U. S. b'ds dep'd to secure circ'n	298,376,850 00	315,850,300 00	326,483,350 00	331,843,200 00
Other U. S. b'ds and securities	142,003,500 00	125,625,750 00	121,152,950 00	94,974,650 00
Oth'r stocks, b'ds, and mortg's	17,483,753 18	17,379,738 92	17,565,911 46	15,887,490 06
Due from national banks	93,254,551 02	87,564,329 71	96,606,482 66	107,650,174 18
Due from other b'ks and b'k'rs	14,658,229 87	13,682,345 12	13,082,613 23	15,211,117 16
Real estate, furniture, &c	15,436,296 16	15,895,564 46	16,730,923 62	17,134,002 58
Current expenses	3,193,717 78	4,927,509 79	3,032,716 27	5,311,253 35
Premiums paid	2,423,918 02	2,233,516 31	2,398,872 26	2,493,773 47
Checks and other cash items	89,837,684 50	105,490,619 36	96,077,134 53	103,684,249 21
Bills of national and other b'ks	20,406,442 00	18,279,816 00	17,866,742 00	17,437,779 00
Specie	19,205,018 75	17,529,778 42	12,029,376 30	9,226,831 82
Legal tenders and fract'l cur'y	187,846,548 82	189,867,852 52	201,425,041 63	205,793,578 76
Total	1,404,776,619 29	1,442,407,737 31	1,476,395,208 13	1,526,962,804 42

1 8 6 7.

	JANUARY 7. 1,648 banks.	APRIL 1. 1,642 banks.	JULY 1. 1,636 banks.	OCTOBER 7. 1,642 banks.
Loans and discounts	$608,771,799 61	$597,648,286 53	$588,450,396 12	$609,675,214 61
U. S. b'ds dep'd to secure circ'n	339,570,700 00	338,803,650 00	337,684,250 00	338,640,150 00
U. S. b'ds dep'd to sec're dep'ts	36,185,950 00	38,465,800 00	38,368,950 00	37,862,100 00
U. S. b'ds and sec'ties on hand	52,949,300 00	46,639,400 00	45,633,700 00	42,460,800 00
Oth'r stocks, b'ds, and mortg's	15,073,737 45	20,194,875 21	21,452,615 43	21,507,881 42
Due from national banks	92,552,206 29	94,121,186 21	92,308,911 87	95,217,610 14
Due from other b'ks and b'k'rs	12,996,157 49	10,737,392 90	9,663,322 82	8,389,226 47
Real estate, furniture, &c	18,925,315 51	19,625,893 81	19,800,905 86	20,639,708 23
Current expenses	2,822,675 18	5,693,784 17	3,249,153 91	5,297,494 13
Premiums paid	2,860,398 85	3,411,325 56	3,338,000 37	2,764,186 35
Checks and other cash items	101,430,220 18	87,951,405 13	128,312,177 79	134,603,231 51
Bills of national banks	19,263,718 00	12,873,785 00	16,138,769 00	11,841,104 00
Bills of other banks	1,176,142 00	825,748 00	531,267 00	333,209 00
Specie	19,726,043 20	11,444,529 15	11,128,672 98	12,798,044 40
Legal tenders and fract'l cur'y	104,872,371 64	92,861,254 17	102,534,613 46	100,556,849 91
Compound interest notes	82,047,250 00	84,065,700 00	75,488,220 00	56,888,250 00
Total	1,511,222,985 10	1,165,451,105 84	1,194,084,526 01	1,499,469,060 17

1 8 6 8.

	JANUARY 6. 1,642 banks.	APRIL 6. 1,643 banks.	JULY 6. 1,640 banks.	OCTOBER 5. 1,643 banks.
Loans and discounts	$616,603,479 89	$628,029,347 65	$655,729,546 42	$657,668,847 83
U. S. b'ds dep'd to secure circ'n	339,064,200 00	339,686,650 00	339,569,100 00	340,487,050 00
U. S. b'ds dep'd to sec're dep'ts	37,315,750 00	37,446,000 00	37,853,150 00	37,390,150 00
U. S. b'ds and sec'ties on hand	44,161,500 00	45,958,550 00	43,068,350 00	36,817,600 00
Oth'r stocks, b'ds, and mortg's	19,365,864 77	19,874,384 33	20,007,327 12	20,693,406 40
Due from national banks	99,311,446 60	95,900,606 35	114,434,097 03	102,278,547 77
Due from other b'ks and b'k'rs	8,180,199 74	7,074,207 44	8,642,456 72	7,848,822 24
Real estate, furniture, &c	21,125,665 68	22,082,570 25	22,699,829 70	22,747,875 18
Current expenses	2,986,893 86	5,428,460 25	2,938,519 04	5,278,911 22
Premiums paid	2,464,536 96	2,660,106 69	2,492,074 37	1,819,815 50
Checks and other cash items	109,390,266 37	114,993,036 23	124,076,097 71	143,241,394 90
Bills of national banks	16,655,572 00	12,573,514 00	13,210,179 00	11,842,974 00
Bills of other banks	261,269 00	196,106 00	312,550 00	222,068 00
Fractional currency	1,927,876 78	1,825,610 16	1,863,358 91	2,262,791 97
Specie	20,981,601 45	18,373,943 22	20,755,919 04	13,003,733 30
Legal-tender notes	114,306,491 00	84,390,219 00	100,166,100 00	92,453,475 00
Compound interest notes	39,997,030 00	38,897,490 00	19,473,420 00	4,513,730 00
Three per cent. certificates	8,245,000 00	24,255,000 00	14,905,000 00	59,080,000 00
Total	1,502,647,644 10	1,499,608,920 97	1,572,107,076 26	1,559,621,773 49

Banks from October, 1863, to October, 1878—Continued.

1 8 6 6 .

Liabilities.	JANUARY 1. 1,582 banks.	APRIL 2. 1,612 banks.	JULY 2. 1,634 banks.	OCTOBER 1. 1,644 banks.
Capital stock	$403,357,346 00	$409,273,534 00	$414,270,493 00	$415,472,369 00
Surplus fund	43,000,370 78	44,687,810 54	50,151,991 77	53,359,277 64
Undivided profits	28,972,493 70	30,964,422 73	29,286,175 45	32,583,486 69
National b'k notes outstanding	213,239,530 00	248,886,282 00	267,798,678 00	280,253,818 00
State bank notes outstanding	45,449,155 00	33,800,865 00	19,996,163 00	9,748,025 00
Individual deposits	522,507,820 27	534,734,950 33	533,338,174 25	564,616,777 64
U. S. deposits	29,747,236 15	29,150,720 82	36,038,185 03	30,420,819 80
Dep'ts of U. S. disb'sing officers			3,066,892 22	2,979,955 77
Due to national banks	94,709,074 15	89,067,501 54	96,496,726 42	110,531,957 31
Due to other b'ks and bankers	23,793,584 24	21,841,641 35	25,951,728 99	26,986,317 57
Total	1,404,776,619 29	1,442,407,737 31	1,476,395,208 13	1,526,962,804 42

1 8 6 7 .

	JANUARY 7. 1,648 banks.	APRIL 1. 1,642 banks.	JULY 1. 1,636 banks.	OCTOBER 7. 1,642 banks.
Capital stock	$420,229,739 00	$419,399,484 00	$418,558,148 00	$420,073,415 00
Surplus fund	59,092,874 57	60,206,013 58	63,232,811 12	66,605,587 01
Undivided profits	26,961,382 60	31,131,034 39	30,656,222 84	33,751,446 21
National b'k notes outstanding	291,436,749 00	292,788,572 00	291,760,553 00	293,887,941 00
State bank notes outstanding	6,061,499 00	5,460,312 00	4,484,112 00	4,092,155 00
Individual deposits	558,699,768 06	512,046,182 47	539,599,076 10	540,797,837 51
U. S. deposits	27,284,876 03	27,473,005 66	29,838,391 53	23,062,119 92
Dep'ts of U. S. disb'sing officers	2,477,509 48	2,650,981 39	3,474,192 74	4,352,379 43
Due to national banks	92,761,998 43	91,150,890 89	89,821,751 60	93,111,240 89
Due to other b'ks and bankers	21,116,588 33	23,138,620 46	22,659,267 08	19,644,940 20
Total	1,511,222,985 40	1,465,451,105 84	1,494,084,526 01	1,489,469,060 17

1 8 6 8 .

	JANUARY 6. 1,612 banks.	APRIL 6. 1,643 banks.	JULY 6. 1,640 banks.	OCTOBER 5. 1,643 banks.
Capital stock	$420,260,790 00	$420,676,210 00	$420,105,041 00	$420,634,511 00
Surplus fund	70,586,125 70	72,349,119 60	75,840,118 91	77,995,761 40
Undivided profits	31,399,877 57	32,861,597 08	33,543,223 35	36,005,883 98
National b'k notes outstanding	291,377,350 00	295,336,044 00	294,908,264 00	295,769,489 00
State bank notes outstanding	3,792,013 00	3,340,177 00	3,163,771 00	2,906,352 00
Individual deposits	534,704,709 00	532,011,480 36	575,842,070 12	580,940,820 85
U. S. deposits	21,305,638 02	22,750,342 77	21,603,676 96	17,573,250 64
Dep'ts of U. S. disb'sing officers	3,208,783 03	1,976,682 31	3,199,389 99	4,570,478 16
Due to national banks	98,141,669 61	91,073,631 25	113,306,316 34	99,414,397 28
Due to other b'ks and bankers	21,867,618 17	21,323,636 60	27,355,204 56	23,720,829 18
Total	1,502,647,644 10	1,499,668,920 97	1,572,167,076 26	1,559,621,773 49

Aggregate resources and liabilities of the National

1 8 6 9.

Resources.	JANUARY 4.	APRIL 17.	JUNE 12.	OCTOBER 9.
	1,628 banks.	1,620 banks.	1,619 banks.	1,617 banks.
Loans and discounts	$644,945,039 53	$662,084,813 47	$686,347,755 81	$682,883,106 97
U. S. bonds to secure circ'lat'n	338,539,950 00	338,379,250 00	338,699,750 00	339,480,100 00
U. S. bonds to secure deposits	34,538,350 00	29,721,350 00	27,625,350 00	18,704,000 00
U. S. b'ds and sec'ties on hand	35,010,600 00	30,226,550 00	27,476,650 00	25,903,950 00
Oth'r stocks, b'ds, and mortg's	20,127,732 96	20,074,435 69	20,777,560 53	22,250,697 14
Due from redeeming agents	65,727,070 80	57,554,382 55	62,912,636 82	56,660,562 84
Due from other national banks	36,067,316 84	30,520,527 89	35,556,504 53	35,393,563 47
Due from State b'ks and b'k'rs	7,715,719 34	8,075,595 60	9,140,919 24	8,790,418 57
Real estate, furniture, &c	23,289,838 28	23,708,188 13	23,850,271 17	25,169,188 95
Current expenses	3,265,990 81	5,641,195 01	5,820,577 87	5,646,382 96
Premiums paid	1,654,352 70	1,716,210 13	1,809,070 01	2,092,364 85
Checks and other cash items	142,605,984 92	154,137,191 23	161,614,852 66	108,809,817 37
Bills of other national banks	14,684,799 00	11,725,239 00	11,524,447 00	10,776,023 00
Fractional currency	2,280,471 06	2,088,545 18	1,804,855 53	2,090,727 38
Specie	29,626,750 26	9,944,532 15	18,455,090 48	23,002,405 83
Legal-tender notes	88,239,300 00	80,875,161 00	80,934,119 00	83,719,295 00
Three per cent. certificates	52,075,000 00	51,190,000 00	49,815,000 00	45,845,000 00
Total	1,540,394,266 50	1,517,753,167 03	1,564,174,410 65	1,497,226,604 33

1 8 7 0.

	JANUARY 22.	MARCH 24.	JUNE 9.	OCTOBER 8.	DECEMBER 28.
	1,615 banks.	1,615 banks.	1,612 banks.	1,615 banks.	1,648 banks.
Loans and discounts	$688,875,203 70	$710,848,609 39	$719,341,186 06	$715,928,079 81	$725,515,538 40
Bonds for circulation	339,350,750 00	339,251,350 00	338,845,200 00	340,857,450 00	344,104,200 00
Bonds for deposits	17,592,000 00	16,102,000 00	15,704,000 00	15,381,500 00	15,189,500 00
U. S. bonds on hand	24,677,100 00	27,292,150 00	28,276,600 00	22,323,800 00	23,893,300 00
Other stocks and b'ds	21,082,412 00	20,524,294 55	23,300,681 87	23,614,721 25	22,686,358 59
Due from red'g agents	71,641,486 05	73,435,117 98	74,635,405 61	66,275,668 92	64,805,062 88
Due from nat'l banks	31,994,609 26	29,510,688 11	36,128,750 66	33,948,805 65	37,478,166 49
Due from State banks	9,319,560 54	10,238,219 85	10,430,781 32	9,202,496 71	9,824,144 18
Real estate, &c	26,002,713 01	26,330,701 24	26,593,357 00	27,470,746 97	28,021,637 44
Current expenses	3,460,588 00	6,683,189 54	6,324,955 47	5,871,750 02	6,905,073 32
Premiums paid	2,439,591 41	2,680,882 39	3,076,456 74	2,491,222 11	3,251,648 72
Cash items	111,624,822 00	11,267,703 12	11,497,534 13	12,536,613 57	13,229,403 34
Clear'g-house exch'gs		75,317,992 22	83,936,515 64	79,089,688 39	76,208,707 00
National bank notes	15,840,669 00	14,226,817 00	16,342,582 00	12,512,927 00	17,001,846 00
Fractional currency	2,476,966 75	2,285,409 02	2,184,714 39	2,078,178 05	2,150,522 88
Specie	48,345,383 72	37,096,543 44	31,099,437 78	18,460,011 47	26,307,251 59
Legal-tender notes	87,708,502 00	82,485,978 00	94,573,751 00	70,324,577 00	80,580,745 00
Three per cent. cert'fs	43,820,000 00	43,570,000 00	43,465,000 00	43,345,000 00	41,845,000 00
Total	1,546,261,357 44	1,529,147,735 85	1,565,756,909 67	1,510,713,236 92	1,538,998,105 93

1 8 7 1.

	MARCH 18.	APRIL 29.	JUNE 10.	OCTOBER 2.	DECEMBER 16.
	1,688 banks.	1,707 banks.	1,723 banks.	1,767 banks.	1,790 banks.
Loans and discounts	$767,858,490 59	$779,321,828 11	$789,416,568 13	$831,552,210 00	$818,996,311 74
Bonds for circulation	351,556,700 00	354,427,200 00	357,388,950 00	364,475,800 00	366,840,200 00
Bonds for deposits	15,231,500 00	15,236,500 00	15,250,500 00	28,087,500 00	23,155,150 00
U. S. bonds on hand	23,911,350 00	22,487,950 00	24,200,300 00	17,753,650 00	17,675,500 00
Other stocks and b'ds	22,763,869 20	22,414,659 05	23,132,871 05	24,517,059 35	23,061,184 20
Due from red'g agents	83,809,188 92	85,061,016 31	92,369,246 71	86,878,608 84	77,985,600 53
Due from nat'l banks	30,201,119 99	38,332,679 74	39,636,579 35	43,525,362 05	43,313,344 78
Due from State banks	10,271,605 34	11,478,174 71	11,853,308 60	12,772,609 83	13,069,301 40
Real estate, &c	28,805,814 79	29,242,762 79	29,637,909 30	30,089,783 85	30,070,339 57
Current expenses	6,694,014 17	6,764,159 73	6,295,099 46	6,153,370 29	7,330,424 12
Premiums paid	3,939,995 20	4,414,755 40	5,026,385 97	5,500,890 17	5,956,079 74
Cash items	11,642,044 74	12,719,280 84	13,101,497 95	14,058,268 86	13,784,424 76
Clear'g-house exch'gs	100,693,917 54	130,855,608 15	102,091,311 75	101,165,854 52	114,538,539 93
National bank notes	13,137,066 00	16,632,323 00	19,101,389 00	14,197,653 00	13,085,904 00
Fractional currency	2,103,298 16	2,135,763 09	2,160,713 22	2,095,485 79	2,061,600 89
Specie	25,760,166 64	22,732,027 02	19,924,955 16	13,252,908 17	20,505,209 56
Legal-tender notes	91,072,349 00	106,219,126 00	122,137,660 00	109,414,745 00	93,942,707 00
Three per cent. cert'fs	37,570,000 00	33,935,000 00	30,690,000 00	25,075,000 00	21,400,000 00
Total	1,627,032,030 28	1,694,440,912 94	1,703,415,335 65	1,730,566,899 72	1,715,861,897 22

Banks from October, 1863, to October, 1878—Continued.

1869.

Liabilities.	JANUARY 4. 1,628 banks.	APRIL 17. 1,620 banks.	JUNE 12. 1,619 banks.	OCTOBER 9. 1,617 banks.
Capital stock	$419,040,931 00	$420,818,721 00	$422,659,260 00	$426,399,151 00
Surplus fund	81,169,936 52	82,653,989 19	82,218,576 47	86,165,334 32
Undivided profits	35,318,273 71	37,489,314 82	43,812,898 70	40,687,300 92
Nat'l bank notes outstanding	294,476,702 00	292,457,098 00	292,753,286 00	293,593,645 00
State bank notes outstanding	2,734,669 00	2,615,387 00	2,558,874 00	2,454,697 00
Individual deposits	568,530,934 11	547,922,174 91	574,307,382 77	511,400,196 63
U. S. deposits	13,211,850 19	10,114,328 32	10,301,907 71	7,112,646 67
Dep'ts U. S. disbursing officers.	3,472,884 90	3,665,131 61	2,454,048 99	4,516,648 12
Due to national banks	95,453,139 33	92,662,648 40	100,933,910 03	95,007,892 83
Due to State banks and b'k'rs	26,984,945 74	23,018,610 62	28,046,771 30	23,849,371 62
Notes and bills re-discounted		2,464,849 81	2,392,205 61	3,839,357 10
Bills payable		1,870,913 26	1,735,289 07	2,140,363 12
Total	1,540,394,266 50	1,517,753,167 03	1,564,174,410 65	1,497,226,604 33

1870.

	JANUARY 22. 1,615 banks.	MARCH 24. 1,615 banks.	JUNE 9. 1,612 banks.	OCTOBER 8. 1,615 banks.	DECEMBER 28. 1,648 banks.
Capital stock	$426,074,954 00	$427,504,247 00	$427,235,701 00	$430,399,301 00	$435,356,004 00
Surplus fund	90,174,281 14	90,229,954 59	91,689,834 12	94,061,438 95	94,705,740 34
Undivided profits	34,300,430 80	43,100,471 62	42,861,712 59	38,608,618 91	46,056,428 55
Nat'l bank circulation	292,838,935 00	292,509,149 00	291,183,614 00	291,798,640 00	296,205,446 00
State bank circulation	2,351,993 00	2,279,460 00	2,222,793 00	2,138,548 00	2,091,799 00
Dividends unpaid	2,299,296 27	1,483,416 15	1,517,595 18	2,462,591 31	2,242,556 49
Individual deposits	546,236,881 57	516,058,085 26	542,261,563 18	501,407,586 90	507,368,618 67
U. S. deposits	6,750,139 19	6,424,421 25	10,677,873 92	6,807,978 49	6,074,407 90
Dep'ts U. S. dis. offi'rs	2,592,001 21	4,778,225 93	2,592,967 54	4,550,142 68	4,155,304 25
Due to national banks	108,351,300 33	109,667,715 95	115,456,491 84	100,348,292 45	106,090,414 53
Due to State banks	28,904,849 14	29,767,575 21	33,012,162 78	29,693,910 80	29,200,587 29
Notes re-discounted	3,842,542 30	2,462,647 49	2,741,843 53	3,843,577 67	4,612,131 08
Bills payable	1,543,753 49	2,873,357 40	2,302,756 99	4,592,609 76	4,838,667 83
Total	1,546,261,357 44	1,529,147,735 85	1,565,756,909 67	1,510,713,236 02	1,538,908,105 93

1871.

	MARCH 18. 1,688 banks.	APRIL 29. 1,707 banks.	JUNE 10. 1,723 banks.	OCTOBER 2. 1,767 banks.	DECEMBER 16. 1,790 banks.
Capital stock	$444,232,771 00	$446,925,493 00	$450,330,841 00	$458,255,696 00	$460,225,866 00
Surplus fund	96,802,081 66	97,620,099 28	98,322,203 80	101,112,671 91	101,573,153 62
Undivided profits	43,883,857 64	44,776,030 71	45,535,227 79	42,008,714 38	48,630,925 81
Nat'l bank circulation	301,713,460 00	306,131,393 00	307,793,880 00	315,519,117 00	318,265,481 00
State bank circulation	2,035,800 00	1,982,580 00	1,968,058 00	1,921,056 00	1,886,538 00
Dividends unpaid	1,263,767 70	2,235,248 46	1,408,628 25	4,540,191 61	1,393,427 98
Individual deposits	561,190,830 41	611,625,174 10	602,110,758 16	600,808,486 55	596,586,487 54
U. S. deposits	6,314,957 81	6,521,572 92	6,265,167 91	29,511,935 98	14,829,525 65
Dep'ts U. S. dis. offi'rs	4,813,016 66	3,757,873 84	4,893,907 25	5,393,508 89	5,399,108 31
Due to national banks	118,904,865 81	128,037,469 17	135,167,847 69	131,730,713 04	118,657,611 16
Due to State banks	37,311,519 13	36,113,290 67	44,219,802 96	40,211,971 67	38,116,950 67
Notes re-discounted	3,256,896 42	3,573,723 02	3,120,039 09	3,964,552 57	4,922,455 78
Bills payable	5,248,206 04	5,740,964 77	5,278,973 72	4,528,191 12	5,374,362 67
Total	1,627,032,039 28	1,694,440,912 94	1,703,415,335 65	1,730,566,899 72	1,715,861,897 22

Aggregate resources and liabilities of the National

1872.

Resources.	FEBRUARY 27. 1,814 banks.	APRIL 19. 1,843 banks.	JUNE 10. 1,853 banks.	OCTOBER 3. 1,919 banks.	DECEMBER 27. 1,940 banks.
Loans and discounts	$839,605,077 91	$844,902,273 49	$871,531,448 67	$877,197,923 47	$885,653,449 62
Bonds for circulation	370,924,700 00	374,428,150 00	377,020,700 00	382,046,400 00	384,458,500 00
Bonds for deposits	15,870,000 00	15,160,000 00	15,409,950 00	15,479,750 00	16,304,750 00
U. S. bonds on hand	21,323,150 00	19,292,100 00	16,458,250 00	12,142,550 00	10,306,100 00
Other stocks and b'ds	22,838,338 80	21,338,914 06	22,270,610 47	23,533,151 73	23,160,557 29
Due from red'g agents	89,548,329 93	82,120,017 24	91,564,269 53	80,717,071 30	86,401,459 44
Due from nat'l banks	38,282,905 86	36,697,592 81	39,468,323 39	34,486,593 87	42,707,613 54
Due from State banks	12,269,822 08	12,299,716 94	13,014,265 26	12,976,878 01	12,008,843 54
Real estate, &c	30,637,676 75	30,809,274 98	31,123,843 21	32,276,498 17	33,014,796 83
Current expenses	6,265,655 13	7,026,041 23	6,719,794 90	6,310,428 79	8,454,803 97
Premiums paid	6,308,821 86	6,544,279 29	6,616,174 75	6,546,848 52	7,097,847 86
Cash items	12,143,403 12	12,461,171 40	13,458,753 80	14,916,784 34	13,696,723 85
Clear'g-house exch'gs	93,154,310 74	114,195,906 36	88,592,800 16	110,086,315 37	90,145,482 72
National bank notes	15,552,087 00	18,492,832 00	16,253,560 00	15,787,206 00	19,070,322 00
Fractional currency	2,278,143 24	2,143,249 20	2,060,464 12	2,151,747 88	2,270,576 32
Specie	25,507,825 32	24,433,899 46	24,256,644 14	10,229,736 70	19,047,336 45
Legal-tender notes	97,865,400 00	105,732,455 00	122,994,417 00	105,121,104 00	102,922,369 00
U. S. cert'fs of deposit				6,710,000 00	12,650,000 00
Three per cent. cert's	18,980,000 00	15,365,000 00	12,005,000 00	7,140,000 00	4,185,000 00
Total	1,719,415,657 34	1,743,652,213 55	1,770,837,269 40	1,755,857,098 24	1,773,556,532 43

1873.

	FEBRUARY 28. 1,947 banks.	APRIL 25. 1,962 banks.	JUNE 13. 1,968 banks.	SEPTEMBER 12. 1,976 banks.	DECEMBER 26. 1,976 banks.
Loans and discounts	$913,265,189 67	$912,064,267 31	$925,557,682 42	$944,220,116 34	$856,816,555 05
Bonds for circulation	384,675,050 00	386,763,800 00	388,080,300 00	388,330,400 00	389,384,400 00
Bonds for deposits	15,035,000 00	16,235,000 00	15,935,000 00	14,805,000 00	14,815,200 00
U. S. bonds on hand	10,436,850 00	9,613,550 00	9,789,400 00	8,824,850 00	8,630,850 00
Other stocks and b'ds	22,063,306 20	22,449,146 04	22,912,415 03	23,709,034 53	24,358,125 06
Due from red'g agents	95,773,077 10	88,815,557 80	97,143,326 94	96,134,120 66	73,032,046 87
Due from nat'l banks	39,183,700 00	38,671,088 63	43,528,792 20	41,413,680 06	40,404,757 97
Due from State banks	13,385,679 17	12,883,353 37	14,073,287 77	12,022,873 41	11,185,253 08
Real estate, &c	34,023,057 77	34,216,878 07	34,820,562 77	34,661,823 21	35,356,746 48
Current expenses	6,977,831 35	7,410,045 87	7,154,211 09	6,985,436 90	8,678,170 39
Premiums paid	7,205,250 07	7,530,987 07	7,890,962 14	7,752,843 87	7,987,707 14
Cash items	11,761,711 50	11,425,209 00	13,636,482 58	11,433,913 22	12,321,972 80
Clear'g-house exch'gs	131,383,860 05	94,132,125 24	90,918,326 59	88,926,063 53	62,881,342 16
National bank notes	15,998,779 00	19,310,202 00	20,394,772 00	16,103,842 00	21,403,179 00
Fractional currency	2,289,680 21	2,198,973 37	2,197,559 84	2,302,775 26	2,287,454 03
Specie	17,777,673 53	16,868,808 74	27,950,086 72	19,868,469 45	26,907,037 58
Legal-tender notes	97,141,960 00	100,605,287 00	106,381,491 00	92,522,663 60	108,719,506 00
U. S. cert'fs of deposit	18,460,000 00	18,370,000 00	22,365,000 00	20,610,000 00	24,610,000 00
Three per cent. cert's	1,865,000 00	710,000 00	305,000 00		
Total	1,839,152,715 21	1,800,303,280 11	1,851,234,860 38	1,830,627,845 53	1,729,380,303 61

1874.

	FEBRUARY 27. 1,975 banks.	MAY 1. 1,978 banks.	JUNE 26. 1,983 banks.	OCTOBER 2. 2,004 banks.	DECEMBER 31. 2,027 banks.
Loans and discounts	$897,850,600 46	$923,347,030 79	$926,105,671 70	$954,394,701 59	$955,862,580 51
Bonds for circulation	389,614,700 00	389,249,100 00	390,281,700 00	383,254,800 00	382,976,200 00
Bonds for deposits	14,600,200 00	14,800,200 00	14,890,200 00	14,491,700 00	14,714,000 00
U. S. bonds on hand	11,043,400 00	10,152,000 00	10,456,900 00	13,313,550 00	15,290,300 00
Other stocks and b'ds	25,305,736 21	25,160,400 20	27,010,727 48	27,807,826 92	28,313,473 12
Due from res've ag'ts	101,502,865 88	94,017,603 31	97,871,517 06	83,885,126 94	80,488,831 45
Due from nat'l banks	36,624,001 39	41,291,015 24	15,770,715 59	39,495,309 47	18,100,842 62
Due from State banks	11,196,711 47	12,374,391 37	12,469,582 33	11,196,611 73	11,655,573 07
Real estate, &c	36,043,741 50	36,768,066 39	37,270,876 51	38,112,926 52	39,190,683 04
Current expenses	6,998,675 73	7,548,748 82	7,559,125 20	7,658,738 82	5,510,566 47
Premiums paid	8,711,028 77	8,680,570 84	8,563,262 27	8,376,659 07	8,626,112 16
Cash items	10,269,955 50	11,949,020 71	10,496,257 00	12,296,416 77	14,005,517 33
Clear'g-house exch'gs	62,768,119 19	94,877,796 52	63,896,271 31	97,383,687 11	112,995,317 55
National bank notes	20,003,251 00	20,673,452 00	23,527,991 00	18,450,013 00	22,552,336 00
Fractional currency	2,300,919 73	2,187,186 69	2,281,808 92	2,224,943 12	2,392,668 74
Specie	33,365,863 58	32,560,969 26	22,193,207 27	21,240,945 23	22,436,761 04
Legal-tender notes	102,717,563 00	161,692,930 00	163,108,350 00	80,021,916 00	82,604,791 00
U. S. cert'fs of deposit	37,235,000 00	40,135,000 00	47,780,000 00	42,825,000 00	33,670,000 00
Dep. with U. S. Treas			91,250 00	20,349,950 15	21,043,084 36
Total	1,808,500,529 16	1,867,802,796 28	1,851,840,913 64	1,877,180,942 44	1,902,409,038 46

Banks from October, 1863, to October, 1878—Continued.

1872.

Liabilities.	FEBRUARY 27. 1,814 banks.	APRIL 19. 1,843 banks.	JUNE 10. 1,853 banks.	OCTOBER 3. 1,919 banks.	DECEMBER 27. 1,940 banks.
Capital stock	$464,081,744 00	$467,924,318 00	$470,543,301 00	$479,629,174 00	$482,606,252 00
Surplus fund	103,787,082 62	104,312,525 81	105,181,943 28	110,257,516 45	111,410,248 98
Undivided profits	43,310,344 46	46,428,590 90	50,234,298 32	46,623,784 50	56,762,411 89
Nat'l bank circulation	321,634,675 00	325,305,752 00	327,092,752 00	333,495,027 00	336,289,285 00
State bank circulation	1,830,563 00	1,763,885 00	1,700,935 00	1,567,143 00	1,511,396 00
Dividends unpaid	1,451,746 20	1,561,011 45	1,454,044 06	3,149,749 61	1,356,934 18
Individual deposits	593,645,666 16	620,775,205 78	618,891,619 49	613,296,671 45	598,114,679 26
U. S. deposits	7,111,893 47	6,355,722 95	6,903,014 77	7,853,772 41	7,863,894 93
Dep'ts U.S.dis.officers	5,024,899 44	3,416,371 16	5,463,953 48	4,563,833 79	5,136,597 74
Due to national banks	128,627,494 44	120,755,565 86	132,804,924 02	110,047,347 67	124,218,392 83
Due to State banks	39,025,165 44	35,005,127 84	39,878,826 42	33,789,083 82	34,794,963 37
Notes rediscounted	3,818,686 91	1,225,622 04	4,745,178 22	5,549,431 88	6,545,059 78
Bills payable	6,062,896 11	5,821,551 76	5,942,479 34	6,040,562 66	6,946,416 17
Total	1,719,415,657 34	1,743,652,213 55	1,770,837,269 40	1,735,857,098 24	1,773,556,592 45

1873.

	FEBRUARY 28. 1,917 banks.	APRIL 25. 1,962 banks.	JUNE 13. 1,968 banks.	SEPTEMBER 12. 1,976 banks.	DECEMBER 26. 1,976 banks.
Capital stock	$484,551,811 00	$487,891,251 00	$490,109,801 00	$491,072,616 00	$490,266,611 00
Surplus fund	114,681,048 73	115,805,574 57	116,847,454 62	120,314,499 20	120,961,267 91
Undivided profits	48,578,045 28	52,415,348 46	55,306,154 69	54,515,131 76	58,375,169 43
Nat'l bank circulation	336,262,459 00	338,163,864 00	338,788,504 00	339,081,799 00	341,320,256 00
State bank circulation	1,368,271 00	1,280,208 00	1,224,470 00	1,188,853 00	1,130,585 00
Dividends unpaid	1,465,993 60	1,162,336 77	1,400,491 90	1,102,547 89	1,269,474 74
Individual deposits	656,187,551 61	616,848,358 25	641,121,775 27	622,685,563 29	540,510,602 78
U. S. deposits	7,044,848 34	7,880,057 73	8,691,001 95	7,829,327 73	7,680,375 26
Dep'ts U.S.dis.officers	5,835,696 60	4,425,750 14	6,416,275 10	8,098,560 13	4,705,593 36
Due to national banks	134,231,842 95	126,631,926 24	137,856,085 67	133,672,732 94	114,996,606 54
Due to State banks	38,124,803 85	35,036,433 18	40,741,788 47	39,298,148 14	36,598,076 29
Notes rediscounted	5,117,810 50	5,403,043 38	5,515,900 67	5,987,512 36	3,811,487 89
Bills payable	5,672,532 75	7,059,128 39	7,215,157 04	5,480,554 09	7,754,137 41
Total	1,639,152,715 21	1,800,303,280 11	1,851,234,860 38	1,830,627,845 53	1,729,380,303 61

1874.

	FEBRUARY 27. 1,975 banks.	MAY 1. 1,978 banks.	JUNE 26. 1,983 banks.	OCTOBER 2. 2,004 banks.	DECEMBER 31. 2,027 banks.
Capital stock	$490,859,101 00	$490,077,001 00	$491,003,711 00	$493,765,121 00	$495,802,481 00
Surplus fund	123,497,347 20	125,561,081 23	126,239,308 41	128,958,106 84	130,485,651 47
Undivided profits	50,236,919 88	54,331,713 13	58,332,965 71	51,484,437 32	51,477,629 33
Nat'l bank circulation	339,602,955 00	340,267,649 00	338,538,743 00	333,225,298 00	331,193,159 00
State bank circulation	1,078,988 00	1,049,286 00	1,009,021 00	964,567 00	860,417 00
Dividends unpaid	1,291,055 63	2,259,129 91	1,242,474 81	3,516,276 99	6,088,845 01
Individual deposits	595,350,334 90	649,286,208 95	622,863,154 44	669,068,995 88	682,846,607 45
U. S. deposits	7,276,959 87	7,991,422 27	7,322,830 85	7,302,153 58	7,492,307 78
Dep'ts U.S.dis.officers	5,634,624 46	3,297,689 24	3,298,639 20	3,927,828 27	3,579,722 94
Due to national banks	138,435,388 39	135,640,418 24	113,033,822 25	125,102,049 93	129,188,671 42
Due to State banks	48,112,223 10	48,693,384 43	50,227,126 18	50,718,607 87	51,626,692 36
Notes rediscounted	3,148,828 92	4,581,420 38	1,136,256 22	4,197,372 25	6,365,652 97
Bills payable	4,275,002 51	4,772,662 59	4,352,590 57	4,950,727 51	5,398,900 83
Total	1,808,500,529 16	1,867,802,796 28	1,851,840,913 64	1,877,180,912 14	1,902,409,638 46

Aggregate resources and liabilities of the National

1875.

Resources.	MARCH 1.	MAY 1.	JUNE 30.	OCTOBER 1.	DECEMBER 17.
	2,029 banks.	2,046 banks.	2,076 banks.	2,088 banks.	2,086 banks.
Loans and discounts	$956,485,939 35	$971,835,208 74	$972,026,532 14	$984,691,434 40	$962,571,807 70
Bonds for circulation	380,082,650 00	378,026,900 00	375,127,900 00	370,321,700 00	363,618,100 00
Bonds for deposits ..	14,492,200 00	14,372,200 00	14,147,200 00	14,097,200 00	13,981,500 00
U. S. bonds on hand	18,062,150 00	14,297,650 00	12,753,000 00	13,989,950 00	16,009,550 00
Other stocks and b'ds	28,268,841 69	29,102,197 10	32,010,316 18	33,505,045 15	31,657,960 52
Due from res've ag'ts	89,991,175 34	80,620,878 75	89,788,903 73	85,701,259 82	81,462,682 27
Due from nat'l banks	44,720,394 11	46,039,597 57	48,513,388 86	47,028,769 18	44,831,891 48
Due from State banks	12,724,243 97	12,094,086 39	11,625,647 15	11,963,768 90	11,895,551 08
Real estate, &c......	39,430,952 12	40,312,285 99	40,969,020 49	42,366,647 65	41,583,311 94
Current expenses....	7,790,581 86	7,706,700 42	4,992,044 34	7,841,213 05	9,218,455 47
Premiums paid......	9,006,880 92	8,434,453 14	8,742,393 83	8,670,091 18	9,442,891 54
Cash items	11,734,762 42	13,122,145 88	12,433,100 43	12,758,872 03	11,238,729 72
Clear'g house exch'gs	81,127,796 39	116,970,819 05	88,924,025 93	75,142,863 45	67,886,967 04
Bills of other banks..	18,909,307 00	19,504,640 00	24,261,961 00	18,528,847 00	17,166,190 00
Fractional currency	3,008,592 12	2,702,326 44	2,620,504 26	2,505,631 78	2,901,023 10
Specie............	16,667,106 17	10,620,361 64	18,950,582 30	8,050,329 73	17,070,905 90
Legal-tender notes. ..	78,508,170 00	84,015,928 00	87,492,895 00	76,458,734 00	70,725,077 00
U. S. cert'fs of deposit	37,200,000 00	38,615,000 00	47,310,000 00	48,810,000 00	31,005,000 00
Due from U. S. Treas	21,007,919 76	21,454,422 29	19,640,785 52	19,686,960 30	19,202,256 68
Total........	1,860,810,753 22	1,909,847,891 40	1,913,239,201 16	1,882,209,307 62	1,823,469,752 44

1876.

	MARCH 10.	MAY 12.	JUNE 30.	OCTOBER 2.	DECEMBER 22.
	2,091 banks.	2,089 banks.	2,091 banks.	2,089 banks.	2,082 banks.
Loans and discounts	$950,205,555 62	$939,895,085 34	$933,086,530 45	$931,304,714 06	$929,066,408 42
Bonds for circulation	354,547,750 00	344,537,350 00	339,141,750 00	337,170,400 00	336,705,300 00
Bonds for deposits...	14,216,500 00	14,128,000 00	14,328,000 00	14,608,000 00	14,757,000 00
U. S. bonds on hand..	25,910,650 00	26,577,000 00	30,842,300 00	31,422,150 00	31,937,950 00
Other stocks and b'ds	30,425,430 43	30,905,195 82	32,482,805 75	34,445,157 16	31,565,914 50
Due from res've ag'ts	99,066,363 05	86,769,083 97	87,080,900 00	87,326,950 48	83,789,174 65
Due from nat'l banks	42,341,542 67	44,328,609 46	47,417,029 63	47,525,089 98	44,011,664 97
Due from State banks	11,180,562 15	11,202,193 96	10,989,507 95	12,061,283 08	12,415,841 97
Real estate, &c.....	41,937,617 25	42,183,958 78	42,722,415 27	43,121,942 01	43,498,445 49
Current expenses....	8,296,207 85	6,820,573 35	5,025,549 58	6,987,644 46	9,818,422 88
Premiums paid......	10,946,713 15	10,414,347 28	10,021,484 00	10,715,251 16	10,831,300 66
Cash items..........	9,517,868 86	9,693,186 37	11,724,502 07	12,043,139 68	10,658,709 26
Clear'g-house exch'gs	58,863,182 43	56,806,632 63	75,328,878 84	87,870,817 06	68,027,016 40
Bills of other banks..	18,536,502 00	20,347,964 00	20,398,422 00	15,910,315 00	17,521,663 00
Fractional currency	3,215,594 30	2,771,866 26	1,987,097 44	1,417,203 66	1,146,741 94
Specie..............	20,077,345 85	21,714,504 36	25,218,469 92	21,360,767 42	32,999,647 89
Legal-tender notes...	76,768,446 00	79,858,661 00	90,836,876 00	84,250,847 00	66,221,400 00
U. S. cert'fs of deposit	30,805,000 00	27,380,000 00	27,955,000 00	29,170,000 00	26,095,000 00
Due from U. S. Treas	18,479,112 79	16,911,680 20	17,063,407 65	16,743,695 40	16,359,491 73
Total..........	1,834,360,941 70	1,793,306,002 78	1,825,760,967 28	1,827,265,367 61	1,787,407,093 76

1877.

	JANUARY 20.	APRIL 14.	JUNE 22.	OCTOBER 1.	DECEMBER 28.
	2,083 banks.	2,073 banks.	2,078 banks.	2,080 banks.	2,074 banks.
Loans and discounts	$920,561,018 65	$911,946,833 88	$901,731,416 03	$891,920,503 54	$881,856,744 87
Bonds for circulation	337,590,700 00	339,658,100 00	337,754,100 00	336,810,950 00	343,860,550 00
Bonds for deposits ..	14,782,000 00	15,084,000 00	14,971,000 00	14,903,000 00	13,538,000 00
U. S. bonds on hand	31,988,650 00	32,964,250 00	32,344,050 00	30,088,700 00	28,470,800 00
Other stocks and b'ds	31,819,930 20	32,554,594 44	35,653,755 29	34,435,995 21	32,169,491 03
Due from res've ag'ts	88,698,308 85	84,942,718 41	82,010,316 18	28,484,133 12	75,960,087 27
Due from nat'l banks	44,844,616 88	42,027,778 81	44,567,303 03	45,217,246 82	44,123,924 97
Due from State banks	13,680,990 81	11,911,437 36	11,246,349 79	11,415,761 60	11,479,945 65
Real estate, &c......	43,704,335 47	44,736,549 09	44,818,722 07	45,229,983 25	45,511,932 25
Current expenses....	4,131,516 48	7,842,296 86	7,910,864 84	6,915,792 50	8,958,903 60
Premiums paid......	10,991,714 50	10,494,505 12	10,320,674 34	9,219,174 62	8,841,939 09
Cash items..........	10,205,464 19	10,410,623 87	10,099,088 46	11,674,587 50	10,205,059 49
Clear'g-house exch'gs	81,117,889 04	85,159,422 71	57,861,481 13	74,525,215 89	64,866,415 01
Bills of other banks..	18,418,727 00	17,942,681 00	20,782,848 00	15,331,467 00	20,312,692 00
Fractional currency	1,238,228 08	1,111,820 09	1,055,123 61	900,805 47	778,084 78
Specie..............	49,709,267 55	27,070,037 78	21,335,006 66	22,658,820 31	32,967,403 70
Legal-tender notes ..	72,680,710 00	72,351,579 00	78,004,386 00	66,920,664 00	70,568,248 00
U. S. cert'fs of deposit	25,470,000 00	32,100,000 00	44,430,000 00	33,410,000 00	26,515,000 00
Due from U. S. Treas	16,441,509 98	16,901,040 84	17,932,574 60	16,021,733 01	16,493,577 08
Total..........	1,818,174,517 68	1,796,603,275 29	1,774,352,833 81	1,741,084,663 84	1,737,205,145 79

Banks from October, 1863, to October, 1878—Continued.

1875.

Liabilities.	MARCH 1. 2,029 banks.	MAY 1. 2,046 banks.	JUNE 30. 2,076 banks.	OCTOBER 1. 2,088 banks.	DECEMBER 17. 2,086 banks.
Capital stock	$496,272,901 00	$498,717,143 00	$501,568,563 50	$504,829,769 00	$505,485,865 00
Surplus fund	131,249,079 47	131,604,608 66	133,169,094 79	134,356,076 41	133,085,422 30
Undivided profits	51,650,243 62	55,907,619 95	52,160,104 68	52,964,953 50	59,204,957 81
Nat'l bank circulation	324,525,340 00	323,321,230 00	318,148,406 00	318,350,379 00	314,979,451 00
State bank circulation	824,876 00	815,229 00	786,844 00	772,348 00	752,722 00
Dividends unpaid	1,601,255 48	2,501,742 39	6,105,519 34	4,003,534 90	1,353,396 80
Individual deposits	647,735,879 69	695,347,677 70	686,478,630 48	664,579,619 39	618,517,245 74
U. S. deposits	7,971,932 75	6,797,972 00	6,714,328 70	6,507,531 59	6,652,556 67
Dep'ts U.S.dis.officers	5,330,414 16	2,766,387 41	3,459,061 80	4,271,195 19	4,232,550 87
Due to national banks	137,735,121 44	127,280,034 02	138,914,828 39	129,810,681 60	110,843,605 44
Due to State banks	55,294,663 84	53,037,582 89	55,714,055 18	49,918,530 95	47,048,174 56
Notes re-discounted	4,841,600 20	5,671,031 44	4,261,464 45	5,254,453 66	5,257,160 61
Bills payable	4,786,436 57	6,079,632 94	5,758,299 85	6,500,234 43	7,056,583 64
Total	1,869,819,753 22	1,909,847,891 40	1,913,239,201 16	1,882,209,307 62	1,823,469,752 44

1876.

	MARCH 10. 2,091 banks.	MAY 12. 2,089 banks.	JUNE 30. 2,091 banks.	OCTOBER 2. 2,089 banks.	DECEMBER 22. 2,082 banks.
Capital stock	$504,818,666 00	$500,982,006 00	$500,393,796 00	$499,802,232 00	$497,482,016 00
Surplus fund	133,091,739 50	131,795,199 94	131,897,197 21	132,202,282 00	131,390,664 67
Undivided profits	51,177,031 26	49,039,278 75	46,609,341 51	46,445,215 59	52,327,715 08
Nat'l bank circulation	307,476,155 00	300,252,085 00	294,444,678 00	291,544,020 00	292,011,575 00
State bank circulation	714,539 00	667,060 00	658,938 00	628,847 00	608,548 00
Dividends unpaid	1,405,829 06	2,325,523 51	6,116,679 30	3,848,705 64	1,286,540 28
Individual deposits	620,674,211 05	612,355,096 59	641,432,886 08	651,385,210 19	619,350,223 06
U. S. deposits	6,606,394 90	8,493,878 18	7,667,722 97	7,256,801 42	6,727,155 14
Dep'ts U.S.dis.officers	4,313,915 45	2,505,273 30	3,392,939 48	3,746,781 58	4,749,615 39
Due to national banks	139,407,880 06	127,880,045 04	131,702,164 87	131,535,969 04	122,351,818 09
Due to State banks	54,002,131 54	46,706,069 52	51,403,995 59	48,250,111 63	48,685,392 14
Notes re-discounted	4,631,882 57	4,653,460 08	3,867,622 21	4,464,407 31	4,553,158 76
Bills payable	6,049,566 31	5,650,126 87	6,173,006 03	6,154,784 21	5,882,672 15
Total	1,834,369,941 70	1,793,306,002 78	1,825,760,967 28	1,827,265,367 61	1,787,407,093 76

1877.

	JANUARY 20. 2,083 banks.	APRIL 14. 2,073 banks.	JUNE 22. 2,078 banks.	OCTOBER 1. 2,080 banks.	DECEMBER 28. 2,074 banks.
Capital stock	$493,634,611 00	$489,684,645 00	$481,044,771 00	$479,467,771 00	$477,128,771 00
Surplus fund	130,224,169 02	127,793,390 52	124,714,072 93	122,776,121 24	121,618,455 32
Undivided profits	37,456,530 32	45,609,418 27	50,508,351 70	44,572,678 72	51,530,910 18
Nat'l bank circulation	292,851,351 00	294,710,313 00	290,602,057 00	291,874,236 00	299,240,475 00
State bank circulation	581,242 00	535,963 00	521,611 00	481,738 00	470,540 00
Dividends unpaid	2,448,909 70	1,853,974 70	1,398,101 52	3,623,703 43	1,404,176 34
Individual deposits	659,891,969 76	641,772,528 08	636,267,529 20	616,403,987 12	604,512,514 52
U. S. deposits	7,234,696 96	7,584,267 72	7,187,431 67	7,972,714 75	6,529,631 09
Dep'ts U.S.dis.officers	3,108,316 55	3,076,878 70	3,710,167 20	2,376,983 02	3,780,759 43
Due to national banks	130,293,566 36	125,422,444 43	121,443,601 23	115,628,951 38	115,773,660 58
Due to State banks	49,965,770 27	48,604,820 09	48,352,583 90	46,577,430 88	44,807,958 79
Notes re-discounted	4,000,063 82	3,985,459 75	2,953,128 58	3,791,219 47	4,651,784 51
Bills payable	6,483,320 92	5,969,241 94	6,249,126 88	6,137,116 83	5,843,107 03
Total	1,818,174,517 68	1,796,603,275 29	1,774,352,833 81	1,741,084,663 84	1,737,295,145 79

Aggregate resources and liabilities of the National

1878.

Resources.	MARCH 15.	MAY 1.	JUNE 29.	OCTOBER 1.
	2.063 banks.	2,059 banks.	2.056 banks.	2,053 banks.
Loans and discounts	$854,750,708 87	$847,620,392 49	$855,078,133 13	$833,988,450 59
Bonds for circulation.........	343,871,350 00	345,256,350 00	347,332,100 00	347,556,650 00
Bonds for deposits	13,329,000 00	19,536,000 00	28,371,000 00	47,936,850 00
U. S. bonds on hand..........	34,881,600 00	33,615,700 00	40,479,900 00	46,785,600 00
Other stocks and bonds	34,674,397 21	34,697,320 53	36,694,996 24	36,859,534 82
Due from reserve agents.....	86,016,990 78	71,331,219 27	78,875,055 92	85,083,418 51
Due from national banks.....	39,692,105 87	40,545,522 72	41,897,858 89	41,492,918 75
Due from State banks........	11,683,050 17	12,413,579 10	12,232,316 30	12,314,698 11
Real estate, furniture, &c....	45,792,363 73	45,901,536 93	46,153,409 35	46,702,476 26
Current expenses	7,786,572 42	7,239,305 78	4,718,618 66	6,272,566 73
Premiums paid	7,806,252 00	7,574,255 95	7,335,454 49	7,134,735 68
Cash items..................	10,107,583 76	10,989,440 78	11,525,376 07	10,982,432 89
Clearing-house exchanges....	66,498,965 23	95,525,134 28	87,498,287 82	82,372,537 88
Bills of other banks..........	16,250,569 00	18,363,335 00	17,063,576 00	16,929,721 00
Fractional currency..........	697,398 86	661,044 69	610,084 25	515,661 04
Specie	54,729,558 02	40,023,756 06	29,251,469 77	30,688,606 59
Legal-tender notes	64,034,972 00	67,245,975 00	71,643,402 00	64,428,600 00
U. S. certificates of deposit...	20,605,000 00	20,995,000 00	36,905,000 00	32,690,000 00
Due from U. S. Treasurer....	16,257,608 98	16,364,039 47	16,798,667 62	16,543,674 36
Total...................	1,729,465,956 90	1,741,898,959 05	1,750,464,706 51	1,767,279,133 21

Banks from October, 1863, to October, 1878—Continued.

1 8 7 8.

Liabilities.	MARCH 15.	MAY 1.	JUNE 29.	OCTOBER 1.
	2,063 banks.	2,059 banks.	2,056 banks.	2,053 banks.
Capital stock	$473,052,541 00	$471,971,627 00	$470,393,366 00	$466,147,436 00
Surplus fund	120,870,290 10	119,231,126 13	118,178,530 75	116,897,779 96
Undivided profits	45,040,851 85	43,938,961 98	40,482,522 64	40,936,213 58
National bank circulation	300,926,284 00	301,884,704 00	299,621,059 00	301,888,092 00
State bank circulation	439,339 00	426,504 00	417,808 00	413,913 00
Dividends unpaid	1,207,472 68	1,930,669 58	5,466,350 52	3,118,389 91
Individual deposits	602,882,585 17	625,479,771 12	621,632,160 06	620,236,176 82
U. S. deposits	7,243,253 29	13,811,474 14	22,686,610 67	41,654,812 08
Deposits U. S. disburs'g officers	3,004,064 90	2,392,281 61	2,903,531 99	3,342,794 73
Due to national banks	123,230,448 50	109,720,396 70	117,845,405 88	122,496,513 92
Due to State banks	43,979,239 39	44,006,551 05	43,360,527 86	42,636,703 42
Notes re-discounted	2,465,390 79	2,834,012 00	2,453,839 77	3,007,324 85
Bills payable	4,215,196 23	4,270,879 74	5,022,894 37	4,502,982 92
Total	1,729,465,956 90	1,741,898,959 05	1,750,464,706 51	1,767,279,133 21

9 C C

ABSTRACT

OF

REPORTS OF THE CONDITION

OF

THE NATIONAL BANKS

ON

DECEMBER 28, 1877, MARCH 15, MAY 1, JUNE 29, AND OCTOBER 1, 1878.

———

Arranged by States, Territories, and Reserve Cities.

———

NOTE.—The abstract of each State is exclusive of any reserve-city therein.

Abstract of reports since October 1, 1877.

MAINE.

Resources.	DECEMBER 28. 72 banks.	MARCH 15. 72 banks.	MAY 1. 72 banks.	JUNE 29. 72 banks.	OCTOBER 1. 72 banks.
Loans and discounts	$14,770,773 20	$14,258,671 39	$14,387,057 92	$14,171,381 30	$13,559,729 60
Bonds for circulation	9,499,250 00	9,510,250 00	9,516,250 00	9,516,250 00	9,616,250 00
Bonds for deposits	170,000 00	170,000 00	170,000 00	170,000 00	195,000 00
U. S. bonds on hand	231,850 00	222,000 00	280,050 00	298,300 00	380,750 00
Other stocks and b'ds	434,243 90	495,562 08	443,856 33	437,838 83	449,946 17
Due from res've ag'ts	1,703,349 24	2,031,123 57	1,836,460 67	1,822,615 30	2,557,353 20
Due from nat'l banks	230,626 21	193,305 61	149,291 48	210,442 59	234,207 89
Due from State banks	12,024 89	12,440 82	7,846 59	15,464 34	4,412 22
Real estate, &c	322,627 86	327,958 26	330,542 43	327,722 95	330,237 95
Current expenses	58,846 98	44,763 13	51,642 25	21,555 01	46,581 70
Premiums paid	103,717 22	89,343 71	80,696 60	62,768 19	53,716 41
Cash items	336,567 34	310,684 16	231,330 07	384,818 89	328,901 63
Clear'g-house exch'gs					
Bills of other banks	384,492 00	308,932 00	364,260 00	304,661 00	327,012 00
Fractional currency	7,698 21	5,150 94	6,717 92	6,141 49	5,154 25
Specie	63,841 44	86,512 77	110,616 82	120,487 12	135,952 39
Legal-tender notes	513,210 00	411,187 00	388,842 00	428,745 00	423,106 00
U. S. cert's of deposit	5,000 00	5,000 00	5,000 00	5,000 00	5,000 00
Due from U. S. Treas.	462,919 21	437,329 02	444,325 87	438,154 57	459,185 85
Total	29,311,037 70	28,929,215 06	28,804,786 95	28,742,346 58	29,112,497 26

NEW HAMPSHIRE.

	46 banks.	46 banks.	46 banks.	46 banks.	46 banks.
Loans and discounts	$6,755,448 74	$6,589,681 01	$6,516,180 41	$6,490,789 54	$6,547,168 78
Bonds for circulation	5,755,000 00	5,755,000 00	5,755,000 00	5,755,000 00	5,755,000 00
Bonds for deposits	337,000 00	362,000 00	372,000 00	407,000 00	475,350 00
U. S. bonds on hand	85,700 00	125,550 00	125,900 00	154,700 00	330,350 00
Other stocks and b'ds	490,423 81	517,897 27	508,141 75	586,196 36	601,755 96
Due from res've ag'ts	1,098,336 30	1,078,698 45	974,926 30	1,128,049 25	1,040,827 86
Due from nat'l banks	22,885 68	8,930 81	50,729 76	37,284 58	67,897 55
Due from State banks	28,151 38	42,252 15	49,245 56	36,750 90	21,735 22
Real estate, &c	259,388 11	256,676 54	254,446 26	248,217 96	258,164 68
Current expenses	54,328 59	45,497 06	46,471 54	41,061 07	44,920 76
Premiums paid	68,952 94	66,060 64	62,955 58	55,587 48	57,400 57
Cash items	107,161 59	123,979 17	104,778 66	93,935 26	114,086 77
Clear'g-house exch'gs					
Bills of other banks	283,259 00	213,602 00	271,077 00	203,435 00	270,292 00
Fractional currency	5,929 57	4,930 86	4,171 95	4,927 92	4,382 96
Specie	29,853 75	54,309 53	62,616 03	65,757 60	74,930 20
Legal-tender notes	171,067 00	148,733 00	144,995 00	134,850 00	139,001 00
U. S. cert's of deposit					
Due from U. S. Treas.	269,625 57	252,625 57	260,525 57	269,725 57	263,925 57
Total	15,822,512 03	15,646,514 06	15,564,161 37	15,713,268 49	16,067,189 88

VERMONT.

	46 banks.	46 banks.	46 banks.	46 banks.	46 banks.
Loans and discounts	$10,821,738 17	$10,499,660 26	$10,556,573 38	$10,523,226 18	$10,320,246 08
Bonds for circulation	7,949,000 00	7,521,060 00	7,636,000 00	7,976,000 00	7,901,600 00
Bonds for deposits	150,000 00	50,000 00	50,000 00	50,000 00	185,000 00
U. S. bonds on hand	275,600 00	636,600 00	680,900 00	380,500 00	353,150 00
Other stocks and b'ds	492,457 50	508,567 10	530,428 10	588,237 87	569,105 99
Due from res've ag'ts	1,123,814 26	930,812 06	774,369 13	947,051 15	982,515 03
Due from nat'l banks	103,528 54	98,485 54	81,070 53	106,547 59	132,742 75
Due from State banks	115 42		10,628 50	387 30	2,753 19
Real estate, &c	315,635 28	355,715 23	352,544 02	352,310 08	355,839 15
Current expenses	45,714 66	25,955 38	33,454 04	38,310 13	31,877 13
Premiums paid	53,252 14	36,943 96	51,054 57	48,349 47	51,088 05
Cash items	95,428 10	82,207 02	100,105 59	85,513 46	78,495 84
Clear'g-house exch'gs					
Bills of other banks	193,651 00	143,049 00	155,310 00	142,712 00	118,257 00
Fractional currency	8,293 56	9,125 12	5,125 44	6,392 05	4,448 61
Specie	33,813 46	38,242 84	42,358 33	58,793 46	84,404 56
Legal-tender notes	306,751 00	326,107 00	298,027 00	315,063 00	310,624 00
U. S. cert's of deposit					
Due from U. S. Treas.	352,513 94	332,343 94	341,216 72	364,467 04	358,012 04
Total	22,320,737 03	21,595,714 45	21,699,165 35	21,992,860 78	21,839,569 42

arranged by States and reserve cities.

MAINE.

Liabilities.	DECEMBER 28.	MARCH 15.	MAY 1.	JUNE 29.	OCTOBER 1.
	72 banks.	72 banks.	72 banks.	72 banks.	72 banks.
Capital stock	$10,760,000 00	$10,760,000 00	$10,760,000 00	$10,760,000 00	$10,760,000 00
Surplus fund	2,369,908 83	2,393,038 75	2,392,188 20	2,383,676 96	2,389,051 62
Undivided profits	1,535,326 50	1,292,190 86	1,283,539 10	1,127,017 86	1,235,439 10
Nat'l bank circulation	8,035,909 00	8,126,829 00	8,215,229 00	8,176,462 00	8,313,222 00
State bank circulation	3,923 00	3,397 00	3,397 00	3,395 00	3,395 00
Dividends unpaid	39,449 95	46,041 97	77,652 20	301,035 34	77,676 64
Individual deposits	5,858,129 65	5,796,443 39	5,600,251 07	5,482,489 65	5,956,171 85
U. S. deposits	59,666 29	72,519 40	79,256 17	68,543 13	85,009 12
Dep'ts U.S.dis.officers	54,242 89	30,797 20	42,440 16	42,503 80	43,537 94
Due to national banks	445,368 57	336,259 73	268,880 16	345,116 96	195,247 52
Due to State banks	24,018 40	23,165 31	42,611 02	19,335 96	40,191 47
Notes re-discounted	115,094 62	36,264 72	34,302 87	32,332 72	13,465 00
Bills payable	10,000 00	12,267 73	5,000 00	437 20	
Total	29,311,037 70	28,929,215 06	28,804,786 95	28,742,346 58	29,112,497 26

NEW HAMPSHIRE.

	46 banks.	46 banks.	46 banks.	46 banks.	46 banks.
Capital stock	$5,740,000 00	$5,740,000 00	$5,740,000 00	$5,740,000 00	$5,740,000 00
Surplus fund	1,010,931 51	1,020,710 85	1,014,387 32	1,025,314 79	1,030,725 86
Undivided profits	650,454 40	553,075 57	529,403 84	508,689 19	539,280 62
Nat'l bank circulation	4,989,133 00	5,038,712 00	5,089,573 00	4,994,362 00	5,047,940 00
State bank circulation	8,874 00	7,803 00	7,803 00	7,787 00	7,717 00
Dividends unpaid	24,020 64	20,326 74	30,862 24	86,007 62	21,802 64
Individual deposits	2,952,769 77	2,759,329 54	2,810,976 28	2,908,906 66	3,165,891 46
U. S. deposits	114,079 50	151,480 98	141,917 47	185,935 68	241,194 03
Dep'ts U.S.officers	134,633 60	152,298 61	34,646 29	107,308 15	101,963 70
Due to national banks	149,382 80	122,990 90	97,327 80	116,709 31	96,170 00
Due to State banks	23,155 90	53,469 38	48,590 73	7,108 83	41,150 29
Notes re-discounted	17,476 91	12,616 49	18,673 40	25,049 26	33,354 28
Bills payable	8,200 00	13,700 00			
Total	15,822,512 63	15,646,514 06	15,564,161 37	15,713,268 49	16,067,189 88

VERMONT.

	46 banks.	46 banks.	46 banks.	46 banks.	46 banks.
Capital stock	$8,568,700 00	$8,568,700 00	$8,568,700 00	$8,568,700 00	$8,466,000 00
Surplus fund	2,124,476 42	2,024,657 21	2,056,301 13	2,051,574 15	2,070,470 24
Undivided profits	756,574 88	567,661 33	577,199 43	600,998 77	534,630 38
Nat'l bank circulation	7,000,218 00	6,663,018 00	6,759,345 00	6,928,688 00	6,939,072 00
State bank circulation	6,195 00	6,195 00	6,195 00	6,193 00	6,193 00
Dividends unpaid	27,894 76	11,419 59	11,026 02	110,653 82	11,088 14
Individual deposits	3,545,915 63	3,587,833 61	3,463,569 32	3,502,101 07	3,589,200 95
U. S. deposits	20,371 68	21,703 03	25,532 98	25,734 69	126,397 64
Dep'ts U.S.dis.officers	8,036 58	4,962 80	7,362 77	4,348 90	7,160 55
Due to national banks	35,431 04	23,673 65	57,137 21	92,249 24	43,156 52
Due to State banks	2,600 26	121 93	52 94	344 40	
Notes re-discounted	3,000 00				4,000 00
Bills payable	221,322 78	115,768 30	166,743 55	101,274 74	42,200 00
Total	22,320,737 03	21,595,714 45	21,699,165 35	21,992,860 78	21,839,569 42

Abstract of reports since October 1, 1877, arranged

MASSACHUSETTS.

Resources.	DECEMBER 28.	MARCH 15.	MAY 1.	JUNE 29.	OCTOBER 1.
	183 banks.	183 banks.	183 banks.	182 banks.	182 banks.
Loans and discounts	$64,648,046 32	$62,392,215 89	$60,902,100 47	$58,870,939 02	$58,948,073 69
Bonds for circulation	40,228,800 00	40,386,800 00	40,507,900 00	40,873,900 00	40,983,900 00
Bonds for deposits...	600,000 00	453,000 00	533,000 00	780,000 00	1,686,750 00
U. S. bonds on hand..	1,865,450 00	2,260,450 00	2,815,000 00	3,885,550 00	4,485,400 00
Other stocks and b'ds	2,133,531 49	2,376,123 97	2,481,744 51	2,731,089 88	2,840,485 49
Due from res'veng'ts	5,872,907 85	7,150,326 09	7,643,215 66	7,052,454 23	7,754,797 95
Due from nat'l banks	652,538 73	820,828 44	675,557 67	662,234 80	702,167 20
Due from State banks	55,909 33	131,183 53	203,222 38	181,866 87	158,280 44
Real estate, &c	2,038,017 14	2,045,716 30	2,080,116 41	2,117,815 11	2,163,876 68
Current expenses....	442,104 66	585,416 71	222,364 32	259,055 53	247,410 18
Premiums paid	633,220 96	581,357 68	498,891 43	517,183 48	507,131 18
Cash items	591,426 98	722,461 73	683,707 20	685,758 72	809,956 10
Clear'g-house exch'gs					
Bills of other banks..	1,177,380 00	887,114 00	1,058,599 00	975,468 00	1,204,973 00
Fractional currency .	44,325 35	42,822 44	35,936 32	31,129 12	27,469 04
Specie	389,867 99	748,190 49	802,966 40	655,281 72	769,933 38
Legal-tender notes ..	1,640,007 00	1,400,383 00	1,467,912 00	1,444,827 00	1,451,782 00
U. S. cert's of deposit	315,000 00	285,000 00	255,000 00	290,000 00	265,000 00
Due from U. S. Treas	1,973,700 45	1,888,520 38	1,881,604 55	1,905,544 45	1,950,449 85
Total	125,302,234 25	125,157,910 65	124,748,838 32	123,920,088 93	126,957,836 18

CITY OF BOSTON.

	55 banks.	55 banks.	54 banks.	54 banks.	54 banks.
Loans and discounts.	$96,484,726 57	$93,508,275 17	$92,818,065 91	$92,795,593 04	$91,408,097 03
Bonds for circulation	29,730,500 00	29,930,500 00	29,873,500 00	30,634,500 00	30,144,500 00
Bonds for deposits...	150,000 00	250,000 00	800,000 00	2,425,000 00	5,952,300 00
U. S. bonds on hand..	1,932,800 00	1,970,600 00	2,661,350 00	4,545,750 00	3,859,000 00
Other stocks and b'ds	1,102,759 07	1,203,110 30	1,344,518 50	1,292,031 13	1,534,434 79
Due from res'veng'ts	6,784,704 23	8,230,207 45	8,186,417 05	8,048,855 22	9,768,490 98
Due from nat'l banks	3,389,316 13	4,772,704 41	5,004,333 17	6,507,645 06	5,381,730 74
Due from State banks	285,275 41	229,217 21	363,816 67	257,871 74	257,007 55
Real estate, &c	3,565,615 06	3,685,268 23	3,731,302 42	3,737,813 37	3,817,483 99
Current expenses....	612,546 03	1,273,348 13	161,814 62	369,579 59	46,077 67
Premiums paid	708,897 52	559,214 74	481,608 90	558,710 53	561,645 02
Cash items	322,435 68	318,371 49	338,988 65	438,969 72	392,813 69
Clear'g-house exch'gs	5,249,633 55	6,044,088 33	5,164,175 00	7,303,196 82	6,560,741 88
Bills of other banks..	1,898,287 00	1,181,194 00	1,022,881 00	1,267,202 00	1,365,072 00
Fractional currency .	12,518 32	12,056 34	11,561 49	10,939 65	8,593 00
Specie	3,743,115 02	6,090,898 44	5,208,122 89	2,814,102 47	3,448,609 15
Legal-tender notes ...	3,340,487 00	2,611,728 00	2,343,505 00	3,730,582 00	3,612,812 00
U. S. cert's of deposit	2,565,000 00	1,235,000 00	775,000 00	2,830,000 00	2,195,000 00
Due from U. S. Treas	1,577,708 50	1,470,919 00	1,425,655 50	1,558,157 00	1,507,539 00
Total	165,456,325 09	164,686,761 24	161,798,616 77	170,546,499 34	171,821,949 39

RHODE ISLAND.

	61 banks.	61 banks.	61 banks.	61 banks.	61 banks.
Loans and discounts	$26,042,752 64	$25,189,375 66	$25,006,536 58	$24,520,543 22	$24,144,486 28
Bonds for circulation	14,245,400 00	14,305,400 00	14,326,400 00	14,451,400 00	14,484,400 00
Bonds for deposits ..	150,000 00	150,000 00	150,000 00	150,000 00	150,000 00
U. S. bonds on hand..	678,000 00	811,500 00	906,500 00	950,000 00	1,220,550 00
Other stocks and b'ds	346,824 36	354,095 85	321,520 85	312,447 35	361,793 35
Due from res'veng'ts	2,117,678 15	1,811,405 91	1,602,550 33	2,370,896 33	2,093,616 63
Due from nat'l banks	524,524 50	418,166 63	546,923 02	391,338 89	465,395 30
Due from State banks	93,596 13	97,689 76	178,803 08	138,925 08	107,229 41
Real estate, &c	679,314 10	667,673 75	675,979 18	719,610 54	732,637 01
Current expenses ...	135,927 63	121,876 43	136,106 65	71,364 96	113,085 88
Premiums paid	102,486 69	108,723 73	115,500 59	101,310 73	120,094 14
Cash items	585,281 80	687,158 48	482,392 88	599,875 89	462,423 80
Clear'g-house exch'gs					
Bills of other banks..	306,609 00	214,384 00	562,840 00	236,464 00	266,608 00
Fractional currency .	12,121 22	11,363 26	11,959 02	9,882 85	9,709 21
Specie	97,623 75	157,665 57	164,367 73	170,430 05	223,944 01
Legal-tender notes ..	524,967 00	408,505 00	462,984 00	409,371 00	376,627 00
U. S. cert's of deposit					
Due from U. S. Treas	659,302 50	634,302 50	646,077 50	647,977 50	698,920 00
Total	47,293,412 47	46,149,316 53	46,352,341 71	46,161,838 39	46,001,711 04

by States and reserve cities—Continued.

MASSACHUSETTS.

Liabilities.	DECEMBER 28.	MARCH 15.	MAY 1.	JUNE 29.	OCTOBER 1.
	183 banks.	183 banks.	183 banks.	182 banks.	182 banks.
Capital stock	$44,347,000 00	$44,297,000 00	$44,297,000 00	$44,197,000 00	$44,165,280 00
Surplus fund.........	13,237,871 81	13,176,617 08	13,011,505 52	12,832,213 40	12,518,881 90
Undivided profits....	4,046,177 87	4,667,504 56	3,121,265 05	3,478,681 69	2,026,081 21
Nat'l bank circulation	34,650,199 00	35,350,743 00	35,788,001 00	35,320,657 00	35,782,746 00
State bank circulation	9,495 00	9,495 00	9,493 00	9,493 00	9,490 00
Dividends unpaid....	88,219 22	77,189 08	205,940 75	293,855 97	748,715 81
Individual deposits ..	26,551,322 42	25,492,649 54	26,260,793 24	25,115,332 50	27,822,202 48
U. S. deposits........	201,242 07	262,080 80	353,921 39	539,764 33	1,718,890 47
Dep'ts U.S.dis.officers	24,693 62	12,128 66	3,759 47	25,296 16	2,995 80
Due to national banks	1,498,156 78	1,275,023 00	1,046,027 61	1,368,921 69	855,416 59
Due to State banks ..	126,933 90	85,550 89	140,407 47	97,445 77	99,254 70
Notes re-discounted..	188,088 74	144,079 45	257,674 23	173,410 75	76,831 23
Bills payable........	242,832 92	306,049 59	253,049 59	468,016 67	230,149 99
Total.	125,302,234 25	125,157,910 65	124,748,838 32	123,920,088 93	126,957,836 18

CITY OF BOSTON.

	55 banks.	55 banks.	54 banks.	54 banks.	54 banks.
Capital stock	$52,850,000 00	$52,350,000 00	$52,125,000 00	$51,825,000 00	$51,050,000 00
Surplus fund.........	11,538,508 87	11,214,931 75	10,717,220 59	10,494,276 30	10,301,059 74
Undivided profits....	2,729,523 39	4,053,235 04	1,855,938 00	2,810,116 62	1,583,759 10
Nat'l bank circulation	24,730,078 00	25,853,724 00	26,018,640 00	25,743,612 00	25,802,794 00
State bank circulation					
Dividends unpaid....	45,272 03	30,064 43	93,404 43	57,239 93	935,061 93
Individual deposits ..	52,266,189 79	50,690,122 81	48,359,617 25	53,483,643 53	52,791,749 31
U. S. deposits	15,790 21	57,441 57	688,822 53	2,305,725 24	5,957,660 60
Dep'ts U.S.dis.officers	7,821 65	7,009 20	8,239 07	7,873 42	20,270 83
Due to national banks	16,613,917 77	15,977,086 24	16,995,764 79	18,627,381 73	17,968,305 24
Due to State banks...	3,626,222 48	3,600,067 78	4,225,219 86	4,221,630 57	4,174,993 78
Notes re-discounted..		23,078 33			37,536 98
Bills payable	1,030,000 00	830,000 00	710,750 25	970,000 00	1,108,757 88
Total	165,456,325 09	164,686,761 24	161,798,616 77	170,546,499 34	171,821,949 39

RHODE ISLAND.

	61 banks.	61 banks.	61 banks.	61 banks.	61 banks.
Capital stock........	$20,009,800 00	$20,009,800 00	$20,009,800 00	$20,009,800 00	$20,009,800 00
Surplus fund.........	3,642,186 78	3,515,093 80	3,572,688 64	3,591,649 44	3,519,078 42
Undivided profits....	1,497,601 57	1,334,976 02	1,333,532 61	1,086,231 98	1,201,561 40
Nat'l bank circulation	12,374,994 00	12,646,437 00	12,738,425 00	12,502,155 00	12,659,739 00
State bank circulation	9,555 00	9,094 00	9,094 00	9,094 00	8,070 00
Dividends unpaid....	117,071 29	134,109 92	121,489 23	360,276 98	206,467 53
Individual deposits...	7,542,625 03	6,921,242 54	6,915,844 22	6,911,658 13	6,794,412 60
U. S. deposits........	59,678 52	53,705 57	72,908 47	60,454 02	70,161 94
Dep'ts U.S.dis.officers	21,817 49	28,414 56	8,166 30	24,405 81	22,779 20
Due to national banks	1,133,713 00	879,802 01	653,843 35	958,365 18	875,109 26
Due to State banks ..	690,939 63	474,870 33	840,549 89	647,657 85	654,531 51
Notes re-discounted..	83,400 07	73,920 78	16,000 00		
Bills payable........	100,000 00	50,000 00	50,000 00		
Total	47,293,412 47	46,149,316 53	46,352,341 71	46,161,838 39	46,001,711 01

Abstract of reports since October 1, 1877, arranged

CONNECTICUT.

Resources.	DECEMBER 28. 81 banks.	MARCH 15. 81 banks.	MAY 1. 81 banks.	JUNE 29. 81 banks.	OCTOBER 1. 82 banks.
Loans and discounts	$33,912,922 04	$32,363,766 03	$32,233,058 36	$31,709,329 45	$30,809,436 65
Bonds for circulation	19,527,100 00	19,790,600 00	19,940,600 00	19,960,600 00	20,119,600 00
Bonds for deposits...	270,000 00	270,000 00	270,000 00	285,000 00	280,000 00
U. S. bonds on hand..	1,438,250 00	1,587,850 00	1,809,500 00	2,021,650 00	2,311,350 00
Other stocks and b'ds	1,092,091 30	1,144,840 61	1,145,258 08	1,283,615 27	1,284,006 38
Due from res've ag'ts	4,116,026 29	5,595,531 42	3,844,638 43	4,971,195 02	4,733,833 25
Due from nat'l banks	1,996,866 57	1,926,193 58	2,035,874 01	1,792,044 55	2,034,155 93
Due from State banks	260,165 65	198,795 13	140,351 65	134,171 29	127,277 09
Real estate, &c	1,453,073 94	1,578,757 75	1,542,004 00	1,583,894 94	1,609,303 19
Current expenses....	285,513 60	191,477 79	246,948 33	104,608 65	228,480 74
Premiums paid	237,002 81	226,445 84	236,250 37	240,983 95	250,916 10
Cash items	563,976 70	516,138 43	587,127 81	679,015 72	720,027 35
Clear'g-house exch'gs					
Bills of other banks .	834,508 00	452,485 00	681,410 00	732,392 00	799,927 00
Fractional currency	25,042 20	18,709 63	19,852 91	18,585 87	16,951 18
Specie	184,991 13	355,539 83	410,900 61	416,574 67	409,103 87
Legal-tender notes ..	1,333,550 00	1,048,747 00	1,168,414 00	1,195,057 00	1,229,765 00
U. S. cert's of deposit	85,000 00	60,000 00	40,000 00	30,000 00	30,000 00
Due from U. S. Treas	808,134 74	884,927 15	929,572 00	918,700 35	961,204 75
Total	68,514,214 97	68,210,805 19	67,299,761 46	68,047,418 73	67,955,338 48

NEW YORK.

	226 banks.	225 banks.	225 banks.	225 banks.	226 banks.
Loans and discounts.	$64,695,463 46	$61,848,572 59	$62,954,481 21	$62,206,208 47	$60,382,873 60
Bonds for circulation	29,683,400 00	29,532,900 00	29,542,900 00	29,620,600 00	29,687,600 00
Bonds for deposits ..	995,500 00	945,500 00	975,500 00	975,500 00	1,025,500 00
U. S. bonds on hand...	2,592,100 00	3,204,650 00	3,420,200 00	3,524,000 00	4,083,900 00
Other stocks and b'ds	2,889,917 47	3,234,154 04	3,341,704 07	3,356,016 93	3,668,581 37
Due from res've ag'ts.	9,473,540 42	10,049,544 54	7,204,569 02	8,297,756 46	7,978,917 34
Due from nat'l banks	1,906,845 42	2,068,129 04	2,019,790 87	1,889,919 94	1,792,039 34
Due from State banks	540,399 32	601,053 53	515,585 02	544,012 01	475,493 75
Real estate, &c	3,147,888 29	3,158,876 90	3,153,010 72	3,182,526 83	3,208,821 37
Current expenses ...	711,420 15	527,488 11	605,359 81	407,666 69	428,842 40
Premiums paid	423,196 79	371,586 82	388,580 40	371,798 47	331,290 57
Cash items	1,393,122 70	1,213,854 82	1,706,784 00	1,441,302 41	1,326,502 88
Clear'g-house exch'gs					
Bills of other banks..	1,189,349 00	830,423 00	890,414 00	919,446 00	774,636 00
Fractional currency .	63,953 77	60,704 13	52,204 61	44,996 75	33,964 54
Specie	426,681 34	990,132 34	1,025,064 90	731,584 81	826,231 68
Legal-tender notes ..¹	3,566,690 00	3,123,053 00	3,353,485 00	3,379,842 00	3,264,997 00
U. S. cert's of deposit.	385,000 00	345,000 00	340,000 00	380,000 00	375,000 00
Due from U. S. Treas.	1,374,692 93	1,386,512 54	1,357,799 15	1,425,108 24	1,399,227 46
Total	125,459,161 06	123,492,135 40	122,847,432 78	122,707,286 01	121,064,419 30

CITY OF NEW YORK.

	47 banks.	47 banks.	47 banks.	47 banks.	47 banks.
Loans and discounts.	$170,414,916 98	$168,694,271 15	$162,623,046 71	$164,380,449 28	$169,716,053 82
Bonds for circulation	24,041,500 00	24,054,000 00	24,400,500 00	24,390,500 00	24,195,500 00
Bonds for deposits...	800,000 00	830,000 00	6,209,000 00	12,799,000 00	26,715,550 00
U. S. bonds on hand ..	9,062,750 00	12,763,350 00	7,911,050 00	8,508,500 00	11,463,900 00
Other stocks and b'ds	7,483,067 79	8,657,685 32	8,270,148 01	9,622,173 07	9,193,663 65
Due from res've ag'ts					
Due from nat'l banks	13,085,608 87	9,992,482 83	11,821,556 40	12,454,285 87	11,365,909 73
Due from State banks	2,485,857 65	2,719,814 23	3,366,216 84	3,646,869 66	2,181,296 75
Real estate, &c	9,437,234 68	9,423,323 96	9,490,772 22	9,455,000 21	9,465,819 80
Current expenses....	2,183,783 22	928,311 87	1,014,625 66	394,366 40	995,332 78
Premiums paid	1,682,218 23	1,585,684 99	1,602,685 76	1,484,109 32	1,767,160 79
Cash items	1,591,748 56	1,706,596 64	2,194,097 22	2,262,610 97	1,765,187 97
Clear'g-house exch'gs	49,526,584 25	52,048,456 44	79,220,337 06	69,419,672 67	62,454,791 59
Bills of other banks..	1,659,078 00	1,510,462 00	2,177,515 00	2,449,245 00	1,560,623 00
Fractional currency	83,056 90	92,253 58	84,948 33	85,995 63	67,702 89
Specie	21,074,826 20	37,432,017 44	28,085,732 06	13,860,205 22	13,204,602 43
Legal-tender notes ..	15,470,946 00	11,967,287 00	16,356,388 00	21,368,416 00	14,803,468 00
U. S. cert's of deposit.	14,590,000 00	9,860,000 00	11,415,000 00	23,830,000 00	21,660,000 00
Due from U. S. Treas.	1,355,423 88	1,269,112 50	1,426,908 00	1,661,352 92	1,221,207 57
Total	346,928,601 21	355,535,109 95	377,679,527 27	381,982,752 22	384,778,766 77

by States and reserve cities—Continued.

CONNECTICUT.

Liabilities.	DECEMBER 28. 81 banks.	MARCH 15. 81 banks.	MAY 1. 81 banks.	JUNE 29. 81 banks.	OCTOBER 1. 82 banks.
Capital stock	$25,448,120 00	$25,448,120 00	$25,448,120 00	$25,424,620 00	$25,504,620 00
Surplus fund	6,274,202 12	6,329,283 21	6,315,756 98	6,270,345 49	6,214,877 70
Undivided profits	1,886,377 39	1,413,991 95	1,559,818 35	1,066,745 28	1,311,239 58
Nat'l bank circulation	17,037,774 00	17,356,241 00	17,432,952 00	17,121,803 00	17,470,928 00
State bank circulation	56,165 00	52,827 00	48,178 00	47,240 00	47,019 00
Dividends unpaid	92,665 25	87,594 05	115,845 37	588,993 67	103,608 40
Individual deposits	15,049,371 14	14,673,865 93	14,848,706 41	14,546,078 04	15,741,172 32
U. S. deposits	105,183 85	139,929 81	115,836 82	144,261 36	121,447 91
Dep'ts U.S.dis.officers	9,696 15	5,757 31	4,155 67	11,732 76	23,434 58
Due to national banks	2,132,425 70	2,238,220 27	1,059,700 61	2,218,654 23	1,082,854 83
Due to State banks	355,158 44	409,898 73	270,933 22	539,469 12	307,286 20
Notes re-discounted	32,075 93	20,075 93	44,758 03	32,475 78	21,849 96
Bills payable	35,000 00	35,000 00	35,000 00	35,000 00	5,000 00
Total	68,514,214 97	68,210,805 19	67,299,761 46	68,047,418 73	67,955,338 48

NEW YORK.

	226 banks.	225 banks.	225 banks.	225 banks.	226 banks.
Capital stock	$33,689,601 00	$33,476,031 00	$33,401,031 00	$33,351,031 00	$33,293,691 00
Surplus fund	7,778,096 43	7,749,923 51	7,744,157 64	7,622,524 90	7,660,665 17
Undivided profits	5,463,824 17	4,421,449 49	4,639,481 67	4,538,689 25	4,465,500 96
Nat'l bank circulation	26,267,107 00	26,115,378 00	26,166,077 00	25,912,180 00	26,166,062 00
State bank circulation	76,861 00	74,743 00	74,723 00	70,951 00	68,931 00
Dividends unpaid	72,199 88	74,213 11	103,826 52	301,599 73	69,084 00
Individual deposits	46,340,211 28	46,962,474 41	46,174,752 30	44,850,251 78	44,981,103 88
U. S. deposits	403,374 03	450,870 39	603,001 91	549,467 82	560,798 04
Dep'ts U.S.dis.officers	102,450 21	76,327 63	81,061 59	93,084 52	78,160 51
Due to national banks	2,989,025 84	2,196,661 73	1,825,081 37	2,797,886 82	1,677,090 85
Due to State banks	1,182,133 21	1,105,754 70	928,053 26	1,060,187 42	906,625 42
Notes re-discounted	315,628 61	148,978 99	396,410 73	421,741 07	249,640 12
Bills payable	778,558 40	639,329 44	709,774 79	1,137,690 70	797,066 35
Total	125,459,161 06	123,492,135 40	122,847,432 78	122,707,286 01	121,064,419 30

CITY OF NEW YORK.

	47 banks.	47 banks.	47 banks.	47 banks.	47 banks.
Capital stock	$56,900,000 00	$55,900,000 00	$55,900,000 00	$55,800,000 00	$53,800,000 00
Surplus fund	16,441,330 14	16,234,656 82	16,071,228 86	16,097,915 49	15,920,230 13
Undivided profits	10,381,866 54	8,305,782 16	8,839,215 24	7,721,009 25	8,659,800 16
Nat'l bank circulation	20,112,856 00	20,284,665 00	20,379,008 00	20,198,648 00	20,025,861 00
State bank circulation	77,230 00	77,158 00	77,156 00	73,360 00	73,339 00
Dividends unpaid	118,521 63	131,383 46	412,484 91	1,114,450 76	190,704 89
Individual deposits	160,333,699 63	163,452,980 32	189,939,804 50	185,625,384 91	172,441,668 96
U. S. deposits	298,871 07	413,661 17	5,513,265 01	12,891,675 71	26,090,296 84
Dep'ts U.S.dis.officers	140,577 99	162,475 86	108,506 77	132,044 06	131,225 18
Due to national banks	59,817,740 89	69,428,129 57	58,828,691 65	61,741,746 83	68,125,941 13
Due to State banks	22,296,904 32	21,120,217 59	21,602,166 33	20,578,517 21	19,311,699 48
Notes re-discounted					
Bills payable		24,000 00	8,000 00	8,000 00	8,000 00
Total	346,028,601 21	355,535,109 95	377,670,527 27	381,982,752 22	384,778,766 77

Abstract of reports since October 1, 1877, arranged

CITY OF ALBANY.

Resources.	DECEMBER 28. 7 banks.	MARCH 15. 7 banks.	MAY 1. 7 banks.	JUNE 29. 7 banks.	OCTOBER 1. 7 banks.
Loans and discounts	$6,236,642 31	$5,763,654 72	$6,401,856 12	$5,807,174 16	$5,492,689 98
Bonds for circulation	1,810,000 00	1,810,000 00	1,810,000 00	1,810,000 00	1,860,000 00
Bonds for deposits	100,000 00	100,000 00	100,000 00	100,000 00	595,000 00
U. S. bonds on hand	1,571,750 00	671,600 00	670,750 00	1,171,150 00	1,555,250 00
Other stocks and b'ds	292,599 21	287,990 97	287,990 97	233,481 62	232,505 62
Due from res'veng'ts.	1,720,335 13	2,432,864 01	2,505,425 70	1,763,909 46	1,680,391 35
Due from nat'l banks	559,947 66	742,755 66	640,454 95	518,791 89	474,082 43
Due from State banks	217,695 29	289,119 06	204,614 93	195,501 86	129,481 67
Real estate, &c	341,884 05	331,784 05	331,784 05	331,082 63	331,682 63
Current expenses	7,649 96	2,383 32	4,951 13		3,700 00
Premiums paid	254,416 88	143,092 48	143,092 48	175,359 98	168,784 41
Cash items	164,327 22	148,975 62	201,332 44	189,348 69	169,654 68
Clear'g-house exch'gs	69,291 48	56,733 22	127,959 61	113,205 12	111,036 71
Bills of other banks	124,259 00	109,010 00	125,160 00	100,453 00	82,123 00
Fractional currency	3,686 96	3,021 37	3,252 55	4,035 90	3,234 66
Specie	50,130 67	120,732 13	154,294 33	166,556 11	209,684 65
Legal-tender notes	510,411 00	402,124 00	421,427 00	434,015 00	419,290 00
U. S. cert's of deposit	475,000 00	425,000 00	475,000 00	470,000 00	430,000 00
Due from U. S. Treas	86,912 80	88,687 06	84,880 76	72,168 86	81,907 26
Total	14,596,939 62	13,989,527 67	14,754,227 02	13,656,744 28	14,030,561 05

NEW JERSEY.

	69 banks.	69 banks.	69 banks.	69 banks.	68 banks.
Loans and discounts	$23,933,147 90	$22,559,764 71	$22,840,238 18	$22,446,645 91	$22,572,215 56
Bonds for circulation	12,589,350 00	12,701,350 00	12,791,350 00	12,881,350 00	12,785,350 00
Bonds for deposits	250,000 00	250,000 00	250,000 00	250,000 00	393,000 00
U. S. bonds on hand	323,600 00	828,950 00	919,900 00	896,550 00	1,069,550 00
Other stocks and b'ds	574,535 16	584,675 44	652,607 91	612,591 44	659,433 87
Due from res'veng'ts	5,489,153 76	5,747,259 49	4,336,350 51	5,298,709 49	5,900,434 70
Due from nat'l banks	1,388,256 09	1,068,664 56	903,183 13	1,026,771 54	1,147,749 29
Due from State banks	236,779 94	230,721 50	177,878 30	249,590 68	224,200 47
Real estate, &c	1,985,732 56	2,003,203 13	1,953,346 43	1,929,333 30	1,965,124 51
Current expenses	314,495 90	189,361 55	200,361 03	133,913 78	177,631 92
Premiums paid	265,784 90	233,210 91	186,757 20	165,482 85	164,530 21
Cash items	597,386 84	563,389 54	621,431 23	732,300 76	591,907 34
Clear'g-house exch'gs					
Bills of other banks	559,388 00	430,159 00	542,820 00	593,184 00	514,099 00
Fractional currency	20,386 18	19,504 57	15,866 32	15,264 84	12,931 91
Specie	253,410 38	340,922 16	406,021 56	441,213 93	472,880 85
Legal-tender notes	1,663,002 00	1,775,184 00	1,820,485 00	1,647,739 00	1,689,088 00
U. S. cert's of deposit	120,000 00	110,000 00	110,000 00	110,000 00	110,000 00
Due from U. S. Treas.	599,563 16	617,763 16	589,972 74	644,655 01	610,535 01
Total	51,164,033 37	50,254,083 72	49,318,575 54	50,075,296 53	51,060,662 64

PENNSYLVANIA.

	179 banks.	179 banks.	179 banks.	180 banks.	181 banks.
Loans and discounts	$47,278,501 79	$46,037,905 96	$46,665,841 75	$44,629,193 69	$43,567,085 32
Bonds for circulation	25,902,600 00	26,037,600 00	26,114,500 00	26,196,950 00	26,396,950 00
Bonds for deposits	580,000 00	580,000 00	580,000 00	580,000 00	605,000 00
U. S. bonds on hand	1,423,850 00	1,283,600 00	1,417,950 00	1,746,550 00	2,016,400 00
Other stocks and b'ds	2,963,732 45	2,972,574 65	3,032,087 34	3,063,773 69	3,225,212 79
Due from res'veng'ts	4,524,905 95	5,499,790 15	3,848,023 50	4,144,244 07	4,324,795 52
Due from nat'l banks	1,665,332 88	1,754,150 12	1,632,379 93	1,583,321 81	1,504,469 51
Due from State banks	801,900 00	832,471 34	838,802 47	910,437 84	854,567 15
Real estate, &c	2,873,091 97	2,909,905 70	2,930,799 94	2,864,816 11	2,978,277 24
Current expenses	333,756 48	465,519 36	587,090 88	327,505 46	493,272 04
Premiums paid	551,523 50	494,352 07	501,159 11	440,159 35	428,878 85
Cash items	498,086 44	557,796 27	505,808 23	559,279 98	567,493 06
Clear'g-house exch'gs					
Bills of other banks	1,060,528 00	767,601 00	857,676 00	943,958 00	765,338 00
Fractional currency	83,382 39	70,599 04	61,904 41	58,980 72	50,866 70
Specie	410,719 52	468,904 87	617,386 81	701,637 77	889,987 18
Legal-tender notes	3,783,400 00	3,570,406 00	3,930,952 00	3,490,604 00	3,329,432 00
U. S. cert's of deposit	100,000 00	100,000 00	130,000 00	105,000 00	95,000 00
Due from U. S. Treas	1,169,193 85	1,188,918 78	1,208,625 44	1,185,960 92	1,205,193 83
Total	96,004,625 22	95,592,215 31	95,461,047 81	93,532,463 41	93,298,219 19

*by States and reserve cities—*Continued.

CITY OF ALBANY.

Liabilities.	DECEMBER 28.	MARCH 15.	MAY 1.	JUNE 29.	OCTOBER 1.
	7 banks.	7 banks.	7 banks.	7 banks.	7 banks.
Capital stock	$2, 000, 000 00	$2, 000, 000 00	$2, 000, 000 00	$2, 000, 000 00	$2, 000, 000 00
Surplus fund.........	1, 470, 000 00	1, 445, 000 00	1, 445, 000 00	1, 445, 000 00	1, 445, 000 00
Undivided profits....	338, 108 52	224, 280 16	214, 678 89	239, 221 54	199, 983 76
Nat'l bank circulation	1, 510, 440 00	1, 606, 690 00	1, 602, 390 00	1, 575, 640 00	1, 602, 460 00
State bank circulation	9, 189 00				
Dividends unpaid....	15, 086 50	980 00	13, 194 50	21, 010 50	17, 819 50
Individual deposits...	5, 801, 824 78	5, 812, 713 52	6, 804, 724 07	5, 592, 709 94	5, 576, 793 12
U. S. deposits	55, 171 37	59, 696 56	57, 558 59	55, 583 04	551, 938 87
Dep'ts U.S.dis.officers	10, 963 70	5, 542 46	5, 265 70	11, 983 84	14, 910 88
Due to national banks	2, 078, 797 46	2, 135, 749 97	1, 908, 859 84	2, 027, 588 77	2, 062, 841 90
Due to State banks ..	607, 358 29	698, 875 00	702, 555 52	688, 006 65	558, 813 02
Notes re-discounted..					
Bills payable........	700, 000 00				
Total	14, 596, 939 62	13, 989, 527 67	14, 754, 227 02	13, 656, 744 28	14, 030, 561 05

NEW JERSEY.

	69 banks.	69 banks.	69 banks.	69 banks.	68 banks.
Capital stock	$14, 203, 350 00	$14, 183, 350 00	$14, 183, 350 00	$14, 183, 350 00	$14, 033, 350 00
Surplus fund.........	3, 843, 527 77	3, 815, 357 17	3, 670, 908 65	3, 640, 895 85	3, 703, 422 53
Undivided profits....	1, 987, 586 42	1, 558, 605 19	1, 568, 415 13	1, 407, 772 78	1, 375, 280 80
Nat'l bank circulation	11, 196, 836 00	11, 256, 011 00	11, 325, 673 00	11, 318, 806 00	11, 278, 693 00
State bank circulation	32, 865 00	32, 815 00	32, 807 00	32, 792 00	32, 454 00
Dividends unpaid....	34, 379 90	47, 587 57	50, 750 10	272, 968 16	83, 460 68
Individual deposits...	17, 534, 296 48	17, 503, 055 96	16, 761, 324 96	17, 421, 454 07	18, 584, 261 36
U. S. deposits........	124, 680 52	141, 600 69	172, 268 04	144, 248 10	284, 097 62
Dep'ts U.S.dis.officers	11, 205 35	5, 051 37	6, 765 31	10, 685 29	6, 146 79
Due to national banks	1, 789, 019 99	1, 369, 554 95	1, 229, 006 23	1, 323, 399 50	1, 357, 944 94
Due to State banks ..	179, 570 38	209, 776 76	163, 613 53	155, 090 96	191, 701 22
Notes re-discounted..	133, 015 56	79, 018 06	80, 215 09	76, 990 82	48, 149 70
Bills payable........	93, 790 00	51, 790 00	73, 478 50	77, 843 00	81, 700 00
Total	51, 164, 033 37	50, 254, 083 72	49, 318, 575 54	50, 075, 296 58	51, 060, 662 64

PENNSYLVANIA.

	179 banks.	179 banks.	179 banks.	180 banks.	181 banks.
Capital stock........	$28, 559, 340 00	$28, 509, 340 00	$28, 509, 740 00	$28, 464, 840 00	$28, 469, 840 00
Surplus fund........	7, 674, 949 42	7, 687, 364 00	7, 697, 713 96	7, 554, 643 21	7, 473, 378 78
Undivided profits....	2, 086, 376 21	2, 022, 587 92	2, 335, 061 07	1, 690, 403 07	2, 092, 043 76
Nat'l bank circulation	22, 933, 611 00	23, 080, 874 00	23, 064, 567 00	22, 864, 743 00	23, 050, 078 00
State bank circulation	40, 830 00	40, 894 00	40, 779 00	40, 717 00	40, 543 00
Dividends unpaid ...	121, 279 25	86, 385 30	95, 494 00	196, 018 50	85, 687 83
Individual deposits ..	31, 801, 335 31	31, 935, 108 08	31, 521, 014 35	30, 158, 759 53	30, 378, 289 63
U. S. deposits........	290, 673 29	293, 448 34	380, 061 55	344, 406 39	370, 222 88
Dep'ts U.S.dis.officers	20, 771 41	8, 495 23	15, 167 34	19, 138 63	11, 901 61
Due to national banks	1, 879, 709 27	1, 388, 774 32	1, 236, 527 23	1, 671, 977 29	1, 031, 724 14
Due to State banks ..	348, 482 30	310, 649 20	270, 123 79	299, 820 93	174, 199 98
Notes re-discounted..	182, 077 76	169, 049 73	191, 798 52	123, 939 26	53, 009 56
Bills payable........	65, 090 00	59, 245 10	103, 000 00	103, 047 60	67, 000 00
Total	96, 004, 625 22	95, 592, 215 31	95, 461, 047 81	93, 532, 463 41	93, 208, 219 19

Abstract of reports since October 1, 1877, arranged

CITY OF PHILADELPHIA.

Resources.	DECEMBER 28. 31 banks.	MARCH 15. 31 banks.	MAY 1. 31 banks.	JUNE 29. 31 banks.	OCTOBER 1. 31 banks.
Loans and discounts.	$44,120,740 38	$43,236,694 36	$42,601,378 45	$40,866,719 61	$42,099,481 19
Bonds for circulation.	13,063,700 00	13,163,700 00	13,263,700 00	13,553,700 00	13,703,700 00
Bonds for deposits ..	250,000 00	250,000 00	250,000 00	250,000 00	250,000 00
U. S. bonds on hand..	1,602,400 00	1,850,400 00	2,187,400 00	2,081,400 00	2,780,450 00
Other stocks and b'ds	1,900,141 02	1,980,316 71	1,833,434 00	1,713,415 09	1,704,513 05
Due from res've ag'ts.	3,791,832 96	4,116,320 04	3,219,302 84	3,966,378 04	4,826,938 02
Due from nat'l banks	2,610,182 21	2,297,617 89	2,797,924 82	2,522,763 20	2,553,683 51
Due from State banks	533,420 08	482,859 69	497,228 83	437,648 25	499,201 62
Real estate, &c	2,610,885 04	2,634,126 00	2,642,540 38	2,643,401 30	2,649,985 13
Current expenses....	205,836 12	487,647 44	505,805 86	240,670 72	565,279 68
Premiums paid	429,369 30	417,610 09	431,938 27	442,119 39	398,468 93
Cash items	326,577 75	269,207 92	331,446 32	431,464 54	404,555 69
Clear'g-house exch'gs	4,599,543 23	3,926,073 81	5,082,987 23	5,439,031 93	6,700,347 32
Bills of other banks..	1,329,019 00	781,533 00	1,084,310 00	939,349 00	775,103 00
Fractional currency.	42,963 97	30,744 67	28,413 19	28,366 21	23,339 61
Specie	1,703,842 10	2,451,061 19	2,265,500 72	2,018,094 32	2,265,692 38
Legal-tender notes ..	5,286,970 00	4,597,827 00	4,285,085 00	4,863,700 00	3,764,554 00
U. S. cert's of deposit	3,880,000 00	3,655,000 00	3,880,000 00	4,800,000 00	3,910,000 00
Due from U. S. Treas.	663,233 03	635,290 21	669,508 41	654,807 01	643,657 01
Total..........	88,950,657 15	87,273,030 02	87,857,904 32	88,493,028 61	90,527,950 14

CITY OF PITTSBURGH.

	22 banks.	22 banks.	22 banks.	22 banks.	22 banks.
Loans and discounts.	$18,798,959 33	$18,078,819 91	$17,961,250 64	$17,497,344 17	$16,670,959 08
Bonds for circulation.	6,104,500 00	6,154,500 00	6,154,500 00	6,354,500 00	6,454,500 00
Bonds for deposits...	200,000 00	200,000 00	200,000 00	200,000 00	304,500 00
U. S. bonds on hand..	554,050 00	561,150 00	563,800 00	587,200 00	678,500 00
Other stocks and b'ds	589,390 29	616,059 50	599,609 50	581,174 50	586,335 33
Due from res've ag'ts.	1,587,225 04	1,939,376 15	1,067,949 92	1,315,426 43	1,712,972 90
Due from nat'l banks.	565,490 43	535,123 04	436,233 79	581,657 18	599,800 12
Due from State banks	249,009 70	188,156 49	241,168 85	183,103 52	208,257 11
Real estate, &c	1,347,486 01	1,349,923 43	1,366,109 37	1,356,873 55	1,471,113 67
Current expenses....	106,876 84	144,706 39	149,693 86	112,006 38	158,409 99
Premiums paid	149,627 83	106,991 98	102,476 91	107,758 46	89,366 40
Cash items	136,975 20	121,825 82	118,289 99	119,488 01	109,562 23
Clear'g-house exch'gs	473,689 92	402,624 36	498,105 91	514,911 72	584,142 99
Bills of other banks..	417,352 00	246,261 00	482,852 00	244,609 00	436,121 00
Fractional currency.	25,347 09	17,162 93	16,900 63	14,112 60	14,192 90
Specie	105,987 07	147,491 71	220,704 30	244,875 42	371,528 16
Legal-tender notes ..	2,115,735 00	1,938,575 00	2,111,256 00	1,704,234 00	2,106,492 00
U. S. cert's of deposit.	100,000 00	100,000 00	100,000 00		
Due from U. S. Treas	292,309 89	300,533 99	296,568 60	304,111 81	306,053 10
Total..........	33,919,991 64	33,169,281 70	32,687,461 27	32,023,386 75	32,862,890 98

DELAWARE.

	13 banks.	13 banks.	14 banks.	14 banks.	14 banks.
Loans and discounts.	$2,797,063 86	$2,846,784 99	$3,004,179 95	$2,990,017 70	$3,028,473 86
Bonds for circulation.	1,534,200 00	1,534,200 00	1,600,200 00	1,600,200 00	1,613,200 00
Bonds for deposits ..	60,000 00	60,000 00	60,000 00	60,000 00	60,000 00
U. S. bonds on hand..	14,150 00	24,150 00	10,150 00	100 00	19,900 00
Other stocks and b'ds	177,369 06	182,295 40	163,292 71	168,148 77	167,863 37
Due from res've ag'ts.	429,242 78	354,707 85	276,517 49	331,884 44	435,258 04
Due from nat'l banks	120,247 59	133,145 09	143,811 79	113,040 45	141,887 34
Due from State banks	88,089 53	61,175 77	62,033 02	68,304 19	43,497 83
Real estate, &c	154,329 42	167,811 20	189,673 51	189,616 67	189,101 22
Current expenses....	23,818 42	14,999 56	22,122 44	25,956 19	22,378 20
Premiums paid	24,719 50	18,697 00	21,200 75	20,538 25	18,326 63
Cash items	44,338 21	53,791 67	48,830 92	62,943 49	73,350 97
Clear'g-house exch'gs					
Bills of other banks..	75,932 00	41,507 00	68,100 00	71,652 00	76,006 00
Fractional currency.	2,728 11	1,786 76	3,017 82	2,257 80	2,224 15
Specie	18,900 86	28,984 35	35,666 86	41,429 39	70,094 34
Legal-tender notes ..	160,266 00	171,870 00	157,983 00	148,354 00	172,439 00
U. S. cert's of deposit.	40,000 00	40,000 00	40,000 00	40,000 00	40,000 00
Due from U. S. Treas.	70,023 40	68,623 75	72,643 50	74,793 75	71,893 75
Total..........	5,844,358 74	5,784,530 39	5,979,423 76	6,018,237 09	6,245,894 70

by States and reserve cities—Continued.

CITY OF PHILADELPHIA.

Liabilities.	DECEMBER 28. 31 banks.	MARCH 15. 31 banks.	MAY 1. 31 banks.	JUNE 29. 31 banks.	OCTOBER 1. 31 banks.
Capital stock	$16,843,000 00	$16,843,000 00	$16,843,000 00	$16,843,000 00	$16,843,000 00
Surplus fund	7,471,730 68	7,423,013 82	7,326,176 40	7,315,970 51	7,313,099 53
Undivided profits	1,211,010 99	1,554,507 78	1,848,508 48	1,236,028 53	1,614,485 51
Nat'l bank circulation	11,371,263 00	11,482,729 00	11,592,336 00	11,402,700 00	11,730,429 00
State bank circulation	21,142 00	21,136 00	13,771 00	13,766 00	13,760 00
Dividends unpaid	55,979 85	38,276 25	34,270 05	51,897 10	41,972 10
Individual deposits	43,326,821 77	39,974,333 44	41,279,507 83	42,412,536 24	42,795,881 25
U. S. deposits	202,937 72	185,712 61	218,877 41	217,130 94	197,946 66
Dep'ts U.S.dis.officers					
Due to national banks	6,441,645 16	7,080,783 23	6,670,481 37	7,063,348 03	7,888,615 63
Due to State banks	1,920,125 98	2,594,537 80	1,955,975 78	1,861,591 26	2,028,760 46
Notes re-discounted		15,000 00	15,000 00	15,000 00	
Bills payable	85,000 00	60,000 00	60,000 00	60,000 00	60,000 00
Total	88,950,657 15	87,273,030 02	87,857,904 32	88,493,028 61	90,527,950 14

CITY OF PITTSBURGH.

	22 banks.	22 banks.	22 banks.	22 banks.	22 banks.
Capital stock	$10,350,000 00	$10,350,000 00	$10,350,000 00	$10,350,000 00	$10,350,000 00
Surplus fund	3,065,998 49	3,026,407 56	3,031,943 37	3,019,328 57	3,036,929 35
Undivided profits	697,395 38	569,000 66	581,830 88	474,760 06	490,505 82
Nat'l bank circulation	5,427,061 00	5,486,986 00	5,463,506 00	5,510,368 00	5,715,216 00
State bank circulation	4,235 00	4,235 00	4,235 00	4,235 00	4,235 00
Dividends unpaid	42,320 50	39,836 50	78,479 50	65,615 00	65,210 25
Individual deposits	11,868,906 99	11,616,590 13	11,430,769 48	11,167,952 65	11,133,314 87
U. S. deposits	6,501 81	97,330 06	102,763 41	10,031 08	121,238 91
Dep'ts U.S.dis.officers	172,912 25	180,070 10	73,441 30	120,644 85	163,824 20
Due to national banks	1,111,648 76	989,201 68	924,632 63	633,264 99	869,425 31
Due to State banks	1,144,411 25	799,624 01	614,739 82	395,218 49	855,984 75
Notes re-discounted	28,567 21		21,146 88	61,968 06	47,006 52
Bills payable		10,000 00	10,000 00	10,000 00	10,000 00
Total	33,919,991 64	33,160,281 70	32,687,461 27	32,023,386 75	32,862,890 98

DELAWARE.

	13 banks.	13 banks.	14 banks.	14 banks.	14 banks.
Capital stock	$1,663,985 00	$1,663,985 00	$1,763,985 00	$1,763,985 00	$1,763,985 00
Surplus fund	447,572 58	449,800 21	452,323 43	450,000 42	454,135 75
Undivided profits	147,085 19	84,719 96	115,849 08	134,830 18	104,591 00
Nat'l bank circulation	1,340,910 00	1,353,420 00	1,349,030 00	1,388,855 00	1,407,620 00
State bank circulation	6,658 00	6,639 00	6,639 00	6,639 00	6,639 00
Dividends unpaid	9,133 50	10,159 90	8,901 90	7,644 40	10,017 50
Individual deposits	1,904,655 16	1,970,446 66	1,924,293 15	1,875,556 05	2,190,040 18
U. S. deposits	35,515 87	34,356 93	40,430 29	44,329 89	49,826 36
Dep'ts U.S.dis.officers	6,662 45	6,372 31	1,149 17	6,068 12	11,263 60
Due to national banks	262,884 53	188,525 62	255,224 95	271,678 76	227,420 72
Due to State banks	19,296 66	10,805 40	2,087 19	12,650 27	11,355 59
Notes re-discounted					
Bills payable		5,000 00	59,500 60	56,000 00	
Total	5,844,358 74	5,784,530 39	5,979,423 76	6,018,237 09	6,245,891 70

Abstract of reports since October 1, 1877, arranged

MARYLAND.

Resources.	DECEMBER 28. 18 banks.	MARCH 15. 18 banks.	MAY 1. 18 banks.	JUNE 29. 18 banks.	OCTOBER 1. 18 banks.
Loans and discounts.	$3,776,502 37	$3,774,780 82	$3,828,898 48	$3,773,569 71	$3,501,186 37
Bonds for circulation.	2,130,550 00	2,130,550 00	2,130,550 00	2,105,550 00	2,066,550 00
Bonds for deposits ..	100,000 00	100,000 00	100,000 00	100,000 00	100,000 00
U. S. bonds on hand..	228,700 00	231,400 00	226,400 00	221,600 00	346,800 00
Other stocks and b'ds	246,539 81	242,166 75	250,119 25	270,186 75	240,688 69
Due from res've ag'ts	537,303 80	450,744 78	337,398 45	316,169 96	517,241 17
Due from nat'l banks	266,022 74	247,814 46	201,838 82	192,137 65	289,509 92
Due from State banks	50,512 10	39,704 14	32,379 49	36,011 24	48,614 01
Real estate, &c	168,502 07	173,982 17	173,845 72	174,916 97	197,401 12
Current expenses....	38,442 28	33,564 39	37,038 63	13,012 41	31,786,54
Premiums paid	14,005 10	12,942 02	12,942 02	7,543 15	9,355 02
Cash items	47,271 26	48,764 81	22,851 16	33,501 91	44,223 04
Clear'g-house exch'gs					
Bills of other banks..	74,017 00	77,036 00	79,445 00	106,352 00	95,935 00
Fractional currency .	4,752 75	5,508 20	3,691 01	3,308 31	3,407 52
Specie	57,195 79	64,623 77	71,012 65	62,628 19	73,976 81
Legal-tender notes ..	287,076 00	258,353 00	310,043 00	271,355 00	297,468 00
U. S. cert's of deposit	10,000 00	10,000 00	10,000 00	10,000 00	10,000 00
Due from U. S. Treas	97,192 26	100,142 21	95,672 50	97,072 50	94,047 50
Total..........	8,134,585 33	8,011,077 52	7,924,126 18	7,794,915 75	7,968,190 71

CITY OF BALTIMORE.

	14 banks.	14 banks.	14 banks.	14 banks.	14 banks.
Loans and discounts.	$19,179,256 57	$19,025,672 91	$18,986,392 21	$18,002,753 04	$18,097,151 73
Bonds for circulation	6,410,000 00	6,410,000 00	6,210,000 00	6,225,000 00	6,265,000 00
Bonds for deposits...	200,000 00	200,000 00	200,000 00	200,000 00	200,000 00
U. S. bonds on hand..	864,000 00	864,000 00	1,064,000 00	1,064,000 00	1,264,000 00
Other stocks and b'ds	664,655 61	674,758 36	690,559 56	560,263 80	487,263 80
Due from res've ag'ts	1,855,690 09	1,745,217 09	1,228,883 83	1,805,675 77	1,780,213 76
Due from nat'l banks	834,893 76	502,582 40	447,957 15	603,108 49	701,555 42
Due from State banks	120,521 33	121,673 55	163,936 28	110,149 70	138,062 86
Real estate, &c	645,735 64	639,005 62	639,095 62	639,102 62	615,069 71
Current expenses....	148,559 20	111,607 14	149,439 08	91,638 02	168,863 05
Premiums paid	35,430 73	35,825 47	36,053 28	35,662 07	60,933 62
Cash items	78,542 29	31,742 92	23,380 79	35,535 77	77,185 10
Clear'g-house exch'gs	1,336,974 51	1,084,959 80	1,894,159 20	1,354,071 86	1,877,978 04
Bills of other banks..	381,721 00	432,199 00	349,070 00	530,482 00	382,879 00
Fractional currency	8,404 12	5,983 54	14,667 55	10,670 21	4,253 87
Specie	212,306 42	280,831 88	319,423 13	318,392 64	273,187 64
Legal-tender notes ..	1,210,679 00	1,110,263 00	1,141,786 00	1,038,042 00	923,564 00
U. S. cert's of deposit	1,750,000 00	2,230,000 00	1,490,000 00	1,515,000 00	1,265,000 00
Due from U. S. Treas	292,612 00	295,512 00	282,312 00	286,987 00	292,462 00
Total..........	36,229,982 27	35,801,984 68	35,331,125 68	34,426,594 99	34,874,623 60

DISTRICT OF COLUMBIA.

	1 bank.	1 bank.	1 bank.	1 bank.	1 bank.
Loans and discounts.	$315,749 14	$271,928 54	$262,221 61	$255,962 79	$248,939 28
Bonds for circulation	250,000 00	250,000 00	250,000 00	250,000 00	250,000 00
Bonds for deposits ..					
U. S. bonds on hand..		50,000 00	100,000 00	100,000 00	200,000 00
Other stocks and b'ds	123,171 26	108,830 01	94,547 51	94,547 51	19,335 00
Due from res've ag'ts	78,367 17	93,582 92	82,800 72	135,628 22	121,950 54
Due from nat'l banks	11,435 46	9,742 01	8,037 26	7,078 67	15,541 22
Due from State banks	284 73	803 36	8,903 68	1,048 69	4,243 35
Real estate, &c	17,550 00	17,550 00	17,550 00	17,550 00	17,550 00
Current expenses ...	35 18	2,554 14	4,316 09	73 84	2,155 92
Premiums paid					
Cash items	1,892 16	4,404 03	10,215 61	16,334 48	8,765 02
Clear'g-house exch'gs					
Bills of other banks..	15,420 00	36,570 00	11,287 00	12,710 00	16,038 00
Fractional currency .	206 90				5 20
Specie	6,930 70	9,200 60	9,378 10	9,330 20	14,370 00
Legal-tender notes ..	79,000 00	75,500 00	73,500 00	79,500 00	75,000 00
U. S. cert's of deposit	30,000 00	30,000 00	30,000 00	30,000 00	30,000 00
Due from U. S. Treas	11,250 00	11,250 00	11,250 00	11,250 00	11,250 00
Total..........	941,298 70	971,915 61	974,207 58	1,021,014 40	1,035,543 53

by States and reserve cities—Continued.

MARYLAND.

Liabilities.	DECEMBER 28. 18 banks.	MARCH 15. 18 banks.	MAY 1. 18 banks.	JUNE 29. 18 banks.	OCTOBER 1. 18 banks.
Capital stock	$2,306,700 00	$2,306,700 00	$2,306,700 00	$2,281,700 00	$2,231,700 00
Surplus fund	668,802 49	669,102 49	660,851 82	669,437 07	676,109 98
Undivided profits	231,154 82	218,025 41	240,879 64	183,380 76	214,602 01
Nat'l bank circulation	1,912,803 00	1,882,308 00	1,884,782 00	1,809,887 00	1,781,452 00
State bank circulation	2,420 00	2,414 00	2,409 00	2,409 00	2,409 00
Dividends unpaid	29,106 51	12,622 90	15,409 84	58,373 03	23,038 58
Individual deposits	2,583,049 41	2,594,730 88	2,492,631 98	2,430,983 16	2,750,479 22
U. S. deposits	61,646 68	48,357 29	48,543 97	40,842 88	46,822 32
Dep'ts U.S.dis.officers	43,004 58	18,968 93	29,345 94	24,461 07	18,732 54
Due to national banks	143,773 06	90,796 89	71,743 70	129,950 44	83,093 26
Due to State banks	34,303 71	27,038 23	40,875 28	31,250 12	21,976 15
Notes re-discounted		37,150 68	22,717 23	21,857 23	17,000 00
Bills payable	117,821 07	103,461 82	98,295 78	101,374 99	100,684 75
Total	8,134,585 33	8,011,077 52	7,924,126 18	7,794,915 75	7,968,190 71

CITY OF BALTIMORE.

	14 banks.	14 banks.	14 banks.	14 banks.	14 banks.
Capital stock	$10,891,985 00	$10,891,985 00	$10,891,985 00	$10,633,310 00	$10,633,310 00
Surplus fund	2,437,984 79	2,428,934 79	2,432,834 26	2,435,383 55	2,354,783 55
Undivided profits	757,242 94	658,120 90	814,815 71	569,314 64	701,571 23
Nat'l bank circulation	5,466,547 00	5,454,792 00	5,427,788 00	5,215,678 00	5,363,348 00
State bank circulation	67,860 00	67,750 00	67,091 00	67,014 00	66,997 00
Dividends unpaid	164,539 79	61,282 53	70,244 48	205,123 86	60,438 32
Individual deposits	13,492,524 04	13,878,490 50	13,484,748 61	13,633,261 30	13,275,700 40
U. S. deposits	93,525 31	93,594 31	135,413 89	108,347 96	100,178 04
Dep'ts U.S.dis.officers					
Due to national banks	2,402,464 97	1,924,132 17	1,758,564 46	1,353,191 48	1,930,145 98
Due to State banks	455,308 43	342,884 48	247,640 27	205,970 11	388,151 06
Notes re-discounted					
Bills payable					
Total	36,220,982 27	35,801,984 68	35,331,125 68	34,426,504 90	34,874,623 60

DISTRICT OF COLUMBIA.

	1 bank.	1 bank.	1 bank.	1 bank.	1 bank.
Capital stock	$252,000 00	$252,000 00	$252,000 00	$252,000 00	$252,000 00
Surplus fund	52,000 00	52,000 00	52,000 00	53,000 00	53,000 00
Undivided profits	20,167 86	27,641 40	33,464 75	21,090 59	30,251 54
Nat'l bank circulation	225,000 00	213,700 00	222,500 00	215,400 00	214,100 00
State bank circulation					
Dividends unpaid	11,208 00	1,288 00	1,160 00	11,108 00	1,220 00
Individual deposits	373,086 22	415,490 73	403,645 02	462,295 81	480,003 85
U. S. deposits					
Dep'ts U.S.dis.officers					
Due to national banks	7,607 46	4,313 95	8,279 50	5,952 82	4,827 14
Due to State banks	229 16	5,481 53	1,158 31	167 18	141 00
Notes re-discounted					
Bills payable					
Total	941,298 70	971,915 61	974,207 58	1,021,014 40	1,035,543 53

Abstract of reports since October 1, 1877, arranged

CITY OF WASHINGTON.

Resources.	DECEMBER 28.	MARCH 15.	MAY 1.	JUNE 29.	OCTOBER 1.
	5 banks.	5 banks.	6 banks.	6 banks.	6 banks.
Loans and discounts.	$1,501,660 77	$1,475,998 10	$1,713,507 30	$1,677,238 63	$1,664,078 19
Bonds for circulation.	750,000 00	765,000 00	860,000 00	900,000 00	900,000 00
Bonds for deposits ..	100,000 00	100,000 00	100,000 00	100,000 00	100,000 00
U. S. bonds on hand..	92,950 00	76,100 00	42,200 00	43,000 00	46,950 00
Other stocks and b'ds	71,702 41	66,489 99	76,317 36	77,935 90	63,703 85
Due from res've ag'ts	228,014 85	296,351 88	240,788 21	277,903 67	298,887 51
Due from nat'l banks	91,211 87	55,519 94	54,563 57	53,875 99	47,452 22
Due from State banks	6,036 66	27,329 87	9,969 72	15,256 45	19,287 36
Real estate, &c	571,117 99	577,862 61	579,563 64	588,905 56	589,978 81
Current expenses....	41,315 38	25,901 62	28,389 37	13,475 08	29,525 97
Premiums paid	14,229 68	14,293 89	19,762 82	15,301 98	12,959 63
Cash items	41,592 56	36,268 27	54,386 19	55,490 02	60,973 59
Clear'g-house exch'gs					
Bills of other banks..	16,673 00	17,335 00	18,002 00	15,474 00	20,273 00
Fractional currency	7,186 58	7,864 41	7,852 15	6,050 06	7,394 18
Specie	31,195 87	31,910 96	57,155 08	52,462 22	33,942 25
Legal-tender notes ..	217,674 00	146,732 00	172,003 00	215,552 00	249,831 00
U. S. cert's of deposit.	35,000 00	35,000 00	35,000 00	35,000 00	35,000 00
Due from U. S. Treas.	33,750 00	33,150 00	31,000 00	38,700 00	44,100 00
Total	3,851,312 02	3,789,108 54	4,100,550 41	4,181,621 56	4,224,337 56

VIRGINIA.

	19 banks.	19 banks.	19 banks.	19 banks.	18 banks.
Loans and discounts	$6,908,215 15	$6,658,513 93	$6,734,924 90	$6,608,348 85	$6,389,170 45
Bonds for circulation	2,547,350 00	2,547,350 00	2,547,350 00	2,497,350 00	2,457,350 00
Bonds for deposits ..	575,000 00	525,000 00	525,000 00	525,000 00	525,000 00
U. S. bonds on hand..	73,800 00	20,900 00	21,500 00	24,800 00	242,300 00
Other stocks and b'ds	127,089 78	116,408 50	108,291 27	115,317 88	130,570 23
Due from res've ag'ts	778,677 41	460,395 19	494,257 92	953,031 65	605,245 90
Due from nat'l banks	264,089 57	300,376 63	164,973 61	219,978 61	199,769 46
Due from State banks	182,306 70	186,050 35	149,333 97	159,580 23	151,959 02
Real estate, &c	380,064 00	375,065 03	384,976 65	398,875 43	351,803 38
Current expenses....	129,154 26	52,402 54	83,244 93	24,743 20	79,101 27
Premiums paid	150,488 42	112,364 62	112,364 62	106,732 33	96,454 47
Cash items	199,685 52	190,528 97	174,507 56	279,905 09	193,529 09
Clear'g-house exch'gs					
Bills of other banks..	176,834 00	103,841 00	152,066 00	130,802 00	195,827 00
Fractional currency.	8,504 29	5,598 85	5,429 47	5,004 21	5,843 34
Specie	54,201 07	52,434 58	46,756 44	51,350 43	75,666 07
Legal-tender notes ..	787,390 00	588,218 00	507,917 00	500,956 00	581,147 00
U. S. cert's of deposit					
Due from U. S. Treas	104,387 23	122,300 40	116,595 60	109,090 05	120,945 85
Total..........	13,456,237 40	12,426,748 59	12,419,489 94	12,711,954 96	12,401,082 53

WEST VIRGINIA.

	15 banks.	15 banks.	15 banks.	15 banks.	15 banks.
Loans and discounts.	$2,557,087 99	$2,574,947 92	$2,549,527 33	$2,505,171 58	$2,380,475 31
Bonds for circulation	1,579,250 00	1,579,250 00	1,579,250 00	1,579,250 00	1,489,250 00
Bonds for deposits ..					
U. S. bonds on hand..	26,350 00	27,950 00	29,950 00	25,700 00	50,800 00
Other stocks and b'ds	35,816 82	34,516 82	34,716 82	36,216 82	47,452 21
Due from res've ag'ts	160,138 53	142,659 40	159,540 46	179,832 46	246,607 93
Due from nat'l banks.	133,247 65	100,570 46	77,022 00	80,723 32	100,938 75
Due from State banks.	40,826 74	32,997 02	31,304 73	29,086 43	44,220 06
Real estate, &c	184,302 27	184,883 40	184,877 40	184,877 40	184,877 40
Current expenses....	44,856 48	24,865 20	30,168 37	26,184 52	25,085 33
Premiums paid	28,787 98	23,504 02	22,203 79	22,177 14	15,200 75
Cash items	18,110 94	14,518 18	16,862 37	9,283 57	11,796 59
Clear'g-house exch'gs					
Bills of other banks..	44,641 00	33,639 00	39,000 00	52,098 00	50,903 00
Fractional currency.	3,611 08	3,074 96	3,618 41	2,911 76	3,017 84
Specie	26,097 11	29,000 12	28,296 01	32,900 91	43,961 71
Legal-tender notes ..	247,596 00	215,912 00	224,788 00	191,196 00	273,778 00
U. S. cert's of deposit.					
Due from U. S. Treas.	73,646 79	69,782 18	73,782 18	67,833 25	71,577 75
Total..........	5,204,367 38	5,092,970 68	5,084,907 87	5,025,443 16	5,058,953 63

by States and reserve cities—Continued.

CITY OF WASHINGTON.

Liabilities.	DECEMBER 28. 5 banks.	MARCH 15. 5 banks.	MAY 1. 6 banks.	JUNE 29. 6 banks.	OCTOBER 1. 6 banks.
Capital stock	$1,180,000 00	$1,180,000 00	$1,270,410 00	$1,255,000 00	$1,255,000 00
Surplus fund.........	288,000 00	280,000 00	280,000 00	280,000 00	289,400 00
Undivided profits....	115,664 04	74,073 42	88,104 93	70,573 12	84,830 55
Nat'l bank circulation	674,000 00	684,500 00	686,200 00	765,000 00	799,600 00
State bank circulation					
Dividends unpaid....	2,456 00	2,519 00	2,367 00	14,226 00	3,335 00
Individual deposits...	1,364,793 18	1,325,521 05	1,592,430 69	1,578,169 91	1,623,850 40
U. S. deposits........	55,354 03	70,801 52	38,765 44	51,249 00	40,596 75
Dep'ts U.S.dis.officers					
Due to national banks	152,437 08	131,702 77	117,015 94	137,130 11	112,725 93
Due to State banks...	18,607 69	20,385 28	16,256 41	21,273 42	14,998 93
Notes re-discounted..		10,515 50			
Bills payable........					
Total	3,851,312 02	3,780,108 54	4,100,550 41	4,181,021 56	4,224,337 56

VIRGINIA.

	19 banks.	19 banks.	19 banks.	19 banks.	18 banks.
Capital stock........	$3,285,000 00	$3,285,000 00	$3,285,000 00	$3,285,000 00	$3,185,000 00
Surplus fund........	811,150 32	810,409 32	810,409 32	811,459 32	810,159 32
Undivided profits....	469,995 28	198,659 64	285,232 70	184,298 91	232,392 02
Nat'l bank circulation	2,249,500 00	2,284,500 00	2,266,500 00	2,218,400 00	2,176,300 00
State bank circulation					
Dividends unpaid....	1,075 00	1,487 00	1,370 00	86,408 00	1,240 00
Individual deposits...	5,579,860 85	4,858,368 39	4,777,188 23	5,000,016 15	4,974,527 41
U. S. deposits........	315,320 78	374,756 98	310,002 49	485,324 18	361,810 44
Dep'ts U.S.dis.officers	86,564 21	61,323 65	57,818 54	59,142 87	92,013 31
Due to national banks	302,329 13	212,511 42	194,825 85	171,924 95	193,746 99
Due to State banks...	276,160 50	256,307 90	238,549 15	240,921 41	248,406 79
Notes re-discounted..	79,272 33	83,424 20	147,593 66	149,059 17	126,086 25
Bills payable........			25,000 00	20,000 00	
Total	13,456,237 40	12,426,748 50	12,419,489 94	12,711,054 96	12,401,682 53

WEST VIRGINIA.

	15 banks.	15 banks.	15 banks.	15 banks.	15 banks.
Capital stock........	$1,746,000 00	$1,746,000 00	$1,746,000 00	$1,746,000 00	$1,656,000 00
Surplus fund........	402,106 79	404,867 07	407,885 66	408,873 15	405,522 48
Undivided profits....	163,971 28	109,323 10	130,636 12	121,689 50	108,996 62
Nat'l bank circulation	1,409,103 00	1,411,136 00	1,402,333 00	1,392,108 00	1,325,803 00
State bank circulation					
Dividends unpaid....	10,515 50	13,537 50	15,557 25	24,303 25	17,412 00
Individual deposits...	1,281,353 23	1,274,507 56	1,232,136 25	1,209,415 12	1,380,690 90
U. S. deposits........					
Dep'ts U.S.dis.officers					
Due to national banks	123,809 80	77,910 04	86,861 23	65,492 35	99,907 97
Due to State banks...	49,890 75	41,989 41	40,468 36	42,931 79	59,320 66
Notes re-discounted..	12,617 03	10,700 00	20,630 00	14,630 00	5,300 00
Bills payable........	5,000 00	3,600 00	3,000 00		
Total	5,204,367 38	5,092,970 68	5,084,907 87	5,025,443 16	5,058,953 63

10 C C

Abstract of reports since October 1, 1877, arranged

NORTH CAROLINA.

Resources.	DECEMBER 28. 15 banks.	MARCH 15. 15 banks.	MAY 1. 15 banks.	JUNE 29. 15 banks.	OCTOBER 1. 15 banks.
Loans and discounts.	$3,634,300 16	$3,617,198 43	$3,690,331 04	$3,883,533 45	$4,049,916 25
Bonds for circulation.	1,454,000 00	1,510,000 00	1,526,000 00	1,650,000 00	1,699,000 00
Bonds for deposits..	150,000 00	150,000 00	150,000 00	150,000 00	150,000 00
U. S. bonds on hand..	44,000 00	44,000 00	96,000 00	95,900 00	75,000 00
Other stocks and b'ds	322,148 08	300,518 03	289,941 00	288,409 14	278,526 29
Due from res've ag'ts.	342,221 36	357,161 48	292,021 13	140,165 86	216,685 11
Due from nat'l banks.	193,857 37	125,966 84	100,978 54	62,813 60	117,381 17
Due from State banks	97,464 89	104,271 37	104,230 04	83,456 32	80,303 04
Real estate, &c	355,951 27	302,016 13	296,066 72	303,637 44	311,762 69
Current expenses....	75,638 51	32,739 53	51,607 31	47,897 57	46,545 16
Premiums paid	118,778 29	108,972 37	108,406 12	96,270 60	97,656 65
Cash items	29,781 00	18,370 42	23,083 13	24,692 56	34,368 04
Clear'g-house exch'gs					
Bills of other banks..	168,815 00	125,740 00	93,703 00	82,701 00	111,997 00
Fractional currency .	5,088 49	7,811 32	8,819 34	6,901 57	7,726 87
Specie	68,525 72	60,690 01	63,698 94	62,224 35	59,432 92
Legal-tender notes ..	357,603 00	431,259 00	399,732 00	311,993 00	250,332 00
U. S. cert's of deposit.					
Due from U. S. Treas.	63,939 00	69,114 00	70,302 03	72,113 96	72,426 04
Total	7,482,112 14	7,365,828 93	7,313,920 34	7,362,710 51	7,659,059 23

SOUTH CAROLINA.

Resources.	12 banks.	12 banks.	12 banks.	12 banks.	12 banks.
Loans and discounts.	$3,622,714 58	$3,297,677 49	$3,233,742 48	$3,480,654 68	$3,765,554 92
Bonds for circulation.	1,435,000 00	1,435,000 00	1,435,000 00	1,435,000 00	1,435,000 00
Bonds for deposits...	150,000 00	150,000 00	150,000 00	150,000 00	150,000 00
U. S. bonds on hand..	40,000 00	40,000 00	35,000 00	35,000 00	35,000 00
Other stocks and b'ds	627,859 33	639,696 38	633,121 27	639,689 86	633,022 05
Due from res've ag'ts.	300,256 79	783,176 66	578,233 85	341,910 59	85,127 41
Due from nat'l banks	408,364 53	272,481 26	257,592 05	180,565 12	156,994 14
Due from State banks	95,156 77	79,129 67	72,378 51	48,745 44	59,918 44
Real estate, &c	242,395 37	240,966 43	241,063 43	252,266 03	251,678 93
Current expenses....	111,919 02	47,261 81	98,731 70	107,865 08	50,068 16
Premiums paid	54,990 01	34,387 50	34,387 50	31,237 59	23,540 39
Cash items	20,018 98	16,220 68	14,761 38	9,799 54	25,720 06
Clear'g-house exch'gs					
Bills of other banks..	203,974 00	208,928 00	153,590 00	91,899 00	88,590 00
Fractional currency .	5,826 46	4,260 49	5,155 15	5,439 51	4,077 27
Specie	40,254 16	40,646 45	51,071 78	70,021 45	48,316 75
Legal-tender notes ..	382,737 00	368,227 00	353,723 00	163,790 00	341,169 00
U. S. cert's of deposit.					
Due from U. S. Treas.	68,626 00	70,410 95	66,401 50	63,946 50	67,412 62
Total	7,810,093 00	7,728,479 77	7,414,555 60	7,107,830 30	7,221,790 14

GEORGIA.

Resources.	12 banks.	12 banks.	12 banks.	12 banks.	12 banks.
Loans and discounts.	$2,754,630 97	$2,243,105 63	$2,355,470 59	$2,379,400 60	$2,580,430 89
Bonds for circulation.	2,004,000 00	1,964,500 00	1,964,500 00	2,075,000 00	2,025,000 00
Bonds for deposits...	125,000 00	125,000 00	131,000 00	131,000 00	131,000 00
U. S. bonds on hand..	500 00	500 00	1,500 00	1,500 00	500 00
Other stocks and b'ds	144,637 51	148,513 45	148,250 95	192,662 49	189,454 63
Due from res've ag'ts.	198,767 37	242,740 12	153,017 23	142,583 37	117,600 55
Due from nat'l banks	186,961 22	245,915 94	176,100 15	123,123 80	156,768 94
Due from State banks	67,809 20	125,098 01	94,413 07	60,056 03	85,420 30
Real estate, &c	229,860 20	231,924 67	227,477 04	223,312 17	220,141 67
Current expenses....	71,335 12	33,815 80	58,188 43	61,804 28	42,223 43
Premiums paid	76,400 79	62,387 08	61,815 23	63,047 02	60,423 58
Cash items	63,963 82	77,061 74	46,331 39	54,105 94	88,465 47
Clear'g-house exch'gs					
Bills of other banks..	314,518 00	390,592 00	270,581 00	194,723 00	233,486 00
Fractional currency .	8,321 45	10,894 73	11,815 16	6,188 05	10,663 91
Specie	59,562 07	68,474 67	66,717 22	87,363 65	71,099 41
Legal-tender notes ..	397,742 00	578,086 00	482,705 00	351,063 00	490,988 00
U. S. cert's of deposit.					
Due from U. S. Treas.	95,653 50	95,396 10	90,696 10	95,874 00	94,101 12
Total	6,799,663 22	6,650,405 94	6,340,527 56	6,243,797 40	6,597,826 90

by States and reserve cities—Continued.

NORTH CAROLINA.

Liabilities.	DECEMBER 28. 15 banks.	MARCH 15. 15 banks.	MAY 1. 15 banks.	JUNE 29. 15 banks.	OCTOBER 1. 15 banks.
Capital stock	$2,601,000 00	$2,551,000 00	$2,551,000 00	$2,551,000 00	$2,551,000 00
Surplus fund	286,534 41	270,333 46	270,333 46	271,333 46	296,945 82
Undivided profits	385,460 15	240,984 99	260,380 32	257,710 54	226,873 13
Nat'l bank circulation	1,302,030 00	1,284,000 00	1,304,210 00	1,372,540 00	1,526,230 00
State bank circulation					
Dividends unpaid	2,030 00	1,849 75	1,640 00	13,600 00	2,220 00
Individual deposits	2,451,853 36	2,739,020 90	2,601,825 52	2,468,935 18	2,442,481 93
U. S. deposits	126,877 61	111,876 13	116,837 42	120,821 78	135,350 60
Dep'ts U.S.dis.officers	18,214 43	13,114 56	7,021 48	11,277 15	13,935 55
Due to national banks	84,017 41	60,389 98	86,412 74	47,070 15	59,870 97
Due to State banks	30,987 70	34,074 20	26,797 06	11,425 51	24,253 40
Notes re-discounted	78,668 98	54,184 96	82,462 34	84,996 74	200,897 83
Bills payable	114,438 09	5,000 00	5,000 00	152,000 00	179,000 00
Total	7,482,112 14	7,365,828 93	7,313,920 34	7,362,710 51	7,659,059 23

SOUTH CAROLINA.

	12 banks.	12 banks.	12 banks.	12 banks.	12 banks.
Capital stock	$2,860,700 00	$2,854,000 00	$2,854,000 00	$2,854,000 00	$2,851,100 00
Surplus fund	415,876 28	425,191 93	425,191 93	426,197 93	433,267 68
Undivided profits	350,755 55	211,603 49	262,509 63	304,271 44	202,635 28
Nat'l bank circulation	1,287,950 00	1,258,196 00	1,239,996 00	1,164,646 00	1,289,751 00
State bank circulation					
Dividends unpaid	12,674 50	16,021 00	14,322 50	24,313 00	14,160 50
Individual deposits	2,298,364 03	2,579,592 95	2,205,766 15	1,917,070 94	1,648,902 97
U. S. deposits	81,853 23	65,363 78	82,372 41	62,504 33	69,660 00
Dep'ts U.S.dis.officers	70,246 52	55,594 52	48,083 19	43,391 10	48,811 70
Due to national banks	221,110 49	98,113 29	88,348 96	66,314 72	156,784 13
Due to State banks	87,071 62	89,802 81	98,787 46	94,079 01	90,755 03
Notes re-discounted	48,490 79		30,177 37	76,041 83	226,961 85
Bills payable	75,000 00	75,000 00	65,000 00	75,000 00	189,000 00
Total	7,810,093 00	7,728,470 77	7,414,555 60	7,107,830 30	7,221,790 14

GEORGIA.

	12 banks.	12 banks.	12 banks.	12 banks.	12 banks.
Capital stock	$2,111,000 00	$2,091,000 00	$2,091,000 00	$2,091,000 00	$2,041,000 00
Surplus fund	347,952 98	357,571 43	357,571 43	361,071 43	367,061 09
Undivided profits	256,880 99	189,599 32	213,882 68	221,878 03	175,694 33
Nat'l bank circulation	1,744,908 00	1,691,806 00	1,673,768 00	1,744,248 00	1,771,575 00
State bank circulation					
Dividends unpaid	1,630 00	5,378 00	5,052 50	29,453 50	11,047 50
Individual deposits	1,753,653 36	2,007,905 20	1,761,577 11	1,516,019 59	1,624,752 61
U. S. deposits	61,714 06	55,889 35	67,933 49	58,044 87	76,255 30
Dep'ts U.S.dis.officers	52,227 83	29,050 10	20,218 21	38,722 27	25,407 43
Due to national banks	205,823 49	71,846 29	89,090 54	66,599 73	197,116 97
Due to State banks	184,778 91	142,835 99	58,433 60	116,759 98	171,436 03
Notes re-discounted	49,093 60	4,614 26	2,000 00		29,390 64
Bills payable					107,000 00
Total	6,799,663 22	6,650,495 94	6,340,527 56	6,243,797 40	6,597,826 90

Abstract of reports since October 1, 1877, arranged

FLORIDA.

Resources.	DECEMBER 28. 1 bank.	MARCH 15. 1 bank.	MAY 1. 1 bank.	JUNE 29. 1 bank.	OCTOBER 1. 1 bank.
Loans and discounts.	$78,159 58	$97,479 11	$91,892 14	$91,653 92	$81,921 00
Bonds for circulation.	50,000 00	50,000 00	50,000 00	50,000 00	50,000 00
Bonds for deposits..					
U. S. bonds on hand..			10,150 00		18,000 00
Other stocks and b'ds	6,966 70	3,264 86	3,534 24	3,480 12	3,354 12
Due from res've ag'ts.	196 02	7,407 75	15,102 65	7,730 32	363 45
Due from nat'l banks	206 37	1,358 33	299 03	924 99	7 20
Due from State banks	1 05	392 24		460 90	712 86
Real estate, &c	11,738 90	11,750 90	11,750 90	11,879 45	11,909 63
Current expenses....	2,726 11	966 60	2,182 37	3,279 02	1,101 15
Premiums paid......	4,356 49	2,656 49	2,938 49	2,663 49	2,758 26
Cash items	387 26	997 66	1,198 85	1,145 66	1,660 28
Clear'g-house exch'gs					
Bills of other banks..	3,503 00	17,646 00	7,268 00	2,678 00	1,281 00
Fractional currency .	354 74	53 02	63 83	50 69	72 99
Specie	633 62	383 77	1,123 91	671 50	465 53
Legal-tender notes ..	8,000 00	15,000 00	15,000 00	10,000 00	9,000 00
U. S. cert's of deposit					
Due from U. S. Treas.	1,070 65	3,221 55	2,417 50	2,250 00	2,250 00
Total..........	168,300 49	212,578 28	214,921 91	188,868 00	184,857 47

ALABAMA.

	10 banks.	10 banks.	10 banks.	10 banks.	10 banks.
Loans and discounts.	$1,550,276 22	$1,554,976 90	$1,579,125 59	$1,628,964 75	$2,133,151 74
Bonds for circulation.	1,621,000 00	1,621,000 00	1,621,000 00	1,621,000 00	1,621,000 00
Bonds for deposits...					50,000 00
U. S. bonds on hand..	35,200 00		40,200 00	53,650 00	20,000 00
Other stocks and b'ds	158,871 25	129,592 86	132,625 76	153,476 60	158,625 35
Due from res've ag'ts.	250,494 53	346,710 03	327,294 89	147,587 31	221,417 10
Due from nat'l banks.	97,130 21	328,358 30	328,608 46	232,432 80	112,024 00
Due from State banks	38,453 62	11,057 74	24,697 50	29,920 74	57,841 23
Real estate, &c	159,743 19	159,379 66	165,003 71	166,117 50	159,282 26
Current expenses....	44,301 76	31,180 16	42,302 82	57,661 61	26,980 08
Premiums paid......	118,242 52	95,057 34	96,889 34	93,862 66	69,427 09
Cash items	26,055 46	91,496 18	91,607 37	35,069 30	31,200 91
Clear'g-house exch'gs					
Bills of other banks..	148,105 00	115,997 00	48,392 00	53,605 00	79,579 00
Fractional currency .	6,429 11	6,333 96	5,353 65	6,135 98	4,300 21
Specie	22,293 85	48,097 59	50,731 83	61,690 75	48,755 42
Legal-tender notes ..	210,605 00	247,632 00	198,930 00	169,024 00	219,027 00
U. S. cert's of deposit.					
Due from U. S. Treas	65,143 65	70,244 60	78,938 45	65,745 00	70,024 00
Total..........	4,552,345 37	4,857,114 32	4,831,701 37	4,573,944 00	5,082,635 99

CITY OF NEW ORLEANS.

	7 banks.	7 banks.	7 banks.	7 banks.	7 banks.
Loans and discounts.	$7,249,190 45	$6,701,422 49	$6,162,710 49	$5,082,014 67	$5,341,301 24
Bonds for circulation.	800,000 00	800,000 00	1,550,000 00	1,700,000 00	1,700,000 00
Bonds for deposits...			25,000 00	25,000 00	25,000 00
U. S. bonds on hand..			326,750 00	191,500 00	55,600 00
Other stocks and b'ds	257,782 09	308,198 08	344,918 08	339,398 08	331,132 08
Due from res've ag'ts.	396,617 42	1,276,992 60	657,185 11	803,604 68	352,683 04
Due from nat'l banks.	51,032 66	139,377 84	232,033 75	163,375 17	59,924 33
Due from State banks	238,328 59	253,427 04	386,338 77	162,754 50	56,125 34
Real estate, &c	532,559 21	519,656 02	519,390 23	437,920 79	437,818 43
Current expenses....	140,093 56	79,723 43	122,076 76	81,409 59	85,339 01
Premiums paid......	52,900 00	39,200 00	67,607 55	72,056 55	65,119 05
Cash items	6,371 87	6,019 51	7,233 15	149,457 90	148,596 65
Clear'g-house exch'gs	1,115,338 08	1,219,462 55	683,516 93	1,167,952 46	332,994 50
Bills of other banks..	131,939 00	116,180 00	162,079 00	230,749 00	105,700 00
Fractional currency .	5,545 31	5,967 79	8,457 78	11,279 53	5,711 87
Specie	89,915 91	192,031 77	204,738 22	230,087 33	164,364 18
Legal-tender notes ..	1,189,188 00	1,237,403 00	1,379,063 00	1,993,097 00	1,199,142 00
U. S. cert's of deposit.					
Due from U. S. Treas	36,400 00	36,500 00	54,540 00	81,500 00	92,500 00
Total	12,292,302 75	12,931,562 12	12,894,238 82	12,914,157 25	10,640,051 72

by States and reserve cities—Continued.

FLORIDA.

Liabilities.	DECEMBER 28. 1 bank.	MARCH 15. 1 bank.	MAY 1. 1 bank.	JUNE 29. 1 bank.	OCTOBER 1. 1 bank.
Capital stock	$50,000 00	$50,000 00	$50,000 00	$50,000 00	$50,000 00
Surplus fund.........	1,660 00	1,810 00	1,810 00	1,810 00	1,980 00
Undivided profits....	4,679 77	2,177 05	3,492 40	5,536 42	2,670 13
Nat'l bank circulation	45,000 00	45,000 00	44,480 00	45,000 00	44,980 00
State bank circulation					
Dividends unpaid....					
Individual deposits...	48,854 07	104,086 17	113,315 25	83,233 00	50,949 35
U. S. deposits........					
Dep'ts U.S.dis.officers					
Due to national banks					114 64
Due to State banks...	3,106 65	7,305 06	1,824 26	288 64	21,450 85
Notes re-discounted..		2,200 00		3,000 00	12,712 50
Bills payable.........	15,000 00				
Total	168,300 49	212,578 28	214,921 91	188,868 06	184,857 47

ALABAMA.

	10 banks.	10 banks.	10 banks.	10 banks.	10 banks.
Capital stock	$1,668,000 00	$1,668,000 00	$1,668,000 00	$1,668,000 00	$1,668,000 00
Surplus fund.........	186,436 84	184,770 85	184,770 85	171,149 20	160,729 52
Undivided profits....	127,769 25	91,789 22	126,914 22	153,880 23	86,092 28
Nat'l bank circulation	1,454,970 00	1,452,030 00	1,445,730 00	1,432,560 00	1,439,240 00
State bank circulation					
Dividends unpaid....	1,678 00	1,300 00	963 00	8,783 00	1,542 00
Individual deposits..	1,016,141 75	1,311,467 21	1,336,459 61	1,082,109 97	1,187,547 74
U. S. deposits........					50,244 45
Dep'ts U.S.dis.officers					
Due to national banks	21,835 11	56,068 26	25,610 62	12,165 88	84,063 18
Due to State banks...	63,797 02	91,688 78	43,253 07	31,854 27	18,615 56
Notes re-discounted..	11,153 40			15,441 45	386,561 26
Bills payable.........	564 00				
Total	4,552,345 37	4,857,114 32	4,831,701 37	4,575,944 00	5,082,635 99

CITY OF NEW ORLEANS.

	7 banks.	7 banks.	7 banks.	7 banks.	7 banks.
Capital stock	$3,300,000 00	$3,300,000 00	$3,300,000 00	$2,875,000 00	$2,875,000 00
Surplus fund.........	515,808 82	508,768 64	508,768 64	573,268 64	573,268 61
Undivided profits....	437,456 55	248,915 13	296,269 36	418,282 28	333,778 55
Nat'l bank circulation	717,445 00	714,300 00	768,710 00	1,260,680 00	1,384,990 00
State bank circulation					
Dividends unpaid....	15,600 95	19,122 96	16,726 96	113,660 61	22,878 06
Individual deposits ..	6,175,067 35	7,361,941 51	7,162,563 95	7,108,324 33	4,838,988 99
U. S. deposits........			34,882 02	44,897 13	24,950 66
Dep'ts U.S.dis.officers					
Due to national banks	356,605 42	194,249 66	175,416 37	211,400 50	190,261 38
Due to State banks...	749,228 66	584,264 22	330,901 52	300,243 64	389,935 44
Notes re-discounted..	25,000 00				
Bills payable.........					
Total	12,292,302 75	12,931,562 12	12,894,238 82	12,914,157 25	10,640,051 72

Abtract of reports since October 1, 1877, arranged

TEXAS.

Resources.	DECEMBER 28. 12 banks.	MARCH 15. 12 banks.	MAY 1. 12 banks.	JUNE 29. 11 banks.	OCTOBER 1. 11 banks.
Loans and discounts.	$1,744,753 88	$1,782,421 56	$1,820,206 97	$1,641,256 79	$1,507,883 74
Bonds for circulation	684,000 00	684,000 00	684,000 00	650,000 00	650,000 00
Bonds for deposits...	175,000 00	175,000 00	175,000 00	175,000 00	175,000 00
U. S. bonds on hand..					
Other stocks and b'ds	82,280 29	94,041 26	85,632 06	102,301 18	104,683 98
Due from res've ag'ts.	249,630 21	102,522 82	133,751 22	51,409 71	256,782 24
Due from nat'l banks.	141,857 42	133,049 27	140,778 00	140,477 35	111,336 50
Due from State banks	117,469 80	117,510 52	114,470 68	108,864 85	167,674 26
Real estate, &c	161,024 76	172,919 80	171,515 74	169,289 99	170,224 12
Current expenses....	50,200 99	33,447 40	39,842 04	19,112 65	27,817 08
Premiums paid......	18,391 19	17,378 28	15,077 32	11,107 66	10,935 52
Cash items	30,571 26	84,550 40	29,216 00	31,309 70	101,586 55
Clear'g-house exch'gs					
Bills of other banks..	216,762 00	128,935 00	162,498 00	148,698 00	146,035 00
Fractional currency .	14,008 63	11,214 45	10,310 91	11,419 29	8,223 17
Specie	86,642 26	118,624 32	134,000 32	132,245 49	110,643 95
Legal-tender notes ..	361,549 00	352,068 00	305,950 00	407,043 00	284,240 00
U. S. cert's of deposit.					
Due from U. S. Treas.	37,008 01	34,317 51	35,915 42	36,237 12	36,102 77
Total..........	4,171,149 70	4,042,009 59	4,148,164 68	3,835,792 78	3,869,108 88

ARKANSAS.

	2 banks.	2 banks.	2 banks.	2 banks.	2 banks.
Loans and discounts.	$213,365 21	$260,889 06	$277,194 76	$304,453 60	$274,404 53
Bonds for circulation	205,000 00	205,000 00	205,000 00	205,000 00	205,000 00
Bonds for deposits...	100,000 00	100,000 00	100,000 00	100,000 00	100,000 00
U. S. bonds on hand..		10,000 00	21,200 00	27,600 00	21,000 00
Other stocks and b'ds	38,002 90	40,878 00	44,601 73	35,973 91	35,405 84
Due from res've ag'ts.	54,011 22	61,177 04	70,672 75	30,950 93	35,947 83
Due from nat'l banks.	25,898 94	36,052 08	31,844 95	23,692 31	5,625 77
Due from State banks	3,307 41	6,016 42	1,790 64	2,135 04	5,464 42
Real estate, &c	2,263 75	1,263 75	1,263 75	1,263 75	1,000 00
Current expenses....	429 23	2,463 53			
Premiums paid......	12,093 95	7,487 50	7,412 50	7,412 50	
Cash items	1,781 66	1,336 53	641 89	521 41	648 72
Clear'g-house exch'gs					
Bills of other banks..	53,928 00	39,170 00	5,520 00	13,271 00	9,082 00
Fractional currency	877 41	784 42	549 88	496 56	540 14
Specie	10,808 95	7,820 73	7,013 30	5,984 80	14,367 35
Legal-tender notes ..	83,600 00	72,700 00	45,280 00	35,350 00	40,900 00
U. S. cert's of deposit.					
Due from U. S. Treas	9,722 00	9,515 16	8,175 00	8,474 94	9,422 80
Total..........	815,990 63	862,563 22	828,161 15	802,580 75	758,809 40

KENTUCKY.

	38 banks.	39 banks.	39 banks.	39 banks.	40 banks.
Loans and discounts.	$8,731,287 72	$8,514,546 49	$8,491,536 98	$8,358,365 88	$7,876,920 90
Bonds for circulation	6,002,650 00	6,157,650 00	6,166,650 00	6,166,650 00	6,151,650 00
Bonds for deposits...	110,000 00	110,000 00	110,000 00	110,000 00	110,000 00
U. S. bonds on hand..	25,500 00	131,350 00	184,000 00	238,750 00	370,850 00
Other stocks and b'ds	94,803 90	182,540 15	273,766 59	325,047 77	371,441 94
Due from res've ag'ts.	791,402 64	563,229 80	487,724 94	647,315 79	867,874 92
Due from nat'l banks.	600,913 87	645,708 27	481,120 17	468,637 40	635,181 03
Due from State banks	292,116 71	294,589 46	178,121 82	242,681 93	277,073 51
Real estate, &c	441,368 31	442,747 38	435,657 13	482,583 70	491,630 98
Current expenses....	90,892 22	79,361 05	99,328 97	45,258 44	69,777 16
Premiums paid......	317,462 30	280,751 67	285,571 92	249,788 13	237,034 10
Cash items	20,820 61	28,098 19	31,553 98	29,050 21	34,294 27
Clear'g-house exch'gs					
Bills of other banks..	283,733 00	219,905 00	225,676 00	213,074 00	234,642 00
Fractional currency .	7,529 95	6,039 95	7,183 28	6,048 35	5,585 59
Specie	61,604 01	60,230 81	60,686 02	61,089 67	84,479 37
Legal-tender notes ..	530,047 00	582,510 00	551,673 00	565,789 00	528,603 00
U. S. cert's of deposit.	30,000 00	30,000 00	30,000 00	5,000 00	10,000 00
Due from U. S. Treas.	269,287 18	288,337 95	276,744 70	283,035 67	277,659 16
Total..........	18,707,419 42	18,618,496 77	18,396,097 50	18,498,166 03	18,634,697 93

by States and reserve cities—Continued.

TEXAS.

Liabilities.	DECEMBER 28. 12 banks.	MARCH 15. 12 banks.	MAY 1. 12 banks.	JUNE 29. 11 banks.	OCTOBER 1. 11 banks.
Capital stock	$1,100,000 00	$1,100,000 00	$1,100,000 00	$1,050,000 00	$1,050,000 00
Surplus fund	294,981 53	300,749 87	299,128 62	292,628 62	296,065 26
Undivided profits	124,615 92	88,291 85	85,085 89	72,804 18	75,978 29
Nat'l bank circulation	610,167 00	596,227 00	587,677 00	536,457 00	533,471 00
State bank circulation					
Dividends unpaid	630 00	262 50	237 50	4,150 00	135 00
Individual deposits	1,441,924 85	1,534,553 42	1,611,932 98	1,562,888 23	1,515,833 20
U. S. deposits	88,095 42	113,688 52	141,207 67	126,818 89	86,302 69
Dep'ts U.S.dis.officers	328,422 02	141,904 33	146,227 79	88,672 53	134,531 73
Due to national banks	21,183 83	19,311 49	41,780 42	26,847 58	33,905 47
Due to State banks	134,229 13	114,070 61	109,103 47	72,025 75	97,886 24
Notes re-discounted	24,400 00	12,950 00	15,450 00	2,500 00	25,000 00
Bills payable	2,500 00	20,000 00	10,333 34		20,000 00
Total	4,171,149 70	4,042,009 59	4,148,164 68	3,845,792 78	3,869,168 88

ARKANSAS.

	2 banks.	2 banks.	2 banks.	2 banks.	2 banks.
Capital stock	$205,000 00	$205,000 00	$205,000 00	$205,000 00	$205,000 00
Surplus fund	30,375 00	31,750 00	31,750 00	31,750 00	31,750 00
Undivided profits	16,603 18	7,315 60	5,776 95	10,797 43	8,036 30
Nat'l bank circulation	184,500 00	180,400 00	144,500 00	164,300 00	184,400 00
State bank circulation					
Dividends unpaid					
Individual deposits	262,225 34	334,172 32	336,258 91	207,521 35	250,164 84
U. S. deposits	83,862 48	72,101 82	83,439 61	75,734 22	54,991 09
Dep'ts U.S.dis.officers	12,235 54	9,240 05	2,778 82	5,172 46	20,821 43
Due to national banks	13,172 75	17,927 80	11,777 35	9,603 40	
Due to State banks	8,016 34	4,655 63	6,879 51	2,701 89	3,645 74
Notes re-discounted					
Bills payable					
Total	815,990 63	862,503 22	828,161 15	802,580 75	758,800 40

KENTUCKY.

	38 banks.	39 banks.	39 banks.	39 banks.	40 banks.
Capital stock	$6,941,000 00	$7,091,000 00	$7,041,000 00	$7,041,000 00	$6,961,730 00
Surplus fund	1,227,550 35	1,242,500 11	1,199,364 90	1,164,999 35	1,124,676 71
Undivided profits	609,850 08	490,723 02	456,297 91	366,857 71	413,654 38
Nat'l bank circulation	5,315,347 00	5,102,207 00	5,494,107 00	5,486,247 00	5,391,407 00
State bank circulation					
Dividends unpaid	12,511 20	12,863 30	8,897 30	80,528 80	8,770 90
Individual deposits	3,834,734 18	3,731,364 69	3,603,824 64	3,742,260 98	4,116,760 07
U. S. deposits	77,929 96	81,954 78	80,598 80	65,709 10	81,822 48
Dep'ts U.S.dis.officers	3,013 00	356 00	2,039 60	720 68	2,611 20
Due to national banks	239,571 86	211,125 93	150,052 83	188,248 32	195,947 32
Due to State banks	416,041 30	386,211 71	324,684 32	290,147 89	304,443 67
Notes re-discounted	8,746 29	7,050 00	5,000 00	4,300 00	
Bills payable	21,130 20	21,130 20	31,130 20	68,146 20	32,874 20
Total	18,707,419 42	18,618,496 77	18,306,997 50	18,498,166 03	18,634,697 93

Abstract of reports since October 1, 1877, arranged

CITY OF LOUISVILLE.

Resources.	DECEMBER 28. 8 banks.	MARCH 15. 8 banks.	MAY 1. 8 banks.	JUNE 29. 8 banks.	OCTOBER 1. 8 banks.
Loans and discounts.	$4,705,424 92	$4,306,348 50	$4,545,668 15	$4,521,747 75	$4,551,089 36
Bonds for circulation.	2,644,700 00	2,644,700 00	2,644,700 00	2,644,700 00	2,644,700 00
Bonds for deposits...	500,000 00	500,000 00	500,000 00	500,000 00	500,000 00
U. S. bonds on hand..	....	....	121,400 00	23,550 00	27,200 00
Other stocks and b'ds	48,759 19	51,690 41	69,061 91	63,241 06	59,393 09
Due from res've ag'ts.	162,736 36	263,606 00	221,341 63	363,141 08	351,915 72
Due from nat'l banks.	125,409 33	98,352 13	151,254 33	134,403 46	128,985 19
Due from State banks	107,732 44	125,032 24	109,759 41	126,268 80	117,512 55
Real estate, &c	240,860 33	225,779 28	226,503 28	220,286 65	208,963 17
Current expenses....	24,621 66	59,678 50	41,823 86	18,496 83	52,443 74
Premiums paid......	235,145 43	227,848 63	173,517 24	167,450 78	159,975 81
Cash items	40,327 47	24,215 33	26,348 66	42,765 53	73,119 13
Clear'g-house exch'gs	....	....	....	....	....
Bills of other banks..	68,609 00	117,512 00	84,025 00	40,500 00	47,113 00
Fractional currency .	828 81	1,552 75	1,410 10	1,307 41	1,308 26
Specie	14,828 45	17,117 25	23,575 37	62,234 68	85,240 76
Legal-tender notes ..	450,123 00	636,053 00	496,050 00	388,200 00	427,210 00
U. S. cert's of deposit.	....	....	....	....	....
Due from U. S. Treas.	117,953 93	120,411 50	121,181 00	126,082 25	116,424 90
Total..........	9,488,060 32	9,419,897 52	9,557,620 14	9,433,376 30	9,552,594 68

TENNESSEE.

	25 banks.	25 banks.	25 banks.	25 banks.	25 banks.
Loans and discounts.	$5,037,242 66	$4,542,002 54	$4,906,618 39	$4,691,289 45	$4,734,719 01
Bonds for circulation	2,614,000 00	2,614,000 00	2,614,000 00	2,744,000 00	2,744,000 00
Bonds for deposits...	400,000 00	390,000 00	430,000 00	550,000 00	620,000 00
U. S. bonds on hand..	229,550 00	316,500 00	337,550 00	304,350 00	202,850 00
Other stocks and b'ds	151,899 30	162,437 65	214,360 20	197,166 56	291,045 78
Due from res've ag'ts	513,126 90	979,192 14	769,943 79	1,010,894 22	829,418 48
Due from nat'l banks.	347,182 40	455,279 17	478,883 16	358,641 31	371,745 62
Due from State banks	154,752 31	172,790 70	186,374 88	120,192 52	119,399 77
Real estate, &c	364,075 87	369,277 62	371,698 30	355,850 10	359,897 94
Current expenses....	118,813 93	83,651 96	95,748 40	63,337 99	59,346 54
Premiums paid......	201,497 84	180,576 09	181,362 67	182,886 13	141,525 05
Cash items	183,038 13	188,612 96	141,206 90	121,616 04	76,874 64
Clear'g-house exch'gs	....	....	....	....	....
Bills of other banks..	485,496 00	471,039 00	466,824 00	350,950 00	501,887 00
Fractional currency .	11,070 43	12,197 42	13,604 52	9,797 71	9,933 23
Specie	82,118 91	87,439 66	129,307 47	145,523 17	182,019 52
Legal-tender notes ..	896,403 00	1,150,800 00	1,157,533 00	1,058,629 00	955,262 00
U. S. cert's of deposit.	....	....	....	....	....
Due from U. S. Treas.	131,941 09	126,712 76	127,115 81	131,612 20	128,898 76
Total	11,922,208 77	12,302,509 67	12,624,221 49	12,405,745 40	12,329,023 34

OHIO.

	153 banks.	152 banks.	150 banks.	151 banks.	151 banks.
Loans and discounts	$32,308,958 39	$30,939,761 75	$30,621,849 53	$29,718,930 47	$29,559,654 58
Bonds for circulation	17,262,250 00	17,249,750 00	17,019,750 00	17,054,750 00	16,950,750 00
Bonds for deposits ..	400,000 00	325,000 00	325,000 00	325,000 00	328,400 00
U. S. bonds on hand..	936,700 00	973,300 00	828,600 00	751,150 00	1,008,550 00
Other stocks and b'ds	808,686 80	904,735 87	846,253 63	845,996 20	795,605 78
Due from res've ag'ts	2,757,630 89	2,903,294 24	1,791,307 49	2,432,926 49	2,841,075 55
Due from nat'l banks.	981,199 37	1,011,179 85	657,347 76	735,383 02	936,121 31
Due from State banks	468,698 10	410,542 88	370,957 43	445,576 79	480,012 05
Real estate, &c	1,612,219 36	1,671,674 05	1,621,210 21	1,654,816 46	1,706,673 93
Current expenses....	218,169 16	382,008 76	395,313 50	204,471 22	388,343 14
Premiums paid......	281,261 75	269,199 52	233,840 42	215,281 23	190,246 50
Cash items	357,603 26	316,520 65	318,389 79	300,000 81	354,572 44
Clear'g-house exch'gs	....	....	....	....	....
Bills of other banks..	854,822 00	891,517 00	854,853 00	626,849 00	891,309 00
Fractional currency .	54,647 83	41,495 12	39,568 55	39,767 40	36,105 60
Specie	283,154 56	401,561 63	406,312 96	391,161 82	483,991 53
Legal-tender notes ..	3,322,270 00	3,374,303 00	3,232,569 00	2,658,357 00	3,249,685 00
U. S. cert's of deposit.	10,000 00	10,000 00	10,000 00	....	....
Due from U. S. Treas.	779,303 75	816,158 70	804,300 00	752,000 84	802,656 33
Total..........	63,697,965 22	62,892,092 32	60,357,436 27	59,133,018 75	61,072,752 83

by States and reserve cities—Continued.

CITY OF LOUISVILLE.,

Liabilities.	DECEMBER 28. 8 banks.	MARCH 15. 8 banks.	MAY 1. 8 banks.	JUNE 29. 8 banks.	OCTOBER 1. 8 banks.
Capital stock	$3, 095, 500 00	$2, 995, 500 00	$2, 995, 500 00	$2, 995, 500 00	$2, 995, 500 00
Surplus fund	342, 212 13	353, 417 31	320, 912 67	317, 333 04	319, 778 62
Undivided profits	174, 486 14	212, 518 23	138, 522 84	130, 035 00	213, 578 98
Nat'l bank circulation	2, 357, 469 00	2, 342, 243 00	2, 329, 203 00	2, 326, 053 00	2, 342, 953 00
State bank circulation					
Dividends unpaid	3, 843 50	4, 202 00	10, 727 00	13, 696 00	9, 391 00
Individual deposits	1, 582, 890 74	1, 548, 674 41	1, 743, 005 62	1, 716, 113 81	1, 719, 520 08
U. S. deposits	201, 861 90	211, 956 91	268, 407 35	207, 050 08	166, 820 01
Dep'ts U.S.dis.officers	226, 885 65	200, 710 73	182, 588 45	201, 870 57	271, 909 90
Due to national banks	637, 011 48	842, 112 14	861, 312 65	713, 890 99	752, 945 03
Due to State banks	672, 954 80	655, 311 09	672, 049 72	679, 388 56	743, 039 50
Notes re-discounted	192, 944 89	53, 251 70	35, 300 84	77, 445 25	17, 068 56
Bills payable				75, 000 00	
Total	9, 488, 060 32	9, 419, 897 52	9, 557, 620 14	9, 453, 376 30	9, 552, 594 68

TENNESSEE.

	25 banks.	25 banks.	25 banks.	25 banks.	25 banks.
Capital stock	$3, 080, 300 00	$3, 080, 300 00	$3, 080, 300 00	$3, 080, 300 00	$3, 080, 300 00
Surplus fund	560, 817 65	529, 946 22	530, 562 35	468, 124 10	478, 899 90
Undivided profits	377, 176 65	228, 614 04	258, 993 52	284, 041 74	211, 080 73
Nat'l bank circulation	2, 345, 601 00	2, 338, 740 00	2, 325, 040 00	2, 419, 860 00	2, 426, 570 00
State bank circulation					
Dividends unpaid	1, 963 50	3, 068 50	2, 478 00	23, 166 00	9, 612 00
Individual deposits	4, 865, 390 99	5, 631, 712 27	5, 872, 149 04	5, 457, 057 12	5, 272, 744 10
U. S. deposits	257, 625 33	239, 031 89	293, 364 93	422, 239 82	493, 373 46
Dep'ts U.S.dis.officers	79, 082 15	58, 194 29	65, 287 63	51, 778 64	81, 222 33
Due to national banks	238, 607 69	132, 122 79	132, 085 51	115, 189 89	154, 103 47
Due to State banks	96, 762 21	56, 579 67	63, 960 51	53, 988 09	108, 692 26
Notes re-discounted	6, 591 60				12, 425 00
Bills payable	12, 200 00	4, 200 00			
Total	11, 922, 208 77	12, 302, 509 67	12, 624, 221 49	12, 405, 745 40	12, 329, 023 34

OHIO.

	153 banks.	152 banks.	150 banks.	151 banks.	151 banks.
Capital stock	$19, 571, 900 00	$19, 461, 900 00	$18, 706, 900 00	$18, 756, 900 00	$18, 636, 900 00
Surplus fund	4, 138, 796 98	4, 100, 596 25	3, 994, 929 35	3, 948, 246 19	3, 945, 493 78
Undivided profits	1, 560, 376 63	1, 752, 139 16	1, 804, 782 42	1, 808, 671 30	1, 706, 056 61
Nat'l bank circulation	15, 313, 908 00	15, 206, 642 00	15, 043, 700 00	15, 062, 508 00	14, 987, 990 00
State bank circulation	36, 043 00	22, 735 00	22, 731 00	22, 723 00	22, 722 00
Dividends unpaid	26, 472 22	17, 249 00	37, 669 72	77, 080 00	26, 818 75
Individual deposits	21, 026, 870 47	20, 725, 841 53	18, 889, 946 84	18, 289, 084 51	20, 108, 630 54
U. S. deposits	259, 322 18	226, 315 33	223, 026 14	210, 675 17	184, 300 60
Dep'ts U.S.dis.officers	33, 091 49	32, 210 86	22, 794 15	30, 549 07	25, 467 27
Due to national banks	612, 016 93	493, 676 43	594, 220 33	486, 768 74	583, 536 85
Due to State banks	470, 443 67	432, 730 63	439, 194 44	367, 000 89	417, 715 01
Notes re-discounted	212, 245 95	167, 557 47	208, 355 08	224, 869 58	108, 515 87
Bills payable	435, 583 70	252, 468 66	369, 183 80	347, 942 30	318, 596 55
Total	63, 697, 065 22	62, 892, 092 32	60, 357, 436 27	59, 133, 018 75	61, 672, 732 83

Abstract of reports since October 1, 1877, arranged

CITY OF CINCINNATI.

Resources.	DECEMBER 28. 6 banks.	MARCH 15. 6 banks.	MAY 1. 6 banks.	JUNE 29. 6 banks.	OCTOBER 1. 6 banks.
Loans and discounts.	$8,506,275 17	$8,661,593 81	$8,414,773 52	$8,253,613 82	$8,369,304 10
Bonds for circulation	3,702,200 00	3,702,200 00	3,702,200 00	3,702,200 00	3,702,200 00
Bonds for deposits ..	825,500 00	825,500 00	825,500 00	865,500 00	890,500 00
U. S. bonds on hand..	336,300 00	419,450 00	451,550 00	473,500 00	331,550 00
Other stocks and b'ds	180,604 92	215,188 54	126,155 65	227,553 59	292,382 08
Due from res've ag'ts	1,628,198 11	1,118,741 19	1,003,360 04	1,274,426 49	1,083,652 66
Due from nat'l banks	491,496 28	341,652 03	333,522 65	313,517 79	550,872 62
Due from State banks	339,783 18	394,755 15	392,541 42	334,197 03	294,058 36
Real estate, &c	200,341 84	238,228 91	238,263 91	258,130 94	250,934 51
Current expenses....	125,815 72	100,025 21	87,860 07	45,330 92	65,996 75
Premiums paid......	24,455 81	14,469 18	13,662 65	8,130 91	....
Cash items	68,159 47	48,843 89	50,017 24	49,794 06	83,728 33
Clear'g-house exch'gs	137,679 47	112,705 68	73,359 28	115,604 96	61,611 10
Bills of other banks..	228,098 00	230,794 00	201,152 00	196,636 00	254,405 00
Fractional currency .	591 22	828 77	1,026 31	1,135 15	925 00
Specie	37,752 35	44,980 58	51,928 35	63,370 12	74,947 19
Legal-tender notes ..	947,720 00	949,000 00	727,114 00	669,158 00	863,000 00
U. S. cert's of deposit.	560,000 00	555,000 00	455,000 00	420,000 00	930,000 00
Due from U. S. Treas.	184,843 50	186,145 45	169,666 95	179,946 95	184,646 95
Total...........	18,525,815 04	18,160,102 39	17,228,654 64	17,451,746 73	18,284,714 65

CITY OF CLEVELAND.

	6 banks.	6 banks.	6 banks.	6 banks.	6 banks.
Loans and discounts.	$7,170,489 55	$7,442,227 69	$6,961,776 95	$6,680,214 93	$6,242,895 78
Bonds for circulation.	2,326,000 00	2,326,000 00	2,267,000 00	2,267,000 00	2,167,000 00
Bonds for deposits ...	225,000 00	225,000 00	225,000 00	225,000 00	225,000 00
U. S. bonds on hand...	116,000 00	119,000 00	104,150 00	87,900 00	328,900 00
Other stocks and b'ds	88,169 59	91,418 34	41,193 34	43,675 84	45,615 83
Due from res've ag'ts	489,858 17	305,455 03	271,132 50	661,795 88	1,673,880 47
Due from nat'l banks	481,929 25	323,977 14	417,497 35	417,138 32	440,675 98
Due from State banks	182,877 68	94,133 37	160,038 60	234,464 33	575,103 65
Real estate, &c	194,104 37	194,111 37	194,116 82	197,125 53	223,131 53
Current expenses....	50,531 58	127,177 55	103,006 22	30,089 58	124,406 64
Premiums paid......	13,767 00	13,767 00	12,423 25	12,423 25	12,423 25
Cash items	116,007 91	62,298 78	47,106 90	64,497 59	66,194 18
Clear'g-house exch'gs	79,809 85	98,176 62	109,686 64	93,531 56	106,618 39
Bills of other banks..	207,313 00	125,866 00	205,966 00	111,304 00	330,830 00
Fractional currency .	10,230 81	8,483 55	10,588 02	8,709 57	9,713 63
Specie	124,877 20	146,844 10	142,297 11	109,192 85	88,964 71
Legal-tender notes ..	690,000 00	830,000 00	920,000 00	820,000 00	1,195,000 00
U. S. cert's of deposit.	35,000 00	30,000 00	5,000 00	5,000 00	15,000 00
Due from U. S. Treas.	98,694 92	101,684 93	103,467 33	94,208 14	94,941 69
Total...........	12,700,660 88	12,665,621 47	12,301,447 12	12,172,271 37	13,965,996 03

INDIANA.

	98 banks.	96 banks.	95 banks.	95 banks.	94 banks.
Loans and discounts.	$24,086,623 32	$22,590,512 30	$22,483,210 49	$21,815,894 01	$20,497,607 78
Bonds for circulation	13,301,700 00	12,937,000 00	13,024,000 00	12,924,000 00	12,882,500 00
Bonds for deposits ...	300,000 00	400,000 00	400,000 00	400,000 00	400,000 00
U. S. bonds on hand..	295,050 00	397,600 00	671,850 00	981,050 00	926,300 00
Other stocks and b'ds	738,680 95	776,363 48	758,752 01	928,533 60	945,042 32
Due from res've ag'ts	1,871,648 65	2,378,602 04	2,378,398 27	2,116,913 09	2,569,243 03
Due from nat'l banks	1,181,543 03	1,390,355 79	1,555,866 34	1,219,201 83	1,979,622 04
Due from State banks	454,666 05	521,189 68	442,942 71	420,127 76	654,826 64
Real estate, &c	1,494,609 63	1,548,826 58	1,599,090 30	1,628,721 50	1,701,078 73
Current expenses....	288,514 47	186,778 46	300,955 58	201,106 13	224,884 06
Premiums paid......	234,006 73	214,975 85	228,616 48	195,358 18	178,887 88
Cash items	238,104 90	247,452 27	290,215 02	324,271 43	352,370 92
Clear'g-house exch'gs	....	....	....	....	....
Bills of other banks..	975,385 00	783,229 00	793,207 00	626,286 00	902,786 00
Fractional currency .	31,201 85	29,964 18	29,822 83	24,669 64	17,920 87
Specie	215,411 41	291,884 28	324,400 53	352,619 73	418,919 57
Legal-tender notes ..	2,488,348 00	2,456,248 00	2,625,308 00	2,228,453 00	2,450,164 00
U. S. cert's of deposit.	70,000 00	70,000 00	15,000 00	15,000 00	5,000 00
Due from U. S. Treas	619,728 71	628,272 55	581,535 56	580,443 46	655,290 07
Total...........	48,884,223 80	47,809,322 90	48,599,201 12	46,982,649 36	47,759,443 91

by States and reserve cities—Continued.

CITY OF CINCINNATI.

Liabilities.	DECEMBER 28. 6 banks.	MARCH 15. 6 banks.	MAY 1. 6 banks.	JUNE 29. 6 banks.	OCTOBER 1. 6 banks.
Capital stock.........	$4,400,000 00	$4,400,000 00	$4,350,000 00	$4,300,000 00	$4,300,000 00
Surplus fund.........	706,200 00	872,400 00	712,400 00	712,400 00	718,300 00
Undivided profits....	688,208 26	395,298 18	542,034 76	577,053 04	463,834 18
Nat'l bank circulation	3,317,070 00	3,318,790 00	3,304,370 00	3,098,970 00	3,096,050 00
State bank circulation					
Dividends unpaid....	5,376 00	4,827 00	3,929 00	3,164 00	5,976 00
Individual deposits ..	5,148,264 11	4,507,771 60	3,893,804 88	4,388,776 17	4,815,127 98
U. S. deposits........	735,000 00	735,000 00	735,000 00	805,512 35	823,675 16
Dep'ts U.S.dis.officers					
Due to national banks	2,160,994 73	2,583,252 97	2,247,098 19	2,103,137 57	2,568,090 18
Due to State banks...	726,151 94	710,312 64	817,567 81	804,263 00	811,891 15
Notes re-discounted..					
Bills payable.........	638,550 00	626,450 00	622,450 00	658,450 00	681,950 00
Total	18,525,815 04	18,160,102 39	17,228,654 64	17,451,746 73	18,284,714 65

CITY OF CLEVELAND.

	6 banks.	6 banks.	6 banks.	6 banks.	6 banks.
Capital stock	$4,350,000 00	$4,350,000 00	$4,350,000 00	$4,350,000 00	$4,350,000 00
Surplus fund........	734,045 90	734,045 90	646,945 90	652,418 39	652,418 39
Undivided profits....	193,426 14	341,652 06	284,512 91	138,762 87	306,945 15
Nat'l bank circulation	2,001,440 00	1,987,240 00	1,967,820 00	1,922,200 00	1,867,500 00
State bank circulation					
Dividends unpaid....	585 00	90 00	42,100 00	18,756 00	18,144 00
Individual deposits...	3,594,933 43	3,645,315 88	3,637,467 15	3,956,528 72	5,341,878 98
U. S. deposits........	85,420 02	35,450 02	124,654 68	85,178 79	123,945 25
Dep'ts U.S.dis.officers	64,161 77	128,328 99	28,893 27	56,517 40	76,175 42
Due to national banks	524,470 00	402,709 45	338,763 17	276,707 02	455,743 21
Due to State banks...	387,878 39	337,901 42	262,290 04	318,202 18	447,245 63
Notes re-discounted..	308,500 14	163,727 75	124,000 00	88,000 00	2,000 00
Bills payable........	455,800 00	539,000 00	494,000 00	300,000 00	324,000 00
Total	12,700,660 88	12,665,621 47	12,301,447 12	12,172,271 37	13,965,996 03

INDIANA.

	98 banks.	96 banks.	95 banks.	95 banks.	94 banks.
Capital stock	$15,998,500 00	$15,512,530 00	$15,321,530 00	$15,191,530 00	$15,034,530 00
Surplus fund........	4,428,905 92	4,443,058 22	4,389,775 17	4,274,406 58	4,116,432 43
Undivided profits....	1,579,803 75	1,239,509 16	1,321,437 52	1,399,909 66	1,294,502 96
Nat'l bank circulation	11,887,759 00	11,529,219 00	11,571,578 00	11,446,453 00	11,435,898 00
State bank circulation					
Dividends unpaid....	22,974 27	47,368 75	18,214 70	52,391 50	14,523 16
Individual deposits...	13,354,003 31	13,238,047 80	14,104,528 10	12,977,292 67	13,839,739 79
U. S. deposits	123,178 65	159,942 95	178,917 58	142,450 25	150,441 01
Dep'ts U.S.dis.officers	180,017 89	381,070 94	60,914 94	116,510 34	157,970 94
Due to national banks	693,051 60	716,058 87	870,137 83	794,408 51	1,055,612 87
Due to State banks ..	485,471 68	453,420 24	635,370 28	537,796 85	604,483 89
Notes re-discounted..	89,113 24	47,831 20	5,800 00	17,500 00	21,500 00
Bills payable........	41,441 29	41,166 80	34,000 00	32,000 00	33,808 81
Total	48,884,223 80	47,809,322 90	48,509,201 12	46,982,649 36	47,759,443 91

Abstract of reports since October 1, 1877, arranged

ILLINOIS.

Resources.	DECEMBER 28. 131 banks.	MARCH 15. 131 banks.	MAY 1. 129 banks.	JUNE 29. 128 banks.	OCTOBER 1. 130 banks.
Loans and discounts.	$20,559,928 97	$19,606,630 78	$19,617,245 29	$19,398,764 85	$18,887,071 71
Bonds for circulation.	8,678,000 00	8,658,000 00	8,520,500 00	8,480,500 00	8,621,500 00
Bonds for deposits...	825,000 00	825,000 00	825,000 00	825,000 00	825,000 00
U. S. bonds on hand..	130,450 00	292,500 00	339,300 00	505,850 00	572,050 00
Other stocks and b'ds	645,401 89	724,903 75	674,927 96	732,786 69	610,468 49
Due from res've ag'ts	2,141,405 60	3,071,043 84	2,692,745 41	3,388,580 12	3,226,831 29
Due from nat'l banks.	847,996 59	911,808 59	866,866 75	1,017,120 08	941,487 01
Due from State banks	194,765 20	168,123 11	174,220 59	163,419 26	155,112 00
Real estate, &c	1,411,935 09	1,418,243 35	1,440,181 42	1,467,508 38	1,492,671 64
Current expenses....	257,508 06	251,738 19	295,750 87	234,796 58	194,045 94
Premiums paid	259,288 84	229,155 41	212,581 27	182,657 45	171,311 86
Cash items	279,427 90	311,230 66	333,397 95	293,776 17	380,977 75
Clear'g-house exch'gs					
Bills of other banks..	686,427 00	801,286 00	714,580 00	671,148 00	632,296 00
Fractional currency .	36,209 84	29,631 36	30,456 21	27,107 65	21,164 50
Specie	199,292 26	268,844 47	361,404 77	409,303 78	482,144 62
Legal-tender notes ..	2,330,943 00	2,763,977 00	2,521,755 00	2,418,475 00	2,488,491 00
U. S. cert's of deposit	20,000 00	20,000 00	20,000 00	20,000 00	20,000 00
Due from U. S. Treas	394,476 09	420,934 77	406,064 27	392,215 99	417,912 81
Total	40,008,456 33	40,773,051 28	40,046,977 76	40,629,010 00	40,140,536 62

CITY OF CHICAGO.

	10 banks.	10 banks.	10 banks.	10 banks.	9 banks.
Loans and discounts.	$15,590,706 52	$15,905,127 38	$15,712,528 46	$15,483,652 95	$15,921,429 72
Bonds for circulation.	950,000 00	950,000 00	950,000 00	950,000 00	800,000 00
Bonds for deposits...			100,000 00	100,000 00	100,000 00
U. S. bonds on hand..	544,500 00	1,156,450 00	1,197,150 00	2,512,750 00	2,596,550 00
Other stocks and b'ds	136,344 08	179,596 08	180,596 08	144,616 08	137,733 68
Due from res've ag'ts.	2,734,494 85	3,120,807 30	2,524,516 14	2,771,867 21	3,024,196 31
Due from nat'l banks	660,159 68	787,136 68	773,525 64	702,327 84	1,091,213 52
Due from State banks	390,669 76	459,317 09	582,159 72	441,974 41	592,140 24
Real estate, &c	607,667 01	709,493 20	606,341 20	742,862 68	723,625 76
Current expenses....	196,391 33	140,051 76	160,001 60	102,937 24	67,817 45
Premiums paid	12,564 72	57,615 40	48,547 81	31,034 98	21,871 71
Cash items	51,725 62	66,855 17	50,872 13	27,790 02	17,976 48
Clear'g-house exch'gs	993,227 16	867,138 39	1,750,408 53	1,064,219 58	2,242,108 88
Bills of other banks.	632,510 00	588,539 00	673,033 00	653,723 00	584,983 00
Fractional currency .	6,643 40	5,676 68	2,468 49	2,511 80	2,780 82
Specie	400,767 39	617,129 12	1,424,138 08	1,292,630 66	1,233,225 56
Legal-tender notes .	3,832,500 00	3,446,042 00	2,443,500 00	2,949,500 00	2,922,190 00
U. S. cert's of deposit	1,165,000 00	1,230,000 00	1,115,000 00	1,560,000 00	990,000 00
Due from U. S. Treas	65,550 00	58,050 00	92,450 00	73,750 00	65,700 00
Total	29,061,421 52	30,344,426 15	30,287,216 88	31,608,148 45	33,155,543 13

MICHIGAN.

	76 banks.	76 banks.	75 banks.	75 banks.	75 banks.
Loans and discounts	$12,129,816 18	$11,948,994 32	$12,102,604 91	$12,306,934 80	$11,818,451 93
Bonds for circulation	4,943,700 00	5,038,700 00	4,923,700 00	4,920,300 00	4,912,350 00
Bonds for deposits...	50,000 00	50,000 00	50,000 00	50,000 00	55,000 00
U. S. bonds on hand..	65,450 00	76,750 00	75,450 00	102,000 00	170,000 00
Other stocks and b'ds	499,470 79	486,407 39	476,803 20	465,896 74	458,924 04
Due from res've ag'ts	1,151,322 03	1,322,541 68	1,061,761 26	1,001,334 36	1,457,020 24
Due from nat'l banks	506,835 66	471,558 29	417,737 45	363,273 64	492,308 97
Due from State banks	103,870 05	95,381 50	67,830 56	102,173 29	83,759 16
Real estate, &c	806,515 37	901,608 78	908,447 27	944,513 52	975,361 62
Current expenses....	181,664 66	118,194 31	155,518 64	67,305 66	133,641 35
Premiums paid	107,358 62	98,091 54	92,539 90	87,437 98	75,130 23
Cash items	132,719 22	114,444 88	109,262 90	104,683 09	109,809 85
Clear'g-house exch'gs					
Bills of other banks.	469,613 00	233,880 00	276,012 00	262,796 00	337,705 00
Fractional currency .	19,557 13	22,162 67	17,709 02	15,794 03	14,603 50
Specie	120,540 45	163,041 73	242,252 79	246,596 87	278,726 49
Legal-tender notes ..	1,064,177 00	935,116 00	987,958 00	889,916 00	1,064,608 00
U. S. cert's of deposit					
Due from U. S. Treas.	227,997 85	245,871 63	226,650 28	221,802 37	227,460 36
Total	22,676,017 61	22,323,434 72	22,192,292 27	22,152,758 35	22,665,820 74

by States and reserve cities—Continued.

ILLINOIS.

Liabilities.	DECEMBER 28. 131 banks.	MARCH 15. 131 banks.	MAY 1. 129 banks.	JUNE 29. 128 banks.	OCTOBER 1. 130 banks.
Capital stock	$11,446,000 00	$11,394,600 00	$11,164,600 00	$11,114,600 00	$11,279,600 00
Surplus fund	3,860,665 92	3,864,012 17	3,805,103 71	3,771,855 77	3,670,099 65
Undivided profits....	1,366,621 64	1,096,789 59	1,143,273 14	1,132,254 15	955,758 99
Nat'l bank circulation	7,745,153 00	7,699,593 00	7,569,078 00	7,487,513 00	7,594,253 00
State bank circulation	....	....	....	....	....
Dividends unpaid....	29,471 65	15,560 53	38,828 00	92,062 00	39,375 50
Individual deposits ..	14,135,405 12	15,451,580 27	15,199,225 51	15,848,074 59	15,468,044 09
U. S. deposits........	613,624 95	625,790 52	534,642 17	572,736 05	620,922 03
Dep'ts U.S.dis.officers	59,787 38	49,087 20	53,780 19	38,394 93	41,415 84
Due to national banks	122,363 15	107,005 39	93,738 86	100,135 20	97,875 96
Due to State banks...	155,230 71	252,887 54	253,064 86	300,802 22	333,492 43
Notes re-discounted..	410,515 25	161,027 51	139,390 91	150,631 42	97,060 46
Bills payable........	153,617 56	53,317 56	52,192 41	19,950 07	2,429 07
Total	40,098,456 33	40,773,051 28	40,046,977 76	40,629,010 00	40,140,536 62

CITY OF CHICAGO.

	10 banks.	10 banks.	10 banks.	10 banks.	9 banks.
Capital stock	$5,150,000 00	$5,150,000 00	$4,650,000 00	$4,650,000 00	$4,450,000 00
Surplus fund........	2,175,000 00	2,200,000 90	2,215,000 00	2,215,000 00	2,200,000 00
Undivided profits....	517,650 61	341,644 19	484,036 80	446,149 97	482,329 02
Nat'l bank circulation	624,600 00	582,900 00	571,600 00	543,900 00	468,500 00
State bank circulation	....	....	....	....	....
Dividends unpaid....	50,020 00	825 00	13,860 00	55,640 00	771 00
Individual deposits ..	12,714,155 06	12,352,348 08	13,361 576 12	13,807,867 13	16,137,159 34
U. S. deposits........				53,011 79	66,032 99
Dep'ts U.S.dis.officers	....	....	....	....	....
Due to national banks	4,464,085 21	5,754,366 81	5,500,132 61	6,080,558 14	5,584,228 57
Due to State banks...	2,950,798 31	3,629,342 07	3,303,511 35	3,741,021 42	3,766,522 21
Notes re-discounted..	415,103 33	243,000 00	97,500 00	15,000 00	....
Bills payable........	....	....	....	....	....
Total	29,061,421 52	30,344,426 15	30,287,216 88	31,608,148 45	33,155,543 13

MICHIGAN.

	76 banks.	76 banks.	75 banks.	75 banks.	75 banks.
Capital stock	$7,663,200 00	$7,678,200 00	$7,463,976 00	$7,558,200 00	$7,528,200 00
Surplus fund........	2,012,082 09	2,005,451 28	2,008,576 39	2,034,793 83	1,994,762 51
Undivided profits....	1,085,122 97	727,552 88	828,443 93	669,641 93	790,316 97
Nat'l bank circulation	4,411,206 00	4,450,755 00	4,348,130 00	4,325,818 00	4,222,880 00
State bank circulation	....	....	....	....	....
Dividends unpaid....	4,062 00	7,084 30	42,485 30	143,825 80	34,496 00
Individual deposits ..	7,140,999 75	7,091,263 63	6,956,367 12	6,938,779 09	7,715,583 60
U. S. deposits........	13,800 93	19,189 92	33,093 35	33,048 06	29,343 79
Dep'ts U.S.dis.officers	14,311 52	12,217 15	6,999 27	8,227 34	23,104 13
Due to national banks	78,826 01	56,674 41	70,271 68	42,216 96	61,938 06
Due to State banks...	68,296 30	91,089 56	46,134 88	35,367 79	40,091 20
Notes re-discounted..	140,997 76	167,584 40	365,005 46	345,207 90	208,678 17
Bills payable........	43,712 28	16,372 19	22,808 89	17,631 56	16,126 22
Total	22,676,617 61	22,323,434 72	22,192,292 27	22,152,758 35	22,665,820 74

Abstract of reports since October 1, 1877, arranged

CITY OF DETROIT.

Resources.	DECEMBER 28. 4 banks.	MARCH 15. 4 banks.	MAY 1. 4 banks.	JUNE 29. 4 banks.	OCTOBER 1. 4 banks.
Loans and discounts	$4,516,024 90	$4,595,179 57	$4,564,132 19	$4,189,613 96	$4,177,269 32
Bonds for circulation	1,303,400 00	1,303,400 00	1,303,400 00	1,303,400 00	1,353,400 00
Bonds for deposits...	500,000 00	500,000 00	500,000 00	500,000 00	500,000 00
U. S. bonds on hand..	....	23,150 00	28,250 00	113,800 00	145,250 00
Other stocks and b'ds	92,926 58	97,226 58	91,433 35	87,469 24	73,115 69
Due from res've ag'ts	888,017 93	922,236 88	805,465 62	853,537 15	1,339,288 80
Due from nat'l banks	461,127 95	842,425 34	733,014 49	621,557 97	627,389 84
Due from State banks	70,138 90	70,230 05	65,329 38	93,912 00	58,993 25
Real estate, &c	91,950 00	91,700 00	91,450 00	92,754 57	91,200 00
Current expenses....	37,088 75	41,682 39	17,989 03	23,388 36	9,355 83
Premiums paid......	8,096 86	5,359 36	5,359 36	89,052 79	5,359 36
Cash items	40,500 41	57,046 49	65,234 69	31,490 08	57,811 08
Clear'g-house exch'gs	162,906 76	149,341 72	228,804 84	170,172 53	240,561 60
Bills of other banks..	166,189 00	48,345 00	168,335 00	91,711 00	80,398 00
Fractional currency .	8,390 63	8,965 39	5,855 24	5,836 34	4,916 45
Specie	48,593 95	108,769 69	114,859 97	128,869 37	136,070 13
Legal-tender notes ..	753,764 00	791,874 00	706,548 00	681,326 00	761,555 00
U. S. cert's of deposit.	....	....	....	....	....
Due from U. S. Treas.	87,292 03	73,053 13	80,633 83	66,293 73	66,138 83
Total..........	9,236,408 65	9,729,985 59	9,576,094 99	9,144,185 69	9,728,073 18

WISCONSIN.

	37 banks.	37 banks.	37 banks.	36 banks.	35 banks.
Loans and discounts.	$5,174,904 58	$5,048,272 75	$5,114,949 41	$5,191,853 12	$5,247,352 14
Bonds for circulation.	2,015,500 00	2,039,500 00	2,039,500 00	2,009,500 00	1,959,500 00
Bonds for deposits...	125,000 00	100,000 00	100,000 00	100,000 00	100,000 00
U. S. bonds on hand..	80,900 00	204,400 00	227,200 00	239,200 00	230,200 00
Other stocks and b'ds	100,081 98	105,566 54	83,764 99	80,505 69	97,719 94
Due from res've ag'ts.	752,114 88	773,321 54	649,153 90	557,980 47	555,425 69
Due from nat'l banks.	311,805 60	439,628 61	285,194 08	235,386 84	381,488 50
Due from State banks	62,565 51	71,357 24	65,994 38	58,849 41	32,286 57
Real estate, &c	339,169 59	341,342 68	336,966 84	332,273 56	322,795 89
Current expenses...	87,288 02	54,624 66	60,435 71	51,603 07	66,285 29
Premiums paid	36,652 63	29,407 74	28,726 66	26,814 22	25,320 32
Cash items	51,529 27	54,559 25	54,150 67	36,649 08	40,333 61
Clear'g-house exch'gs	....	....	....	....	....
Bills of other banks..	261,053 00	194,182 00	144,443 00	138,575 00	116,932 00
Fractional currency .	9,700 28	9,059 86	8,183 72	8,577 87	6,392 66
Specie	65,820 56	134,991 76	141,703 16	131,607 40	159,938 01
Legal-tender notes ..	718,870 00	674,612 00	607,369 00	491,438 00	490,026 00
U. S. cert's of deposit.	....	....	....	....	....
Due from U. S. Treas.	97,534 07	101,190 60	98,711 25	91,865 67	93,213 99
Total..........	10,290,489 97	10,376,017 23	10,046,448 77	9,782,679 40	9,925,210 61

CITY OF MILWAUKEE.

	3 banks.	3 banks.	3 banks.	3 banks.	3 banks.
Loans and discounts.	$2,028,387 62	$2,060,760 60	$2,093,555 54	$1,866,355 40	$2,138,291 46
Bonds for circulation.	285,000 00	285,000 00	285,000 00	285,000 00	235,000 00
Bonds for deposits ..	400,000 00	450,000 00	450,000 00	450,000 00	450,000 00
U. S. bonds on hand..	104,800 00	20,950 00	16,200 00	14,650 00	12,000 00
Other stocks and b'ds	76,100 00	70,000 00	75,000 00	55,000 00	39,000 00
Due from res've ag'ts.	359,820 99	511,203 50	440,060 07	438,436 13	379,218 03
Due from nat'l banks	203,618 64	384,563 32	165,577 66	329,646 45	83,566 00
Due from State banks	10,925 04	11,014 64	19,197 19	8,019 89	10,010 91
Real estate, &c......	136,017 17	148,029 98	142,937 48	137,795 98	127,578 48
Current expenses....	10,550 38	9,347 53	9,619 85	9,271 12	4,393 56
Premiums paid	5,387 99	6,282 10	5,092 71	5,927 62	4,403 67
Cash items	7,450 86	7,567 87	4,370 08	2,471 06	4,419 62
Clear'g-house exch'gs	108,209 47	91,037 07	147,951 29	139,519 04	367,887 35
Bills of other banks..	22,481 00	9,733 00	13,422 00	6,219 00	9,022 00
Fractional currency .	1,118 39	658 99	1,013 25	1,025 56	673 46
Specie	25,392 05	22,581 40	89,000 57	78,125 12	73,828 76
Legal-tender notes ..	625,606 00	461,167 00	428,738 00	420,087 00	236,798 00
U. S. cert's of deposit.	35,000 00	35,000 00	....	....	50,000 00
Due from U. S. Treas	12,825 00	13,325 00	13,525 00	13,525 00	10,575 00
Total..........	4,458,590 60	4,598,222 00	4,400,260 79	4,262,004 37	4,236,666 30

by States and reserve cities—Continued.

CITY OF DETROIT.

Liabilities.	DECEMBER 28. 4 banks.	MARCH 15. 4 banks.	MAY 1. 4 banks.	JUNE 29. 4 banks.	OCTOBER 1. 4 banks.
Capital stock	$2,100,000 00	$2,100,000 00	$2,100,000 00	$2,100,000 00	$2,100,000 00
Surplus fund	925,000 00	965,000 00	965,000 00	715,000 00	715,000 00
Undivided profits	476,290 67	454,352 31	382,571 46	387,167 95	295,853 93
Nat'l bank circulation	1,147,400 00	1,132,200 00	1,132,895 00	1,063,795 00	1,156,900 00
State bank circulation					
Dividends unpaid	1,967 00	1,075 00	3,402 00	282,052 00	24,306 00
Individual deposits	3,333,599 97	3,625,883 93	3,710,349 06	3,473,313 54	3,944,191 33
U. S. deposits	88,531 49	212,770 77	231,219 29	128,031 62	132,551 33
Dep'ts U.S.dis.officers	264,844 58	213,808 41	156,883 85	205,722 09	237,790 41
Due to national banks	465,251 63	557,031 95	459,501 71	391,683 28	632,976 19
Due to State banks	433,323 31	457,863 22	434,272 62	387,415 21	488,503 99
Notes re-discounted		10,000 00		10,000 00	
Bills payable					
Total	9,236,408 65	9,729,985 59	9,576,094 99	9,144,185,69	9,728,073 18

WISCONSIN.

	37 banks.	37 banks.	37 banks.	36 banks.	35 banks.
Capital stock	$2,750,000 00	$2,750,000 00	$2,725,000 00	$2,665,000 00	$2,615,000 00
Surplus fund	746,037 98	748,124 05	745,624 05	739,924 05	739,501 38
Undivided profits	402,029 04	262,894 49	273,131 99	283,877 02	303,578 65
Nat'l bank circulation	1,786,334 00	1,781,249 00	1,795,629 00	1,769,746 00	1,756,476 00
State bank circulation					
Dividends unpaid	31,574 00	33,009 50	31,563 50	44,663 50	34,678 50
Individual deposits	4,370,581 75	4,592,463 93	4,312,167 89	4,076,874 87	4,273,679 64
U. S. deposits	60,021 40	66,115 39	51,977 64	75,853 65	65,153 89
Dep'ts U.S.dis.officers	11,015 42	7,580 26	17,667 26	10,831 96	13,490 73
Due to national banks	14,451 18	18,002 70	9,087 13	10,138 47	12,912 53
Due to State banks	65,207 11	95,378 46	64,666 47	65,813 20	73,246 00
Notes re-discounted	38,911 80	17,018 71	10,813 10	25,835 84	19,830 00
Bills payable	14,326 29	4,120 74	9,120 74	14,120 84	15,663 20
Total	10,290,489 97	10,376,017 23	10,046,448 77	9,782,679 40	9,925,210 61

CITY OF MILWAUKEE.

	3 banks.	3 banks.	3 banks.	3 banks.	3 banks.
Capital stock	$650,000 00	$650,000 00	$650,000 00	$650,000 00	$650,000 00
Surplus fund	230,000 00	215,000 00	215,000 00	215,000 00	215,000 00
Undivided profits	87,748 97	51,121 35	51,319 76	65,490 57	56,346 09
Nat'l bank circulation	234,000 00	234,000 00	235,300 00	235,600 00	202,700 00
State bank circulation					
Dividends unpaid					
Individual deposits	1,995,759 41	2,124,028 82	2,152,996 48	2,041,376 06	1,933,435 48
U. S. deposits	168,208 82	219,006 50	231,133 17	244,172 84	204,449 29
Dep'ts U.S.dis.officers	211,542 12	197,936 29	126,491 40	144,144 59	267,233 63
Due to national banks	561,659 04	626,683 31	418,354 02	446,358 84	396,001 10
Due to State banks	316,672 24	286,142 73	269,635 96	199,861 47	193,707 46
Notes re-discounted					117,733 25
Bills payable					
Total	4,458,590 66	4,598,222 00	4,400,260 79	4,262,004 37	4,236,666 30

Abstract of reports since October 1, 1877, arranged

IOWA.

Resources.	DECEMBER 28. 78 banks.	MARCH 15. 77 banks.	MAY 1. 77 banks.	JUNE 29. 77 banks.	OCTOBER 1. 76 banks.
Loans and discounts.	$10,060,176 84	$9,687,731 67	$9,538,056 20	$9,445,394 16	$9,634,751 27
Bonds for circulation	4,435,500 00	4,355,500 00	4,380,500 00	4,477,000 00	4,507,000 00
Bonds for deposits...	140,000 00	75,000 00	75,000 00	75,000 00	75,000 00
U. S. bonds on hand..	219,950 00	245,000 00	282,600 00	310,150 00	315,850 00
Other stocks and b'ds	311,456 38	368,580 08	396,967 18	459,899 71	423,517 36
Due from res've ag'ts	755,090 86	1,319,689 64	1,266,047 06	1,268,245 87	718,128 50
Due from nat'l banks.	413,777 63	736,383 97	657,255 83	617,995 26	470,261 96
Due from State banks	160,943 80	187,398 14	181,501 48	219,902 61	145,790 88
Real estate, &c	933,776 09	892,467 71	922,194 08	921,791 72	936,688 12
Current expenses....	177,745 44	206,646 90	207,470 00	145,615 19	170,729 25
Premiums paid	171,943 24	130,810 45	132,013 06	118,438 95	110,787 25
Cash items	93,463 98	123,442 73	112,749 83	126,463 35	110,371 71
Clear'g-house exch'gs					
Bills of other banks..	477,740 00	504,918 00	505,243 00	405,158 20	340,885 00
Fractional currency	21,495 23	14,068 59	15,942 12	15,929 11	10,757 91
Specie	150,719 43	130,399 81	204,507 10	251,090 19	298,187 13
Legal-tender notes ..	1,381,517 00	1,494,705 00	1,545,544 00	1,395,447 00	1,130,504 00
U. S. cert's of deposit.					
Due from U. S. Treas	204,471 23	218,750 00	207,859 88	227,168 42	219,400 84
Total..........	20,109,767 15	20,092,402 69	20,631,450 82	20,410,630 54	19,618,611 18

MINNESOTA.

	31 banks.	30 banks.	30 banks.	31 banks.	31 banks.
Loans and discounts	$8,521,396 11	$8,831,333 10	$9,066,059 28	$9,461,823 15	$9,982,572 39
Bonds for circulation	2,603,500 00	2,503,500 00	2,563,500 00	2,613,500 00	2,623,500 00
Bonds for deposits...	460,000 00	465,000 00	465,000 00	465,000 00	465,500 00
U. S. bonds on hand	37,900 00	44,650 00	3,450 00	8,000 00	4,900 00
Other stocks and b'ds	112,537 34	76,386 50	100,761 50	96,775 90	91,502 10
Due from res've ag't	957,038 98	677,029 79	503,317 03	727,138 87	648,864 35
Due from nat'l banks	430,416 98	347,785 86	292,180 22	470,301 80	206,125 76
Due from State banks	74,185 61	74,963 76	86,910 24	87,707 78	43,250 08
Real estate, &c	448,828 70	423,853 79	422,768 54	424,009 50	425,216 15
Current expenses....	146,620 70	116,377 08	150,862 73	84,974 50	91,572 67
Premiums paid	128,950 51	91,677 33	93,594 08	89,783 08	70,878 84
Cash items	101,611 19	72,344 11	159,510 78	131,967 22	125,027 25
Clear'g-house exch'gs					
Bills of other banks..	319,873 00	196,672 00	333,967 00	150,028 00	104,430 00
Fractional currency.	10,315 07	6,309 35	5,428 52	6,673 97	6,238 34
Specie	56,793 19	56,314 33	47,308 36	72,087 68	91,814 69
Legal-tender notes ..	941,879 00	644,221 00	631,258 00	858,752 00	651,846 00
U. S. cert's of deposit.					
Due from U. S. Treas.	119,674 46	112,356 00	118,195 60	123,556 91	132,464 11
Total..........	15,471,520 84	14,740,114 00	15,044,071 88	15,872,080 36	15,765,702 73

MISSOURI.

	24 banks.	20 banks.	20 banks.	19 banks.	17 banks.
Loans and discounts	$4,847,815 10	$2,608,090 82	$2,543,792 75	$2,373,933 28	$2,090,909 30
Bonds for circulation	1,680,000 00	1,450,000 00	1,410,000 00	1,360,000 00	1,280,000 00
Bonds for deposits...					
U. S. bonds on hand	49,450 00	39,250 00	68,200 00	74,150 00	114,200 00
Other stocks and b'ds	620,695 07	549,162 99	587,897 80	553,102 39	537,513 79
Due from res've ag'ts	257,865 50	373,796 63	406,887 36	462,329 55	349,304 34
Due from nat'l banks	146,969 94	124,965 98	100,386 87	133,872 21	131,102 48
Due from State banks	190,747 26	101,192 55	85,074 22	100,684 38	81,560 19
Real estate, &c	393,600 02	282,424 81	278,307 96	277,649 35	261,903 28
Current expenses....	126,448 34	47,568 51	71,776 26	52,839 58	37,824 17
Premiums paid	88,789 61	51,256 00	42,343 33	43,116 76	28,353 20
Cash items	157,433 67	54,068 52	43,129 68	67,752 79	24,782 59
Clear'g-house exch'gs					
Bills of other banks..	152,337 00	108,972 00	117,079 00	112,270 00	87,013 00
Fractional currency.	5,976 80	2,421 54	2,012 89	1,953 33	1,559 08
Specie	57,552 33	42,639 59	42,274 03	47,341 78	47,716 06
Legal-tender notes ..	397,349 00	347,497 00	327,334 00	303,481 00	291,292 00
U. S. cert's of deposit.	5,000 00				
Due from U. S. Treas.	78,353 03	69,494 71	67,757 46	67,317 68	59,553 68
Total..........	9,256,352 67	6,252,801 65	6,194,253 61	6,040,194 08	5,424,688 16

by States and reserve cities—Continued.

I O W A.

Liabilities.	DECEMBER 28. 78 banks.	MARCH 15. 77 banks.	MAY 1. 77 banks.	JUNE 29. 77 banks.	OCTOBER 1. 76 banks.
Capital stock	$6, 057, 000 00	$6, 057, 000 00	$6, 057, 000 00	$6, 037, 000 00	$5, 957, 000 00
Surplus fund	1, 487, 520 07	1, 453, 407 75	1, 439, 971 98	1, 436, 188 51	1, 414, 473 19
Undivided profits	792, 322 53	640, 624 32	685, 843 62	630, 020 98	573, 966 54
Nat'l bank circulation	3, 936, 244 00	3, 851, 077 00	3, 851, 405 00	3, 918, 135 00	3, 966, 175 60
State bank circulation					
Dividends unpaid	29, 276 66	44, 599 10	42, 795 10	60, 531 10	29, 721 66
Individual deposits	7, 086, 486 05	8, 029, 626 68	7, 932, 378 58	7, 751, 876 08	7, 129, 047 33
U. S. deposits	38, 856 17	40, 073 53	32, 386 73	40, 941 25	36, 092 09
Dep'ts U.S.dis.officers	80, 382 28	4, 288 26	17, 124 44	3, 889 86	6, 196 10
Due to national banks	154, 827 24	162, 738 25	180, 117 97	156, 721 34	131, 220 58
Due to State banks	114, 841 05	288, 690 65	357, 550 75	337, 013 22	166, 335 88
Notes re-discounted	237, 111 10	69, 277 15	21, 376 65	18, 313 20	188, 382 81
Bills payable	74, 900 00	51, 000 00	13, 500 00		20, 000 00
Total	20, 109, 767 15	20, 692, 402 69	20, 631, 450 82	20, 410, 630 54	19, 618, 611 18

M I N N E S O T A.

	31 banks.	30 banks.	30 banks.	31 banks.	31 banks.
Capital stock	$4, 430, 000 00	$4, 730, 000 00	$4, 710, 000 00	$4, 770, 000 00	$4, 770, 000 00
Surplus fund	814, 911 32	782, 104 84	782, 604 84	766, 701 81	770, 283 93
Undivided profits	615, 829 90	368, 041 03	475, 926 35	511, 882 53	437, 386 93
Nat'l bank circulation	2, 325, 461 00	2, 236, 211 00	2, 268, 326 00	2, 204, 561 00	2, 345, 171 00
State bank circulation					
Dividends unpaid	7, 776 50	5, 469 50	3, 810 50	23, 235 50	7, 349 50
Individual deposits	6, 206, 954 97	5, 714, 836 83	5, 634, 047 32	6, 390, 878 20	6, 191, 480 13
U. S. deposits	69, 278 22	103, 236 06	216, 478 92	176, 544 11	114, 049 09
Dep't's U.S.dis.officers	276, 628 61	136, 175 17	196, 574 55	201, 566 99	190, 957 73
Due to national banks	245, 942 09	227, 240 34	186, 144 90	323, 256 74	209, 504 81
Due to State banks	286, 547 33	229, 659 04	221, 103 16	333, 058 25	246, 829 42
Notes re-discounted	172, 190 81	169, 639 29	314, 546 34	66, 395 23	455, 190 19
Bills payable	20, 000 00	37, 500 00	34, 500 00	14, 000 00	18, 500 00
Total	15, 471, 520 84	14, 740 114 00	15, 044, 071 88	15, 872, 080 36	15, 765, 702 73

M I S S O U R I.

	24 banks.	20 banks.	20 banks.	19 banks.	17 banks.
Capital stock	$2, 425, 000 00	$1, 725, 000 00	$1, 725, 000 00	$1, 675, 000 00	$1, 475, 000 00
Surplus fund	471, 360 55	396, 261 59	396, 261 59	378, 424 42	347, 173 20
Undivided profits	379, 155 90	199, 539 44	246, 971 84	255, 215 54	217, 877 97
Nat'l bank circulation	1, 507, 237 00	1, 299, 332 00	1, 252, 158 00	1, 191, 948 00	1, 128, 791 00
State bank circulation					
Dividends unpaid	815 00	7, 794 50	243 00	2, 743 00	178 00
Individual deposits	3, 430, 071 07	2, 405, 668 95	2, 351, 617 08	2, 399, 041 06	2, 164, 758 00
U. S. deposits					
Dep'ts U.S.dis.officers					
Due to national banks	227, 361 58	13, 354 20	22, 450 17	24, 482 23	1, 883 05
Due to State banks	220, 404 54	42, 074 29	74, 721 05	41, 371 93	17, 788 73
Notes re-discounted	415, 128 58	66, 128 58	40, 600 00	39, 000 00	54, 100 00
Bills payable	176, 818 45	97, 648 10	84, 827 90	32, 967 90	16, 838 21
Total	9, 256, 352 67	6, 252, 801 65	6, 194, 253 61	6, 040, 194 08	5, 424, 688 16

11 C C

Abstract of reports since October 1, 1877, arranged

CITY OF ST. LOUIS.

Resources.	DECEMBER 28. 6 banks.	MARCH 15. 5 banks.	MAY 1. 5 banks.	JUNE 29. 5 banks.	OCTOBER 1. 5 banks.
Loans and discounts.	$6,365,964 35	$5,947,146 96	$5,581,886 77	$5,447,724 59	$5,941,051 12
Bonds for circulation.	460,000 00	410,000 00	410,000 00	410,000 00	410,000 00
Bonds for deposits...	300,000 00	300,000 00	300,000 00	300,000 00	300,000 00
U. S. bonds on hand..	7,950 00	600 00	83,100 00	337,500 00	228,100 00
Other stocks and b'ds	580,257 47	536,010 49	572,909 38	833,581 98	650,847 41
Due from res'v eag'ts	724,937 21	765,648 90	607,708 00	465,529 66	736,095 18
Due from nat'l banks.	338,093 89	296,542 55	219,961 15	313,822 37	327,622 90
Due from State banks	95,207 78	72,380 55	117,268 29	92,046 78	142,061 40
Real estate, &c	316,095 07	275,890 02	275,848 78	274,723 17	276,891 89
Current expenses....	136,739 96	64,963 94	76,794 64	55,961 73	129,039 15
Premiums paid	50,790 31	48,863 40	51,318 57	61,496 09	57,296 49
Cash items	11,024 72	17,195 35	25,246 61	33,544 29	14,016 14
Clear'g-house exch'gs	518,891 07	326,987 22	454,303 48	530,515 95	552,333 05
Bills of other banks..	217,549 00	442,217 00	365,075 00	267,817 00	148,487 00
Fractional currency .	3,959 00	6,346 30	5,865 29	4,952 89	4,291 49
Specie	68,404 83	73,842 21	87,509 91	86,066 87	77,704 92
Legal-tender notes ..	1,125,626 00	1,196,600 00	1,231,500 00	934,000 00	732,000 00
U. S. cert's of deposit	100,000 00	100,000 00	215,000 00	400,000 00	215,000 00
Due from U. S. Treas	24,312 50	26,478 25	51,386 55	30,590 60	25,880 00
Total..........	11,445,804 06	10,906,813 14	10,732,682 42	10,879,673 97	10,968,718 14

KANSAS.

	14 banks.	12 banks.	12 banks.	12 banks.	11 banks.
Loans and discounts.	$1,991,528 36	$1,607,373 78	$1,485,648 81	$1,504,728 38	$1,331,576 98
Bonds for circulation.	830,000 00	730,000 00	730,000 00	730,000 00	680,000 00
Bonds for deposits...	300,000 00	300,000 00	300,000 00	300,000 00	350,000 00
U. S. bonds on hand..	25,000 00	....	21,500 00	22,000 00	4,950 00
Other stocks and b'ds	71,209 38	40,204 36	41,801 97	43,984 89	32,438 49
Due from res'v eag'ts	282,093 79	159,585 63	294,619 07	296,805 48	278,459 26
Due from nat'l banks	131,185 90	99,572 58	152,739 34	168,698 30	114,014 31
Due from State banks	73,285 71	67,957 22	108,052 53	119,176 34	140,460 24
Real estate, &c......	284,473 46	266,682 20	262,649 46	256,514 40	232,161 09
Current expenses....	46,533 07	23,897 82	35,250 28	34,865 84	25,648 28
Premiums paid	66,976 78	53,372 07	49,067 70	49,067 70	20,911 58
Cash items	29,270 87	30,045 05	39,833 19	33,255 40	25,606 11
Clear'g-house exch'gs					
Bills of other banks..	68,408 00	74,020 00	63,548 00	63,215 00	31,381 00
Fractional currency .	2,346 23	2,478 54	2,239 49	2,159 64	1,467 17
Specie	21,293 20	29,110 81	38,045 04	46,455 24	27,568 31
Legal-tender notes ..	253,464 00	254,811 00	263,604 00	254,323 00	303,631 00
U. S. cert's of deposit					
Due from U. S. Treas	47,121 22	37,950 00	35,541 36	36,175 61	33,590 00
Total..........	4,524,189 97	3,777,061 06	3,924,140 44	3,961,425 22	3,653,863 82

NEBRASKA.

	10 banks.	10 banks.	10 banks.	10 banks.	10 banks.
Loans and discounts.	$2,358,587 00	$2,135,265 02	$2,065,078 07	$2,089,845 84	$2,483,410 75
Bonds for circulation.	764,000 00	764,000 00	764,000 00	784,000 00	784,000 00
Bonds for deposits ..	300,000 00	303,000 00	355,000 00	358,000 00	378,500 00
U. S. bonds on hand..	125,300 00	123,400 00	42,000 00	40,450 00	25,350 00
Other stocks and b'ds	366,494 60	318,630 39	333,658 00	341,825 12	335,060 27
Due from res'v eag'ts	260,644 99	312,856 03	411,765 70	646,413 19	341,250 92
Due from nat'l banks.	123,975 68	75,668 86	112,515 88	205,894 34	124,607 97
Due from State banks	80,181 60	147,167 05	218,939 16	286,117 24	200,561 91
Real estate, &c......	203,573 71	212,426 41	220,703 30	221,506 07	221,116 30
Current expenses....	32,173 78	36,140 01	22,289 70	42,065 46	36,529 19
Premiums paid	41,756 02	37,506 03	31,903 76	30,313 05	20,355 12
Cash items	107,055 82	24,244 50	122,146 61	78,783 45	47,581 81
Clear'g-house exch'gs					
Bills of other banks..	117,237 00	124,467 00	119,022 00	108,373 00	116,205 00
Fractional currency .	5,723 91	5,150 31	4,098 79	5,096 46	4,349 61
Specie	38,720 95	37,420 35	88,763 32	125,922 08	152,129 06
Legal-tender notes ..	391,687 00	376,487 00	376,386 00	387,254 00	304,608 00
U. S. cert's of deposit.					
Due from U. S. Treas.	39,120 63	40,104 13	33,493 53	40,490 84	40,373 44
Total	5,350,232 69	5,073,733 39	5,321,763 82	5,792,410 14	5,616,049 35

by States and reserve cities—Continued.

CITY OF ST. LOUIS.

Liabilities.	DECEMBER 28. 6 banks.	MARCH 15. 5 banks.	MAY 1. 5 banks.	JUNE 29. 5 banks.	OCTOBER 1. 5 banks.
Capital stock	$2, 850, 000 00	$2, 650, 000 00	$2, 650, 000 00	$2, 650, 000 00	$2, 650 000 00
Surplus fund	564, 712 69	568, 816 35	550, 788 33	655, 149 68	555, 140 68
Undivided profits	403, 231 25	295, 191 21	328, 375 99	132, 996 59	322, 747 51
Nat'l bank circulation	410, 500 00	365, 500 00	362, 400 00	354, 600 00	352, 900 00
State bank circulation					
Dividends unpaid	3, 410 18	4, 899 68	4, 056 68	43, 827 68	5, 841 68
Individual deposits	4, 060, 525 87	4, 062, 613 41	3, 727, 562 91	3, 604, 900 02	3, 563, 056 17
U. S. deposits	219, 542 26	233, 603 85	272, 380 02	132, 212 05	209, 142 16
Dep'ts U.S.dis.officers					
Due to national banks	1, 072, 019 02	1, 143, 454 79	1, 212, 869 72	1, 331, 709 20	1, 398, 079 15
Due to State banks	1, 479, 883 70	1, 582, 733 85	1, 624, 248 77	1, 974, 278 75	1, 911, 801 79
Notes re-discounted	331, 979 09				
Bills payable	50, 000 00				
Total	11, 445, 804 06	10, 900, 813 14	10, 732, 082 42	10, 879, 673 97	10, 968, 718 14

KANSAS.

	14 banks.	12 banks.	12 banks.	12 banks.	11 banks.
Capital stock	$1, 015, 000 00	$900, 000 00	$900, 000 00	$900, 000 00	$800, 000 0
Surplus fund	236, 080 58	224, 374 00	178, 374 00	178, 374 00	179, 314 00
Undivided profits	156, 388 41	82, 977 15	76, 207 88	73, 027 46	60, 580 13
Nat'l bank circulation	746, 080 00	653, 020 00	650, 720 00	655, 500 00	564, 400 00
State bank circulation					
Dividends unpaid					
Individual deposits	1, 908, 215 35	1, 474, 400 28	1, 579, 906 87	1, 667, 503 09	1, 578, 747 20
U. S. deposits	80, 336 64	142, 258 13	135, 549 66	119, 076 50	158, 688 29
Dep'ts U.S.officers	228, 430 04	100, 648 26	187, 360 46	184, 787 31	138, 335 01
Due to national banks	17, 829 29	17, 414 18	26, 017 92	26, 421 22	6, 031 90
Due to State banks	95, 729 66	94, 769 06	133, 103 65	123, 735 64	141, 080 29
Notes re-discounted	34, 200 00	51, 200 00	20, 000 00	5, 000 00	10, 000 00
Bills payable	5, 000 00	36, 000 00	36, 000 00	25, 000 00	16, 637 00
Total	4, 524, 189 97	3, 777, 061 06	3, 924, 140 14	3, 961, 425 22	3, 653, 863 82

NEBRASKA.

	10 banks.	10 banks.	10 banks.	10 banks.	10 banks.
Capital stock	$950, 000 00	$950, 000 00	$950, 000 00	$950, 000 00	$950, 000 00
Surplus fund	174, 000 00	175, 200 00	175, 200 00	225, 975 00	222, 775 00
Undivided profits	168, 009 05	149, 722 16	120, 165 51	146, 387 85	154, 968 35
Nat'l bank circulation	686, 520 00	687, 060 00	686, 610 00	696, 750 00	703, 930 00
State bank circulation					
Dividends unpaid	66 00	105 00	60 00		400 00
Individual deposits	2, 499, 896 45	2, 330, 069 68	2, 594, 305 76	2, 938, 200 10	2, 719, 382 37
U. S. deposits	48, 595 66	101, 783 99	169, 362 60	132, 438 34	143, 293 49
Dep'ts U.S.officers	233, 121 56	153, 350 08	213, 173 71	262, 185 55	230, 579 71
Due to national banks	268, 880 10	174, 014 99	124, 598 05	224, 154 61	236, 467 16
Due to State banks	202, 754 73	206, 752 54	229, 574 89	216, 318 69	201, 720 41
Notes re-discounted	178, 389 14	126, 674 95	48, 713 27		52, 532 86
Bills payable		10, 000 00	10, 000 00		
Total	5, 350, 232 69	5, 073, 733 39	5, 321, 763 82	5, 792, 410 14	5, 616, 049 25

Abstract of reports since October 1, 1877, arranged

COLORADO.

Resources.	DECEMBER 28.	MARCH 15.	MAY 1.	JUNE 29.	OCTOBER 1.
	13 banks.	13 banks.	13 banks.	12 banks.	13 banks.
Loans and discounts	$2,541,641 13	$2,374,969 34	$2,482,171 26	$2,550,345 63	$2,762,494 37
Bonds for circulation	649,000 00	740,000 00	740,000 00	710,000 00	740,000 00
Bonds for deposits...	100,000 00	100,000 00	100,000 00	100,000 00	100,000 00
U. S. bonds on hand..			300 00	2,200 00	6,700 00
Other stocks and b'ds	150,842 84	218,917 31	230,738 27	240,189 35	227,221 83
Due from res've ag'ts	417,878 27	282,239 63	282,666 62	291,495 46	513,079 26
Due from nat'l banks	564,887 46	321,386 07	285,167 79	322,762 66	457,653 26
Due from State banks	226,837 61	189,837 34	192,873 37	206,969 91	252,901 20
Real estate, &c	192,581 85	202,258 79	202,480 91	182,428 12	182,328 79
Current expenses....	66,859 71	48,456 60	41,438 47	29,607 93	19,497 09
Premiums paid......	40,131 88	45,976 88	44,914 38	32,539 38	30,329 74
Cash items	59,994 62	54,563 18	70,251 41	50,436 73	95,931 93
Clear'g-house exch'gs					
Bills of other banks..	93,601 00	85,399 00	66,741 00	55,021 00	71,171 00
Fractional currency .	4,261 26	2,957 40	2,908 43	1,513 77	1,257 31
Specie	35,494 25	46,283 08	40,798 76	44,423 96	62,685 43
Legal-tender notes ..	502,678 00	470,331 00	443,899 00	375,133 00	465,920 00
U. S. cert's of deposit					
Due from U. S. Treas	40,321 46	39,190 97	37,870 48	43,218 92	47,156 89
Total..........	5,705,301 34	5,222,716 59	5,265,219 55	5,247,285 82	6,036,328 10

OREGON.

	1 bank.	1 bank.	1 bank.	1 bank.	1 bank.
Loans and discounts	$785,315 97	$764,542 68	$832,507 49	$884,012 93	$882,574 13
Bonds for circulation	250,000 00	250,000 00	250,000 00	250,000 00	250,000 00
Bonds for deposits...	200,000 00	200,000 00	225,000 00	225,000 00	225,000 00
U. S. bonds on hand..	51,050 00	81,550 00	76,550 00	51,650 00	64,950 00
Other stocks and b'ds	144,713 93	262,930 15	267,873 32	132,863 32	91,285 26
Due from res've ag'ts	368,425 89	206,302 49	106,131 92	85,503 61	138,674 95
Due from nat'l banks	5,171 50	6,819 95	8,393 86	4,603 34	2,133 82
Due from State banks	324,945 64	171,478 20	6,591 14	29,770 21	144,037 03
Real estate, &c	4,232 50	2,000 00	2,000 00	2,000 00	
Current expenses....	12,812 58	4,381 83	8,276 67	13,357 75	7,355 93
Premiums paid......	38 50	6,530 22	7,598 05		432 67
Cash items	46 25	55 50		99 50	36 00
Clear'g-house exch'gs					
Bills of other banks..	5,270 00	4,100 00	7,050 00	8,100 00	1,870 00
Fractional currency					
Specie	132,825 05	166,358 18	97,548 44	71,777 60	77,778 36
Legal-tender notes ..	83,200 00	51,340 00	46,300 00	57,520 00	34,540 00
U. S. cert's of deposit					
Due from U. S. Treas	19,150 00	19,650 00	13,550 00	12,850 00	14,250 00
Total	2,387,197 81	2,198,039 20	1,955,370 89	1,829,108 26	1,934,918 15

CALIFORNIA.

	7 banks.	7 banks.	7 banks.	7 banks.	7 banks.
Loans and discounts	$2,263,925 51	$2,150,513 44	$2,251,432 68	$2,238,596 89	$2,325,141 53
Bonds for circulation.	938,000 00	938,000 00	938,000 00	938,000 00	984,000 00
Bonds for deposits...					
U. S. bonds on hand..	40,100 00	40,100 00	40,100 00	40,100 00	40,600 00
Other stocks and b'ds	95,898 06	65,069 45	134,960 00	83,334 29	118,906 72
Due from res've ag'ts	220,487 90	203,603 39	119,434 59	163,546 57	174,585 68
Due from nat'l banks	13,654 53	23,956 39	21,434 30	24,642 16	22,600 88
Due from State banks	80,608 41	156,795 18	129,211 31	62,082 23	119,816 81
Real estate, &c	205,763 76	214,651 04	214,951 04	214,851 04	215,616 24
Current expenses....	32,660 61	17,251 40	24,733 88	30,571 05	22,420 38
Premiums paid......	7,394 00	7,437 86	6,009 74	7,694 70	8,283 94
Cash items	39,480 96	64,214 75	34,062 05	37,680 94	20,383 99
Clear'g-house exch'gs					
Bills of other banks..	5,715 00	5,995 00	12,146 00	13,641 00	8,922 00
Fractional currency	12 33	3 74	3 55	6 05	2 20
Specie	508,980 60	540,658 52	471,920 87	535,870 45	452,984 27
Legal-tender notes ..	34,997 00	15,668 00	16,373 00	10,575 00	14,642 00
U. S. cert's of deposit					
Due from U. S. Treas.					
Total..........	4,487,678 67	4,443,318 16	4,414,776 01	4,401,192 37	4,528,906 64

by States and reserve cities—Continued.

COLORADO.

Liabilities.	DECEMBER 28. 13 banks.	MARCH 15. 13 banks.	MAY 1. 13 banks.	JUNE 29. 12 banks.	OCTOBER 1. 13 banks.
Capital stock	$1,010,000 00	$1,010,000 00	$1,010,000 00	$900,000 00	$1,010,000 00
Surplus fund	159,100 00	164,100 00	164,100 00	164,100 00	166,000 00
Undivided profits	186,115 09	110,623 45	103,132 24	93,894 71	89,055 23
Nat'l bank circulation	578,955 00	648,600 00	657,150 00	635,400 00	635,140 00
State bank circulation					
Dividends unpaid	415 00	280 00	240 00	190 00	
Individual deposits	3,193,837 56	2,887,291 95	2,974,858 53	2,971,011 17	3,634,710 84
U. S. deposits	42,937 69	61,239 23	67,151 32	49,325 51	51,283 98
Dep'ts U.S.dis.officers	11,158 38	5,899 02	9,018 15	10,518 34	22,319 09
Due to national banks	318,380 83	200,846 13	138,989 58	190,039 52	228,407 56
Due to State banks	199,401 79	123,636 81	139,379 73	163,117 45	198,243 40
Notes re-discounted	5,000 00	4,200 00	1,200 00	9,689 12	1,177 00
Bills payable					
Total	5,705,301 34	5,222,716 59	5,265,219 55	5,247,285 82	6,036,328 10

OREGON.

	1 bank.	1 bank.	1 bank.	1 bank.	1 bank.
Capital stock	$250,000 00	$250,000 00	$250,000 00	$250,000 00	$250,000 00
Surplus fund	50,000 00	50,000 00	50,000 00	50,000 00	50,000 00
Undivided profits	279,692 21	266,005 09	270,541 45	290,161 94	283,924 02
Nat'l bank circulation	215,700 00	219,800 00	208,200 00	197,000 00	202,000 00
State bank circulation					
Dividends unpaid	4,312 00	5,524 00	1,836 00	1,836 00	2,832 00
Individual deposits	1,127,537 54	1,025,308 10	765,691 76	655,868 75	707,825 24
U. S. deposits	92,479 65	110,455 56	115,760 78	56,988 08	333,314 67
Dep'ts U.S.dis.officers	304,366 69	175,193 88	172,619 69	252,145 48	353,673 44
Due to national banks					686 96
Due to State banks	63,109 69	95,602 57	120,721 21	75,107 11	50,661 82
Notes re-discounted					
Bills payable					
Total	2,387,197 81	2,498,039 20	1,955,370 89	1,820,108 26	1,834,918 15

CALIFORNIA.

	7 banks.	7 banks.	7 banks.	7 banks.	7 banks.
Capital stock	$1,550,000 00	$1,550,000 00	$1,550,000 00	$1,550,000 00	$1,550,000 00
Surplus fund	107,094 69	132,385 92	132,385 92	138,889 22	141,985 07
Undivided profits	185,210 02	96,459 32	90,702 38	130,630 03	105,429 13
Nat'l bank circulation	746,680 00	748,220 00	747,220 00	748,015 00	707,565 00
State bank circulation					
Dividends unpaid	1,788 00	3,048 00	1,923 00	6,332 00	1,619 00
Individual deposits	1,721,049 72	1,850,982 73	1,742,910 93	1,676,646 80	1,874,172 97
U. S. deposits					
Dep'ts U.S.dis.officers					
Due to national banks	24,459 18	9,694 14	2,313 85		9,690 14
Due to State banks	151,397 06	82,528 05	147,319 93	150,679 32	78,445 33
Notes re-discounted					
Bills payable					
Total	4,487,678 67	4,443,318 16	4,414,776 01	4,101,192 37	4,528,006 64

Abstract of reports since October 1, 1877, arranged

CITY OF SAN FRANCISCO.

Resources.	DECEMBER 28.	MARCH 15.	MAY 1.	JUNE 29.	OCTOBER 1.
	2 banks.	2 banks.	2 banks.	2 banks.	2 banks.
Loans and discounts	$2,828,621 69	$3,023,814 60	$3,115,063 08	$3,018,334 46	$3,064,661 14
Bonds for circulation	850,000 00	850,000 00	850,000 00	850,000 00	850,000 00
Bonds for deposits					
U. S. bonds on hand					
Other stocks and b'ds	24,308 00	24,245 50	24,245 50	24,245 50	20,393 50
Due from res've ag'ts	19,717 63	21,534 16	26,647 29	30,887 13	51,028 82
Due from nat'l banks	63,043 89	21,023 45	38,540 50	46,114 09	44,360 23
Due from State banks	203,251 09	170,331 70	228,912 97	213,797 21	267,279 56
Real estate, &c	74,449 70	74,364 23	97,123 59	96,868 79	92,766 52
Current expenses	3,610 03	3,299 79	663 75	1,504 34	882 45
Premiums paid	11,379 44	11,153 20	10,920 00	10,920 00	10,920 00
Cash items	53,244 10	7,065 38	17,800 27	30,623 94	51,545 58
Clear'g-house exch'gs	292,635 61	71,180 02	89,379 18	72,681 62	170,382 48
Bills of other banks	11,225 00	2,939 00	3,445 00	4,473 00	5,870 00
Fractional currency	33 24	106 23	52 25	25 66	28 40
Specie	689,630 20	645,638 50	507,535 94	676,930 77	868,323 21
Legal-tender notes	35,598 00	68,460 00	41,053 00	32,720 00	42,387 00
U. S. cert's of deposit					
Due from U. S. Treas.					
Total	5,160,747 62	4,995,155 76	5,051,382 32	5,110,126 51	5,540,837 89

NEW MEXICO.

	2 banks.	2 banks.	2 banks.	2 banks.	2 banks.
Loans and discounts	$333,868 96	$371,157 95	$342,587 67	$356,890 10	$331,402 16
Bonds for circulation	300,000 00	300,000 00	300,000 00	300,000 00	300,000 00
Bonds for deposits	160,000 00	160,000 00	160,000 00	160,000 00	160,000 00
U. S. bonds on hand					
Other stocks and b'ds	1,002 60	1,090 47	1,252 87	2,135 16	5,657 60
Due from res've ag'ts	34,447 40	21,947 54	38,717 78	31,845 27	66,891 40
Due from nat'l banks	21,890 15	23,548 44	23,016 07	46,621 73	27,898 00
Due from State banks	36,304 28	42,016 43	44,539 28	61,957 77	44,180 23
Real estate, &c	5,544 89	5,544 89	5,544 89	5,544 89	5,579 89
Current expenses	4,957 28	6,268 51	2,579 44	5,403 03	9,378 50
Premiums paid	45,471 17	35,310 60	32,310 60	32,310 60	25,850 38
Cash items	885 20	720 84	892 13	317 59	11,528 96
Clear'g-house exch'gs					
Bills of other banks	4,986 00	11,015 00	7,938 00	11,826 00	8,963 00
Fractional currency	1,629 76	995 73	864 04	569 90	239 56
Specie	25,866 30	21,866 35	14,572 45	14,248 65	18,290 69
Legal-tender notes	70,401 00	51,004 00	28,361 00	44,442 00	38,048 00
U. S. cert's of deposit					
Due from U. S. Treas.	14,200 00	14,200 00	14,500 00	14,500 00	14,300 00
Total	1,061,483 99	1,066,686 75	1,017,586 22	1,088,612 69	1,068,298 37

UTAH.

	1 bank.	1 bank.	1 bank.	1 bank.	1 bank.
Loans and discounts	$303,696 49	$325,960 98	$341,529 28	$297,420 80	$218,300 75
Bonds for circulation	50,000 00	50,000 00	50,000 00	50,000 00	50,000 00
Bonds for deposits					
U. S. bonds on hand					
Other stocks and b'ds	5,631 85	10,945 40	11,644 42	11,921 37	88,183 80
Due from res've ag'ts	4,114 79	4,067 30	3,721 41	2,962 36	8,538 37
Due from nat'l banks	22,119 05	21,798 88	3,482 27	24,073 26	45,997 93
Due from State banks	52,918 53	53,044 34	20,533 28	11,499 25	26,607 62
Real estate, &c	55,000 00	55,000 00	45,000 00	45,000 00	45,000 00
Current expenses	1,002 16	5,474 62	266 25	1,974 95	6,814 16
Premiums paid					
Cash items	3,643 60	1,425 00	11,041 12	13,175 43	748 10
Clear'g-house exch'gs					
Bills of other banks	3,003 00	8,918 00	2,597 00	7,658 00	8,782 00
Fractional currency	506 92	206 11	79 55	298 95	70 70
Specie	33,222 20	19,894 16	17,606 16	27,943 15	29,396 75
Legal-tender notes	88,331 00	99,727 00	127,651 00	137,918 00	109,208 00
U. S. cert's of deposit					
Due from U. S. Treas.	2,250 00	2,250 00	2,250 00	2,250 00	2,250 00
Total	625,439 59	658,711 79	637,401 74	634,995 52	639,898 36

by States and reserve cities—Continued.

CITY OF SAN FRANCISCO.

Liabilities.	DECEMBER 28. 2 banks.	MARCH 15. 2 banks.	MAY 1. 2 banks.	JUNE 29. 2 banks.	OCTOBER 1. 2 banks.
Capital stock	$2,750,000 00	$2,750,000 00	$2,750,000 00	$2,750,000 00	$2,750,000 00
Surplus fund	121,748 43	131,748 43	133,081 77	135,748 43	142,542 23
Undivided profits	98,918 42	61,617 66	71,708 90	67,401 93	66,879 86
Nat'l bank circulation	654,735 00	664,270 00	657,915 00	667,400 00	668,980 00
State bank circulation					
Dividends unpaid	8,097 36	18,701 01	12,739 03	17,685 88	15,504 44
Individual deposits	1,308,394 12	1,134,332 79	1,105,273 26	1,197,080 88	1,528,805 00
U. S. deposits					
Dep'ts U.S.dis.officers					
Due to national banks	173,382 64	152,371 06	182,858 19	162,996 23	203,123 68
Due to State banks	43,471 65	82,114 81	137,806 17	111,813 16	165,002 68
Notes re-discounted					
Bills payable					
Total	5,160,747 62	4,995,155 76	5,051,382 32	5,110,126 51	5,540,837 89

NEW MEXICO.

	2 banks.	2 banks.	2 banks.	2 banks.	2 banks.
Capital stock	$300,000 00	$300,000 00	$300,000 00	$300,000 00	$300,000 00
Surplus fund	32,095 17	33,724 12	34,786 53	34,786 53	37,670 20
Undivided profits	31,600 74	37,241 31	30,509 22	39,949 66	35,338 18
Nat'l bank circulation	264,630 00	267,430 00	266,700 00	263,010 00	266,340 00
State bank circulation					
Dividends unpaid					
Individual deposits	279,710 15	287,495 74	266,321 45	301,326 95	280,937 92
U. S. deposits	85,989 05	73,027 88	68,135 45	87,809 59	100,931 11
Dep'ts U.S.dis.officers	66,401 42	65,450 89	49,899 12	60,613 65	47,080 96
Due to national banks		80 43	80 87		
Due to State banks	1,048 46	2,227 36	1,153 58	1,116 31	
Notes re-discounted					
Bills payable					
Total	1,061,483 99	1,006,686 75	1,017,586 22	1,088,612 69	1,068,298 37

UTAH.

	1 bank.	1 bank.	1 bank.	1 bank.	1 bank.
Capital stock	$200,000 00	$200,000 00	$200,000 00	$200,000 00	$200,000 00
Surplus fund	40,000 00	40,000 00	40,000 00	40,000 00	40,000 00
Undivided profits	26,881 64	34,172 37	24,605 60	18,836 97	34,303 18
Nat'l bank circulation	34,700 00	42,400 00	44,300 00	45,000 00	39,600 00
State bank circulation					
Dividends unpaid	162 00	150 00	90 00	174 00	96 00
Individual deposits	322,166 42	340,839 98	321,353 43	328,617 52	319,910 75
U. S. deposits					
Dep'ts U.S.dis.officers					
Due to national banks	103 31	5 00			
Due to State banks	1,426 22	1,144 44	7,052 71	2,367 03	5,988 43
Notes re-discounted					
Bills payable					
Total	625,439 59	658,711 79	637,401 74	634,995 52	639,898 36

Abstract of reports since October 1, 1877, arranged

IDAHO.

Resources.	DECEMBER 28.	MARCH 15.	MAY 1.	JUNE 29.	OCTOBER 1.
	1 bank.	1 bank.	1 bank.	1 bank.	1 bank.
Loans and discounts.	$92,308 68	$75,651 65	$82,107 17	$92,805 75	$103,122 75
Bonds for circulation.	100,000 00	100,000 00	100,000 00	100,000 00	100,000 00
Bonds for deposits....					
U. S. bonds on hand..					
Other stocks and b'ds	76,538 70	74,441 25	73,930 00	74,743 26	90,153 81
Due from res've ag'ts					
Due from nat'l banks.	2,097 99	53 50	53 50	10,980 07	12,397 43
Due from State banks	2,046 76	38,053 72	44,796 99	32,474 42	17,337 36
Real estate, &c	7,033 33	7,000 00	7,000 00	7,000 00	7,000 00
Current expenses....	6,617 73	1,772 22	2,690 62	4,275 86	4,658 98
Premiums paid					
Cash items	1,007 57	1,099 66	380 47	115 23	354 53
Clear'g-house exch'gs					
Bills of other banks..	9,078 00	5,855 00	6,200 00	8,748 00	4,851 00
Fractional currency .	118 50	72 00	70 00	63 00	52 00
Specie	21,099 00	10,250 00	9,925 00	9,050 00	5,515 00
Legal-tender notes ..	32,150 00	17,878 00	17,555 00	15,338 00	8,975 00
U. S. cert's of deposit.					
Due from U. S. Treas.	4,855 49	3,901 49	4,499 99	4,500 00	4,595 00
Total	354,951 75	336,028 49	340,209 34	360,093 59	359,012 86

MONTANA.

	5 banks.	5 banks.	5 banks.	5 banks.	3 banks.
Loans and discounts.	$893,086 18	$1,022,309 44	$1,014,424 42	$1,086,644 11	$867,836 34
Bonds for circulation.	236,000 00	236,000 00	280,000 00	280,000 00	130,000 00
Bonds for deposits ..	130,000 00	130,000 00	140,000 00	150,000 00	100,000 00
U. S. bonds on hand..					
Other stocks and b'ds	53,805 48	52,814 32	74,914 54	80,139 97	66,714 31
Due from res've ag'ts	76,426 86	60,179 61	51,994 75	39,980 67	11,561 84
Due from nat'l banks	70,763 22	56,697 96	33,254 20	48,746 72	27,114 70
Due from State banks	97,756 44	98,584 83	70,634 22	46,402 16	87,375 58
Real estate, &c	41,180 61	38,960 61	40,164 71	39,794 71	26,291 91
Current expenses....	24,022 12	11,763 55	18,178 57	4,097 92	10,479 53
Premiums paid	39,040 00	36,039 00	31,021 50	29,184 00	19,687 36
Cash items	93,104 95	94,794 36	47,500 74	53,881 17	41,302 99
Clear'g-house exch'gs					
Bills of other banks..	20,150 00	18,639 00	37,792 00	25,896 00	14,137 00
Fractional currency .	2,926 50	2,687 12	2,423 06	218 95	552 63
Specie	15,569 38	9,497 95	13,072 66	21,936 84	20,966 33
Legal-tender notes ..	109,700 00	100,900 00	139,280 00	139,500 00	96,500 00
U. S. cert's of deposit					
Due from U. S. Treas.	11,620 00	10,620 00	13,200 00	14,400 00	7,650 00
Total..........	1,915,160 83	1,989,547 75	2,007,945 37	2,060,823 22	1,528,170 52

DAKOTA.

	1 bank.	2 banks.	2 banks.	2 banks.	3 banks.
Loans and discounts	$85,671 59	$116,266 95	$148,294 07	$167,414 83	$233,404 81
Bonds for circulation.	50,000 00	80,000 00	80,000 00	80,000 00	110,000 00
Bonds for deposits ..	50,000 00	50,000 00	50,000 00	50,000 00	50,000 00
U. S. bonds on hand..				50 00	12,500 00
Other stocks and b'ds	2,448 71	2,710 35	3,467 63	3,563 63	5,388 65
Due from res've ag'ts	29,372 06	26,304 61	21,908 10	34,851 04	137,659 34
Due from nat'l banks	43,771 03	37,389 10	52,969 08	43,486 87	64,095 24
Due from State banks			4,193 19	1,150 00	125,445 50
Real estate, &c	10,692 04	12,790 98	13,135 63	17,123 08	29,036 68
Current expenses....	5,341 14	3,013 49	4,575 70	2,601 13	5,859 70
Premiums paid	10,000 00	10,300 00	10,300 00	10,300 00	5,732 50
Cash items	1,500 48	1,798 73	2,216 18	10,401 26	7,750 84
Clear'g-house exch'gs					
Bills of other banks..	287 00	4,358 00	4,085 00	4,798 00	39,203 00
Fractional currency .	183 50	172 98	162 67	72 66	101 00
Specie	743 40	1,655 17	2,646 28	4,960 12	11,564 49
Legal-tender notes ..	14,220 00	27,420 00	30,636 00	19,335 00	68,030 00
U. S. cert's of deposit.					
Due from U. S. Treas.	2,250 00	2,250 00	3,600 00	3,600 00	4,950 00
Total..........	304,480 95	376,460 36	431,589 53	453,707 62	930,721 93

by States and reserve cities—Continued.

IDAHO.

Liabilities.	DECEMBER 28. 1 bank.	MARCH 15. 1 bank.	MAY 1. 1 bank.	JUNE 29. 1 bank.	OCTOBER 1. 1 bank.
Capital stock	$100,000 00	$100,000 00	$100,000 00	$100,000 00	$100,000 00
Surplus fund........	20,000 00	20,000 00	20,000 00	20,000 00	20,000 00
Undivided profits....	16,396 13	3,699 39	5,383 49	8,131 35	11,330 49
Nat'l bank circulation	82,100 00	85,700 00	84,750 00	77,350 00	83,680 00
State bank circulation					
Dividends unpaid....					
Individual deposits..	120,730 10	122,846 12	134,925 61	137,013 18	135,721 40
U. S. deposits........					
Dep'ts U.S.dis.officers					
Due to national banks					
Due to State banks...	15,725 52	3,782 98	4,150 24	7,599 06	8,280 97
Notes re-discounted..					
Bills payable........				10,000 00	
Total............	354,951 75	336,028 49	349,209 34	360,093 59	359,012 86

MONTANA.

	5 banks.	5 banks.	5 banks.	5 banks.	3 banks.
Capital stock	$350,000 00	$350,000 00	$350,000 00	$350,000 00	$200,000 00
Surplus fund........	83,462 00	88,500 00	88,500 00	90,000 00	75,000 00
Undivided profits....	107,812 28	87,975 44	102,664 33	87,237 48	107,860 32
Nat'l bank circulation	206,534 00	204,134 00	243,134 00	234,934 00	109,934 00
State bank circulation					
Dividends unpaid....					
Individual deposits...	903,780 22	1,078,473 78	952,642 36	933,644 09	746,731 10
U. S. deposits........	75,719 36	63,065 13	70,440 66	48,723 04	7,523 06
Dep'ts U.S.dis.officers	78,304 80	56,648 01	99,793 74	134,741 51	114,570 14
Due to national banks	73,281 36	26,990 60	35,090 53	58,581 05	13,972 45
Due to State banks...	36,266 81	27,460 79	59,370 75	73,744 05	125,911 45
Notes re-discounted ..				26,218 00	26,668 00
Bills payable........		6,300 00	6,300 00	23,000 00	
Total	1,915,160 83	1,989,547 75	2,007,945 37	2,060,823 22	1,528,170 52

DAKOTA.

	1 bank.	2 banks.	2 banks.	2 banks.	3 banks.
Capital stock	$50,000 00	$111,500 00	$125,000 00	$125,000 00	$175,000 00
Surplus fund........	10,000 00	10,000 00	10,000 00	10,000 00	10,000 00
Undivided profits	9,519 01	9,275 99	12,938 46	14,049 82	17,920 02
Nat'l bank circulation	44,000 00	45,000 00	45,350 00	60,350 00	98,400 00
State bank circulation					
Dividends unpaid....	600 00	650 00			920 00
Individual deposits...	143,173 26	149,337 17	175,542 06	186,974 24	578,149 53
U. S. deposits........	38,776 47	38,937 94	51,972 45	15,812 56	10,241 98
Dep'ts U.S.dis.officers	8,412 21	10,310 71	10,786 56	39,763 74	39,739 85
Due to national banks				841 86	158 59
Due to State banks...		1,448 55		915 40	191 96
Notes re-discounted ..					
Bills payable........					
Total	304,480 95	376,460 36	431,589 53	453,707 62	930,721 93

12 C C

Abstract of reports since October 1, 1877, arranged

WYOMING.

Resources.	DECEMBER 28. 2 banks.	MARCH 15. 2 banks.	MAY 1. 2 banks-	JUNE 29. 2 banks.	OCTOBER 1. 2 banks.
Loans and discounts	$230,363 68	$251,435 32	$281,248 51	$273,637 71	$285,035 25
Bonds for circulation	60,000 00	60,000 00	60,500 00	60,000 00	60,000 00
Bonds for deposits					
U.S. bonds on hand					
Other stocks and b'ds	15,342 53	20,240 26	25,709 15	32,109 50	32,650 02
Due from res've ag'ts	46,048 01	4,872 57	1,126 16	13,907 68	24,024 79
Due from nat'l banks	93,460 60	65,060 11	36,014 11	44,239 86	81,450 37
Due from State banks	263 39	1,039 64	9,839 51	3,121 20	8,886 86
Real estate, &c	19,798 45	19,798 45	19,798 45	19,708 45	19,798 45
Current expenses	21,282 69	3,479 70	5,703 20	5,738 21	19,370 04
Premiums paid	7,748 75	6,396 25	6,396 25	5,726 90	5,726 90
Cash items	4,106 33	5,031 73	5,622 66	5,402 86	8,830 65
Clear'g-house exch'gs					
Bills of other banks	20,478 00	7,795 00	10,674 00	18,162 00	21,891 00
Fractional currency	324 75	271 45	327 30	320 30	265 00
Specie	10,276 60	6,686 25	12,853 36	18,254 48	25,625 65
Legal-tender notes	46,722 00	57,492 00	67,289 00	67,456 00	66,733 00
U.S. cert's of deposit					
Due from U.S. Treas	2,700 00	2,998 25	3,497 05	4,397 05	5,897 05
Total	587,915 78	512,596 98	546,098 71	572,272 20	657,185 03

WASHINGTON.

			1 bank.	1 bank.	1 bank.
Loans and discounts			$59,973 24	$81,817 33	$125,521 60
Bonds for circulation			50,000 00	50,000 00	50,000 00
Bonds for deposits				50,000 00	50,000 00
U.S. bonds on hand					1,156 85
Other stocks and b'ds				1,055 64	18,273 99
Due from res've ag'ts			19,997 86	1,500 00	8,717 21
Due from nat'l banks			15,584 97	7,866 70	5,109 89
Due from State banks			648 64	971 84	1,050 40
Real estate, &c			122 10	813 62	2,806 29
Current expenses				2,124 99	2,124 99
Premiums paid			2,111 09	240 37	512 30
Cash items					
Clear'g-house exch'gs			880 00	20 00	7,557 00
Bills of other banks					
Fractional currency			21,783 95	40,391 70	60,058 80
Specie			4,174 00	27,520 00	18,021 00
Legal-tender notes					
U.S. cert's of deposit				3,250 00	2,250 00
Due from U.S. Treas					
Total			175,275 85	267,372 19	353,160 32

by States and reserve cities—Continued.

WYOMING.

Liabilities.	DECEMBER 28. 2 banks.	MARCH 15. 2 banks.	MAY 1. 2 banks.	JUNE 29. 2 banks.	OCTOBER 1. 2 banks.
Capital stock	$125,000 00	$125,000 00	$125,000 00	$125,000 00	$125,000 00
Surplus fund	25,000 00	25,000 00	25,000 00	25,000 00	25,000 00
Undivided profits	77,319 93	66,705 69	72,849 95	73,088 66	80,495 56
Nat'l bank circulation	49,000 00	47,400 00	45,900 00	43,600 00	42,400 00
State bank circulation					
Dividends unpaid					
Individual deposits	301,562 51	244,026 47	252,780 67	301,446 41	368,690 37
U. S. deposits					
Dep'ts U.S.dis.officers					
Due to national banks	6,675 69	1,651 34	20,284 95	1,891 42	39 48
Due to State banks	2,457 65	2,813 18	4,283 14	2,245 71	6,565 62
Notes re-discounted					
Bills payable					
Total	587,915 78	512,596 98	546,098 71	572,272 20	657,185 03

WASHINGTON.

			1 bank.	1 bank.	1 bank.
Capital stock			$150,000 00	$150,000 00	$150,000 00
Surplus fund					
Undivided profits			160 75	2,983 11	7,737 18
Nat'l bank circulation				32,800 00	44,500 00
State bank circulation					
Dividends unpaid					
Individual deposits			24,815 10	71,583 38	91,527 27
U. S. deposits				10,201 51	52,980 64
Dep'ts U.S.dis.officers				4 19	4,950 75
Due to national banks					1,461 48
Due to State banks					
Notes re-discounted					
Bills payable					
Total			175,275 85	267,572 19	353,160 32

*9 7 8 3 7 4 1 1 8 2 4 2 6 *